Thomas Ruggles

The history of the poor; their rights, duties, and the laws respecting

them

In a series of letters

Thomas Ruggles

The history of the poor; their rights, duties, and the laws respecting them
In a series of letters

ISBN/EAN: 9783337306205

Printed in Europe, USA, Canada, Australia, Japan

Cover: Foto ©ninafisch / pixelio.de

More available books at **www.hansebooks.com**

THE

HISTORY

OF THE

POOR:

THEIR RIGHTS, DUTIES,

AND

THE LAWS RESPECTING THEM:

IN A SERIES OF LETTERS.

————————————

A NEW EDITION CORRECTED, AND CONTINUED TO THE PRESENT TIME.

————————————

By THO. RUGGLES, Esq. F.A.S.

One of his Majefty's Juftices of the Peace for the Counties of Effex and Suffolk.

————————————

London:

PRINTED FOR W. RICHARDSON, ROYAL EXCHANGE.

M.DCC.XCVII.

TO THE PUBLIC.

WHEN I at firſt determined to reviſe the follow-ing Letters, and to publiſh them in a volume diſtinct from that uſeful Agricultural Regiſter* wherein they firſt appeared, it was my intention to addreſs them to Mr. Pitt, under an abſurd perſuaſion that a miniſter of ſtate is expected, as it were, *ex officio*, to read thoſe treatiſes which are, through the medium of the preſs, directed for his peruſal; and alſo from a belief that, if he did peruſe, he might, from the detail of what has been done by the legiſlature for the poor, has been writ-ten by thoſe whoſe obſervations on the ſubject have been preſerved in print, or from the hints and obſervations ſcattered throughout the publication itſelf, find ſomewhat upon the ſubject, which, when improved by his ſolid judgement, matured by long experience, might, in the form of an act of the legiſlature, meliorate and improve

* The Annals of Agriculture, by A. Young, Eſq.

the

the fituation of the poor, and diminifh the expenfes of their maintenance.

But reflection foon cured me of that prefumption : a minifter of ftate is the laft perfon in the kingdom who can be expected to read books; he has more upon his hands, to read men, than he can eafily get over in the daily routine of bufinefs. In the mean time, with refpect to the *ardua regni*, he cannot poffibly attend to a more irrefiftible monitor than the public voice ; by which expreffion neither the howling of a favage and licentious mob, or the cries of pretended patriotifm, are intended ; but the voice of that general opinion, which arifes from general knowledge of the fubject, that fpeaks always in a tone, and with an authority, which is irrefiftible, and then truly is not the *vox populi* alone, it is the *vox Dei.*

To the Public, therefore, this hiftory of, and thefe obfervations on, the police refpecting the poor, are properly dedicated. If any part of the detail contained in the following pages, if any of the obfervations, are worth the attention of the Public ; if any of the hints here thrown out tend, in the leaft degree, to meliorate the condition of the poor themfelves, or to fave the Public any part of the vaft expenfe which lies fo heavy on the fhoulders of the landed intereft, confiftent with the general comfort of the fociety at large, their difcernment will fee it, their good fenfe will apply it, and their voice will

fpeak,

fpeak, with irrefiftible perfuafion, to our rulers, that it may be done.

If nothing in thefe pages is worthy their attention, if no ideas can be collected from the variety of matter treated of which tend to throw light on this fubject of fo great confequence to us and to our pofterity, the contrary prefumption will be properly punifhed by the public neglect, and the infignificance of the publication will doom it to that oblivion in which many other tracts on the fame topic are buried.

In fuch a cafe, the writer would have offended ftill more againft the public advantage, had he, by an addrefs to the minifter, taken up any of his valuable time; but yet he wifhed, through the medium of the prefs, to talk with him on the fubject; to afk him whether that vaft increafe of the poor's rate, which became known to the public by the means of the returns from the overfeers in the year 1787, is not worth his notice? Whether the fubject itfelf is of fo trifling an import as to be always left to the determination of a number of members of the Houfe of Commons, fcarcely greater than would meet as a committee on a private bill? Or, whether he receives any fatisfaction from a conduct fimilar to that of the dog in the manger; doing nothing himfelf, and not permitting any other perfon to be active on the fubject?

The fate of Mr. Gilbert's bill and Sir William Young's plan fhews fomewhat of this difpofition: the firft probably
fell,

fell, like other mifhapen and difproportionate buildings,
mole ruit fua; the laft certainly contained fome good
regulations, was calculated to give a fpur to our activity in the adminiftration of the poor-laws, and to recal
into the execution of them fomewhat of their original intent ; the promotion of induftry, and the encouragement
of labour.

But public rumour then reported that the minifter intended to take the bufinefs under his own infpection, and,
for that reafon, he difcountenanced the indigefted fchemes
of private individuals; we know not, indeed, but at this inftant
he may be employed in digefting a code which fhall comprehend in its fcope every thing that can be expected from
the union of great ability with an intimate knowledge of
the fubject ; or, poffibly, his mind may be made up, and,
after much inveftigation of and attention to the matter,
he may have come to this prudent refolution : I will do
nothing ; leaft done, like leaft faid, is fooneft mended.
But yet this important bufinefs preffes ; the poor-rates are
ftill rifing throughout that part of the kingdom which cannot employ its poor in manufactures, and manufactures
are by no means general, but local: befides, while not one
quarter of the ifland receives any immediate benefit from
the very flourifhing ftate of our trade and manufactures,
the three-fourths which are in ftill water feel themfelves in
danger from the very caufe which creates the calm, and,
oppreffed with an additional weight by the furges which
                                                    circle

circle round the pool, find it is with difficulty they can keep the head above water.

While the diftant rumour of large wages makes the poor diffatisfied with thofe which agriculture can afford, it creates a diflike to that labour which in their opinion, judging by comparifon from vague report, how manufacture pays its workmen, is fo poorly recompenfed: this gives rife to idlenefs, which creates a call on the fund raifed for their fupport; hence arife rates to which a four fhilling land-tax is a trifling object; hence we know of inftances where the poor-rates amount to the annual rent of lands. Is not this a fact? Is it not a grievance? If this is not corrected in time of peace, where will the financier find the dividends in any future war to pay the intereft of an increafed debt? Does not the fubject, therefore, on this account, demand the attention of a minifter during the halcyon days of peace?

The natural and political liberty of the mafs of the people is clogged and diminifhed by the law of fettlements; and, in the opinion of fome of the beft writers and ftrongeft reafoners on this important topic, it is unneceffarily and unwifely abridged. Do not the poor-laws on this account, alfo, demand the attention of the ftate? Is it not juft that every individual of the kingdom fhould enjoy as much free-dom as is confiftent with the fafety of the whole? But it may poffibly be replied in the language of ftate-prudence, This is not the time; fee what the cry of liberty and the call

for

for freedom have done upon the Continent! The anfwer is obvious; the cafes are widely different; the one is a temporary anarchy arifing from the abolition of all government, the other would be a recovery from a reftraint inimical to the interefts of labour and induftry, flowing from the power and enlightened mind of the legiflature itfelf: the one *would be* legal liberty, the other *is* exceffive licentioufnefs; therefore, let us not, by fuch a fuperabundant caution, fuffer ftate-prudence to rivet our fetters clofer, in proportion as our neighbours acquire a freedom, which they have not yet learned how to ufe with propriety or to exercife with dignity.

This language proceeds on the prefumption, that it is a point proved in the following fheets, that a partial repeal of the law of fettlement, or fuch a modification of it as would permit the poor man to go where he could beft find employment, would be beneficial to the intereft of the ftate as well as favourable to the liberty of the fubject; and furely the point is fully and fatisfactorily proved, if the united opinion of men of the moft enlightened minds and moft inftructed judgement does, in any cafe, amount to proof; or if the wealth and profperity of a kingdom increafes in a ratio with the aggregate of the money earned within the kingdom by the labour and employment of its inhabitants.

But while this claim for a greater degree of freedom is made for the poor, and a melioration of their condition is propofed in this refpect, care has been taken to point out the

the means of preventing fuch a degree of liberty, generating licentioufnefs, by recommending the erection of fchools of induftry, on the bafis of the power given by the ftatute of Elizabeth, to raife by affeffment a fum of money to purchafe a ftock of wool, hemp, flax, &c. for their employment; an object which feems fcarcely attended to by thofe who now carry into execution the poor-laws, as appears by the very trifling total returned to the Houfe of Commons by the overfeers, as expended on that account throughout the kingdom. This furely is another object worthy the attention of a great minifter, and it is an object that cannot generally be enforced without the affiftance of the legiflature; none of the fubfifting ftatutes pointing out the means of doing it, diftinct from thofe pefts to the morals, health, induftry, and activity, of the rifing generation, — work-houfes; which are horrible, although, as the police refpecting the poor is at prefent regulated, neceffary evils.

The claims of the poor on fociety have alfo been glanced at in the following pages. . By this expreffion, no abftract ideas of a claim to equality, either in legiflation or property, has been canvaffed; but fimply that claim to a fair retribution for their ftrength and ability to labour, which is their only birth-right; for, it is a principle arifing from neceffity, that, in all civilized focieties, there muft be hewers of wood and drawers of water; but thofe who fill up the lower, though ufeful, rank of our fellow-fubjects, infinitely exceed in number and in actual utility all the other claffes

a   of

of fociety put together; their claims are, therefore, as
ferious rights, and they demand from the ftate full as
ferious a confideration as any other claim upon it, for
fecurity of political liberty or private property; the right
to receive a compenfation for their labour, adequate to
their neceffary wants, while they have a capability of labour, is certainly due to them, and the right of maintenance
from the more opulent claffes of fociety, when that capability to labour is paffed, is another debt which fociety owes
them.

In the difcharge of this demand, has arifen that burthen
which the landed intereft in particular have great caufe to
complain of, the poor's rates; which, in many diftricts, when
united with the land-tax and tithes, amount almoft to a dif-
inherifon; for, although the occupier or tenant nominally
pays the tithes and poor-rates, the land in fact bears the
weight, and the total is taken from the landlord's pocket;
therefore, while we are finking under this treble load, is it
not natural, is it not juft, that we fhould inquire into the
tranfactions of paft times, and fearch the records of antiquity, to explore on what principle of legiflation, from what
confent, virtual or implied, of our forefathers, from what
fyftem of laws, human or divine, this ruinous fact, though
apparent paradox, fhould happen? That, from the fame
circle of land, the ecclefiaftics claim a tenth of the produce,
in moft inftances equal to a half of the rent; the ftate one-
fifth; and the remainder of the referved rent will not always

ways fatisfy the demand of the poor's rate. In the following pages, that inquiry has been made, and the myftery has
been, in fome degree, developed.

Another objeƌ worth the attention of the minifter of a
great nation has been comprehended in this inquiry; an
objeƌ not confined folely to any particular code of laws,
but embracing all legiflative aƌs whatfoever; the whole
force and the energy of which lie entirely in the means
provided for infuring their exaƌ and uniform execution.
What are all aƌs of parliament, which profefs to comprehend every rank and denomination of fubjeƌs, but a rule
of municipal conduƌ which *all* are to guide themfelves by?
and the vindicatory fanƌion contained in them is the compelling power. Now, if that fanƌion is fuch, as when called
into ufe, indicates a prefuppofed depravity in thofe who
are to be governed, an injury is done in the very prelude;
and the teft of the ordinance is vitiated *ab initio*, becaufe
the moral delinquency of the fociety is prejudged. Such is
the fanƌion which is expeƌed to enforce the execution,
not only of the poor-laws, but of moft of the penal claufes
in the Statutes at Large; they are to be enforced by penalties,
on the information of fellow-fubjeƌs, who the legiflature
fuppofes will degrade themfelves to become informers; not
for the good of the public, not from patriotic, moral, or
religious, motives, but from the vileft of all, from the fordid
motive of gain, it is fuppofed that a fubjeƌ of the ftate
will place his neighbour under the correƌion of the law.

This

This general idea difgraces the nation, and the principle is proved by experience to be ineffectual.

The manufacturing and commercial interefts of the nation feem to have underftood mankind better than the ftatefman, or at leaft they have formed a better opinion of their neighbours; for, in the acts of parliament to prevent frauds and abufes amongft the manufacturers and artizans, they have modelled the penal fanction on a different principle; the whole penalty is given to the poor, and they are, in a committee, empowered to appoint an infpector, whofe duty it is to go his rounds, to fee the regulations enforced, lay his informations, and fee the penalty diftributed according to the act. The ftrict execution of thefe acts of the legiflature is a proof of the efficacy of the means ufed; for, the penal fanction of laws is not intended, like cobwebs, to catch flies only, and fuffer the larger infects to break through the web; it is a net for all, and equally intended as a compulfive regulation to the *poor* as to the *rich*, to the *overfeer* as to the *magiftrate:* a hint, therefore, from thefe regulating ftatutes, might give energy to the poor-laws and vigour to the execution of them, or at leaft would increafe the revenue for their maintenance from the proper fources, --- the pockets of thofe who undertake an office, but neglect the duties annexed to it.

On the whole, the public will read, in the following pages, a fummary hiftory of the duties of the poor to, and their claims from, fociety, throughout that part of this

kingdom

kingdom fubject to the poor-laws, traced from the earlieft times in which the poor, and their interefts, have been confidered by the legiflature, and continued to the clofe of the laft parliament ; together with a tranfient view of the thoughts and opinions of thofe whofe writings on the fubject have been handed down to us ; interfperfed with obfervations as the fubject gave rife to them ; together with fuch reflections as have arifen from an attention to the whole of the evidence here fubmitted to the public, compared with the opinions of thofe men, eminent for their abilities and the purity of their intentions, who have made this inquiry an object of their contemplation.

The prefent critical fituation of this kingdom, fo different from that peaceful and profpering ftate which it occupied during the period through which much the greateft part of the following treatife was written, calls upon every man, whatever may be his clafs or condition of life, to fupport, by all the means in his power, the conftituted government of his country, which can no way be fo effectually done as by promoting induftry, economy, and good morals, among the poor. If, in times of peace and profperity, this is the more particular duty of the magiftrate, in the commencement of a war, the principle of which is as novel as its event is uncertain, it becomes a crime to neglect that which, in times of peace, would be thought no immaterial obligation ; and, if the duty of a minifter fhould impel him, in thofe times, to

make

make fuch regulations in the internal police of the kingdom as to call forth the greateft poffible production of
its induftry, with which the profperity and happinefs of
all ranks in the ftate muft be connected, much ftronger
fhould he feel that impulfe in the beginning of fuch a
war as the prefent, the confequences of which to our
religion, our morals, our laws and conftitution, no human
eye can forefee ; but the immediate effect of which on
our trade, our commerce, our eftates, and our property,
we muft all foon feel : therefore, there can be no time
or fituation more proper than the prefent for an inquiry of
the kind here offered to the public ; although there may be
many enlightened minds in this kingdom whofe abilities and
means of information may qualify them to offer a more fatisfactory treatife.

CLARE,   T. R.
March 12, 1793.

PREFACE

SECOND EDITION.

SOME reafon may be expected by the public for the alterations contained in this Second Edition of the Hiftory of the Poor, &c. and, probably, fome account of the motive which influenced the author to its continuation. The firft is, undoubtedly, due to his readers as a matter of right : the fecond he rather confiders as an act of choice, on his part, with which he can have no objection to comply.

The courfe of inquiry which the inveftigation of this fubject naturally pointed out brought me to the knowledge of the ancient mode of diftributing the revenues of the church. This branch of the hiftory of elder times caught my attention by bringing to view an obfolete

folete claim, on a certain part of the ecclefiaftical revenues, towards the maintenance of the poor; and, although many generations are paffed away fince fuch a
claim was exemplified by the practice of the age, yet it
ftruck me as fufficient to found an equitable expectation
of the affiftance of the parochial clergy in the management and regulation of the domeftic habits of that clafs
of our fellow-fubjects to whom they were, in remote days,
not only fpiritual paftors, but diftributors of relief in times
of diftrefs.

The office which is intended to be trufted to the clergy
in the management of the poor, if the Bill now before
the Houfe of Commons, or any other on a fimilar principle, fhould pafs into a law, renders it unneceffary to
dwell on this fubject, as it will be a proof that the expectation of parliament fixes itfelf on the parochial clergy,
as gentlemen eminently qualified by fituation, education,
and principle, to take fome fhare in that moft neceffary
and important point of our internal police, to which we
ought all to pay our moft active attention; --- the regulation of the poor. And, as there exifts no doubt but that
the clergy, on their parts, are as *willing* as they are *able*
to give their affiftance, the prefling for it, on the principle
of an equitable right or duty, is become an ungenerous
furplufage: befides, the attempt to fix this claim, in order
to engraft a duty, has been thought by many, to whofe
opinions I pay much deference, a topic more replete with
harm

harm than good, and has occasioned a publication which, probably, would otherwise have been more honourably noticed, to be passed over almost in silence, although by no means in contempt; while the principles of its author, as a friend to the hierarchy, have been somewhat called in question.

That part of the Inquiry into the History of the Poor, their Rights and Duties, is, therefore, in this Edition, omitted.

With respect to the author's motive for the continuation of his History to the present day, he candidly confesses two impelling reasons. The first, he hopes, will be allowed, as founded on public principle; to give more light on this important subject than was in his power at the time of his writing the Letters contained in the former Edition. This country has now experienced the effect of the present system, through a time of scarcity, till lately unfelt; it has seen, that, as the skin of the infant expands itself to the stature of the man, so does the principle of charity, which now has, for near two centuries, become, to the immortal honour of this nation, the law of the land, expand itself to those stretches of imperious necessity which admit of the expenditure of additional millions to preserve our poor countrymen from want; and that at a time while the political necessities of the state press upon all ranks of people with a force hitherto incredible, and have, unitedly, occasioned a mag-

b   nitude

nitude of expenfe, which all the abilities of an able financier can fcarcely provide ways and means to anfwer.
But, at the fame time that *humanity* feels gratified, our
prudence fhould alfo be able to concur in approbation of
the vaft expenditure which has been, and may continue in a certain degree to be, incurred in the maintenance of the poor. This will not be the cafe until,
by fome actively-efficient meafure, the induftry of the
lower claffes is called out to do its beft, before the pockets
of the next clafs of ufeful fubjects of the ftate are emptied
to the relief of their poorer neighbours.

The writer muft alfo confefs a tacit pleafure in committing to the prefs the laft fheets of the continuation of
his Hiftory, as it will appear from them that the firft
edition of this tract has not been written in vain, but
that our countrymen will probably reap fome advantage
from this employment of his hours of leifure, as it may
have been the means of exciting the firft abilities in the
nation to an inveftigation of the fubject, and occafioned
Defire to be united with Power in the fervice of the
caufe. And although the prefent Bill, which is now
before the Houfe, the firft public refult of that union,
may not meet the ideas and expectations of all parts of
the kingdom fubject to the poor-laws, which cannot be
a matter of our wonder, the intricacy of the fubject,
the wide extent of its operations, the number of interefts any rule which regulates the conduct of fo many

millions

millions of people, in different fituations, muft clafh with, and the little pains which is taken by people in general to underftand an act of parliament of fome intricacy, being confidered; yet we may, with confidence, truft that the meafure is now in good hands; becaufe this nation, after the lapfe of near two hundred years, has again feen, in The Bill, for the better Support and Maintenance of the Poor, now before the Houfe of Commons, an inftance of a minifter of ftate, in the midft of innumerable difficulties attendant on our prefent arduous political fituation, taking upon himfelf the burthen of a meafure of the firft impor- tance to the internal happinefs of the nation, which has been from that remote time till now left to the ftraggling attention of any member of parliament; and, when this fact recalls to our memory the wifdom which characterized the minifters of the reign of Elizabeth, (and the parliamen- tary journals of thofe times inform us that the famous forty- third ftatute of her reign, the prefent corner-ftone of our poor-laws, was not the produce of one feffion, but the col- lected valuable remnants of many bills on the fubject, which had been, in the parliamentary language of the day, *dafhed*,) let us not defpair of the beft confequences arifing from the prefent united application of abilities, knowledge, and per- feverance, to the better fupport, maintenance, and educa- tion, of the poor.

LETTERS

LETTERS

𝔒𝔫 𝔱𝔥𝔢 𝔓𝔬𝔬𝔯;

THEIR

RIGHTS, DUTIES,

AND THE

LAWS RESPECTING THEM.

LETTER I.

DEAR SIR,   *Clare*, 1791.

HEREWITH you receive the firſt letter of a ſeries, which ſhall comprehend an inveſtigation of the cauſes that produce ſo much miſery and diſtreſs among our poor; which will be accompanied, during the continuation of the ſubjeʤ, with hints tending to a plan, that, it is imagined, may render their ſituation more comfortable, and leſſen that heavy burthen of rates, which impoveriſh the landed intereſt, and, in faʤ, anticipate the ſource of our political expenditure.

I began the inquiry during the former part of the winter, with the intent of ſending it to the Editor of the Annals of Agriculture; but doubted with reſpeʤ to the propriety of the ſubjeʤ for that compilation; until, having the pleaſure of your company at Clare, you indicated a wiſh that it might be ſent you.

B

It

It very forcibly ſtruck me, that, during the ſolitude of a long winter, ſpent in the country, in the lapſe of time which daily paſſes away between the hours allotted to refreſhment and repoſe; that mind muſt be torpid and inactive, in which many ideas do not ariſe that cannot be referred to perſonal views or ſelfiſh conſiderations, and which are not occaſioned by objects of buſineſs or pleaſure, but take their origin from better motives, and impulſes of a higher nature; from reflections on the relative ſtate our happineſs is placed in, with reſpect to that of our friends and more immediate neighbours, in the firſt place; of our countrymen, in the next; and, ultimately, not only of the human race, but of the whole animal creation.

One ſerious cauſe muſt, therefore, ariſe from this ſource, to taint the happineſs of a life paſſed in retirement; as our ideas take their colour from the more immediate objects of our obſervation, it is impoſſible but that ſomething of a ſombrous and unpleaſant hue muſt tinge the mind, while it attends to what paſſes in that claſs of ſociety which is more immediately ſubject to our obſervation; and while we perceive and feel, as it were, the ſordid miſery and diſtreſs of our near, though humble, neighbours, it is impoſſible that a mind, rightly diſpoſed, whoſe beſt energy is to be alive to the woes of others, can enjoy uninterrupted eaſe, while ſo much miſery is ſo near the threſhold; charity can do much, but cannot do every thing, nor for every body, although ſeconded by the beſt intentions and moſt liberal purſe; objects of miſery, like mountain above mountain to the weary traveller, ariſe to the view; creating deſpair of attaining to the end of their wiſhes, even in thoſe who poſſeſs the ſtrongeſt and moſt liberal minds, and recalling neceſſary and honeſt Prudence to her ſeat. But ſtill one ſource of beneficence may be opened without fear of impoveriſhment, and the powers of the mind may be called to the aid of charity. Is it impoſſible to explore the cauſes of that miſery which we diſcern among our poor neighbours? And, the cauſes being explored, may not a remedy be

pointed

pointed out? The attempt is worth the labour, although the event should not be succefsful; this one fact being too glaring for humanity to be blind to, that, while a tenth part of our countrymen enjoy the comforts or revel in the luxuries of life, the patient and industrious multitude are sinking beneath a load of poverty and wretchednefs.

Reflections, fuch as the preceding, gave rife to this inquiry; I thought that a few of the leifure hours of a country life could not be better employed than in an attempt to investigate the caufes of that mifery which we fee among our working poor, and to point out fome probable and practicable means of relief and amendment of their condition; conceiving, alfo, that the ideas and hints, which might arife from fuch an inquiry, could not make their appearance with fo much propriety in any publication as in the Annals of Agriculture; becaufe the object of it refpects the happinefs of a clafs of our fellow-creatures, without whofe manual labour the fruits of the earth could neither be fowed or reaped; and alfo re-collecting, that, if a ray of reafon is elicited in the progrefs of the inquiry, it is due to the fhrine of Agriculture, which, if not Wifdom herfelf, bears a ftrong refemblance of her divine original: I therefore dedicate the following pages, on this too-much-neglected fubject, to your fervice, and your reader's patient candour.

The page of hiftory reveals to us this melancholy and awful truth, that the happinefs of millions has, in all ages, been at the beck and in the power of units, and thofe often the meaneft and worft of mankind; myriads have fallen by the fword, difeafe, and famine, the victims of war, led on to their deftruction by wretches who have difgraced the human race; but our inquiry has nothing to do with the dire effects of zeal, defpotifm, or political revolution; our employment lies in the vales of peace and plenty; our purpofe is to inveftigate this problem, Why our laborious poor are fo wretched? Does the complaint arife from phyfical caufes, or from the regulations of fociety? Can fociety, by laws, regulations,

example,

example, or by any and what means, meliorate their condition?

The unceafing laws of nature muſt, in every climate, have their energy; effects muſt every where be analogous to, and flowing from, their caufe; gradations of comfort arife in civilized fociety in due proportion to the degree of civilization; the fqualid inhabitant of Magellan's Streights, although fo wretched and negatived in appearance, in all that makes life fupportable, fhares, doubtlefs, a degree of happinefs in proportion to his capacity of enjoyment; that capacity enlarges as civilization prevails, and means of obtaining the objects of our wifhes alfo increafe. In this ifland, a difpofition to relifh the comforts of life, the meaneſt of us equally poffeffes with the greateſt; furely, therefore, thofe comforts correfpondent with our fituation, fhould not be removed at fuch a diſtance from the grafp of any of us, as to be attainable only by a breach of the laws of fociety. — In fome climes, favoured by a more direct approach of the folar ray, the various articles of drefs are an incumbrance, and the native has no care what raiment he fhall clothe himfelf with: in fuch climate he may, literally, imitate the lilies of the field, which neither toil nor fpin, and are clothed only in the attire Nature prepared for them. How different is the neceſſity in this higher latitude; fcarce a natural day paſſes away, even during the fummer folſtice, but our comfort and health require that clothing, to obtain which the price of many days' labour muſt be paid. How much ſtronger does urgent neceſſity require warmth of clothing in the dreary leaflefs winter, when every gale wafts rheumatifm and ague; and what is effential to the health and prefervation of the parent, is furely not lefs fo for the child. Hence, in this country, arifes one unceafing call for no inconfiderable fhare of the price of labour; a call fanctioned as well by an attention to the prefervation of life as by the dictates of decency, the refult of ideas connected with civilization.

Another

Another ftrong and urgent demand on the fcanty revenue of the poor man, is the expenfe of fire. In more fouthern latitudes, the whole year may be paffed, and it may not be an article effential to the life or health of the inhabitant: poffibly, in climates included in ninety of the one hundred and eighty degrees of north and fouth latitude, the lower claffes of fociety fee not the blazing hearth, or have no occafion for it in their domiciles throughout the year: their habits of life are different; their fimple food, confifting principally of the fruits of the earth, requires not much affiftance from fire to make it fuitable to the palate or proper for digeftion; we read that the inhabitants of the iflands in the South Sea* knew not the ufe of hot water; but, in this ifland, fire is neceffary, at times, throughout the whole year; in fummer, for preparing the food, and in fpring, autumn, and winter, for the comfort alfo, if not for the prefervation, of the cottager.

Our climate alfo occafions another demand to fcreen the poor man from its rigours. Throughout a confiderable part of the habitable world, the genial warmth of the atmofphere is fuch, that the human race requires fcarce any protection from the common air and fky: in thofe climes, man may wander with man, joint tenants of the fhade; but here, a domicil is neceffary; although the hardy aborigines of the ifland might not require fuch a fhelter, yet man, tamed and made tender by the arts of civilization, demands a threfhold, within whofe facred bounds the domeftic hearth may be fheltered, as well from the affaults of the weather, as thofe of his boifterous or impertinent neighbour; hence, therefore, arifes another call on his flender income, an income earned by the labour of his hands and the fweat of his brow.

Thefe three neceffary and unavoidable calls on the finances of the poor have been already ftated, in the articles of clothing, fire, and dwelling: but a much larger and more important de-

* Cook's Voyage.

mand

mand remains to be mentioned,—the daily fupply of food; the fupply of fuch meat and drink, as fhall enable him, day after day and year after year, to pafs through a life of hard labour and conftant fatigue; a degree of labour which the ftrongeft of us, whofe mufcles have not been trained to the purpofe, would fhrink from in the experiment of a day, perhaps of an hour; and the produce of this labour, the reward of thefe toils, to be expended, not on himfelf only, but frequently to be divided with a wife and family of children, who often have no honeft means of increafing their hufband's and parent's income.

But this is not all: the occupation of the labourer, as well as the nature of his being, fubjects him to acute illnefs, to chronic diforders, and at length to old age, decrepitude, and impotence; the inftant any of thefe unavoidable misfortunes of life attack him, the fource of every comfort is ftopped, and without the aid of his more opulent neighbours, or, what is infinitely to the credit of this nation, without the interference of the godlike laws of his country, this ufeful clafs of our countrymen would fink in the arms of famine or defpair.

Thefe, I apprehend, are the phyfical caufes of that depth of wretchednefs and mifery which we too often fee in the cottages of the poor; not to mention the wayward nature of the human difpofition; the example and prevalence of vicious habits; the facinating charms of intoxication; the confequential habits, idlenefs and diffipation; the indolence which is concomitant with a broken fpirit; and that careleffnefs and indifference to what may happen in future, which is too apt to arife in the mind that cannot fee its way through prefent difficulties: thefe are frailties infeparable from the nature of human beings, which increafe and aggravate their diftrefs, and which nothing but a proper fenfe of religion can remove; and neither the power of the legiflature or the wifdom of the philofopher can teach to alleviate.

But

But it is not from climate, it is not from the frailties of human nature alone, or the neceſſary wants and demands which the preſervation of life and health inculcates to the mind of man, and the inſufficiency of the earnings of bodily labour to attain the gratification of them, that the appearance of the labourer indicates ſuch wretchedneſs; the laws, the cuſtoms, and habits of ſociety, are all contributory to this effect; and the exceſs of civilization occaſions diſtreſſes ſuperior, yet ſimilar, to what the ſavage experiences in his ſtate of nature; ſuperior, becauſe *his* diſtreſs is not aggravated by a near view of the tantalizing contraſt, the enjoyments of opulence and luxury; ſimilar in the effects, which are, cold, hunger, and diſeaſe; in the one inſtance, the ſavage muſt be ſatisfied with the order of nature, which eſtabliſhes no law of appropriation, but occupancy; he, conſequently, cannot blame the laws and habits of ſociety, which aggravate, if they do not, in fact, give riſe to, the misfortunes of the Engliſh labourer: this is an aſſertion which demands an inquiry; and, if the principle is eſtabliſhed by ſuch an inveſtigation, ſhould not thoſe laws, habits, and cuſtoms, be modified, to correſpond with the feelings of humanity?

In the firſt place, it is apparent that bodily ſtrength is the only patrimony the labourer enjoys; this is to ſupply him and his family with the neceſſaries of life: the ſame patrimony, in conjunction with the opportunity of exerting the faculties of the mind, the inhabitant of an uncivilized country poſſeſſes; the firſt is reſtrained by the laws from treſpaſſing on *appropriated* property; and, in this country, all that can be called property, is *appropriated*; the other has ample ſcope for the exerciſe of his faculties, both of body and mind; the gifts of nature lying open to the firſt man who has ſtrength or dexterity ſufficient to occupy them. Here is a manifeſt advantage which the ſavage poſſeſſes, and the laws of his country have taken from the Engliſh labourer: but have not the laws, the maxims, or the benevolence, of ſociety, given to the poor ſome equivalent,

equivalent, inftead of the opportunity of obtaining property by occupancy ? the objects of which being, in every inftance, already occupied, he is reduced to the fole means of bartering the fweat of his brow for the neceffaries of life; they furely have, and an attempt fhall be made to point out the fubftitutes.

The labourer is worthy of his *hire*, becaufe he gives for it his fole property, his ftrength and his time, referving to himfelf only fufficient intervals for refrefhment and repofe : what ought therefore to be his *hire?* The anfwer is obvious : the neceffaries and comforts of life, equal to the reafonable wants of that clafs of fociety among which he ranks. Does he receive recompenfe for his labour equivalent to fuch a reafonable expectation ? The examination of the fact fhall be the anfwer to the queftion ; and, that the inquiry may be as clofe to the point as poffible, let us examine, in the firft place, how the retributions for labour were paid in days of yore; whether they then ftood in the fame proportion with the neceffaries of life, in times when luxury was not fo univerfally diffufed, and the cottager, not having the fight of the rich man's enjoyments fo immediately under his eye, might be fuppofed to be better contented with his homely fare, than in thefe days, when the ftrong expreffions of the poet are verified in every village :

—— Sævior armis
Luxuria incubuit, victumque ulcifcitur orbem.

——————————

L E T T E R   II.

FLEETWOOD's Chronicon Pretiofum will affift us in this inquiry; and, that the conclufion of the argument may not be fuppofed to reft on the foundations of fancy, fome extracts from that ufeful compilation fhall be produced.

The

The intention of the author was not much diffimilar to that of the prefent tract, except that he had a point to prove, we have only a fubject to examine; and, to prove his point, he has fearched not only all the publications then extant on the fubject, but alfo many manufcript accounts of different monafteries, where the prices of the different articles of life were regularly inferted, and in fome inftances where the prices of labour formed alfo part of the account. But no certain comparative view can be formed on this head until about the middle of the fourteenth century; when, by an act of parliament paffed in the 23d year of Edward the Third, the wages of the labourers were regulated, on account, as the preamble of the ftatute recites, of the great increafe of wages occafioned by the plague:* by the firft chapter, every perfon able of body, and under the age of fixty, not having means of maintaining himfelf, is bound to ferve thofe who are willing to employ him, at the wages which were ufually given fix years before the plague, and ftated to be,

	s.	d.
To haymakers and weeders, by the day - -	0	1
Mowing meadows, by the acre or day - - -	0	5
Reapers of corn, in the firft week in Auguft, by the day,	0	2
In the fecond week, and to the end of the month -	0	3
Threfhing a quarter of wheat or rye - - -	0	$2\frac{1}{2}$
Threfhing a quarter of barley, beans, peafe, or oats -	0	$1\frac{1}{2}$

That excellent model for all parochial antiquities, Sir John Cullum's Hiftory and Antiquities of Hawftead, will alfo affift in forming a more accurate idea of the proportional prices of labour and provifions in Suffolk throughout fome part of this century:

* This preamble indicates the caufe of the advance in the price of labour, a decreafe of the number of hands, and proves the policy of the act to decreafe, not increafe, wages.

						s.	d.
1387. Wheat threfhed, per quarter	-		-			0	4
Other grain	-	-	-	-		0	2
A reaper, per day	-	-	-	-		0	4
Man filling dung-cart three days		-		-		0	10½
1389. Wheat reaping, per acre	-		-		-	0	7
Mowing an acre of grafs	-		-		-	0	6

Thefc prices are without meat, drink, or other courtefy demanded. *

The prices of provifions, and the neceffaries and comforts of life, were, during the fame century, as follow :

A. D.				£.	s.	d.
1309. A pair of fhoes	-	-	-	0	0	4
1314. A ftalled, or corn-fed, ox	-		-	1	4	0
1314. A grafs-fed ox	-	-	-	0	16	0
A fat ftalled cow	-	-	-	0	12	0
A fat fheep unfhorn	-	-	-	0	1	8
A fat fheep fhorn	-	-	-	0	1	2
A fat hog, two years old	-		-	0	3	4
A fat goofe	-	-	-	-	0	0	2¼
Ale regulated by proclamation, in refpect to price, a gallon	-	-	-	0	0	1
1338. Wheat, a quarter	-	-	-	0	3	4
Barley, a quarter	-	-	-	0	0	10
Peafe and beans, a quarter	-	-	0	1	0
Oats, a quarter	-	-	-	0	0	10
White wine, a gallon	-	-	-	0	0	6
Red wine, a gallon	-	-	-	0	0	4
1387. Barley, at Leicefter, a quarter	-	-	0	2	0
1388. Lactage of a cow with its calf, one year, and a hen,	0	6	8

* Hiftory and Antiquitics of Hawftead, p. 188, 190.

1388. Wheat,

				£.	s.	d.
1388. Wheat, per quarter	-	-	-	0	4	0
Oats, per quarter	-	-	-	0	2	0
An ox	-	-	-	0	13	6
A boar	-	-	-	0	1	8*

It is not an eafy matter to determine, from the prices fpecified in Fleetwood, what was the average-rate, at which provifions were fold, the year parliament regulated the price of labour; for, about the middle of this century, years of dearth and plenty almoft alternately follow each other, and the peftilence alfo occafioned a confiderable difference; but the articles extracted are in thofe years, when none of thefe caufes affected the price of provifions, and may therefore be efteemed a tolerable exact average for the fourteenth century.

In the beginning of the next century in the year 1404, the pay of a labourer was fometimes two-pence, fometimes three-pence, as appears from a computus of the Prior and Canons of Burchefter; and in

				£.	s.	d.
1446. Labourers without diet	-	-	-	0	0	3½
From Michaelmas to Eafter, 1d. lefs.						
A mower in harveft, without diet	-	-	0	0	6
A reaper and carter, without diet	-	-	0	0	5

The prices of neceffaries and provifions from the fame computus:

				s.	d.
1407. A cow	-	-	-	7	0
Two bufhels of wheat	-	-	-	0	10
Five bufhels and a half of falt	-	-	3	4¼
1425. Peafe, per quarter	-	-	-	2	2
Gallon of ale, from 1d. to	-	-	0	1¼

			s.	*d.*
1425. Gallon of red wine	-	-	0	8
Gallon of sweet wine	-	-	1	4
Two yards of ruffet cloth for the fhepherd	-	2	2
Thirty pair of winter gloves for the fervants	-	4	0

The following from other computus's:

				s.	*d.*
1444. Wheat, a quarter	-	-	-	4	4
Malt, a quarter	-	-	-	4	0
Oats, a quarter	-	-	-	1	8
Flitch bacon	-	-	-	1	8
1445. Wheat, a quarter	-	-	-	4	6
Oats, a quarter	-	-	-	2	0
Gallon of ale	-	-	-	0	1½
1447. Wheat, a quarter	-	-	-	8	0
Oats, a quarter	-	-	-	2	1¼
1448. Wheat, a quarter	-	-	-	6	8
Oats, a quarter	-	-	-	2	0
1449. Wheat, a quarter	-	-	-	5	0
1450. Wheat, a quarter	-	-	-	8	0
Oats, a quarter	-	-	-	2	0
Gallon of ale	-	-	-	0	1
1463. Wheat, a quarter	-	-	-	2	0*

In the fixteenth century, only two inftances are to be found of the wages of a labourer, one in 1514, the other in 1557.

A. D.			*s.*	*d.*
1514. Labourers from Eafter to Michaelmas, except in harveft,	0	4
Ditto from Michaelmas to Eafter	-	-	0	3
A mower in harveft, with diet, 4*d*. without	-	0	6
A reaper and carter in harveft, with diet, 3*d*. without,	0	5

* Fleetwood's Chron. Pret.

1514. A

					s.	d.
1514.	A woman-labourer, and other labourers, with diet,					
	2½d. without	-	-	-	0	4½
1557.	Threfhing a quarter of wheat	-	-	1	1
	Ditto of rye	-	-	-	0	10
	Ditto of barley	-	-	-	0	5

Prices of provifions, &c. in the 16th century:

					£.	s.	d.
1512.	Oats, a quarter	-	-	-	0	2	0
	Beans, a quarter	-	-	-	0	4	0
1513.	Oats, a quarter	-	-	-	0	2	4
	Beans, a quarter	-	-	-	0	4	2
1515.	Beans, a quarter	-	-	-	0	4	2
1533.	Fat oxen	-	-	-	1	6	8
	Fat wethers	-	-	-	0	3	4
	Fat calves	-	-	-	0	3	4
	Fat lambs	-	-	-	0	1	0
	Beef in London 2½lb. or 3lb.	-	-	0	0	1
	Mutton, per quarter, in London	-	-	0	0	8
1557.	Wheat, a quarter before harveft	-	-	0	8	0
	Wheat, a quarter after harveft	-	-	0	4	0
	Malt, a quarter before harveft	-	-	0	5	0
	Malt, a quarter after harveft	-	-	0	4	8
1558.	A good fheep	-	-	-	0	2	10

In this inquiry there is no occafion to enter into an explanation of the comparative value of money in the three centuries, through a great part of which thefe notices have been taken ; becaufe the prices of labour and provifions have been valued by the fame fpecies of real or imaginary coin; and therefore the value of fuch, although very different from what bears the fame denominations in this century, is quite competent to illuftrate the ratio the prices of labour bore at thefe periods to the prices of the neceffaries of life.

LETTER

LETTER III.

INSTANCES of the prices of labour, and the cotemporary prices of provifions have been continued, by the affiftance of the *Chronicon Pretiofum*, to a later æra than that in our ecclefiaftical hiftory; when the 31ft ftatute of Henry VIII. ch. 13. laid the axe to the root of all monaftic poffeffions in this kingdom, and transferred their eftates and rights to the crown. The effect this total change of property had on the fituation of the poor remains to be confidered.

It will, at firft fight, be thought, and is indeed believed to be the fact, by thofe who have fuperficially inveftigated the hiftory of this period, that this act, at once, ftruck off many of their comforts, and deprived them of many fources of affiftance, which are fup-pofed to have flowed to the poor in numberlefs ftreams, from the kitchens, refectories, ftores, and cellars, of the monafteries; and that the different acts of parliament for their relief, which reflect honour on the annals of our hiftory, towards the end of the fix-teenth and beginning of the enfuing century, arofe from a neceffity, occafioned by this capital ftroke of the 8th Henry's defpotic au-thority; but the hiftory of the times does not authorize the con-clufion.

It rather appears that what ftreams did, in fact, flow from thefe ecclefiaftical fraternities, to the poor of the kingdom, were fhallow and penurious; at the beft, the coarfe offal of a homely board; indeed, if the mode of life which was purfued by the nobility and gentry of this age be confidered; if we recollect, that the metropolis was not then, and, indeed, has not been till lately, that overgrown monfter, which engluts, within its maw, a property that, fpread on the humble board of the cottager, would feed millions; but, on the contrary, almoft every village then boafted, as its conftant inhabitant, one or more fubftantial, if not ennobled, landlord, whofe

whofe hofpitable feat bore a femblance, according to the riches and rank of the owner, to that economic profufion, which, by the inftance fo happily preferved for the information of pofterity, by Dr. Percy,* appears to have graced the character of the fifth Earl of Northumberland, who lived near the beginning of this century; we fhall not, if fimilar inftances, in proportion to rank and fortune be fuppofed to be prevalent, imagine the poor to have much felt the want of fuch affiftance, as the heads of monafteries permitted to be given away at their gates; which, from the relations of modern travellers, who have lately vifited thofe countries on the continent, where monaftic inftitutions are ftill in full force, and efpecially from the obfervations of Dr. Ducarel, in his tour through Normandy, where the cuftoms, endowments, and charitable donations, of the monafteries and priories may be fuppofed, from their former connection with, to be fimilar to, what was experienced in this country, appear to be infignificant and trifling, always excepting thofe inftances where the particular motive of the endowment was to enfure a hofpitable reception to the traveller. Tanner alfo, by a note in the preface to *Notitia Monaftica*, appears to be of opinion, that it cannot be attributed to what the poor received from the religious houfes, that no parochial affeffments for their relief were found neceffary during the prevalence of the monaftic inftitutions; although it appears that fome of the larger priories dignified one of their officers with the name of almoner.

But, be this fact as it may, it is to be prefumed, that, if the poor did not fuftain any great lofs from the abolition of the monafteries, in the article of any confiderable relief, they might have received from them, in provifion or alms; they certainly felt one great inconvenience from the number of the neceffitous being con-

* The Regulations and Eftablifhment of the Houfehold of Henry Algernon Percy, 1512. Printed for Dr. Percy, the prefent Bifhop of Dromore, but not publifhed.

fiderably

fiderably increafed; becaufe, on the diffolution of the fmaller monafteries, in the year 1535, whofe revenues did not exceed two
hundred pounds a year, it is faid, that not lefs than ten thoufand
perfons were fent to feek their fortunes in the wide world, without
any other allowance than forty fhillings and a new gown; and
a revenue of thirty or thirty-two thoufand pounds a year was
vefted in the crown; and, when the greater monafteries were diffolved, in the year 1539, and a revenue of one hundred and
four thoufand nine hundred and nineteen pounds was diverted
from the maintenance of people in idlenefs, and began to flow in
different channels,* if the number of the poor, thrown upon the
public by the diffolution of the leffer monafteries, be added to the
number which may alfo be fuppofed to have become a burthen
to the public by the diffolution of the greater monafteries, computing that number by the proportional revenue vefted in the
crown by the latter event to the revenue alfo vefted in the crown
by the former, amounting to a total of near forty-three thoufand
perfons, who in the lapfe of a few years had become additional
objects of charity; for, although many of the members of the
greater monafteries were allowed penfions, yet, if it be confidered
that they now enjoyed the liberty of becoming fathers of families, fuch a calculation will not appear to be extravagant; it
will then not occafion our furprife, that a few years after this
event, the legiflature fhould find occafion to interfere in their
behalf, when probably not lefs than a hundred thoufand perfons,
who had no vifible means of maintenance, preffed on the diftribution of the charitable fund vefted in truft with the ecclefiaftics, now in part wrefted from their gripe; and alfo became importunate fuitors to the defultory feelings of charitable individuals, who might naturally be moved with compaffion at the
fight of their father-confeffors now become needy fathers of a
young offspring.

* Notitia Monaftica, Preface.

Befides,

Befides, the wars, which, from the conqueft, had kept our population thin; a number of lives having been thrown away in
the different contefts, within the kingdom, for the fceptre; on
the continent of Europe, for foreign poffeffions; and in Afia, on
romantic principles of religious chivalry; had now, for a confiderable period, ceafed; and near a century had elapfed fince the
battle of Bofworth had feated Henry the Seventh on the throne,
who, by his marriage with Elizabeth, the heirefs of the York
family, had united the claims of the two houfes in his perfon;
and no internal commotion having, fince that event, occafioned
any confiderable wafte of blood; and, except at the battle of
Flodden-Field, which feems, for a time, to have quelled the
animofity of our northern neighbours, the nation having fuffered
no lofs of inhabitants from foreign wars; peace, of courfe, and
its concomitant, population, had increafed the riches of thofe
who poffeffed the opportunity of acquiring, and, at the fame
time, the number of thofe, whofe humble fituation precluded
them from fuch attempts; the number of inhabitants, therefore,
who had no means of fupport, except from their labour, confequently was confiderably increafed, * and, moft probably, among
the crowd which preffed on the public from the diffolved monafteries, few were there who could handle the plough, the flail,
or the fpade; but many, who, if they could not dig, were not
afhamed to beg; a privilege which different acts of parliament
had already laid under certain reftrictions.

---

* In 1377, the number of inhabitants in England and Wales amounted to 2,092,978.
In 1583, to 4,688,000.

CHALMERS'S ESTIMATE.

LETTER

LETTER IV.

THE situation of the poor, with respect to the price of labour and the necessaries of life, their claims also on the charity of those in whose possession was centred the property of this kingdom, having been considered; it will now be a topic worthy our attention to relate, briefly as possible, the notice the legislature of the kingdom has taken of them, from the period when they first became objects of legislation, unto the present time when they participate of a revenue amounting to near three millions sterling per annum, raised for their employment and relief by the authority of the state.

This inquiry may, with great propriety, pass over that distant æra, the transactions of which history has preserved in very faint and doubtful records; and, indeed, it is not probable that, in times when this island enjoyed not any regular form of government, a great attention should be paid by our governors to the welfare of the poor; nor is it matter of wonder that while the petty reguli of the heptarchy were contesting the boundaries of their insignificant dominions; or while a foreign family, attended by a swarm of martial and needy followers, were contending for the throne of England, or disputing among themselves for the prize they had obtained; that any humane or wise regulations should take place with respect to the poor, who were then only considered as the means by which the claims of their respective lords might either be enforced or defended; and, viewed in that light, they rank in a different class of citizens, and are distinguished by epithets different from, but not more respectable in society, than that of husbandmen.

After the family of William, the Norman, had been established on the throne for several generations, and Edward the First,

having

having made the conquest of North Wales, turned his attention to the defencelefs fituation of the lower clafs of his Welch fubjects, and produced, with the aſſiſtance of his parliament, that code of laws known in our ſtatute-books by the name of *Statutum Walliæ* ; in which were regulated the modes by which they might obtain redrefs of private and public wrongs ; and in which it is enacted, that a poor man, inſtead of putting in pledges to profecute a fuit, on fuing out a writ, ſhould only pledge his faith : from the date of this ſtatute, which was paſſed in 1284, no mention appears of the poor in the acts of parliament until 1349, when the ſtatute of labourers regulated their wages, as has been already mentioned, and in ſtrong language declared that their labour, while they were able to work, ſhould be their only refource, by the following words : " That no one, under pain of impriſonment, by pretence of piety or charity, ſhould prefume to give any thing to thofe who were able to labour, to encourage them in idlenefs and floth, that by thofe means they might be compelled to work for the neceffaries of life." Another ſtatute paſſed in the fame reign, which gave the poor the right of an attaint in pleas, real and perfonal, without fine, and the ſtatute of labourers, alfo, was confirmed, and the obfervance of it enforced by an impriſonment of fifteen days, and alfo by the puniſhment of burning them in the forehead, with an iron in the form of the letter F, if they left their work and went away into different towns, or into another country ; and alfo obliged the officers of cities or boroughs, in which they might refide, to deliver them up.

From this period, until the 2d of Richard the Second, the ſtatute-book is filent with refpect to them ; the parliament then, 1378, confirmed the ſtatute of the 23d of Edward the Third, and the other ſtatutes of labourers, and ten years afterwards repeated the confirmation ; and farther directed that no fervant or labourer ſhould depart from one hundred, rape, or wapentake, to another,

D 2   to

to ferve, or live elfewhere, or under pretence of going a pilgrimage, without a letter patent, containing the caufe of his going,
and the time of his return, on pain of being put in the ftocks until he finds furety for his return. This act of parliament alfo
regulated the wages of yearly fervants, in hufbandry, allowing to
the bailiff 13s. 4d. and clothing once a year; to the mafter-hind,
10s.; the carter, 10s.; fhepherd, 10s.; oxherd, 6s. 8d.; the deye, 6s.;
plough-driver 7s.: their wages were enforced, and the people were
reftrained from giving *more* by pecuniary penalties: for the firft
tranfgreffion, forfeiture of the overplus; fecond tranfgreffion, double the overplus; third offence, treble the overplus, or imprifonment of forty days. By the fame ftatute, thofe who had ferved in
any agricultural occupation, until they were twelve years of age,
were reftrained from being put out to any trade or myftery, on
penalty of the indenture, or covenant, being void; and all fervants
in hufbandry, and labourers, were prohibited to wear any fword,
buckler, or dagger, except for defence of the realm in the time
of war; but they were permitted to have bows and arrows, and to
ufe them on Sundays and feaft-days : all unlawful games were
alfo prohibited : the feventh chapter of this ftatute alfo directed,
that impotent beggars fhould live in the cities and villages where
they were refident at the time of paffing the act, and if the inhabitants of the faid cities and villages *ne voilent ou ne poient fuffir
de les trover*, i. e. were not willing or able to maintain them, *
they fhould be taken to other towns in the hundred, rape, or
wapentake, or to the towns where they were born, within forty
days after proclamation of the act, where they fhould continue
for life.

Three years after the date of this act, the legiflature made a
laudable provifion for the poor, from the appropriations of bene-

---

* This tranflation may poffibly be inaccurate.—I have fearched the French dictiona-
ries and gloffaries in my poffeffion, and confefs I cannot find fuch a meaning affixed to the
verb *trover*, but know of none fo proper.

fices,

fices, which was confirmed in the beginning of the reign of Henry the IVth; at which time it was enacted, that no labourer should be retained to work by the week; but for what reason it is not easy, at this distance of time, to conjecture.

The legislature remained silent on the subject from this period until 1414, when, by the second statute of Henry the Vth, justices of the peace are directed to send their writs for fugitive labourers and servants to every sheriff in England, and are also empowered to examine labourers, servants, and their masters, on their oaths, of all things done by them contrary to the ordinances and statutes, and to punish them, on their confession, as though they were convicted by inquest; which power is also recognized in the second year of Henry the VIth, with respect to those who take wages *superior* to what are allowed by statute; and, in the sixth year of the same reign, it is enacted, that justices of peace, in their counties, and the mayors and bailiffs, in every city, borough, and town, shall have power to make proclamation in every county, city, borough, and town, in full session, once a year, how much every servant, in husbandry, should take for his service for the year ensuing; and that two proclamations should be made between the feasts of Easter and Michaelmas for that purpose; which act is confirmed in the eighth year of the same reign.

In the year 1436, wheat and barley, being at a small price, (that is to say, wheat at 6s. 8d. and barley at 3s. per quarter,) are permitted, by a statute of the same date, to be exported without licence. Six years afterwards this statute is confirmed for ten years; and, in 1444, it is made perpetual; and, in this year, the legislature also enacted, that the wages of husbandmen, in harvest-time, should not *exceed* the following rates: a reaper, 4d. a day with board; without board, 6d.: a harvest-man, or driver, 3d. with board; without, 5d.: women-labourers, 2½d. with board; without, 4½d.: and that the wages of servants in husbandry, by the year, should not *exceed* the following prices; a bailiff, 23s. 4d. with

board, and 5s. for clothes; a chief hind, carter, or fhepherd,
20s. with board, and 4s. for clothes; a common fervant, 15s. a
year, board, and 3s. 4d. for clothes; a woman-fervant, 10s. board,
and 4s. for clothes; a child, under 14 years of age, 6s. with board,
and 3s. for clothes; and alfo directed that a fervant, in hufbandry, purporting to depart from his mafter at the end of the
year, fhould give him half a year's warning, or elfe ferve him the
year following.

From this time, no notice is taken of the agricultural poor,
and no new regulations which could affect them are to be found
in the ftatutes at large, until the eleventh of Henry the VIIth,
1494, except an act which paffed three years before, prohibiting
pulling down, or fuffering to decay, houfes of hufbandry; by
which means, the preamble to the act fays, in fome towns, where
upwards of two hundred perfons *were* occupied, and lived by
their lawful labour, *now* only two or three herdfmen are employed,
and the reft fall into idlenefs.* By the fecond chapter of the
eleventh of Henry the VIIth, vagabonds, and idle and fufpected
perfons, fhall be fet in the ftocks three days and three nights, and
have no other fuftenance but bread and water, and be then put out
of the town; and every beggar, not able to work, fhall refort to
the hundred where he laft dwelt, is beft known, or was born, and
there remain, on pain of like punifhment: and no artificer, or labourer, fhall play at any unlawful games, except during Chriftmas.
Two juftices are alfo, by the fame act, empowered to reftrain
the common felling of ale.   It is curious to fee how early, after the
relief of the poor became an object of the legiflature, the regu-

*. The legiflature, two centuries ago, feems to have been aware of the bad confe-
quences, to population and induftry, that arife from the confolidation of fmall farms,
which, where general, is a meafure which ftrikes at the root of every ftimulus to agricultural induftry among the poor, by excluding all profpect of ufing the plough and fickle
for themfelves.

                                                            lation

lation of alehoufes was alfo a fubject of their attention, and with what an equal ftep the laws refpecting vagabonds and alehoufes proceed together.

The parliament alfo, in the fame year, enabled poor perfons to fue out writs of fubpœna againft thofe that may give them caufe of complaint, and counfel fhall be appointed them, taking nothing for the fame, at the difcretion of the chancellor. The prices of labour were again regulated by the fame parliament.

In the 6th year of Henry the VIIIth, the wages of fervants, in hufbandry, are again regulated, as are the hours they fhall work, have for their meals, and fleep; and, by the twenty-fecond of the fame reign, juftices of the peace are empowered to licence, under their feals, fuch poor, aged, and impotent perfons, to beg within a certain precinct, as they fhall think to have moft need; and if any beg, without fuch licence, he fhall be whipped, or elfe fet in the ftocks; and a vagabond. taken begging fhall be whipped, and then fworn to return to the place where he was born, or laft dwelt, for the fpace of three years, and there put himfelf to labour.

All the other parliamentary regulations which refpect the poor labourers, between the interval of this laft-mentioned act and thofe of the 28th and the 31ft years of the fame reign; the firft of which vefted the fmaller monafteries, and the laft diffolved the whole ftructure of, monaftic inftitution, and vefted all their eftates in the crown; may be found in a capitular of ftatute 27th, Henry VIII. cap. 25, which directed, that all governors of fhires, cities, hamlets, parifhes, &c. fhall find and keep every aged, poor, and impotent perfon, who was born or dwelt three years within the fame limit, by way of voluntary and charitable alms, in every of the fame cities, parifhes, &c. with fuch convenient alms as fhall be thought meet by their difcretion, fo as none of them fhall be compelled to go openly begging: and alfo fhall compel every fturdy vagabond to be kept in continual labour. Children under

14

14 years of age, and above five, that live in idlenefs, and are taken begging, may be put to fervice by the governors of cities, towns, &c. to hufbandry, or other crafts or labours. A vagabond fhall, the firft time, be whipped, and fent to the place where he was born, or laft dwelled, by the fpace of three years, there to get his living; and, if he continue his roguifh life, he fhall have the upper part of the griftle of his right ear cut off; and if, after that, he is taken wandering in idlenefs, or doth not apply to his labour, or is not in fervice with any mafter, he fhall be adjudged and executed as a fe-lon. No perfon fhall make any open or common dole, nor fhall give any money in alms, but to the common boxes and common gather-ings, in every parifh, on pain of forfeiting ten times as much. Un-lawful games are alfo prohibited.

These, as far as they refpect the fubject of this inquiry, are the leading points, in which the legiflature of other times interfered in the regulations of the rights, claims, and conduct, of that clafs of the community, whofe only property is their perfonal ftrength, and whofe fole employment through life is hard labour : but there alfo exifted a defcription of fellow-fubjects, whofe rights were ftill more circumfcribed, and the exiftence of which clafs of men in this ifland is, much to the honour of the prefent age, proved at this day only by the page of hiftory, and fuch notices as are preferved in the black-lettered law-books of paft times.

They were called villains. The word has refpect to the nature of the tenure and the locality of their fervices, rather than to any par-ticular ideas of difgrace which were attached to their perfon; *villani quia villa adfcripti,* fays Lord Coke: they were in fome inftances the property of the lord, were transferred like other property, and that particular defcription of them, called villains in grofs, were in many refpects in a fimilar fituation to thofe Africans, who are objects of our commerce, and tranfported to the Weft Indies; but it appears, from Littleton's Tenures, that their perfonal fafety was guarded, and no inftances are to be found where they were exempted

empted from the general benefit of the laws of their country, unlefs where the laws and cuftoms, of a particular tenure, interfered,
and reduced them, in thofe inftances, almoft to a ftate of flavery.
It may be prefumed, therefore, that in all other refpects they had
an equal claim, with the reft of our fellow-fubjects, to a compenfation for their labour, while they were able to do any; and, when they
were incapacitated, they then claimed from the hand of charity
equally with their neighbours.

LETTER V.

AT this period, fo interefting to the feelings of all Englifh
Proteftants, when that vaft fuperftructure of Papal influence and grandeur, reared on the foundation of fear and fu-
perftition, which had exifted fo many centuries, fell, as it were,
by the magic touch of Henry VIII. to the ground, and an edifice more confonant to the principles of fober piety and good fenfe
arofe in its ftead; let us paufe awhile, and reflect on the different fituations the poor were in, both with refpect to their wants
and demands on fociety *then*, and that ftation which they *now*
hold : the contraft will appear ftriking, and fome ufeful reflections
may arife from it.

Their wages had uniformly hitherto borne a proportion to the
neceffaries of life; and, that fuch proportion might be preferved,
independent of the capricious or felfifh will of an interefted
mafter, and the impofing demands of fturdy lazinefs, the price
of labour had frequently been regulated by the legiflature, which
had alfo paid a conftant attention to the prices of provifions; and
all the neceffaries of life had been attainable hitherto, throughout
the whole period which has been fubject to our review, (except

E   in

in times of cafual dearth,) by a proportion of labour which left a furplus for accidents or illnefs; but, at the fame time that the legiflature had this equitable attention to their interefts, it enforced the neceffity of labour and employment, by corporal punifhments of the idle and wanderer, and by reftraining the hand of charity from giving perfons of fuch defcription any affiftance.

Through the fame æra we alfo find that the infirm, the aged, and the impotent, had no claims of affiftance from fociety, except on that portion of the poffeffions of the ecclefiaftics which feems to have been adequate, under the management of the clergy, to the demand on it; and the jealoufy of the legiflature, left the attempt made by the monafteries on that fund, by the appropriation of the great tithes to themfelves, might, in the end, divert it from its proper application, is very apparent, by that act of parliament which paffed in the 15th of Richard II. and was confirmed by the 4th of Henry IV.

Another circumftance well deferves our notice:—the luxuries of life were hitherto but little, if at all, in ufe among the poor; no deleterious fnuff or tobacco, no debilitating tea, no liquid fire, commonly called gin, or fpirits; thofe banes of health and morals, thofe fure deftroyers of the conftitutions of the prefent and of the rifing generations; and it is late in the period that we find any mention made of ale-houfes, recepticles of vice and immorality! from whence the Treafury draws a confiderable revenue, and at the fame time drains the poor of their property, conftitution, and morals.

Manufactures had alfo made but little progrefs among us, which, however they may enrich individuals, or increafe the fources of our commerce, are, to the labouring poor, when they are the means of congregating them to work in parties, or are introductory of fedentary employment, moft ferious evils; in as much as they are by long experience found to affect, moft materially, the health and morals of thofe employed in them; and when, which has happened
pened

pened in many places, they leave the parishes which have, for a time, been their refidence, (for, manufactures are naturally defultory,) thofe parifhes are left in miferable poverty and haplefs wretchednefs.

The means of intercourfe with popular cities were alfo lefs obvious; of confequence, all thofe crimes, which, being committed in a crowd, may efcape cenfure, were lefs practifed; and that evil example, which is always to be found where many idle people are affembled, was lefs before their eyes; befides, the moral conduct of the individual was more under the guidance of the ecclefiaftical director of his confcience, during the exiftence of the Roman Catholic perfuafion; which circumftance muft be allowed to have been a caufe of ftricter moral conduct among the poor than at prefent prevails.

It has been already hinted, that the population of the kingdom, particularly among the lower claffes of fociety, has confiderably increafed fince the abolition of monafteries; and that whatever alms the poor then received from thofe focieties of regular clergy, as well as the crumbs which fell from the tables of the opulent, who now expend their incomes in cities and places of public refort, are at prefent withdrawn; and the very numerous poor of this kingdom are, now, left a very heavy burthen on the landed property alone, while manufactures and commerce enjoy a confiderable portion of the benefit arifing from their labour.

At the fame time, a principle deftructive to the rights, and particularly affecting the lower claffes of fociety, feems now to pervade the whole fyftem of the management of the poor; a principle which is inherent to defpotic governments, but clafhes with the rights of a fubject under a limited monarchy, and which has, neverthelefs, increafed in this country in a direct proportion with the liberality and freedom of our excellent conftitution. The principle alluded to is that which leaves a chafm between the different orders of the ftate, and operates to this effect: that thofe who are born to hard

labour

labour for their maintenance fhall never have an opportunity of emerging from their low condition; the artizan or manufaßurer, the farmer or tradefman, may rife to the confequence of a legiflator: opulence will raife the poffeffor to diftinßions in fociety; an individual of every profeffion may look up with the well-grounded hope of becoming, in maturer age, of more importance among the higher claffes of the ftate than when he began his career; but between the labourer and any fuperior fituation among his countrymen there is now a dreadful gulph, which none, or fcarce any, can pafs. — During the æra which has been examined, fuch a principle does not appear to have prevailed, and yet the rights of the fubjeß were not then fo well defined as at prefent; the wages received, under fanßion of ftatute-laws, by the labourer, enabled the prudent to fave fomething; that fomething might *then* be applied to profit, in fmall occupations of land; a fmall bufinefs leads the way to a greater: — by thefe means the door was open to riches and authority; and honeft ambition was a fpur even to the cottager, of which he is now deprived; for, the induftrious man in thefe days feldom receives any affiftance from the overfeer, in the cafualties to which human nature is fubjeß, until every farthing of his favings is exhaufted, and he becomes, with refpeß to his poverty, on a level with the idle and the drunkard; and if he is fortunate enough, by many years induftry and economy, to accumulate a few pounds, no fmall bufinefs, in his line of life, is now open to him; the confolidation of fmall farms has precluded all hopes of employing his money in that bufinefs with which he has had moft experience; all, therefore, he can do is to buy a cottage, which the parifh-officers too often fix their attention on, as a fufficient reafon why he and his family, numerous as they may be, fhall not receive relief, becaufe he has vifible property. This chafm between the labourer and the other claffes in fociety, it is prefumed, may do more mifchief to the ftate, by deftroying every ftimulus to induftry, except dire neceffity, and actually become a more ferious caufe of
the

·the furprifing increafe of the poor's rates than even thofe inducements to diffipation and enervating luxury, which the policy of
finance holds out to them in the fhape of tea, fpirits, and ale-
houfes.

No wonder, therefore, that thofe who lead a life of retirement,
far from the haunts of the ambitious or voluptuous, who retreat
from bufinefs or pleafure, either to cultivate a more intimate knowledge of themfelves or to deceive the paffing hours by an attention
to the improvement or embellifhment of their eftates, fhould
have their fenfibility wounded by being not only hearers, but eye-
witneffes, of the mifery of their fellow-creatures. — No wonder
that thofe who have been nurfed in the lap of luxury fhould avoid
thofe fcenes which otherwife, it is probable, they would embellifh
by their tafte; and defert thofe manfions, now untenanted and
dreary, which, when occupied by the hofpitable owners, diffufed a
gleam of chearfulnefs through the country. It furely is not beneath the office of humanity, at times, to hold converfation with
the peafant, whofe labour improves or embellifhes our demefnes;
but the topic of fuch converfation too often diftreffes humanity,
and fends the hearer home dejected and diffatisfied.

Probably fome reflections may then arife in his mind not very
favourable to the prefent fyftem of poor-laws: being a witnefs of
their wretched fituation, he may reafonably conclude that the fum,
immenfe as it is, which the poor's rate, together with the charitable
donations of our anceftors, raifes for them, is not fufficient, or
that it is much mifapplied; for the rate itfelf is certainly an
enormous burthen, rifing from two or three fhillings in the pound,
upon the actual rental, up to fixteen, eighteen, or more, in fome
parifhes; and the whole of this revenue has increafed to the prefent
bulk, from nothing, in lefs than two centuries, and no part of it is
mortgaged, but the whole applied, or prefumed to be applied, to
their maintenance and relief.

Their

Their wages, it is true, are lefs in proportion to the value of money or the neceffaries of life, than they were in times antecedent to the prefent fyftem, probably lefs by one-third; and they alfo, in thofe times, received affiftance from the clergy, who, by their advice, then regulated their religious and moral principles, which are confiderable prefervers of induftry and good economy; therefore, raifing their wages would not alone be of fervice to them at prefent, becaufe the religious fentiment feems·extinct throughout the multitude in general, and morality has unawares expired with it; confequently thofe principles, which, if active, would kindle a fpark of honeft induftry among them, are totally inert; and additional wages, it is feared, would only induce additional excefles.

If education will fix habits unconnected with the moral fentiment; if Mr. Pope's maxim is true, that

> Juft as the twig is bent, the tree's inclin'd;

an opening is furely left which may be applied to the beft of purpofes, without raifing the wages of the labourer, without calling for affiftance from the clerical poffeffions, or expecting the clergy to attempt again the office of ghoftly directors with refpect to their poor parifhioners.

Induftry, early induftry, keeps the rifing age from prefent mifchief, and fafhions the future man to a life of honefty; and, depend on it, the religious principle, together with every refpected moral virtue, may be reared on the bafis of habitual induftry.

" To teach the young idea how to fhoot" is among the moft pleafing and important offices of life; how excellent muft be a plan formed on that fentiment, which would comprehend, and, in a manner, infure, the future well-being of fo large a portion of this nation; would deliver them from a childhood and youth, paffed in idlenefs and theft, to a manhood formed from the earlieft years to habits of induftry; would, in the mean time, render

their

their hours of fome value to their parents, which are now an incumbrance to them, and a peft to their neighbours.

Much has been done, it may be faid, for the rifing generation
within thefe few years, by Sunday-fchools; it is very far from my
intention to call in queftion either the principle on which the
patrons of Sunday-fchools proceed, or to difpute the fact that
they have done fervice; but, as the intention of Sunday-fchools is
to inculcate a religious principle, to give early habits of religious
duties, and to open the mind of the poor to religious inftruction, furely thofe feminaries are at prefent incomplete. Shall
the fix days be fpent in idlenefs, perhaps in theft and immorality,
while the feventh alone is taken care of ? May not the child who
is left to itfelf in a ftate of idlenefs, or, poffibly, for fo we know
it too often happens, fent out to fteal firing for its parents, or
encouraged to pilfer for its fuftenance through the other fix days
in the week, and who attends at the Sunday-fchools, where, from
fuperior readinefs and regularity of attendance there, and at church,
it is praifed by the mafter or miftrefs for reading and behaving well
on the Sunday; may not fuch a child, from fuch practice, im-
bibe habits of hypocrify, at the fame time that it is educated in a
regular attendance to religious duties ? Surely there is fome danger
that he may, in mature life, make ufe of this church-going habit,
as a cloak for his conduct the reft of the week; befides, it fhould
be confidered that the accomplifhments of reading and writing are
not effentially neceffary for all people; there muft always be in all
focieties of mankind fome who are hewers of wood and drawers
of waters; to whofe fum of happinefs, or honeft means of getting
their bread, thefe accomplifhments will not add an unit; and to
all the children of that clafs in fociety, for whofe benefit Sunday-
fchools have been with fo much well-meaning humanity encouraged;
fix days induftrious habits are recommended as a better preparation
to a feventh of religious duties and inftruction, than fix days paffed
in vice or idlenefs. But this topic fhall be dropped for the prefent,
and

and the utility of Sunday-fchools acknowledged on this general
principle,

Eft quodam prodire tenus, fi non detur ultrà.

In the mean time, the inquiry into the actual ftate and fituation
of the poor, as far as they are affected by the prevailing habits of
the times, as well as by the laws of their country; together with
the opinion which thofe who have paid any attention to the fubject, and have laid the refult of that attention before the public,
have formed of the caufes of their increafing wretchednefs and
our increafing expenfes; fhall be purfued, from the period at which
this paufe has been made, through the fucceeding years to the
prefent time; in full confidence that fome ufeful knowledge on
this important fubject may be gained; and in hopes that while we
are amufed we may be inftructed.

L E T T E R   VI.

WHEN I fent you the laft letter on this fubject, the difficulty of meeting with fufficient information in refpect
to the price of labour, and the neceffaries of life, from the period
which has hitherto been the object of this inquiry, unto the end
of the reign of Elizabeth, did not then occur to me; nor did I
forefee that I fhould be left in the dark on that fubject, when
Fleetwood's *Chronicon* ceafed to give me any longer its fteady and
faithful light. The record of the prices of wheat at Windfor-
market, which has been regularly taken by the Burfer of Eton-
College to fix the corn-rents for the year, is the only exact account, fo far back as it goes, in this kingdom; and that extends
only to the year 1595; but, not being able to accompany the
                                                                price

price of wheat from that period, which was only nine years anterior to the 43d of Elizabeth, with any certain cotemporary account of the price of labour; although I have taken every means
in my power to obtain such information as might be depended on
with respect to the concurrent price of labour and provisions to
the 43d year of Elizabeth, hitherto without effect; and being fearful that those among your readers, who have paid any attention to
what has already been said on the subject, may conceive it is de-
serted, and my word not intended to be kept with them; I determined to send you a few pages on that part of the inquiry, which
my library will enable me to elucidate, and my reason is adequate
to explain.

On perusing the English historians of the age antecedent to
that when the parliament of Elizabeth interwove the preservation
of the poor with the constitution of the kingdom; the assertion,
made in a former part of this tract, that the monks, if they could
not dig, were not ashamed to beg, is found to be well authorized
by history; for, it appears that the multitudes of idle people, which
the dissolved monasteries had vomited forth on the public, were
become a serious burthen on society, and occasioned the passing an
act in the first parliament of Edward the Sixth, which is as curious
in the preamble, as it is inconsistent, in the enacting part, with
every principle of humanity and justice: the preamble states, that
" forasmuch as idleness and vagabondry is the mother and root
of all thefts, robberies, evil acts, and other mischiefs, and yet idle
and disorderly persons, being unprofitable members, or rather
enemies, of the commonwealth, have been suffered to increase,
and yet do so, whom if they should be punished with *death*, whipping, imprisonment, and other corporal pain, it were not without
their deserts," be it enacted, &c.

In short, this curious piece of legislation makes a man who
liveth idly three days, the slave for two years of him who informs
against such an idler, he being first branded with a red-hot iron

F

on

on the breaft with the letter V ; during which two years he fhall be fed with bread and water, and *refufe*-meat, and caufed to work by beating, chaining, and otherwife, in any work, be it ever fo vile ; and, if he runs away from his mafter for the fpace of fourteen days, he fhall become his *flave* for life; after being branded on the cheek with the letter S ; and, if he runs away a fecond time, he fhall be adjudged a felon.

This act of parliament, fo difcreditable even to that age of diforder and defpotifm, arofe, as Rapin fays, from the neceffity the government experienced of obliging the monks to work, who were little inured to labour, but employed themfelves in going from houfe to houfe, infpiring people with the fpirit of rebellion ; and thus much is certain, let the caufe of fuch feverity have been what it may, that the act itfelf was fo diametrically oppofite to every juft principle of legiflation, that it was repealed in the third year of the fame reign, and during the adminiftration of thofe by whofe authority it had been paffed ; and the poor were then left by the legiflature much in the fame fituation as before the abolition of monafteries ; although certainly deprived of a fource of maintenance, and the number of them confiderably increafed by that diffolution.

Thofe to whom Henry the Eighth had left the care of his infant fon, even when affifted by the council, among whom many names of refpectable memory appear, feem to have been as infufficient to that department of government, which refpects the interior police of the kingdom, as we may reafonably fuppofe the minor king could have been, had he himfelf wielded the fceptre. What elfe but complete ignorance could have induced them to permit fo unpopular and unjuft an act to be paffed in the firft year of their young fovereign's reign, as has been alluded to ? which law they were fo foon obliged to repeal ; and, in the year following, the repeal, as an encouragement (as the preamble fays) to, and promotion of, induftry, an act was paffed which obliged fervants in

hufbandry

hufbandry to ferve the whole year, and not by days' wages; the occafion of which curious reftraint, it is difficult at this diftance of time to guefs; the ftatute-book, as well as hiftory, being filent on the fubject.

That the poor were now in a diftreffed fituation throughout the kingdom, is very apparent; they had loft fuch relief, whatever it might have been, as they had been accuftomed to receive from the monafteries; they had alfo loft a confiderable fource of employment, by the lands of the monafteries being granted to the nobles and followers of the court; who left the hufbandry of their newly-acquired domains to chance and negleft, which had been more attended to, and well cultivated, when under the infpection of the monafteries, and their tenants; and thofe alfo, who were lately their confeffors and fpiritual directors, who, while it was their intereft, influenced the poor to a life of induftry and content, ftill retained the fame influence over their minds, and made ufe of it now, to incite them to faction and fedition; certain confequences of that diftrefs, which arifes from idlenefs and diffipation; while the legiflature, to mitigate and allay the turbulent and diffatisfied fpirit then prevalent among the lower orders of the ftate, with an abfurdity fcarcely credible, paffed a law, that the poor of every parifh fhall be relieved, " with that which every parifhioner of his charitable devotion *will give*." 5th and 6th Edward VI. cap. 2.

As a top to the climax of their abfurdities in legiflating for the poor, during this fhort and unpropitious reign, parliament firft inftituted licenfed ale-houfes, and fanctioned them by an act which has the following preamble, as a reafon for the ftatute: " Forafmuch as intolerable hurts and troubles to the commonwealth of this realm doth daily grow and increafe, through fuch abufes and diforders as are had in common ale-houfes, and other houfes, called tippling-houfes." A preamble which fhould have preceded a prohibition, not a licenfe, or permiffion.

F 2

The short reign of Mary was paſſed in the regulation of what appeared to her, and her advifers, of much more importance than the feeding of millions; the bending the ſtubborn opinions of a few, in matters of religious controverſy.—And, can it be ſup-poſed, that either legiſlators or ecclcſiaſtics, who were employed in bringing heretics to the ſtake, could clevate their attention to the divine office of inveſtigating the means to preſerve the multitudes of their poor brethren from idlenefs and want ?   However, before all the perverted faculties of their minds were totally abſorbed in the taſk of regulating matters of religious opinion, with the accu-racy that their cotemporary legiſlator, Charles the Fifth,* regu-lated the motion of time-keepers, they had ſufficient leiſure to leave matters in the ſame ſtate, with reſpect to the poor, as they werc in the two laſt reigns ; except that they invented the ſcheme of expoſing thoſe who begged ; which, at that time, muſt, of ne-ceſſity, have been as well the aged and infirm, as the idlc; by obliging them to wear a badge on their breaſt and back openly, by an act of the ſecond year of the reign of Philip and Mary ; but, in theſe days, when the rights of human nature are ſo well underſtood, and, with ſuch merited ſuccefs, wreſted from the ſtrongeſt gripe of power, it will not ſtrike us with ſurpriſe, that, in thoſe times of ignorance, ſuperſtition, and deſpotiſm, the rights of the many ſhould be but little underſtood, and lefs attended to, by the few who held the iron rod of power.

The kingdom felt, during the reigns of theſe two children of the Eighth Henry, moſt ſerious effects from the ignorance of govern-ment in, or its inattention to, the regulation of the interior po-lice; being, at times, convulſed by inteſtine commotions, from its centre to its circumference ; as the rebellions of Kett, in Nol-folk ; that of Arundel, in Devonſhire ; and inſurrections in many

* Robinſon's Hiſtory of the Emperor Charles V. 4to edit. vol. iii. book 12.

counties, in the year 1549; and thofe of Wyatt, in Kent and Surrey, and Carew, in Cornwall, in 1554, plainly evidence.

It is no wonder, therefore, that in an early part of the reign
of Elizabeth, after the affairs of religion were fettled to the general fatisfaction of the nation, by the eftablifhment of the Pro-
teftant faith, according to the ritual of the church of England;
and foon after the Queen had entrufted the affairs of the kingdom
to the management of a Bacon and a Cecil; that we find the attention of parliament occupied on the fubject of the poor, with
a ferioufnefs of application that proved their conception of the
importance of the object to the univerfal welfare of the nation;
and which gave rife to three acts, that were paffed in the fifth
year of her reign; by the firft of which, thofe regulations made in
the feveral parliaments of the fourth of Henry the Seventh, and
the feventh and twenty-feventh of Henry the Eighth, for keeping
in repair farm-houfes, and maintaining of tillage, were enforced;
and all that was enacted, during the laft two reigns, on this fubject, was repealed. By the fecond act, the poor were to be relieved by what every perfon gives weekly; and, if any parifhioner
fhall refufe to pay, reafonably, towards the relief of the poor, or
fhall difcourage others, then the juftices of the peace, at their
quarter-feffions, may tax him a weekly fum; which, if he refufes
to pay, they may commit him to prifon: and, if any parifh has
more poor than they are able to relieve, juftices of the peace may
licenfe fo many of them, as they fhall think good, to beg within
the county.

The next act, which is the 5th of Elizabeth, cap. 4. is in force
at this day; and produces many ufeful regulations, as well in refpect to what perfons are compellable to ferve in any crafts or trades,
as in hufbandry: the conduct of the mafter and fervant, reciprocally to each other, is regulated; the production of teftimonials of
a fervant's conduct enforced by a penalty; the time during which
labourers

labourers fhall continue at work; befides many other heads of regulation; for all which, it is better to refer your readers to that excellent compendium, Burn's Juftice, or to the ftatute itfelf, than take up their time, or my own, in recapitulating its contents.—One feƈion, however, I muft call forth to their notice : the wages of fervants, labourers, and artificers, as well by the day as year, fhall be limited, rated, and appointed, by the juftices of the peace of the county, they having refpeƈt to the plenty, or fcarcity, of the times, &c. : and this feƈion is enforced by a penalty on the juftices, for not attending at the time required by the aƈt ; and alfo on the mafter for giving, and the fervant for taking, more than fuch rated wages. — Seƈt. 15.

The wifdom and humanity of government, during this long and profperous reign, engrafted, by degrees, fome of the beft moral principles of the Chriftian religion into the ftatute-law of the land. Our Saviour, in his converfations with his d'fciples, lays very great ftrefs on the duty of giving to the poor, adminiftering to the fick, and relieving the prifoner ; as may be feen in the 25th chapter of Matthew, and many other places in the New Teftament : and the parliament of Elizabeth fanƈioned that, which was before only a moral duty, by a law of the ftate ; for, by the 14th of Elizabeth, cap. 5. affeffments are direƈed to be made of the parifhioners of every parifh, for the relief of the poor of the fame parifh ; and a provifion is alfo made for the relief of the prifoners in common gaols. The mode, alfo, of treating 'that clafs, or defcription, of our fellow-creatures, called, by the law, vagabonds, feemed alfo much better underftood than in former reigns; but ftill was tinged with too much feverity, againft thofe members of fociety, who are guilty of a negative offence only, — that of want of induftry ; which, in faƈt, punifhes itfelf; and is, with juftice, punifhed by the municipal laws ; as it is certainly a crime, and fo confidered by one of the beft writers on that fubjeƈt this age has produced —

Beccaria;

Beccaria;* who, in his excellent treatife, *Dei Delitti e delle Pene,* exactly defcribes thofe ufelefs, and culpable, members of fociety, under the title of *oziofi,* whom we include by the word *vagabonds;* and indicates an opinion, that their offence to fociety is fomewhat fimilar to that of men who are probably guilty of crimes, but againft whom there is no certain pofitive proof. This ftatute of Elizabeth orders vagabonds to be grievoufly whipped, and burned through the griftle of the righr ear, for the firft offence, if above fourteen years of age, unlefs fome creditable perfon will take them into fervice for a year; and, if of eighteen years of age, and he falls again into a roguifh life, he fhall fuffer death as a felon, unlefs fome creditable perfon will take him into fervice for two years; and, if he falls a third time into a roguifh life, he fhall be adjudged a felon.

Government, after experiencing the effects arifing from what had been done in the fourteenth year of this reign, again took up the fubject; and we find, in the eighteenth ftatute, the firft idea of natural children being maintained at the expenfe of their mother, or reputed father, who appear before this time to have been maintained at the expenfe of the parifh; or, at leaft, there was no pofitive law of the ftate enforcing the contrary. This ftatute alfo provides for the punifhment of the father and mother; and has ftood the teft of time, being the rule for the conduct of magiftrates at this day.

In this parliament, alfo, arofe the firft idea of providing a ftock to fet the poor at work. Indeed, it is fcarcely credible, that legiflators fhould, for centuries, have punifhed *idlenefs* and *vagabondry* fo feverely, and not have provided a certainty, that thofe members of fociety, who, from their fituation, are ftrongly tempted to incur the crime, fhould have the means put in their power, by induftry, of avoiding it.

* Beccaria dei Delitti e delle Pene, fect. 24.

Houfes

Houfes of induftry are now mentioned, for the firft time; and lands in focage are permitted, during twenty years, to be given towards their maintenance, and to provide ftock for the poor to work up. But what principle could induce the parliament to prohibit building cottages, unlefs four acres of land were laid to each of them, it is impoffible at this diftance of time to tell; the hiftory of that period taking no notice of the fubject; and the preamble to the act itfelf ftating only general inconvenience; yet fuch a regulation paffed into a law, in 1589; together with a prohibition againft more families, or houfeholds, than one, inhabiting the fame cottage.

The parliament of this wife and happy æra were as progreffive in improving the fituation of the poor, and in laws replete with tendernefs and humanity, affecting the lower claffes of the ftate, as were the parliaments under the two preceding reigns retrogreffive and deficient in thofe refpects. In the thirty-fifth year of Elizabeth, we find them turning again their attention to hufbandry, and repealing feveral former ftatutes affecting it; repealing, alfo, that part of the ftatute-law refpecting vagabonds, which retained any unneceffary, and therefore improper, feverity; regulating the management of thofe poor and impotent perfons, who are compelled to live by alms; and enlarging the term, during which it fhould be lawful to give land towards the maintenance of houfes of correction, or of the poor: and, after having tried, for four years, the effect of all the laws then in force, relative to this important department of the police, and having called, as it were, practical experience, in aid of theoretic legiflation; we find, towards the end of the fixteenth century, and in the beginning of the thirty-ninth year of this reign, thefe various matters and important regulations taking fomewhat the appearance of a code or fyftem of laws, as they were contained in the firft fix and the feventeenth chapters of this feffion.

A re-

A recapitulation of the heads of thefe feveral ſtatutes would be tedious, and is unneceſſary to the purpoſe of this tract; which is intended to inquire into the relative fituation of the poor, in time paſt, and at prefent: but one circumſtance, on the revifal of the hiftory of thefe ftatutes, ſtrikes the mind ſtrongly; that the 43d of Elizabeth, which is confidered by many as the fountain and origin of the poor's rate, is in fact not fo, but is the refult of the collected wifdom, obfervation, and experience, of the fame, or nearly the fame, individual ſtateſmen; and thofe, men of acknowledged wifdom and prudence, attending to the fame object, the general good of fociety, in this moſt important article of police, during the term of almoſt half a century.

Although fome fenfible and enlightened minds have appeared to doubt, whether this ſtatute has, in its prefent confequences, brought upon that portion of fociety, which, by the law of the land, is fubject to its influence, more good than evil; reafoning from the great burthen it impofes on the landed intereſt in particular; the knowledge alfo that in other countries no fuch law fubfifts; that until a certain æra it was not the law here; till when no collections, but fuch as are voluntary, were gathered for the poor; knowing withal, that mifery and diftrefs, arifing from poverty, are the lot of too many; although fuch an immenfe revenue is raifed for their relief: yet fo great was the neceſſity of raifing a certain revenue for them, and fo gradually and ſtrongly did fuch neceſſity enforce itfelf through the period which has juſt been fubject to our attention, by a kind of divine right, on the confcience of the legiſlature, who difputed and yielded, ſtep by ſtep, to its powerful energy, during a long reign; which all our hiftorians teach us to remember with reverence, for the wifdom and prudence fo vifibly prevalent throughout that age; this aſſertion may now be ventured, that a tax upon fociety, for the relief of the poor, was, in the age of Elizabeth, expedient and neceſſary; and that the regulations of the 43d ftatute of her reign were then the beſt mo-

G   dification

dification of fuch a tax, and well calculated to enforce habits of induftry, and all thofe exertions to maintain themfelves before they became a burthen upon their fellow-fubjects, which fell within the fcope of their power and ability: whether they are fo now, and whether the prefent enormous burthen of the poor's rates arifes from this ftatute being put in force, or from other caufes, fhall be the object of a fubfequent inveftigation.

<hr>

LETTER VII.

TO form an accurate judgement on any fubject, it is neceffary that the mind fhould have been as fully attentive to the defign of each part and proportion in detail as to the fpirit and effect of the whole; the fly on the dome of St. Paul's might, with equal reafon, be fuppofed able to form a fenfible and critical opinion of that magnificent fabric, as the mind of that man be conceived equal to form an adequate conception of the intent of the legiflature in the ftatute alluded to, who has only read detached parts of it, or haftily, from the practice of modern days, formed a conception of the fpirit and intentions which impreffed the parliament when it became the law of the land, in the beginning of the laft century.

It is neceffary, therefore, in fome part of this inquiry, to declare what was the intent of the legiflature when they paffed this act; and to point out the means made ufe of by them to enforce the execution of that intent; or, in other words, to explain the fpirit of this humane and wife code.

In the execution of this tafk, reference fhall be made to the ftatute itfelf, as divided by its fections, that the reader may examine, if he thinks proper, how far the following abridgment

is

is warranted by the words of the act itself;* which is here printed, as it cannot, I believe, be purchased singly, or unconnected with other matter; and Burn's Justice, which is in every body's hands,

G 2   contains

---

* In confequence of fome converfation with feveral gentlemen of the Royal and Antiquary Societies, who meet at a coffee-houfe in the Strand after thofe focieties are broken up, and fpend the evening together; I was induced, principally on the affertion of Mr. Godfchell, (a worthy and very intelligent magiftrate in the county of Surrey, who publifhed, in 1787, a General Plan of Parochial and Provincial Police,) that Sir Edward Coke was the framer of the 43d Eliz. cap. 2, to fearch the Journals of the Houfe of Lords and of the Commons of that time, but was not able either from them, or any other fource of printed information in my power to fearch, to prove, with certainty, that we owe this act of parliament to the abilities of that great lawyer folely; that he, being at that time the Queen's attorney-general, might have perufed and fettled the act, is probable.

The Journals of the Houfe of Commons unfortunately are imperfect at the period when this meafure was in agitation in parliament, there being a chafm from the year 1580 to 1603.

In Sir Simon D'Ewe's Journal the following notices are found, 43d Eliz. 1601, November 5.

" Upon motion this day, a committee was appointed to confider of the ftatute for the relief of the poor, viz. Sir Robert Wroth, Mr. Phillips, Sir Edward Hobbie, Sir Francis Haftings, Sir George Moore, and others, who were appointed to meet on Thurfday next in the Exchequer-Chamber, at two o'clock in the afternoon.

" December 10, P. M. The bill for the relief of the poor was read the fecond time, and committed to Mr. Comptroller, Sir Robert Wroth, Sir Francis D'Arcie, Mr. Francis Bacon, Mr. Lieutenant of the Tower, and others, who were appointed to meet to-morrow, in the afternoon, at two of the clock, in the Court of Words.

" December 11, P. M. Sir Robert Wroth, a committee in the bill for the relief of the poor, brought in the bill with amendments, and a provifo added by the committee.

" The provifoes and amendments were read, and the bill ordered to be engroffed."

It appears that there was another bill brought into the Houfe for avoiding idlenefs, and fetting the poor to work. This was read the fecond time December 15; and, on the queftion for committing it for engroffing, was dafhed.

JOURNALS OF THE HOUSE OF LORDS.

1601. December 16. 1ma *Vice lecta eft Billa*, " An Act for the Relief of the Poor."
December 17. 2da *Vice lecta eft Billa*, " An Act for the Relief of the Poor."
Expedit. *Hodie*: 3a *Vice lecta eft Billa*, " An Act for the Relief of the Poor."

" *Anno*

contains only detached parts of it; and it certainly is a ſtatute which is intimately connected with the intereſts of all owners and occupiers

"*Anno quadrageſſimo tertio Reginæ* Elizabethæ.

C A P. II.

"*An Act for the Relief of the Poor.*

" BE it enacted, by the authority of this preſent parliament, That the church-wardens of every pariſh, and four, three, or two, ſubſtantial houſeholders there, as ſhall be thought meet, having reſpect to the proportion and greatneſs of the ſame pariſh and pariſhes, to be nominated yearly, in *Eaſter*-week, or within one month after *Eaſter*, under the hand and ſeal of two or more juſtices of the peace of the ſame county, whereof one to be of the *quorum*, dwelling in or near the ſame pariſh or diviſion where the ſame pariſh doth lie, ſhall be called overſeers of the poor of the ſame pariſh : and they, or the greater part of them, ſhall take order from time to time, by and with the conſent of two or more ſuch juſtices of the peace as is aforeſaid, for ſetting to work the children of all ſuch whoſe parents ſhall not, by the ſaid church-wardens and overſeers, or the greater part of them, be thought able to keep and maintain their children ; and alſo for ſetting to work all ſuch perſons, married or unmarried, having no means to maintain them, and uſe no ordinary and daily trade of life to get their living by : and alſo to raiſe, weekly or otherwiſe, (by taxation of every inhabitant, parſon, vicar, and other, and of every occupier of lands, houſes, tithes impropriate, propriations of tithes, coal-mines, or ſaleable underwoods, in the ſaid pariſh, in ſuch competent ſum and ſums of money as they ſhall think fit,) a convenient ſtock of flax, hemp, wool, thread, iron, and other neceſſary ware and ſtuff, to ſet the poor on work : and alſo competent ſums of money for and towards the neceſſary relief of the lame, impotent, old, blind, and ſuch other among them, being poor, and not able to work : and alſo for the putting out of ſuch children to be apprentices, to be gathered out of the ſame pariſh, according to the ability of the ſame pariſh, and to do and execute all other things, as well for the diſpoſing of the ſaid ſtock as otherwiſe, concerning the premiſes, as to them ſhall ſeem convenient.

II. " Which ſaid church-wardens and overſeers, ſo to be nominated, or ſuch of them as ſhall not be let by ſickneſs, or other juſt excuſe, to be allowed by two ſuch juſtices of peace or more as is aforeſaid, ſhall meet together, at the leaſt once every month in the church of the ſaid pariſh, upon the *Sunday*, in the afternoon, after divine ſervice, there to conſider of ſome good courſe to be taken, and of ſome meet order to be ſet down in the premiſes ; and ſhall, within four days after the end of their year, and after other overſeers nominated as aforeſaid, make and yield up to ſuch two juſtices of peace as is aforeſaid, a true and perfect account of all ſums of money by them received, or rated and ſeſſed and not received, and alſo of ſuch ſtock as ſhall be in their hands, or in the hands

of

occupiers of land and houfes, and, in fact, with the beft interefts of the whole kingdom.

It

of any of the poor to work, and of all other things concerning their'faid office; and fuch fum or fums of money as fhall be in their hands, fhall pay and deliver over to the faid church-wardens and overfeers newly nominated and appointed as aforefaid; upon pain that every one of them abfenting themfelves without lawful caufe as aforefaid, from fuch monthly meeting for the purpofe aforefaid, or being negligent in their office, or in the execution of the orders aforefaid, being made by and with the affent of the faid juftices of peace, or any two of them before-mentioned, to forfeit, for every fuch default of abfence or negligence, twenty fhillings.

III. " And be it alfo enacted, That if the faid juftices of peace do perceive that the inhabitants of any parifh are not able to levy among themfelves fufficient fums of money for the purpofes aforefaid; that then the faid two juftices fhall and may tax, rate, and affefs, as aforefaid, any other of other parifhes, or out of any parifh, within the hundred where the faid parifh is, to pay fuch fum and fums of money to the church-wardens and overfeers of the faid poor parifh for the faid purpofes, as the faid juftices fhall think fit, according to the intent of this law: and, if the faid hundred fhall not be thought to the faid juftices able and fit to relieve the faid feveral parifhes not able to provide for them-felves as aforefaid; then the juftices of peace, at their general quarter-feffions, or the greater number of them, fhall rate and affefs, as aforefaid, any other of other parifhes, or out of any parifh, within the faid county, for the purpofes aforefaid, as in their difcretion fhall feem fit.

IV. " And that it fhall be lawful, as well for the prefent as fubfequent church-wardens and overfeers, or any of them, by warrant from any two fuch juftices of peace, as is aforefaid, to levy as well the faid fums of money, and all arrearages, of every one that fhall refufe to contribute according as they fhall be affeffed, by diftrefs and fale of the offender's goods, as the fums of money or ftock which fhall be behind upon any account to be made as aforefaid, rendering to the parties the overplus: and, in defect of fuch diftrefs, it fhall be lawful for any fuch two juftices of the peace to commit him or them to the common gaol of the county, there to remain, without bail or mainprize, until payment of the faid fum, arrearages, and ftock : and the faid juftices of peace, or any one of them, to fend, to the houfe of correction or common gaol, fuch as fhall not employ themfelves to work, being appointed thereunto, as aforefaid : and alfo any fuch two juftices of peace to commit to the faid prifon every one of the faid church-wardens and overfeers which fhall refufe to account ; there to remain, without bail or mainprize, until he have made a true account, and fatisfied and paid fo much as upon the faid account fhall be remaining in his hands.

V. " And

It is remarkable that the ſtatute opens without any preamble whatever: moſt acts of our parliament, in the preamble, give a ſummary

V. " And be it further enacted, That it ſhall be lawful for the ſaid church-wardens and overſeers, or the greater part of them, by the aſſent of any two juſtices of the peace aforeſaid, to bind any ſuch children, as aforeſaid, to be apprentices, where they ſhall ſee convenient, till ſuch man-child ſhall come to the age of four-and-twenty years, and ſuch woman-child to the age of one-and-twenty years, or the time of her marriage ; the ſame to be as effectual to all purpoſes, as if ſuch child were of full age, and, by indenture of covenant, bound him or her ſelf. And to the intent that neceſſary places of habitation may more conveniently be provided for ſuch poor impotent people ; be it enacted by the authority aforeſaid, That it ſhall and may be lawful for the ſaid church-wardens and overſeers, or the greater part of them, by the leave of the lord or lords of the manor, whereof any waſte or common within their pariſh is or ſhall be parcel, and upon agreement before with him or them made, in writing, under the hands and ſeals of the ſaid lord or lords, or otherwiſe, according to any order to be ſet down by the juſtices of peace of the ſaid county, at their general quarter-ſeſſions, or the greater part of them, by like leave and agreement of the ſaid lord or lords, in writing, under his or their hands and ſeals, to erect, build, and ſet up, in fit and convenient places of habitation in ſuch waſte or common, at the general charges of the pariſh, or otherwiſe of the hundred or county, as aforeſaid, to be taxed, rated, and gathered, in manner before expreſſed, convenient houſes of dwelling for the ſaid impotent poor; and alſo to place inmates, or more families than one, in one cottage or houſe ; one act made in the one-and-thirtieth year of her Majeſty's reign, intituled, *An Act againſt the erecting and maintaining of Cottages*, or any thing therein contained to the contrary notwithſtanding : which cottages and places for inmates ſhall not, at any time after, be uſed or employed to or for any other habitation, but only for impotent and poor of the ſame pariſh, that ſhall be there placed from time to time by the church-wardens and overſeers of the poor of the ſame pariſh, or the moſt part of them, upon the pains and forfeitures contained in the ſaid former act made in the ſaid one-and-thirtieth year of her Majeſty's reign.

VI. " Provided always, That if any perſon or perſons ſhall find themſelves grieved with any ſeſs or tax, or other act done by the ſaid church-wardens and other perſons, or by the ſaid juſtices of peace ; that then it ſhall be lawful for the juſtices of the peace, at their general quarter-ſeſſions, or the greater number of them, to take ſuch order therein, as to them ſhall be thought convenient; and the ſame to conclude and bind all the ſaid parties.

VII. " And be it further enacted, That the father and grandfather, and the mother and grandmother, and the children of every poor, old, blind, lame, and impotent, perſon, or other poor perſon not able to work, being of a ſufficient ability, ſhall, at their own

charges,

fummary view of the evils intended by the legiflature to be corrected, or the good which is expected to enfue from the regulations
to

charges, relieve and maintain every fuch poor perfon in that manner, and according to
that rate, as by the juftices of peace of that county where fuch fufficient perfons dwell, or
the greater number of them, at their general quarter-feffions, fhall be affeffed; upon pain
that every one of them fhall forfeit twenty fhillings for every month which they fhall
fail therein.

VIII. " And be it further hereby enacted, That the mayors, bailiffs, or other head-
officers, of every town and place, corporate and city, within this realm, being juftice or
juftices of peace, fhall have the fame authority by virtue of this act, within the limits and
precincts of their jurifdictions, as well out of feffions as at their feffions, if they hold any,
as is herein limited, prefcribed, and appointed, to juftices of the peace of the county, or
any two or more of them, or to the juftices of peace, in their quarter-feffions, to do and
execute for all the ufes and purpofes in this act prefcribed, and no other juftice or juftices
of peace to enter or meddle there : and that every alderman of the city of *London*,
within his ward, fhall and may do and execute, in every refpect, fo much as is appointed
and allowed by this act to be done and executed by one or two juftices of peace of any
county within this realm.

IX. " And be it alfo enacted, That if it fhall happen any parifh to extend itfelf
into more counties than one, or part to lie within the liberties of any city, town, or
place corporate, and part without, that then as well the juftices of peace of every county
as alfo the head-officers of fuch city, town, or place corporate, fhall deal and intermeddle
only in fo much of the faid parifh as lieth within their liberties, and not any further : and
every of them refpectively within their feveral limits, wards, and jurifdictions, to execute
the ordinances before-mentioned concerning the nomination of overfeers, the confent to
binding apprentices, the giving warrant to levy taxations unpaid, the taking account of
church-wardens and overfeers, and the committing to prifon fuch as refufe to account, or
deny to pay the arrearages due upon their accounts; and yet, neverthelefs, the faid
church-wardens and overfeers, or the moft part of them, of the faid parifhes that do extend into fuch feveral limits and jurifdictions, fhall, without dividing themfelves, duly
execute their office in all places within the faid parifh, in all things to them belonging,
and fhall duly exhibit and make one account before the faid head-officer of the town or
place corporate, and one other before the faid juftices of peace, or any fuch two of them,
as is aforefaid.

X. " And further be it enacted, by the authority aforefaid, That if, in any place
within this realm, there happen to be hereafter no fuch nomination of overfeers yearly,
as is before appointed, that then every juftice of peace of the county, dwelling within the
divifion where fuch default of nomination fhall happen, and every mayor, alderman, and
head-

to be enforced; but here is no preamble, unlefs the title can be
called one, which is in fo many words, " An Act for the Relief of
the

head-officer, of city, town, or place-corporate, where fuch default fhall happen, fhall
lofe and forfeit, for every fuch default, five pounds, to be employed towards the relief of
the poor of the faid parifh, or place-corporate, and to be levied, as aforefaid, of their
goods, by warrant from the general feffions of the peace of the faid county, or of the fame
city, town, or place-corporate, if they keep feffions.

XI. " And be it alfo enacted, by the authority aforefaid, That all penalties and forfeitures before-mentioned in this act, to be forfeited by any perfon or perfons, fhall go and
be employed to the ufe of the poor of the fame parifh, and towards a ftock and habitation
for them, and other neceffary ufes and relief, as before in this act are mentioned and expreffed : and fhall be levied by the faid church-wardens and overfeers, or one of them, by
warrant from any two fuch juftices of peace, or mayor, alderman, or head-officer of city,
town, or place-corporate, refpectively, within their feveral limits, by diftrefs and fale
thereof, as aforefaid ; or, in defect thereof, it fhall be lawful for any two fuch juftices of
peace, and the faid aldermen and head-officers, within their feveral limits, to commit the
offender to the faid prifon, there to remain, without bail or mainprize, till the faid forfeitures fhall be fatisfied and paid.

XII. " And be it further enacted, by the authority aforefaid, That the juftices of peace
of every county or place-corporate, or the more part of them, in their general feffions to
be holden next after the feaft of Eafter next, and fo, yearly, as often as they fhall think
meet, fhall rate every parifh to fuch a weekly fum of money as they fhall think convenient; fo as no parifh be rated above the fum of fix-pence, nor under the fum of a halfpenny, weekly to be paid, and fo as the total fum of fuch taxation of the parifhes, in
every county, amount not above the rate of two-pence for every parifh within the faid
county ; which fums fo taxed fhall be yearly affeffed by the agreement of the parifhioners
within themfelves, or, in default thereof, by the church-wardens and petty conftables of
the fame parifh, or the more part of them ; or, in default of their agreement, by the order
of fuch juftice or juftices of peace as fhall dwell in the fame parifh, or (if none be there
dwelling) in the parts next adjoining.

XIII. " And if any perfon fhall refufe or neglect to pay any fuch portion of money fo
taxed, it fhall be lawful for the faid church-wardens and conftables, or any of them, or,
in their default, for any juftice of peace of the faid limit, to levy the fame by diftrefs and
fale of the goods of the party fo refufing or neglecting, rendering to the party the overplus ; and, in default of fuch diftrefs, it fhall be lawful to any juftice of that limit to commit fuch perfon to the faid prifon, there to abide, without bail or mainprize, till he have
paid the fame.

XIV. " And

the Poor." The enacting part inftantly commences. Induftry,
and principally early induftry, is the firft object under their contemplation:

H

XIV. " And be it alfo enacted, That the faid juftices of peace at their general quarter-
feffions, to be holden at the time of fuch taxation, fhall fet down what competent fums of
money fhall be fent quarterly out of every county or place-corporate, for the relief of the
poor prifoners of the King's Bench and Marfhalfea, and alfo of fuch hofpitals and alms-
houfes as fhall be in the faid county, and what fums of money fhall be fent to every one of
the faid hofpitals and alms-houfes, fo as there be fent out of every county, yearly, twenty
fhillings, at the leaft, to each of the faid prifons of the King's Bench and Marfhalfea ;
which fums, ratably to be affeffed upon every parifh, the church-wardens of every parifh
fhall truly collect, and pay over to the high-conftables in whofe divifion fuch parifh fhall be
fituate, from time to time, quarterly, ten days before the end of every quarter ; and
every fuch conftable, at every fuch quarter-feffions in fuch county, fhall pay over the fame
to two fuch treafurers, or to one of them, as fhall, by the more part of the juftices of
peace of the county, be elected to be the faid treafurers, to be chofen by the juftices of
peace of the faid county, city, or town, or place-corporate, or of others which were feffed
and taxed at five pounds lands, or ten pounds goods, at the leaft, at the tax of fubfidy
next before the time of the faid election to be made ; and the faid treafurers fo elected to
continue for the fpace of one whole year in their office, and then to give up their charge,
with a due account of their receipts and difburfements, at the quarter-feffions to be holden
next after the feaft of *Eafter* in every year, to fuch others as fhall, from year to year, in
form aforefaid, fucceffively be elected treafurers for the faid county, city, town, or place-
corporate ; which faid treafurers, or one of them, fhall pay over the fame to the Lord-
Chief-Juftice of *England*, and Knight-Marfhal for the time being, equally to be divided
to the ufe aforefaid, taking their acquittance for the fame, or, in default of the faid chief-
juftice, to the next antienteft juftice of the King's Bench, as aforefaid : and, if any
church-warden or high-conftable, or his executors or adminiftrators, fhall fail to make
payment in form above fpecified, then every church-warden, his executors or adminiftrators, fo offending, fhall forfeit, for every time, the fum of ten fhillings ; and every high-
conftable, his executors or adminiftrators, fhall forfeit, for every time, the fum of twenty
fhillings ; the fame forfeitures, together with the fums behind, to be levied by the faid
treafurer and treafurers, by way of diftrefs and fale of the goods, as aforefaid, in form
aforefaid, and by them to be employed towards the charitable ufes comprifed in this act.

XV. " And be it further enacted, That all the furplufage of money, which fhall be remaining in the faid ftock of any county, fhall, by difcretion of the more part of the
juftices of peace, in their quarter-feffions, be ordered, diftributed, and beftowed, for the
relief of the poor hofpitals of that county, and of thofe that fhall fuftain loffes by fire,

water,

templation : the fetting to work children, whofe parents fhall not
be thought able to maintain them, and alfo the putting poor
children

water, the fea, or other cafualties, and to fuch other charitable purpofes, for the relief of
the poor, as to the more part of the faid juftices of peace fhall feem convenient.

XVI. " And be it further enaeled, That if any treafurer eleeted fhall wilfully refufe to
take upon him the faid office of treafurerfhip, or refufe to diftribute and give relief, or to
account, according to fuch form as fhall be appointed by the more part of the faid juftices
of peace ; that then it fhall be lawful for the juftices of peace, in their quarter-feffions, or,
in their default, for the juftices of affize, at their affizes, to be holden in the fame county,
to fine the fame treafurer by their difcretion; the fame fine not to be under three pounds,
and to be levied by fale of his goods, and to be profecuted by any two of the faid juftices of
peace whom they fhall authorize. Provided always, that this aet fhall not take effeet until
the feaft of *Eafter* next.

XVII. " And be it enaeted, That the ftatute made in the nine-and-thirtieth year of her
Majefty's reign, intituled, *An Aet for the Relief of the Poor*, fhall continue and ftand in
force until the feaft of *Eafter* next ; and that all taxations heretofore impofed, and not paid,
nor that fhall be paid before the faid feaft of *Eafter* next, and that all taxes hereafter, before
the faid feaft, to be taxed by virtue of the faid former aet, which fhall not be paid before
the faid feaft of *Eafter*, fhall and may, after the faid feaft of *Eafter*, be levied by the overfeers, and other perfons in this aet, refpeetively appointed to levy taxations, by diftrefs,
and by fuch warrant, in every refpeet, as if they had been taxed and impofed by virtue of
this aet, and were not paid.

XVIII. " Provided always, That whereas the ifland of *Fowlnefs*, in the county of
Effex, being environed with the fea, and having a chapel of eafe for the inhabitants thereof,
and yet the faid ifland is no parifh, but the lands in the fame are fituated within divers parifhes far diftant from the faid ifland ; be it therefore enaeted, by the authority aforefaid,
that the faid juftices of peace fhall nominate and appoint inhabitants within the faid ifland,
to be overfeers for the poor people dwelling within the faid ifland ; and that both they, the
faid Juftices, and the faid overfeers, fhall have the fame power and authority to all intents,
confiderations, and purpofes, for the execution of the parts and articles of this aet, and
fhall be fubjeet to the fame pains and forfeitures, and likewife that the inhabitants and occupiers of lands there fhall be liable and chargeable to the fame payments, charges, expenfes,
and orders, in fuch manner and form as if the fame ifland were a parifh ; in confideration
whereof, neither the faid inhabitants, or occupiers of land, within the faid ifland, fhall
not be compelled to contribute towards the relief of the poor of thofe parifhes, wherein their
houfes or lands which they occupy within the faid ifland are fituated, for or by reafon of their
faid habitation or occupyings, other than for the relief of the poor people within the faid
ifland, neither yet fhall the other inhabitants of the parifhes, wherein fuch houfes or lands

are

children out apprentice; fetting the idle, whether from choice or neceffity, to work; for which purpofe a fum was to be raifed by affeffment, to purchafe a ftock of flax, hemp, wool, thread, iron, and other neceffary ware and ftuff:—the next confideration was to raife a competent fum of money, by the fame means, for the neceffary relief of the lame, old, impotent, blind, and fuch others as are poor, *and not able to work.* Sect. 1.

This intent was to be carried into execution by the church-wardens and overfeers; which laft were yearly to be appointed by the neighbouring magiftrates, whofe particular duty in this act is declared to be, to give order, direct, and infpect, the proceedings of the churchwardens and overfeers; and that this plan may, in all its

are fituated, be compelled, by reafon of their refiancy or dwelling, to contribute to the relief of the poor inhabitants within the faid ifland.

XIX. " And be it further enacted, That if any action, or trefpafs, or other fuit, fhall happen to be attempted and brought againft any perfon or perfons, for taking of any dif-trefs, making of any fale, or any other thing doing, by authority of this prefent act, the de-fendant or defendants, in any fuch action or fuit, fhall and may either plead not guilty, or otherwife make avowry, cognifance, or juftification, for the taking of the faid diftreffes, making of fale, or other thing doing, by virtue of this act, alleging, in fuch avowry, cog-nifance, or juftification, that the faid diftrefs, fale, trefpafs, or other thing, whereof the plaintiff or plaintiffs complained, was done by authority of this act, and according to the tenor, purport, and effect, of this act, without any expreffing or rehearfal of any other matter or circumftance contained in this prefent act : to which avowry, cognifance, or juftification, the plaintiff fhall be admitted to reply, that the defendant did take the faid dif-trefs, made the faid fale, or did any other act or trefpafs fuppofed in his declaration, of his own wrong, without any fuch caufe alleged by the faid defendant ; whereupon the iffue in every fuch action fhall be joined, to be tried by verdict of twelve men, and not otherwife, as is accuftomed in other perfonal actions ; and, upon the trial of that iffue, the whole mat-ter to be given on both parties in evidence, according to the very truth of the fame ; and, after fuch iffue tried for the defendant, or nonfuit of the plaintiff after appearance, the fame defendant to recover treble damages, by reafon of his wrongful vexation in that behalf, with his cofts alfo in that part fuftained, and that to be affeffed by the fame jury, or writ to inquire of the damages, as the fame fhall require.

XX. " Provided always, That this act fhall endure no longer than to the end of the next feffion of parliament. 3 *Car. I. c.* 4. *Continued until the end of the firft feffion of the next parliament, and further continued by* 16 *Car. I. c.* 4."

parts, be carried by the overfeers, under the direction of the juftices, into execution, they are ordered to meet on this bufinefs, at leaft once in the month, on a Sunday, after divine fervice in the church; and, within four days after the year is expired, yield up to two juftices an account of all things concerning their office. Provifion is alfo made in thofe inftances where parifhes may not be able among themfelves to levy the neceffary fums of money, by calling in aid other parifhes. Sect. 1, 2, 3, 5, 6, 7.

That the expenfe for the relief of thofe who are poor, and not able to work, may be felt as little as poffible by the community at large, parental and filial affection is compelled to do its duty before the public is burthened; and for that purpofe grandfathers, fathers, and children, are reciprocally called forth to fupport each other if able. Sect. 7.

And, that neceffary habitations may be provided for the poor and impotent, it is made lawful for the overfeers, with leave of the lord of the manor, and under the control of the magiftrates, to build convenient places of habitation on the wafte, and to place inmates, or more families than one, in the fame cottage or houfe; notwith-ftanding an act paffed in the 30th year of the fame reign, which has already been alluded to. Sect. 6.

Another object was, to raife a fum of money from every parifh, by a weekly rate, not exceeding fixpence, or under two-pence, for the relief of the poor prifoners in the King's Bench and Marfhalfea; and alfo fuch hofpitals and alms-houfes as fhall be in each county; fo as that there be fent out of every county yearly not lefs than twenty fhillings to each of the faid prifons; and the furplus-mo-ney fhall, at the difcretion of the juftices of the peace, in their quarter-feffions, be diftributed for the relief of the poor hofpitals of the county; and of thofe who fhall fuftain loffes by fire, water, the fea, or other cafualties; and to fuch other purpofes for the relief of the poor, as to the moft part of the faid juftices fhall feem convenient. Sect. 12, 13, 14, 15, 16.

The

The island of Fowlnefs, in the county of Effex, being extra-parochial, it was thought neceffary to include it by name; and the general regulations of the act are alfo extended to that ifland. Sect. 18.

The fanction by which the legiflature has enforced their regulations principally refts in pecuniary penalties, to which all defcriptions of perfons, called on to the performance of any part of the act, are liable: thefe forfeitures rife from twenty fhillings to five pounds, which is the penalty to which the magiftrates are fubject if they neglect to appoint overfeers; and are directed to be applied in aid of the fund, which is ordered to be raifed for the employment and relief of the poor. Sect. 2, 10, 11, 14, 16.

The fummary mode of diftrefs, by warrant, from two magiftrates, enforces the payment of the affeffments, and alfo of the penalties, except in the inftances of the penalties incurred by the magiftrates, and the treafurer of the county-ftock, raifed by virtue of Section 12, which are directed to be levied, by warrant, from general or quarter feffions. Sect. 4, 10, 13.

Imprifonment, in default of fufficient diftrefs, is called in aid of the revenue thus to be raifed for the benefit of the poor; and, alfo, as a punifhment to thofe who fhall not employ themfelves, work being firft found for them; and as a punifhment to fuch overfeers, as may refufe to give account; until their contumacy is overcome, and they have paid the arrears due. Sect. 4, 13.

An appeal is given to the quarter-feffions, to any perfon who fhall find himfelf aggrieved by any cefs or tax, or by any other act, done by the church-wardens, overfeers, juftices of the peace, or any other perfon. Sect. 6.

To enforce obedience in corporate towns and cities, the head-officers, within their jurifdictions, fhall have the fame authority as juftices of the peace, within their refpective counties; and, where parifhes extend into two counties or liberties, the head-officers fhall have

have authority only within their refpective counties and liberties, and not farther. Sect. 8, 9.

It is declared at what time this act fhall commence, and 39 Eliz. cap. 3. ceafe to be in force. Sect. 17.

Then follow directions for the defendant's plea, in any fuit commenced againft him on this ftatute; the replication of the plaintiff; the iffue to be joined; and, on verdict for defendant, or nonfuit of plaintiff, treble damages and cofts are given; the whole calculated to come eafily at the real fact, and to protect thofe, who are employed under the act, from being molefted by vexatious fuits; and the act itfelf is intended to be experimental only, and declared to endure no longer than to the end of the next feffion of parliament. Sect. 19, 20.

Thefe few preceding paragraphs contain a fummary of the contents of this ftatute,—the bafis of all future regulations with refpect to the poor, their employment, and relief; and, to ufe the words of that excellent writer on the laws and conftitution of this kingdom, the late Judge Blackftone, " the farther any fubfequent plans for maintaining the poor have departed from this inftitution, the more impracticable, and even pernicious, their vifionary attempts have proved:" nor could any thing fhort of prophecy have foretold, in the beginning of the feventeenth century, that, in confequence of thefe wife and humane regulations, above 3,000,000l. would, towards the clofe of the eighteenth century, be raifed in England and Wales, for the relief of the poor, exclufive of numerous hofpitals, largely endowed; charity-fchools; annual value of landed eftates, given to charitable purpofes; fums of money at intereft in the funds; charities, fupported by voluntary contribution; private charities; the income of the whole, probably, not fhort of 5,000,000l. a year; and, after all, fo much mifery and diftrefs, arifing from extreme poverty, would then remain among us.

It

It furely muft be obvious to the meaneft capacity, after the moft trifling attention to the great purpofe of the legiflature, in this act of parliament, that the burthen of the poor's rates, which is, with fo much reafon, complained of, and the prefent diftreffed fituation of fo many of the poor, *cannot arife from this ftatute being fully, and in every part of it, carried into ftrict execution, but from a practice totally the reverfe.—Nor can it be afferted, with truth or reafon, that any one regulation contained in it is impracticable in thefe times, or that any one is impolitic, or dangerous to be executed, either to the individual executing it, the poor, who are the objects of it, or the nation at large, who are interefted in the confequences arifing from it.—* Thofe fections which relate to the raifing a fum of money, by affeffments on the occupiers, are, moft certainly, executed with all ftrictnefs : but the firft great purpofe of the money fo raifed,—*the purchafing ftock to fet to work thofe children whofe parents are not able to maintain them, and, alfo, the idle, whether from choice or neceffity,* is too much neglected : although there is no doubt but the habit of early induftry once obtained, by an application of fome part of the money thus raifed ; and, by thefe means, the poor being inured to an induftrious way of life ; would, of itfelf, amply compenfate the parifhes for the purchafe of a ftock of materials; although the manufactures thus fabricated might not meet with a ready fale, at a price which will allow of a computation for much profit.

It is a well-known fact, that confiderable fums are expended in every parifh, in the purchafe of articles for the clothing of the poor, which are bought of the retail fhop-keeper, in the country, at a fair average of thirty per cent. more than the prime coft of the materials and fabric to the manufacturer : in this article, therefore, a very great faving may be made, by employing the hands of children now in idlenefs, or mifchief, in fuch a manufactory, as might comfortably and neatly, although coarfely, clothe their relations and themfelves, at a much cheaper rate, with clothing

thing which would wear much longer than what is now bought at the shops: in the mean time, the habit of induſtry would be obtained, and the firſt great objeᨏ of this ſtatute put in force, which now is almoſt generally negleᨏed; and the clothing of the poor would form no inconſiderable ſource of conſumption for thoſe manufaᨏures which might be produced by the early induſtry of their children.

———————

L E T T E R   VIII.

TO prove, in ſome degree, that the idea thrown out in the preceding letter is not founded in theory or vain ſpeculation only, one experimental inſtance ſhall be given, too trifling, it is acknowledged, for the notice of the public, but much in point.

Having ſeen, in the ſummer of 1787, the good effeᨏs ariſing from the ſchools of induſtry, throughout the ſouthern diſtriᨏ of Lindſey, in the county of Lincoln, it determined me to try, on a very ſmall ſcale, the experiment in my own pariſh; and, accordingly, in the winter of the ſame year, a perſon was perſuaded to undertake the teaching ſix boys, of about the age of ſeven years, to ſpin what is called top-work, although it was deſired the yarn might not be twiſted ſo cloſe as in that fabric, it being intended for knitting. A woman was alſo found to teach the ſame number of girls, of the ſame age, to knit ſtockings. Forty-two pounds of wool were bought at Bury for the experiment. The account, when manufaᨏured, ſtood as follows:

Combed

	£.	s.	d.
Combed wool, 42 lb. at 11d. per lb. - -	1	18	6
Spinning ditto, by boys, at 4¼d. per lb. fome deductions made for wafte included - - - -	0	14	3
Twifting and reeling 33 lb. 14 oz. of yarn, at 2½d. and 3d. per lb. - - - - - -	0	8	0
Knitting 10 lb. 12 oz. at 1s. 4d. - - -	0	14	4
Ditto 23 lb. 2 oz. at 1s. 6d. - - - -	1	14	7¼
Total expended - - -	5	9	8¼
34 pair of children's ftockings, and 43 pair of men's, weighing 33 lb. 14 oz. fold to the work-houfe,	5	13	8
Ends of wool, 7 lb. made into mops, at 4d. per lb. 1 lb. 2 oz. wafted and loft.	0	2	4
Total produce - - - -	5	16	0
Profit - - - - -	0	6	3¼

By which it appears, that a profit of above fix fhillings refulted from the experiment, in which only 5l. 9s. 8¼d. was employed.

	£.	s.	d.
Six boys were taught to fpin, nine weeks, and earned	0	14	3
Six girls learned to knit, 27 weeks, and earned -	2	8	11¼

Suppofing a capital of 5l. employed fix months, in this infant manufactory, on which the clear profit was 6s. 3¼d. (and five pounds is above the fum actually employed that length of time,) a profit of 20l. 19s. 5d. will arife on 100l. thus employed for one year; and one hundred and twenty boys, and an equal number of girls, will be induftrioufly employed in learning an occupation:

I   fome

fome money will be earned for their parents, by honeft induftry; and clothing, at a much cheaper rate than what is bought at the fhops, will be manufactured for the poor; for, it is prefumed, that under proper management, no inconfiderable quantity of the yarn produced may be wove into a fabric which would make excellent, ftrong, and warm, clothing.

This experiment would have been continued; but the man who taught the boys, and the woman who taught the girls, did not think fo fmall a number worth their attention; confequently, their fcholars were neither regular in their attendance, or induftrious while they did attend.

The falary paid to the mafter and miftrefs is not brought into the account; becaufe it is conceived, that the price given on fo fmall a fcale is not a rule on a large one; and there is reafon to believe, that the profits of fuch a manufactory will more than pay the falary to the inftructors.

This idea of employing the children of the poor would extend itfelf, under good management, to other manufactures, befides thofe of wool; why not to coarfe linens; and to fhoes, for which the poor pay an extravagant price?

If this be the cafe; if fo much good might probably arife from putting in execution the leading idea in this ftatute; of employing the children of the poor; which is an inconfiderable part only, of what was wifely enacted by our forefathers, and foolifhly neglected by ourfelves, it furely, to thofe who complain of the burthen of the poor's rates, and, at the fame time, neglect to execute the laws for promoting induftry among the poor, may be objected in the words of Seneca, " *Sanabilibus ægrotamus malis; ipfaque nos in rectum genitos natura, fi emendari velimus, juvat:*" but, alas! what is the bufinefs of all is the employment of none; we fuffer an immenfe revenue to be raifed on us, for two good purpofes — for induftry and charity; and permit the perverfion of half of it; for, was one half of this revenue honeftly and fairly applied to the purpofes -
of

of the act, the poor would be more creditably and comfortably maintained; and the other half might remain in the pockets of that class of the community, from whom the whole is, with such strictness, exacted.

If it should be objected, that no sufficient demand would be found for such a manufactory by children, the answer is obvious; there is a point to which the experiment might be pushed, and it will be time enough to stop when we can go no farther: — it is not a sufficient excuse for our doing nothing, that we cannot do every thing. An account printed by the society, for the promotion of youthful industry in the county of Lincoln, has, among many other excellent observations, pointed out the means of promoting a consumption of this produce of their manufactory, which may be seen in the margin;* and some good consequences would certainly result to the poor themselves, as well as to those who are so heavily taxed for their maintenance; for, if the infant poor could, by their industry, clothe their parents and themselves, by this leading principle of the statute being put in force; the overseers would have smaller bills with the shop-keepers, whose livelihood principally arises from supplying the poor at exorbitant prices with their daily wants; the rising generation would be educated in more regular habits of industry; and the poor themselves would be better clothed, and at a cheaper rate.

That the good resulting from the execution of that section of the 43d of Elizabeth, which respects the employment of the infant

* With all those who have the good of their country at heart, it should be an object of constant attention to promote the consumption, no less than the sale, of wool. A parish-officer, who was mindful of this, would never purchase a cotton or linen gown for the poor instead of a woolsey one, which is much stronger, cheaper, and more comfortable; nor would he give them coarse cloth aprons, when blue woollen aprons would answer every purpose much better, and save washing; nor, lastly, would he suffer the the money of the parish to be laid out in thread stockings instead of worsted ones: all which things have been but too frequently practised.

poor, may appear in a ftronger light, it may be worth while to
call to mind what is, in fact, at this day the employment of the
rifing generation of the poor in that part of England where manufactures do not thrive, and where the operations of hufbandry
are the principal fources of induftry and labour : there, in fuch
diftricts which comprehend above a moiety of the kingdom, the
children of the parifh are encouraged by their parents to employ
themfelves in every act of peculation which is in their power, and
which, from the infignificance of the property ftolen, individually,
is an object fcarcely worthy the attention of the magiftrate ; and to
which, if he, on complaint made, did attend, he could not correct ;
becaufe the little culprits are not objects of legal punifhment ; children of five, fix, or feven, years of age being fent out in parties to
pilfer.

But if the individual inftance is too trifling for our notice, the
aggregate forms no inconfiderable mifchief done to the public, and
property purloined from fociety by thefe little thieves : a child
fteals a turnip or two daily for its parent's dinner, it is nothing ;
but the practice, continued through a winter by hundreds of them,
will confume fome acres ; it carries, with the affiftance of its play-
mates, the ftakes from the hedges, and loofe bars or rails from the
fences ; the value of the property is fmall, though to repair the
mifchief done is expenfive ; and, when thefe depredations are
carried on in the vicinity of a town or parifh, where the population of this clafs of people are hundreds or thoufands, the total of
mifchief is confiderable ; and, though the crime is an object of
civil punifhment, the child is not ; and the encouragement or con-
nivance of their parents cannot fall under the magiftrates authority ; for, the property ftolen is inftantly confumed, before any
fearch-warrant can operate.

In the mean time, the material injury is done to the morals ;
the rifing generation are, in early youth, accuftomed to habits
which turn them, from the path of honeft induftry, to the high
road

road which leads, through every species of depredation on society, to the gallows.

LETTER IX.

THE neceſſary relief of ſoldiers and mariners, which is enforced in a chapter immediately following the act, that has been the ſubject of our attention; and a law to redreſs the miſemployment of lands, goods, and ſtocks of money, heretofore given to certain charitable uſes, which follows chap. 4th; complete the plan of that parliament which ſat till near the cloſe of the reign of Elizabeth; *the latter ſtatute being at preſent as neceſſary to be called into practice, and, if executed, as well calculated for bringing to light any perverſion of that vaſt property which has been left by our forefathers for charitable purpoſes, as any plan that the ingenuity of the legiſlature could in theſe days invent;* and it ſtill remains the law of the land; and the authority of the chancellor might at any time call it into uſe, by an appointment of commiſſioners, according to the act, within the different dioceſes.

Theſe, with many more ſtatutes for the regulation of the internal police of the kingdom, were the production of the laſt parliament which ſat in the reign of Elizabeth; an æra, with no extravagance of metaphor, called *golden*, if applied either to the glory of her reign, with reſpect to the ſucceſs of her ſubjects arms; the importance of it, with reſpect to foreign powers; or its utility and happineſs as it regarded thoſe who lived under her dominion: whatever may have been her private character as a woman; whatever intrigues, which may have ariſen from love, jealouſy, or the other baſer paſſions that diſgraced her court; a lapſe of near two hundred years has with propriety removed, as with a veil, from our eyes; and they now only remain in the pages of the noveliſt or the

the retailer of frivolous anecdote; but her laſt words to her laſt
parliament, while coupled with ſuch laws as do honour to human
nature, and are a ſevere ſatire on the load of revenue-acts, with
which our modern ſtatute-books abound, ought to remain with
grateful recollection fixed on the minds of all poſterity; " I know
that the commonwealth is to be governed for the good and advantage of thoſe who are committed to me ; not of myſelf to whom it
is entruſted ; and that an account is one day to be given before
another judgement-ſeat."

During the reign of James the Firſt, very little was done by the
legiſlature in the regulation of the internal police; the jealouſy,
which aroſe both in the mind of the King and the Commons, occaſioned that prince to avoid, as much as his neceſſities would permit him, meeting his parliament; while the Houſe of Commons,
who early in the reign felt the effects of thoſe high notions of prerogative which diſturbed the repoſe, equally of the prince as of
his ſubjects, were too intent on the preſervation of their own pri-
vileges to attend to the general welfare of the people ; yet one of
their firſt acts of legiſlation related to rating the wages of artiſts
and labourers ; and, by ſtat. 1. cap. 6. parliament enlarged the
powers of juſtices of the peace with reſpect to the rating the wages
of workmen, as directed by 5th of Eliz. cap. 4. extending the ſame
to all manner of workmen whatever, " either working by the day,
week, month, or year, or taking any work at any perſon's hand
whatſoever, to be done by the great or otherwiſe," rendering alſo
the return of the certificate of ſuch rates of wages into Chancery
unneceſſary; by directing them to be proclaimed, engroſſed in
parchment, and kept, by the Cuſtos Rotulorum of the county,
among the records.

This attention to, and enlargement of, the powers of the 5th
of Elizabeth, is a proof that good aroſe to the public from the
rating of wages ; becauſe, if the experience of forty years had
proved it to be replete with more miſchief than uſe, it cannot be

ſuppoſed

suppofed that the legiflature would have extended the practice, and made the power general, which had been hitherto confined to particular claffes of workmen ; nor would the execution of the act have been rendered more eafy to the magiftrates ; yet there is rea-fon to believe, that the juftices feldom enforced the execution of thefe acts ; becaufe, on a fearch made in the office of the clerk of the peace for the county of Effex, only one inftance could be found ; and that at Eafter-feffions, 1661 : and Sir John Cullum, in his Hiftory of Hawftead, in the county of Suffolk, whofe in-tention, in that excellent model of parochial hiftory, was, among other objects, to give the reader information on the fubject of wages of the poor, in times now far removed, and the cotempo-rary prices of the neceffaries of life, mentions alfo but one in-ftance, viz. in Eafter-feffions, 1682.

Other ftatutes, affecting the lower claffes of our fellow-fubjects, although not immediately relative to the topic in queftion, were alfo paffed in the beginning of this reign : the 39th of Elizabeth, with refpect to the punifhment of rogues and vagabonds, was ex-plained and continued, by chap. 7th ; haunting and tippling in ale-houfes was alfo reftrained, by chap. the 9th of the fame feffions ; an act, the preamble to which is curious, and ftates, very properly, the only proper ufe of fuch places ; " Whereas the antient, true, and principal ufe of inns, ale-houfes, and victualling-houfes, was for the receipt, relief, and lodging, of wayfaring people, travel-ling from place to place, and for fuch fupply of the wants of fuch people as are not able, by greater quantities, to make their provifion of victuals ; and not meant for entertainment and harbouring of lewd and idle people, to fpend and confume their money, and their time, in lewd and drunken manner," Be it enacted, &c.

As this act punifhes the keeper of the ale-houfes permitting un-lawful drinking, fo does chapter the fifth, of the ftatute paffed in 1606, punifh the tippler, or drunkard, himfelf ; both which

ftatutes,

ſtatutes, although at preſent the law of the land, and well calculated to prevent drunkenneſs, the root of much evil, yet are no
more attended to by the magiſtrate of theſe days than as vain and
nugatory founds, of the regulation of other times, which are long
paſſed away, and the memory of which remains not, except in the
page of hiſtory.

In the ſeventh ſtatute of this reign, chapter the third, directions
are enacted, how the money, given for the binding poor children
apprentices, ſhall be employed; by the preamble to which, it appears, that great ſums of money had then been given, and more
was likely to be given, for the purpoſe of binding poor children
apprentices unto needful trades and occupations; a purpoſe to
which the charity of modern times, although in many inſtances
profuſe, and in ſome redundant, has not in the leaſt attended; and,
therefore, this ſtatute, except as far as it may reſpect ſums of
money then given, and ſtill in ſtock, or lands, bought therewith,
is now not in uſe.

The fourth chapter of this ſeſſion has ſomewhat of a reference
to the 43d of Elizabeth; as that directed a ſtock to be raiſed, to
ſet the idle, whether from choice or neceſſity, to work, ſo this
ſtatute directs houſes to be builded, to receive thoſe who are idle,
by choice, in which they may be compelled to work; and gives
birth to houſes of correction, and the regulations reſpecting them;
for, although, by the 39th ſtatute of the late reign, juſtices of the
peace were empowered to erect houſes of correction; yet it appears, by Lord Coke's reading on this ſtatute, that thoſe powers
were not carried into execution; and a penalty of 5*l.* is now laid
on every juſtice, within every county of the realm, where ſuch
houſe ſhall not be erected or provided.

One moſt ſevere clauſe is inſerted in this act of parliament,
affecting the mothers of baſtard-children; a ſeverity totally incompatible with any idea of a juſt proportion of puniſhments to crimes,
and diametrically oppoſite to every principle of moral rectitude:
that

that claufe is alluded to, which empowers magiftrates to commit to the houfe of correction, to be punifhed and fet to work, for the term of a whole year, any woman who fhall have a baftard, which may be chargeable to the parifh; and this, without any authority of mitigation, for the firft offence; and, for the fecond offence of this kind, " eftfoons if fhe fhall offend again," fhe is to be committed, *until fhe fhall find fecurities not to offend again*; fo that, for the firft inftance of immorality, fhe is to fuffer a feverity of punifh-ment infinitely difproportionate to the offence: for the fecond, or any future inftance of fimilar mifconduct, her punifhment, if fhe be a proftitute to a man of property, may be nothing: a fevere and foolifh law; one much more honoured in its neglect, than in the obfervance.

After the diffolution of this parliament, in 1609, none other was called for fourteen years; and, in the mean time, James had full opportunity of giving his fubjects a fufficient fpecimen of king-craft, as he was ufed to call it, or art of government; but, in the twenty-third year of his reign, he found himfelf obliged to affemble the parliament, which continued fitting until his death: that happened in 1625. In this parliament, nothing was done, with refpect to the interefts of the lower claffes of the people, except another act to reprefs drunkennefs.

LETTER X.

THE reign of Charles the Firft continues the acts already in force, with refpect to the poor, but produces nothing new on this fubject, except a farther reftraint on tippling in inns and ale-houfes. The former acts had reftrained, by penalty, his majefty's fubjects only; this, which paffed in the firft year of his

K   reign,

reign, extended to foreigners alfo. It is curious to obferve, that as foon as ale-houfes had obtained a legal fanction, under the licenfe of the neighbouring magiftrates; the bad confequences refulting from them; in promoting idlenefs, debauchery, drunkennefs, and all manner of mifchief, was feverely felt by the nation, and frequent attempts were made by the legiflature to reftrain thofe abufes, but, it is feared, with little effect; becaufe-it may be perceived, that additional reftraints on perfons who haunted thofe pefts of all good order were impofed, year after year, by the parliament; and facility of conviction was confulted, almoft at the expenfe of religious obligations. Thefe ftatutes remain in full force at this day;* and it is in the knowledge of us all, how much fociety hourly fuffers in its morals and induftry, from thefe too frequent and too much frequented places of licenfe and ebriety; but the financier will tell us, that, by thefe and fimilar enormities, the revenue is increafed, and the treafury makes up a good account : to which the proper reply of a good fubject and a good citizen may be,

Non tali auxilio nec defenforibus iftis,
Tempus eget.

The fcene of confufion and civil difcord, which followed the parliament that was held in the 16th of Charles the Firft, and the inteftine wars, which defolated this kingdom, during a period of near twenty years, until the reftoration of the fecond Charles, forbid any expectation of feparating, during their continuation, the concerns of the poor from the miferies of the foldier : *inter arma*

---

* By the 21ft of James the Firft, chap. the 7th, which is continued by an act in the third of Charles the Firft, and again by an act in the fixteenth of the fame reign; the oath of a tippler, having firft confeffed that he was tippling in an ale-houfe, fhall be fufficient proof againft others of the offence ; which incurs, to thofe tippling, a penalty of five fhillings ; and, to the ale-houfe-keeper permitting it, a difability to keep an ale-houfe for three years enfuing the offence.

filent

filent leges, fays Lord Coke; and the maxim has ever been found true by experience, which has alfo proved to us, that, in all civil commotions, where the folly of the million has been made fub-fervient to the purpofes of the few, the rights of the citizen fall before the felf-interefted purpofes of individuals.

Until the Reftoration, which was above half a century from the 43d year of the reign of Elizabeth, the parliament had made no alteration in the laws with refpect to the maintenance and employ-ment of the poor; and that ftatute remained the law in that re-fpect; nor has there been preferved to us any pamphlet or fugitive tract, which, during that period, has reflected on this ftatute, as being deficient either in policy or prudential regulation; on the contrary, it has been continued, from time to time, without any comment whatever, and particularly by ftat. 3. Charles I. chap. 4. and 5.; a filent but a ftrong prefumption, that it had been hither-to found equal to the great purpofe expected from it; the exten-fion of charity by the means of induftry.

Soon after the reftoration of Charles the Second, that is to fay, in the 13th and 14th year of his reign, which takes its date in the ftatute-book from the death of his father, it was perceived that partial inconvenience had rifen, in a manner, from the general good effects of this act of Elizabeth, as an extract from the pre-amble to chap. 12th of the ftatute of that date will plainly demon-ftrate; which ftates, that " whereas poor people are not reftrained from going from one parifh to another, and therefore do endea-vour to fettle themfelves where there is the beft ftock and largeft commons and waftes to build cottages." It appears by this pre-amble, that a good ftock of materials to work up, and a chance of obtaining habitations, occafioned the poor to migrate, from thofe parifhes where the overfeers were negligent in thefe matters, to other parifhes where they had a chance of a domicile and em-ployment; and furely every principle of freedom and every duty of reciprocal juftice fhould permit the poor who live by their

K 2   labour

labour to remove *ad libitum* to thofe parifhes where they may find
labour to live by; notwithftanding the partial inconvenience felt
by particular parifhes, when the general good will be fo much
better promoted, both in principle and practice. This is the firft
act which refpects the fettlements of the poor, but does not attempt in any inftance an alteration of the 43d of Elizabeth, and
may rather be called, with no impropriety, a ufeful addition to
that venerable edifice; comprehending in it the origin of fettlements, work-houfes, and the laws refpecting rogues and vagabonds, together with regulations as to the maintenance of natural
children.

The dignity of hiftory very feldom ftoops to record the diftreffes
or comforts of the bulk of the people; the bufinefs of the hiftorian is with wars and revolutions, treaties and the infringement
of them, the intrigues of party, and the exceffes of the higher
orders of the ftate; but rarely does he condefcend to relate,

The fhort and fimple annals of the poor.

It is, therefore, from other fources our information muft be fupplied; from the pamphlet, or the newfpaper of the day; and,
hitherto, but few of thefe have come to hand, of fo remote a date
as the middle of the laft century; from the only exifting inftance
on record, that could be found, of the juftices rating of wages, in
the county of * Effex, compared with the cotemporary prices of
wheat

* Effex, Eafter-Seffions, 1661.
Common labourers, fellers, and makers up of wood, ditches, and hedges; threfhers, and
all other common labourers, by the day (the time of harveft excepted).

	With Board.		Without Board.	
	s.	d.	s.	d.
From the middle of March to the middle of September	0	8	1	2
From the middle of September to the middle of March	0	6	1	0
Man hay-maker	0	8	1	0
Woman hay-maker	0	5	0	10
Weeders of corn	0	4	0	9

Mowers

wheat and malt, a reafonable conclufion may be drawn, that the proportion, between the fcarcity of the *neceſſaries* of life and price of labour, was by that means more exactly preferved than in thefe times; for, although the price of wheat is very high, yet, in the other articles of the confumption of a poor family, in candles, foap, beer, no fuch excife-duties took place then as now do ; nor was tea and gin fo much their beverage ; nor had paper-credit fo much depreciated the value of money, by raifing ideal riches, as at prefent ; for, in fuch a proportion it is fuppofed the value of gold and filver to be decreafed, and confequently the money-price

	s.	d.		s.	d.
Mowers of corn and grafs	0	10	—	1	6
A fallower	0	6	—	1	3
Man-reaper	1	0	—	1	10
Woman-reaper	0	8	—	1	2

LABOURERS BY TASK.

	s.	d.
Mowing an acre of grafs	1	10
Well-making, clean raking, and cocking, an acre of grafs, ready to carry,	2	0
Reaping, or fhearing, well-binding, cocking, or fhocking, an acre of wheat, rye, or meflin	4	0
Reaping, or fhearing, an acre of barley, or bullymony, binding and fhocking the fame	2	6
The fame to oats	2	6
Reaping and well-binding an acre of beans	3	6
Mowing an acre of barley or oats	1	2
Making an acre of peafe, vetches, or tares	1	9
Making and ditching a rod of new ditch, 4 feet wide, out of the whole ground, 3 feet deep, 1½ foot at bottom, double-fet with quick, and fetting a hedge upon it, after the rate of 16½ feet a rod, with gathering fets for the fame,	1	2
A rod of ditch, of like breadth and depth, without quick	0	6
Threfhing wheat and rye, the quarter	1	10
———— barley and oats	0	10
———— beans, peafe, bullymony, tares	0	10

	£.	s.	d.
The prices of wheat, this year, as appears by Fleetwood's Chronicon, per quarter	3	10	0
Malt, per quarter	1	13	4

of

of the neceffaries of life increafed, that a poor family which could, in the middle of the laft century, earn 20*l.* a year, was in a better fituation than the fame family would be now with earnings amounting to 50*l.* a year; therefore, the prices of labour were more adequate to fupply their wants,* although the price of wheat was very high, than the prevailing prices in this county at prefent; befides, at this time, a poor family might, without the fear of being fent back by the parifh-officers, go where they chofe, for better wages, or more certain employment; whereas, fince the year 1662, the law of fettlements, introduced by 13th and 14th Charles II. chap. 12. has much abridged their liberty in that re-fpect; made them of neceffity ftationary, and obliged them to reft fatisfied with thofe wages they can obtain where their legal fettle-ment happens to be; a reftraint on them which ought to infure to them wages, in the parifh where they muft remain, more adequate to their neceffities, becaufe it precludes them in a manner from bringing their labour, the only marketable produce they poffefs, to the beft market. It is this reftraint which has, in all manufactu-ring-towns, been one caufe of reducing the poor to fuch a ftate of miferable poverty; for, among the manufacturers, they have too frequently found mafters who have taken, and continue to take, every advantage, which ftrict law will give; of confequence, the prices of labour have been, in manufacturing-towns, in an in-verfe ratio of the number of poor fettled in the place; and the fame caufe has increafed that number, by inviting foreigners, in times when large orders required many workmen; the mafters themfelves being the overfeers, whofe duty, as parifh-officers, has been oppofed by their intereft in fupplying the demand.

But, on the other hand, the queftion, What are the neceffaries of life? fhould be taken into confideration; and this is a point not

---

* *Wants:* this expreffion is underftood to comprehend not neceffaries alone, but the comforts and indulgences of life. .

eafily

eafily fettled ; the rigid rule of juftice fo conftantly militating with the laudable, but defultory, feelings of humanity. When we affert that nothing is a neceffary to life but what fupports the ftream of life, we confine the number of articles within a narrow limit ; and poffibly to thofe articles alfo whofe price is not much rifen, or the ufe of which is trifling in a poor family, as linen, foap, leather ; but when, with a wider fcope of humanity, we take in the comforts of life which were in contemplation in the preceding paragraph, the expenfes of the poor are very confiderably increafed. To fettle our ideas on this fubject, Adam Smith may be thought no improper moderator ; at leaft his high character for ftrong fenfe, combined with deep knowledge of the topic, point him out as of the beft authority : he reckons as neceffaries to the poor in England, linen, foap, leather fhoes ; he claffes beer, ale, tobacco, tea, fugar, and fpirituous liquors, among the luxuries of life, but profeffes he means to throw no reproach on a temperate ufe of them.

Although the reign of Charles II. extended to the year 1680, and the parliament regularly fat every year, except the 21ft, 24th, 26th, and 28th, of his reign, yet but little more was enacted refpecting the poor : in the 23d feffion, by chap. the 18th, fome farther regulations with refpect to work-houfes were thought expedient, and paffed into a law ; and, in the 19th, the 22d, and 30th, feffion, the fituation of poor prifoners was taken into confideration, and fome good regulations made to give them means of employing themfelves while in confinement ; to prevent the fpreading of infectious diftempers, and to expedite the difcharge of prifoners, when liberated by courfe of law ; yet, as they do not fall under the particular object of this inquiry, there is no occafion to make any obfervations on them ; but let us pafs on to the enfuing reign, ftopping only to inquire whether any treatifes have been printed before the Revolution, and preferved to the prefent time, which may throw light on this important fubject.

LETTER

LETTER XI.

THE information which may be gleaned on the subject of the poor of this kingdom, from the earliest time, until the close of the last century, by tracts, pamphlets, or fugitive publications, is not much more satisfactory and particular, than what the pages of the history of this country afford. It should seem, that, excepting here and there, a mind thirsty after that information, which may be serviceably applied to the benefit of our fellow-creatures; people, in general, of all denominations, at all times, recede with disgust from inquiries of this nature, and throw aside that book, whose periods remind them of the miseries attendant on the great mass of human lives within this kingdom; or vainly, although with a good intent, attempt to point out some means to mitigate or avert them : the result of every inquiry a country-life could afford, together with an unlimited order to one of the first bookfellers in town, to collect every thing that has been written on the subject, to the close of the last century, has produced a very insignificant list; more tracts must certainly have been published, but it is supposed not many worth notice, because scarcely any are quoted or mentioned in the pages of those which have been collected. Among the farrago of pamphlets published during the last century, which the British Museum possesses, many, it is possible, whose titles would not otherwise have existed to this time, have been preserved; but neither time or opportunity have offered to search that immense arsenal of literature; in the mean time, the subject itself presses on the mind; and some apprehension left the illness of my friend* should occasion a temporary discontinuance of that useful publication, on account of which the inquiry was first begun, before it is brought to a conclusion, which would, in

* At this time Mr. A. Young was dangerously ill.

some

some respect, leave the Annals of Agriculture imperfect; a work which reflects lasting honour on *him*, who, with such success, has brought, as it were, under a glance of the eye, a mass of agricultural information, that will long remain a valuable treasure to the kingdom. These reasons have urged me to continue the plan hinted at a few pages back, although at present so indifferently provided with materials on the subject.

It creates no small degree of surprise, that a mind so capacious as the Viscount St. Alban's, who lived cotemporary and was art and part with that parliament which passed the famous statute of Elizabeth, among the voluminous pages of his writings and the vast variety of subjects his almost omnipotent abilities comprehended and his indefatigable pen treated of, should not have left a single tract on this important subject : one paragraph alone can be found, a mere drop, amidst the ocean of five quarto volumes of his work; and this drop is in his advice to the king, touching Mr. Sutton's* estate; but by this it is apparent, that his ideas were not well digested on this subject, nor was the topic closely entered on. The only passage worth extracting is the following : " But chiefly it were to be wished such beneficence towards the relief of the poor were so bestowed, as not only the mere and naked poor should be sustained, *but also that the honest person which has hard means to live, upon whom the poor are now charged, should be, in some sort, eased:*† for that were a work generally acceptable to the kingdom, if the public hand of alms might spare the private hand of tax; and, therefore, of all other employments of that kind, I commend most *houses of relief and correction*, which are *mixed hospitals*; where the impotent person is relieved, and the sturdy beggar buckled to work,

* The founder of the Charter-House.

† This sentiment is amazingly prophetic of the experienced pressure of the poor-rates in modern times : the *poor* pay to the rates for the maintenance of the *poorer*, and are themselves sinking from want of maintenance and relief.

and

and the unable perfon alfo not maintained to be idle, which is ever joined with drunkennefs and impurity, but is forted with fuch work as he can manage and perform; and where the ufes are not diftinguifhed, as in other hofpitals, whereof fome are for aged and impotent, and fome for children, and fome for correction of vagabonds, but are general and promifcuous, that may take off poor, of every fort, from the county, as the county breeds them; and thus the poor themfelves fhall find the provifion, and other people the fweetnefs of the abatement of the tax. Now if it be objected, that houfes of correction in all places have not done the good expected; as it cannot be denied, but in moft places they have done much good; it muft be remembered, that there is a great difference between that which is done by the *diftracted government of juftices of peace*, and that which may be done by a *fettled ordinance*, fubject to a regular vifitation, as this may be."

When Sir Francis Bacon, as attorney-general, drew up this letter of advice for his mafter James the Firft, he muft furely have conceived in his mind fome idea of *incorporated houfes of induftry*; and anticipated, as it were, by prophetic forefight, fomewhat of thofe excellent regulations, which, through the aufpices of a reverend and worthy magiftrate, have brought the poor under fuch good order, and fo reduced the rates in thofe parifhes, whofe houfe of induftry he, with fuch attention, at prefent, prefides over.*

The words *diftracted government of juftices of peace* are worth our notice: it is to be feared that the obfervation would equally apply, through the many years that have paffed fince this advice was given, as it did then; a farther comment on this expreffion would be indecorous; but it warrants this fingle obfervation, that, as the *gratis* opinion of a lawyer is not thought fo good as that which *a fee* commands, fo poffibly the *gratis* or *voluntary attention* of the gentlemen in the commiffion of the peace is likely to be more

* The Rev. Mr. Cooke, of Semer, in Suffolk.

defultory

defultory and diftracted than that which a falary might purchafe.

My Lord Hale is the firft great name on the lift of thofe
who have turned their attention to the employment and relief of the
poor. The year his plan firft appeared in is not apparent in the
copy, but it certainly preceded any other in my poffeffion, as it
muft have been written before 1676, that being the year in which
he died: it would ta.e up too much time to tranfcribe all in this
excellent tract, which is deferving our attention; therefore thofe
parts only fhall be taken notice of which are moft to our purpofe;
he fays, " The only ftatute which provides univerfally for the
poor is the forty-third of Elizabeth, which generally makes two
provifions.

" *Firft*, for the impotent poor that are not able to work;
and for thefe it is a good and effectual provifion, if duly executed.

" *Second*, for thofe *that are able*. The defects of this provifion
are, firft, in the execution; the fecond defect is in the law itfelf;
which is, that there is no power in the juftices of peace, or fome
fuperintendent power, to compel the raifing of a ftock, where the
church-wardens and overfeers neglect it. — 2. The act chargeth
every parifh apart, where it may be they are able to do little
towards it; neither would it be fo effectual as if three, four, five,
or more contiguous parifhes, did contribute towards the raifing of
a ftock, proportionable to the poor refpectively. — 3. There is no
power for hiring or erecting a common houfe, or place, for their
common work-houfe; which may be, in fome refpects and upon
fome occafions, ufeful and neceffary, as fhall be fhewn.

" The remedies are:

" 1. That the juftices of the peace, at the quarter-feffions, do
fet out and diftribute the parifhes, in their feveral counties, into
feveral divifions, in each of which there may be a work-houfe
for the common ufe of the refpective divifions, wherein they are
refpectively placed; to wit, one, two, three, four, five, or fix,

parifhes

parishes to a work-houfe, according to the greatnefs or fmallnefs, and accommodation, of the feveral parifhes.

" 2. That, at the feffions, the church-wardens and overfeers of the poor of the refpective parifhes, bring in their feveral rates for the relief of their refpective poor, upon oath. And that the faid juftices do affefs three, four, or five, yearly payments, to be levied and collected at one or two entire fums, within the time prefixed by them, for the raifing a ftock, to fet the poor, within thofe pre- cincts, on work; and to build or procure a convenient work- houfe, for employing the poor (if need be) in it, and for lodging materials, and for inftructing children in trade or work.

" 3. That there be yearly chofen, by the faid juftices, a mafter for each work-houfe, with a convenient falary, out of the faid ftock, or the produce thereof, to continue for three years; and two overfeers, to fee the iffuing and return of the faid ftock, and to take the accounts quarterly or monthly of the mafter, as they fhall think fit.

" 4. That the ftock be delivered to the overfeers, and by them iffued to the mafter, as there fhall be occafion; and that they alfo, from time to time, receive the produce of the faid ftock, and the accounts for the fame.

" 5. That, at the end of every year, the mafter and overfeers give up their accounts to the two next juftices of the peace, at times by them prefixed, and publicly notified to the inhabitants of each precinct, to the end that they may take any exceptions to fuch accounts, if there be caufe.

" 6. That the mafter and overfeers of every refpective work- houfe ftand, and be incorporate, by the name of the mafter and overfeers of their refpective precincts, and capable to take in fuc- ceffion, by will or otherwife, lands, goods, or money, or other legacies or gifts, for the benefit of the poor within their refpective precincts.

" 7. That

" 7. That they alſo be accountable, as well to their reſpective ſucceſſors, as to the juſtices of the peace at their quarter-ſeſſions, for the benefit, and produce, and employment, of ſuch gifts and bequeſts.

8. " That they be diſabled to grant any lands, to them given or bequeathed, for any longer term than one year, and at an improved rent.

" 9. That if any perſon, that is able to work, and not able to maintain himſelf, ſhall refuſe to do ſo, he may be forced thereto, by warrant of two juſtices of peace, by impriſonment, and moderate correction in ſuch work-houſe.

" 10. If any perſon, employed by the maſter, ſhall embezzle, or wilfully prejudice, or ſpoil, his work, he ſhall, upon complaint and proof thereof, by the party grieved, to any juſtice of peace, and by warrant from him, receive impriſonment, or moderate correction, by warrant of ſuch juſtice.

" Theſe are the heads of that proviſion I could wiſh for the ſetting the poor to work, which is but an eſſay, and may receive alterations or additions upon conſideration."

This excellent man then ſpeaks of the benefits ariſing from his plan, and anſwers ſome objections to it; and then concludes, that ſuch a plan, if it could be accompliſhed, would be a work of great humanity, which would become a Chriſtian and a good Engliſhman. In this plan, the idea ſuggeſted by Sir Francis Bacon is improved, matured, and digeſted into ſome regularity; and, under this form, it preſents to our view a prototype, as it were, of Mr. Gilbert's ſcheme, which has lately attracted the attention of the public.

The next publication which has been collected, in point of time, is by _Andrew Yarrington_, who appears, by his own account, to have been a linen-draper, and afterward employed by ſome gentlemen to bring a manufacture into England, from Bohemia and Saxony, made (to uſe his own words) of iron and tin: it appears alſo,

that

that he was a furveyor to fome iron-works in Ireland; he certainly
poffeffed great information on matters of trade, and a clear un-
derftanding : the imprimatur of his book bears date 1676; the title
is an epitome of its motley contents, " England's Improvement,
by Sea and Land, to outdo the Dutch without fighting, to pay
Debts without Money, and to fet at work all the Poor in England,
with the Growth of our own Lands," *cum multis aliis*; in this
curious and, in fome refpect, inftructive book, may be found the
firft idea of a *fchool for induftry*, according to the practice in Hol-
land and Flanders, which, the author takes great pains to prove,
might with profit be carried into effect in England.   He alfo, in a
vifion of future glory, anticipates, in profpect, the extent of our
paper-credit, our numerous inland navigations, the full employment of the infant poor, and our confequential riches.   His vifion
is completely verified in the two firft inftances, and their confequences ; why it may not, in the other, remains probably for another century to prove.   But, furely, as the complaint, that the
poor are not employed, and that idlenefs prevails among them,
may be now made, with at leaft equal truth, towards the clofe of
the eighteenth century, as it was about the middle of the feventeenth ; why the other part of his prophecy fhould not be brought
to pafs remains in nothing but experience itfelf to fhew, and it
is to be hoped that the Sunday-fchools will prove harbingers to the
attempt.

Mr. Thomas Firmin, a friend of Archbifhop Tillotfon, is the
next writer on this fubject.   His two letters to that prelate, entitled, " Some Propofals for the Employment of the Poor, efpecially
in and about the city of London," bear date in the years 1678 and
1681 : he appears to have been a man of refpectable character, and
frequently to have been employed in diftributing private charity :
in his firft letter, he fpeaks of his fuccefs attending a plan for a
kind of work-houfe, in the parifh of Alderfgate, to employ the
poor in fpinning flax and hemp at their own houfes.   His expe-

rience,

rience, in this bufinefs, is great; and fo is his fuccefs. He perceives, he fays, by his experiment, " that the only way to provide
for the poor, and to bring them to labour, is to provide fuch work
for them as they may do at their own homes, which, though never
fo mean and homely, is more defired than any other place; and the
way which feveral perfons have propofed of bringing them to a
work-houfe will never effect the end intended: for, fuppofe a woman hath a fick hufband, or child, or fome infirmity upon herfelf,
in all fuch cafes fhe may do fomething at home, but cannot leave
her own houfe. True, indeed, for vagrants, or fturdy beggars,
who have no habitation, and muft be held to their labour, as gal-
ley-flaves are tied to their oars, fuch public work-houfes are very
neceffary; and I wifh we had more of them, and that thofe we
have were employed to this purpofe, to which they were at firft
defigned and intended: but for fuch poor people as have habitations of their own, and who are known in the parifh where they
live, and would take pains at home, it is altogether unreafonable
and unprofitable (in my judgement) to force them to a public work-
houfe.

" If any parifh that abounds with poor people *would fet up a
fchool, in the nature of a work-houfe, to teach poor children to work,*
who wander up and down the parifh, and parts adjacent, and between begging and ftealing get a forry living, but never bring any
thing unto their parents, nor earn one farthing towards their own
maintenance, *it would, in a fhort time, be found very advantageous,*
not only to the poor children, who, by this means, whilft young,
fhould be inured to labour, and taught to get their own living,
but alfo to their parents, who fhould hereby both be freed from any
charge by keeping them, and alfo in time be helped by their labour,
as it is in other places.

" And, farther, the parifh would, by this means, be freed from
much charge, that now they are at, either to keep thefe children,
or to allow their parents fomething toward it, nothing being
                                                                        thought

thought a greater argument for a large penfion, than that a man or
woman hath fix or feven children; whereas, unlefs they were all
born at one time, or come fafter into the world than ordinarily fo
many children do, it is very hard if fome of them be not able to
work for themfelves. I myfelf have, at this time, fome children
working to me, not above feven or eight years old, who are able
to earn 2*d*. a day; and fome, that are but a little older, 2*s*. a
week; and I doubt not to bring any child, about that age, to do
the like: and ftill as they grow up, and become proficients, even
in this poor trade of fpinning, they will be able to get more, and
to fpin better, than older people. Neither would I have thefe
fchools confined only to fpinning, but to take in knitting, and
making of lace, or plain-work, or any other work which the children fhall be thought moft fit for: and this is that, which (as I
am informed) is practifed in other countries with fo great advantage, that there are few poor children, who have attained the age
of feven or eight years, that are any charge to the parifh or burthen to their poor parents: and Mr. Chamberlain (in his book,
entitled, The prefent State of England, p. 137) hath obferved,
that, in the city of Norwich, it hath been of late years computed"
and found, that (yearly) children, from fix to ten years of age,
have gained twelve thoufand pounds more than what they have
fpent, and that chiefly by knitting fine Jerfey ftockings."

To this plan he fuppofes objections to be made. He anfwers
them all, except the laft queftion, which is:—

" What will you do with all the yarn thefe poor people fhall
fpin? If you weave it into cloth, the commodity is brought
over fo cheap, that you will never be able to fell, without much
lofs?

" *Anfwer*. I muft confefs this objection hath too much of
truth in it, to be wholly removed. The beft anfwer I can make
to it, at prefent, is this:—That we had much better lofe fomething by the labour of the poor, than lofe all by letting them live

in

in floth and idlenefs : for, fuppofe you fhould give 6*d.* for that work which is really worth but 5*d.* ; hence will 5*d.* really be got to the nation, though 1*d.* fhould be loft to the parifh. Yet, befides, let it be confidered, that, if this perfon had not been employed, there would not lefs have been fpent, but rather more; forafmuch as 6*d.* that is got by labour, doth many times go farther than 12*d.* given for doing nothing. All the time people are idle, they will be fpending, if they have it ; and, if they have it not, it is like they will be worfe employed."

It alfo appears, from this letter, that no great good was conceived to arife from work-houfes in the metropolis, of which they now had received fome years experience ; the act of parliament, authorizing incorporated work-houfes within the bills of mortality, having paffed in 1662.

In this letter is alfo the idea of a *badge* on thofe among the poor, who, being incapable of labour, are maintained by the parifh ; and, by the badge, it was imagined, they would not be likely to receive much from begging ; it being apparent, by the badge, that their parifh maintains them.

The fecond letter, which appeared in 1681, feems much to our purpofe, as it contains a plan of a School of Induftry; but it would be of little fervice to give his intentions in detail, not only on account of the length of quotation which would be neceffary, but becaufe it does not appear that his fcheme was ever carried into execution ; and it is apprehended that a more perfect plan actually is now in practice through many parts of Lincolnfhire, which, if any wifh to eftablifh fuch a fchool of induftry fortunately prevailed, might be obtained from fome of the worthy truftees ; and fuch a fchool might be applied to fpinning flax, as well as wool, knitting of ftockings, winding of filk, making of lace, or plain-work, and the like. In this letter, alfo, Mr. Firmin fuppofes objections to his plan, and anfwers them all, except the laft, which is the fame as has been noticed in his firft letter, and which he confeffed himfelf unable *perfectly* to anfwer ; and here he gives the fame reply as he did to the fame queftion before, which has been already mentioned.

On the whole, his feveral fchemes are practicable ; and they fall from the pen of an honeft and experienced man. His reafons in favour of them, anfwering the objections which he fuppofes may be made, are, in general, conclufive, except in the inftance which has been recited ; and the objection itfelf, as to the difficulty of finding a fale for the goods manufactured, would not probably be fo ftrong at prefent, as it was a hundred and twelve years ago ; nor would it apply fo much to a *county*-fchool of induftry, as to one in *London :* the parents and relations of the poor children, whom their parifhes now clothe at an expenfe much above the prime-coft of the wares manufactured, would, it is apprehended, give vent to a confiderable quantity of the goods ; more efpecially if the fale was encouraged by the parifh-officers and farmers recommending the manufacture to their labourers.

<hr/>

L E T T E R   XII.

SIR JOSIAH CHILD, who has, in his *new difcourfe of trade*, given one chapter on the relief and employment of the poor, fhall be now attended to. It does not appear, by the edition whence this note is taken, which is the fourth, exactly when the firft edition was publifhed ; although, as the parliament which fat in 1669 was not diffolved until 1679, it appears moft probable, from the beginning of the preface, that it was publifhed about the laft date ; and, therefore, does not improperly follow Mr. Firmin's Letters.

In

In the chapter which relates to the poor, Sir Jofiah begins by intimating to the reader, that this is a *calm* fubject, and thwarts no *common* or *private* intereft among us, except that of the common enemy of mankind, the devil. It muft ftrike every reader, that things are ftrangely altered fince this tract was written, as the fubject is in thefe days by no means *calm*, and thwarts many private interefts in every parifh; although, it muft be confefled, that, in fome refpect, thefe are the interefts of the devil, as they are oppofite to every intereft of integrity and common honefty.

He argues for a defect in the poor-laws, from the failure in execution of thofe ftatutes which relate to the poor, and refts the proof of his argument on this fact, that, in every change of parties this nation may have experienced, all parties had thefe laws to fteer by, and none of them fufficiently maintained the impotent and employed the indigent. Could this worthy merchant be a member of parliament? Did he live in the world, and not know, by conftant experience, that the maintenance of the impotent, or the employment of the indigent, is the very laft object to which leaders of parties will attend? At leaft the experience of the prefent æra would prove the fact; however it might have been in the reign of Charles the Second. On the day when the Houfe of Commons debated on the motion of Mr. Gilbert, refpecting his bill, which was to determine whether it fhould be read a fecond time or be rejected, about forty-four members attended; not a member who ranked high on the treafury-bench, or in the phalanx of oppofition; but Mr. Gilbert and Mr. Young, who oppofed the bill, had nearly the debate to themfelves; and this bill, which involved in its confequences the material interefts of the nation, was thrown out, by a divifion of thirty-four to ten.

But, laying afide this objection to Sir Jofiah's argument, and fuppofing that the parties in the ftate would attend to thefe regulations, and have attended to them, and that they are ftill badly executed, the fame obfervation might be made with refpect to the

M 2

laws

laws of the Deity, the general received rules of morality, the Ten Commandments. All claffes and conditions of men have long poffeffed all that is contained in the Decalogue, to regulate their conduct by; and all nations experience daily the faulty execution, or rather the conftant breach, of thefe facred laws; to argue from the faulty execution of breach of a municipal rule, the inefficacy or impropriety of that rule is bad logic; it is not the conclufion naturally following from the premifes.

He fays, the radical error is the leaving it to the care of every parifh to maintain their own poor only.

To correct this error, he propofes a plan of a fociety, who are to be incorporated by act of parliament, by the name of *Fathers of the Poor*; to whom all church-wardens, overfeers, and other officers, fhould be fubordinate; gives them powers fuperior to the magiftrates; and confumes many pages in forming rules for the conduct of this incorporation; which is apparently intended, in the firft place, for the city of London and its vicinity, although, in the end, the whole kingdom is fuppofed to embrace the plan.

Here furely may be feen the outline from which Mr. Gilbert's late plan was filled up; or at leaft from hence frefh hints were taken; which, had it paffed into a law, would probably have introduced throughout the kingdom general confufion.

It would fcarcely be worth the trouble for the writer to tranfcribe, or the reader to perufe, the plan of Sir Jofiah Child in the detail; as, it is conceived, it never ought to be carried into execution, by the force of law, in this kingdom; fome parts of it, which fhall be juft glanced at, will be an apology for this opinion.

" 1ft. That the faid fathers of the poor may have liberty to affefs all parifhes within their diftrict, fo much as they yearly paid to that purpofe any three years preceding.

" 2. That they may receive charitable contributions *on the Lord's day*, and at any other times they may think fit.

" 3. That they may have all the power juftices have.

" 4. That

" 4. That they may have power to fend fuch poor, as they fhall think fit, into *any of his Majefty's plantations.*

" 5. That they may have petty banks or lumbards, for the benefit of the poor ; may have *half what is paid at play-houfes,* and a *patent for farthings."*

In the fame manner as Mr. Firmin, Sir Jofiah afks and anfwers queftions with refpect to his propofed plan: two of the queftions, together with part of the anfwers, are as follow:

" What will be the advantage to the kingdom in general, and to the poor in particular, that will accrue by fuch a fociety of men, more than is enjoyed by the laws at prefent?"

Part of the anfwer. — " Poor children will be inftructed in learning and arts, and thereby rendered ferviceable to their country.

" What fhall all the poor of thefe cities and counties, being very numerous, be employed about?"

Part of the anfwer. — " The girls may be employed in mending the clothes of the aged, in fpinning, carding, and other linen manufactories ; and many in fewing linen for the exchange, or any houfekeepers that will put out linen to the matrons, that have the government of them.

" The boys in picking oakum, making pins, rafping wood, making hangings, or any other manufacture of any kind, which, *whether it turns to prefent profit or not, is not much material* ; the great bufinefs of the nation being, firft, *to keep the poor from begging and ftarving, and enuring fuch as are able to labour and difcipline that they may be hereafter ufeful members to the kingdom."*

This maxim deferves to be written in letters of gold in all work-houfes, houfes of induftry, fchools of induftry, and to be engraved in capitals in the overfeers books in every parifh in the kingdom ; this is the great and leading principle in the forty-third of Elizabeth ; it is for this purpofe the ftock of wool, flax, hemp, thread, iron, is *there* directed to be purchafed ; not for the view of

immediate

immediate gain only, *but for the enuring such as are able to labour and difcipline, that they be hereafter ufeful members to the kingdom.*

Two capital objections are obvious to any one who confiders what has been tranfcribed of this plan.

The firft is, that it propofes to raife a revenue for the maintenance and employment of the poor, in addition to that enormous one which we now complain of; and that by a *new* tax, and by a *patent for coining farthings: church-collections* are alfo propofed, which were the very ground-work of the prefent poor's rate.

The fecond objection is founded on the little regard paid to the liberty of the fubject; as it propofes to give the unconftitutional power to this fociety of tranfporting the poor to our colonies, without a crime charged, merely from fuch conceptions of convenience that might arife in the breafts of thefe *fathers of the poor.*

The tendency of opulence to taint the honefteft principles, and to operate as a draught of the river Lethe, in producing among the *rich* a total oblivion of the rights of the *poor*, is here well exemplified. — The merchant, rolling in wealth, forgets that banifhment is a very ferious punifhment for a crime of fome enormity; to fuch a degree is it dreaded, that fome criminals have preferred death, the legal punifhment of their crimes, rather than accept of pardon, on terms of tranfportation : he has alfo forgot, that, to tranfport a fellow-fubject, a crime committed, indictment, verdict of their countrymen, and the fentence of the laws, are neceffary.

Thefe are all the publications, which have fallen under our obfervation, before that memorable æra in our hiftory—*the Revolution.* An event, taken together with thofe laws and regulations, fo favourable to the liberties of the fubject, which accompanied it, as to demand our moft humble thanks to the Almighty Governor of kings and ftates ; and alfo our grateful remembrance of thofe who were his immediate agents, in fixing our liberties on their prefent folid bafis ; placed in a happy medium between *defpotifm* and *licentioufnefs* ; a medium fo difficult to be hit on, and fo conducive to pub-

lic

lic happinefs, when eftablifhed, that philanthropy excites our wifhes, poffibly at the expenfe of our political intereft, in favour of fo
many millions of our fellow-creatures as people the extenfive kingdom of France; that they may, at length, find a haven of fecurity
to their liberties, in a conftitution fimilar to what we now enjoy;
equally removed from the anarchy of democracy, as the flavery of
defpotifm.   In the mean time, it fhall be the fixed point in view
of this tract, to continue the inquiry with refpect to the poor-
laws, and the relative fituation of the poor themfelves in fociety,
from this period to the prefent day; and then offer fome general
principles, as a refult from the whole of this inveftigation, in full
confidence that the remedy, as well as the mifchief, may be made
apparent; and alfo with fome rays of hope, that the vacant hour
of a retired life may be made conducive to a diminution of the train
of evil fo large a mafs of our fellow-fubjects fuffer under, as well
as to a prevention of the increafe, if not to a diminution, of the
prefent load of expenfe attending their maintenance and fupport;
which will foon pre-occupy the fources of revenue; and, in fome
future day of misfortune, may fall on us when we are lefs able to
fupport it; and, in falling, crufh us with its weight; entail in its
confequences a long and tremendous ruin on all ranks of our fellow-fubjects, together with a demolition of this much-admired conftitution, and involve us in a fcene of univerfal confufion.

LETTER XIII.

THE law of fettlements, introduced by parliament in the reign
of Charles the Second, was a ferious abridgement of the liberty of our fellow-fubjects; but was, at the fame time, a confequence

quence refulting from that humane confideration, which our forefathers felt, for their prefervation from actual want. It became a
prudential caution, from the time that parifh-rates were firft collected for the relief of the poor, that the money raifed in a parifh
fhould be applied to the relief of thofe only who belonged to that
parifh; hence has arifen a reftraint on the poor, in many inftances
cruel; in all, unjuft; a great additional expenfe on thofe on whom
the rate is levied, arifing from cofts of law, in determining fettlements; an additional trouble to the magiftrates; and, to the gentlemen of the profeffion, much bufinefs, and many fees. Settle-
ments now occupy no fmall portion of the attention of the King's
Bench; and reports of the determinations in that court, refpecting
them, are become voluminous; and form a topic, of no fmall confequence, in the common-place-book of the gentlemen of the
long robe.

That a great part of the reftraint on the poor, or, at leaft, that
which bears hardeft on them, by preventing them living in parifhes
where they may beft get their bread, unlefs it happens to be their
place of fettlement, or they have a certificate of the confent of
their parifh to live there, may, with equal convenience and fafety,
be removed; and that much of the expenfe attending contefts between parifhes, with refpect to fettlements, may be faved, is certain. The heads of the bill brought into the Houfe of Commons,
by Sir William Young, immediately after the difmiffion of Mr.
Gilbert's plan, warrant this affertion. To fpeculate on the reafons
why fo much of that bill as relates to certificates did not pafs, is
not the bufinefs of this invefligation; which now procceds to the
firft fanction the law of fettlements received from the legiflature
after the Revolution.

Hitherto but little had been done to confine the poor within
their own parifhes. The ftatute, which paffed in the reign of
Charles the Second, empowering two juftices, on complaint of the
overfeers, within forty days after any poor perfon had come to in-
                                                                    habit

habit in their parifh, in any tenement under the annual value of ten pounds, that they were likely to become chargeable, to remove them to their laft legal place of fettlement, was, at the Revolution, the only law extant on that fubject; and being, together with the alteration, by the 17th of James the Second, directing that the forty days fhould be accounted, from the time of delivery of notice in writing, about to expire; the 3d of William and Mary, chapter 11, again takes up the fubject; and directs that the notice fhould be read in the church, immediately after fervice, on the next Lord's day after it fhall have been delivered; and, then, that it fhall be regiftered in the poor's book; and inflicts a penalty on the church-warden and overfeer neglecting to read and regifter it: and alfo enacts, that ferving a parifh-office, paying parifh-duties, and hiring and fervice for a year, of a perfon not having a wife or child, and ferving an apprenticefhip by indenture, fhall alfo gain a fettlement. In thefe feveral cafes, the appeal lies from the two magiftrates, adjudging the fettlement, to the quarter-feffions.

A regulation, which is intended to act as a reftraint on the parifh-officers, in the diftribution of the parifh-money, is alfo enacted in this ftatute; a regifter is directed to be kept in every parifh of the names of fuch as receive collections; and the parifhioners are ordered to meet in the veftry yearly, in Eafter-week, before whom this regifter is to be produced; and perfons receiving collections are to be called over, the reafons of their taking relief examined, a new lift made and entered, and no other perfons but fuch as are in the lift fhall be allowed to receive collections, except in cafe of peftilential difeafes, and the fmall-pox, without authority, under the hand of one juftice of the peace, refiding within fuch parifh, or the parts adjoining.

Soon did experience prove the mifchief of the acts, with refpect to the fettlements of the poor; fo early did the hardfhip on them, and the inconvenience to the parifhes, arifing from thefe reftric-

N tions

tions on their natural liberty, to get their bread where they could
beft find employment, appear ; that it was found neceffary, in the
year 1697, to open the door a little wider to them ; and to let out
of their parifhes fuch as the church-wardens, overfeers of the
poor, and a neighbouring magiftrate, fhould grant a certificate to ;
under the authority of an act paffed in this year, for fupplying
fome defects in the poor-law ; by which, fuch perfons as may come
to inhabit in any parifh, bringing with them a certificate, properly
attefted, owning them to be inhabitants of the parifh granting it,
and engaging to provide for them whenever they afk relief of the
parifh in which they refide, fhall not be removed until actually
chargeable.

This act alfo directs badges to be worn on the fhoulder of the
right fleeve, by all thofe who receive alms from the parifh ; and
inflicts a penalty on the parifh-officers relieving a perfon not wearing fuch a badge, and a punifhment on the pauper refufing to wear
it : — a good regulation, formed on wife principles, but almoft
univerfally neglected.

Perfons, to whom poor children are bound apprentice, purfuant
to the 43d of Elizabeth, are alfo, by this act, obliged to receive
and to provide for their apprentices, under a penalty of ten pounds,
to be applied to the ufe of the poor.

The legiflature of this reign gives us no other regulations, with
refpect to the poor ; and the general neglect of thofe which have
hitherto been enacted, either as checks on the difhonefty, felfifhnefs, and indolence, of the parifh-officers, or on the impofitions,
debauchery, and lazinefs, of the poor themfelves, ought to be a
matter of ferious aftonifhment to thofe who reflect on the general
complaint of the expenfe attending their maintenance and relief.
What levity ! what abfurdity ! in our lazy complaints of the
weight of the poor's rate ; let us but clap our fhoulders to the
wheel ; the burthen is enormous, but might be fhaken off, or
greatly lightened, by thofe who adminifter the laws ; were thofe
laws,

laws, in fact, administered. Why do we throw the blame from where it ought to fall, and charge the laws themselves with the consequences flowing from a breach of them ? They form, in general, a code replete with humanity in their principle, wise in their regulations, which uniformly tend to discourage idleness and unnecessary expense, throughout the whole scope of their legiflation ; and are now charged with all those destructive evils they were intended, and are calculated, to prevent : the burthen of the poor's rate is heavy, and daily increasing, by a rapid accumulation ; and the cause does not lie in a defect of the *laws* for the maintenance of the poor, but in a defect of the *execution* of those laws : we are affected with a similar impression as those weak minds, which, while the body is haftening to the grave, in a deep decline, have not energy enough to redeem returning health, by a course of exercise and virtuous temperance ; but lazily fuffer the vital principle to be extinguished, by continuing in a habit of indolence and debauchery : in short, we are infected by the *very vices*, which we fo loudly cry out againft, in thofe who are fupported at our expenfe.

The fame wretched principle appears to have pervaded the execution of the poor-laws, towards the end of the laft century; and fimilar complaints of the increafing burthen of expenfe prevail ; as may be feen in a pamphlet, named, *Bread for the Poor*, printed at Exeter, in 1698, by Samuel Darker, figned by the initials of the author's name, R. D. : he fays, in a kind of introduction, that " whoever takes the fmall trouble of infpecting the poor-accounts, of a few parifhes, may foon obferve, that the charge of maintaining them, in fome places, is, within fixty years paft, advanced from forty fhillings to forty pounds yearly ; in others, twice that fum ; and moftwheres double, — within twenty years paft, and like to double again in a fhort time ; and, notwithftanding fuch advance in maintaining the poor, yet the wages they receive is greater than formerly, work more plentiful, and provifions cheaper."

Where

Where there is an effect, the author very properly fays, there muſt be a cauſe; and that the cauſes are,

Profuſeneſs of diet; inſtanced by the bread they eat, being of the fineſt flour; their drink, ale and ſpirits; ſpending their money in alehouſes, to the amount of an incredible ſum, as appears from the payments to the exciſe, very little of which is ſpent by travellers or houſekeepers; and that they pay a price for what they drink, in theſe places, vaſtly ſuperior to its real value.

As a remedy to this cauſe, relief in houſe-rent, meat, drink, clothes, *and not money*, is propoſed.

The ſecond cauſe is idleneſs: this ariſes from receiving pay from the pariſh: people of this deſcription, ſoon conceiving, that the pariſh is *obliged* to maintain them; therefore, their work is ſo much gained from them by the pariſh.

The remedy is; due care to employ the poor conſtantly, and oblige them to do ſuch work as they can perform.

Giving exceſſive pay is another cauſe; by which is meant pariſh-allowance: under this head the common outgoings of a day-labourer is computed; but the computation proceeds on an idea of expenſes, ſo much beneath what is neceſſary at preſent, and ſeems to be calculated for the county of Devon only, that it would be futile to inſert it.

The remedy propoſed is, frugal allowance in quantity, kind, and value.

The fourth cauſe is; living in ſeparate houſes; whereas, did three or four families live together, fire, candle, and attendance, might be ſaved.

The author then explains the method of providing diet for the poor; gives many reaſons why ſuch a management ſhould take place; and anſwers objections which he ſuppoſes may be made to relieving them in the neceſſaries of life rather than in money, which enables them to purchaſe the ſuperfluities:—he alſo recommends

badges,

badges, which, as we have feen, were about this time enforced by parliament.

It appears, from this pamphlet, that the poor's rates for the county of Devon amounted, in the year 1698, to 38,991*l.* 13*s.* 5*d.* a year; which is afferted to be 30,000*l.* a year more than they were fifty or fixty years before; and that the whole amount of the poor's rates in the kingdom was then above twenty-one times as much, or more than 819,000*l.* a year; that, as *one age* had given a *fourfold advance* in Devonfhire, it is worth confideration whether or not the public be in danger: for, if the rates of the whole kingdom increafe proportionably, they will amount in another age to 3,276,000*l.* — Such is the reafoning in this pamphlet; let us now examine the fact.

	£.
About the middle of the 17th century, the affeffment for the poor, in the county of Devon, was annually about - - - - - - - -	8,291
In the year 1698, about - - - - -	38,991
In the year 1785, by the return of the overfeers -	85,492

Therefore the gradual rife in this county was, in the firft fifty years, about 30,000*l.*; in the next eighty-feven years 46,501*l.*

Taking the fame dates for the poor's rates of the whole kingdom, the account will ftand:

	£.
About the year 1650, at - - - -	188,811
In the year 1698, about - - - -	819,000
In the year 1785, by the overfeers returns - -	2,184,904

In the firft fifty years the rife is 730,189*l.*; — in the next eighty-feven years 1,265,904*l.*

The fact does not turn out quite fo deftructive to the interefts of the public as the writer of this pamphlet prognofticated; but it prefents a tremendous advancing increafe, as well in an individual county, as throughout the kingdom.

Let

Let us now examine the prices of wheat at thefe three feparate periods. The table of the price of wheat at Windfor-market, in vol. xiv. p. 227, of the Annals of Agriculture, will enable us to do it accurately.

		£.	s.	d.
Average-prices of wheat, from 1630 to 1654, by the quarter - - - - - - -		2	9	10
Ditto, from 1687 to 1711 - - - -		2	4	2
Ditto, from 1765 to 1789 - - - -		2	6	11

The expenfe attending the maintenance of the poor does not, therefore, arife from the increafed price of wheat ; becaufe, by this table, wheat is cheaper on the average of the laft twenty-five years, ending in 1789, than in that of the firft, ending in 1654 ; and but a little dearer than that ending in 1711.

The aftonifhing increafe towards the clofe of the laft century can be accounted for much more reafonably than that which has arifen in this. When the firft eftimate was taken, towards the middle of the century, the civil war, and its confequential depre-. dations, found employment and fuftenance for a very confiderable body of the poor. The foldier is not maintained by the poor's rate; and the wages of thofe who remained to till the lands, or were employed in our then-mouldering manufactures, were proba- bly raifed on account of the want of hands. No fuch caufe ex- ifted in 1698 or in 1785 ; and the price of wheat in 1698, refer- ring to the fame table, was 3l. 0s. 9d. a quarter; and, in 1785, 1l. 16s. 11d. a quarter. It appears, therefore, that the price of wheat has no effect on the expenfe attending the maintenance of the poor; and wheaten bread is, and long has been, the principal part of their food: this, although it appears a paradox, is a truth. When wheat was 3l. 0s. 9d. a quarter, the expenfes of the poor amounted to but little more than one-third as much as in 1785, when the price of wheat was only 1l. 16s. 11d. a quarter.

As,

As, by this ftatement, it appears that the price of bread has no effect on the poor's rate; and it is believed that, all things confidered, the expenfe of *neceffary* clothing is not more increafed than the laft article (an affertion, the proof of which fhall not now be entered on); and the article of firing remains alfo nearly at the fame price, it was a hundred years ago, theft fupplying (in woodland-countries particularly) an ample fuccedaneum for price; it follows, that we fhould find out the probable caufe of this alarming fact: alas! a fuperficial obferver may read it as he runs, that indolence and luxury are the too-obvious caufes: indolence forces numbers on our rates, which induftry would maintain; luxury ufes profufely what economic temperance would fave: the one adds a million paupers to be maintained by us; the other expends, in the maintenance of that million, what ought to maintain double the number: the one, brings the multitude; the other, imaginary wants.*

Juvenal exclaims, when contemplating the decadency of the Roman empire, ftrongly typified by Britain, in its profufe extravagance,

———Sævior armis
Luxuria incubuit, victumque ulcifcitur orbem.

The fact comes home to *us*, in every clafs and defcription of people; as well poor as rich, the governors and the governed. The confequence is alfo approaching; and our duty will be to fubmit, with refignation to that cataftrophe, which we cannot fufficiently roufe our energy to oppofe.

* The reader fhould be reminded, that this calculation, and the conclufion refulting from it, was written before the extreme high price of wheat, and a proportional dearnefs of every other grain, together with meat, had reduced the poor to extremity of diftrefs, in the years 1795 and 1796. The various confequences refulting to the nation, from that moft grievous affliction, will be obferved upon, in its proper place, in the continuation of this hiftory to the prefent day.

LETTER.

NEXT, in order of time to this publication, follows an Eſſay towards regulating the Trade, and employing the Poor of this Kingdom; written, about the year 1700, by John Cary, Eſq.; an abſtract from which may be ſeen in Dr. Burn's Hiſtory of the Poor-Laws; a publication which, had it been in my poſſeſſion when this inquiry was firſt inſtituted, would have diverted me from the inveſtigation; as I ſhould have ſcarcely choſen to have gone over that ground, which ſo able a writer had beaten before me.

Mr. Cary attributes the burthen of the poor's rates to idleneſs; and inquires,

1. What hath been the cauſe of this idleneſs; and how hath it crept in upon us?

2. What muſt be done to reſtrain its going farther?

3. What methods are proper to be uſed to make proviſion for thoſe who are paſt their labour?

The cauſe of idleneſs, he ſays, is the abuſe of the poor-laws we have, and want of better; the encouragement of ale-houſes, on account of the revenue; but, above all, our laws to ſet the poor at work are ſhort and defective, tending rather to maintain them as poor, than to raiſe them to a better way of living; rendering the poor more bold, by their knowing that the pariſh-officers *muſt either find them work or give them maintenance.*

Nothing but good laws can reſtrain idleneſs; ſuch as may provide work for thoſe that are willing, and force thoſe to work who are able. For this purpoſe work-houſes are recommended, where the poor may be employed in manufactures.

The poor ſhould alſo be employed in navigation, huſbandry, and handicrafts.

The

The juftices of peace fhould have power to affign youth to artificers, hufbandry, manufacturers, and to bind them apprentice.

As to thofe of elder years, who will rather beg than work, let them be forced to ferve the king in his fleet, or the merchants on board their fhips.

Young people fhould be prohibited from hawking and finging ballads about the ftreets; ftage-plays, *lotteries*, and *gaming-houfes*, fhould be ftrictly looked after.

Alms-houfes are recommended for thofe who are not able to work, or whofe work is not fufficient for their maintenance. Poor's rates fhould be affeffed with greater equality in cities and manufacturing-towns, where the poor are ferviceable to the rich manufacturers, by carrying on their trade; yet, when age, ficknefs, or a numerous family, make them defire relief, their chief dependence muft be on thofe who are but a ftep above their own condition.

Mr. Cary fpeaks, with praife, of an act of parliament which paffed in the 7th and 8th year of William and Mary, for eftablifhing a work-houfe at Briftol; which, he fays, was pretty much on the plan propofed by Sir Jofiah Child for the cities of London and Weftminfter; but, as this act is calculated for cities and great towns only, and cannot be a model for counties, he fubjoins the following propofal, to carry this defign on throughout the kingdom:

That power be given, by act of parliament, for parifhes to incorporate for building hofpitals, work-houfes, and houfes of correction, for employing the poor, under the management of guardians of the poor: the incorporation to be by hundreds.

The guardians to be the juftices of the peace within the diftrict, together with a number of the inhabitants, chofen out of each parifh, in proportion to the affeffment the parifhes refpectively pay.

The election of guardians to be every year, or two years.

O   The

The guardians to have power to choofe a governor, deputy-governor, treafurer, and affiftants, yearly; and be empowered to hold courts, make bye-laws, have a common feal; to order affeff-ments to be levied; to fummon the inhabitants of the parifhes within the hundred; to compel thofe who feek relief to dwell in their hofpitals and work-houfes; to take in young people, and bring them up to work; to teach them to read and write, and then bind them out apprentices; to provide for the aged and impotent; to affift thofe whofe labours will not maintain their families; to apprehend rogues, vagabonds, and beggars, and fet them to work; to inflict reafonable correction.

This plan, by Mr. Cary, may probably have given the hint to thofe gentlemen who applied to parliament, in the twenty-ninth year of his late majefty's reign, for the act for the better relief and employment of the poor in the hundreds of *Colneis* and *Carlford*, in the county of Suffolk. Whether incorporations of diftricts for thefe purpofes have produced a greater proportion of good than evil; whether they have tended to introduce, among the lower claffes of this country, more induftry, better health, better morals, more comfort; and whether, on the whole, the fum of their happinefs is increafed; cannot be determined by any other means than an exa-mination of their effects after thofe years of experience which have paffed fince their firft inftitution in the counties of Norfolk and Suffolk, where they were firft introduced: that they have generally tended to deprefs the poor's rate may be granted; but gold may be bought too dear.

It has been faid in a publication,* the author of which founded, or might have founded, his obfervations on an actual examination of the facts, after many years experience, that they have injured the principle of induftry, deftroyed the health and the hardinefs of the

* The true Alarm, or an Effay fhewing the pernicious Influence of Houfes of In-duftry. 1787.

adult

adult living in, and the youth brought up in them; have introduced bad morals, fhocking habits of indecency; have occafioned a decreafe of population; and would, if they became general, fo deftroy the moral fentiments and happinefs of the country, as to affect the political liberties and patriotic fpirit of the nation, by bringing up the rifing generation with fentiments and habits fo difpirited and debilitated, as to render them only fit flaves of defpotifm; for, the author fays, and with much feeming juftice of obfervation: Of what moment can it poffibly be to a wretch who has not the liberty of walking out beyond a certain boundary, that the kingdom becomes a prey to foreign invaders, or is torn to pieces by an inteftine commotion, unlefs you may fuppofe that he is more likely to rejoice at a fcene of perfect confufion, as he might then entertain a hope, that, in a general wreck, where he had nothing to lofe, he might feize upon fomething worth having.

But let us hope and believe that the confequences actually felt from thefe houfes of induftry are not fo deplorable; let us recollect, that, when a man undertakes in the title-page of a pamphlet to prove a point, as this writer does, it is plain he has a point to prove; and in which, if he fails in inftances or arguments, he may expect to meet with fome degree of public derifion; the fear of this twifts his facts, turns his arguments, and points his periods, and no longer is he fo friendly to truth as to fyftem.

LETTER XV.

IN expectation of finding, among the various fubjects which fell under the pen of the celebrated Mr. Locke, fome ideas which might ferve as firft principles on this interefting fubject; I turned over his

works, and particularly attended to thofe tracts which he wrote
on lowering the intereft of money, and raifing its value; a fpeculation which occupied the attention of the nation towards the clofe
of the laft century; but the actual fituation of the poor not
coming under his confideration, nothing very applicable to the
fubject is to be found; although a confufed recollection ftrikes me,
that fome modern pamphlet on the poor-laws, or their regulation,
had ftated Mr. Locke's ideas on the fubject as erroneous: whether
fo or not, it became me, while in purfuit of this inquiry, to know
what thofe ideas were, which, had they been found among his
works, whether wrong or right, demanded, on account of his great
name, that they fhould be noticed; for fuch a mind as his, on
every topic which may have been the object of its difquifition, is a
polar ftar to the ignorant wanderer: although nothing directly
applicable to the police of the poor is found, yet a comparifon
which he makes between a kingdom and a farmer is fo much in
point with their prefent profligate fituation, the carelefs conduct of
their overfeers, and that fpirit which has unhappily got head
among our rulers, of encouraging the commercial world, at the
expenfe of agriculture, and every principle of internal economy;
while, at the fame time, it fo ftrongly authenticates the alarming
prognoftics of our decadency, alluded to a few pages back; that
the whole paffage, falling from the height of that great name, muft
make an impreffion, and occafion it to be worth tranfcribing.*

" A kingdom grows rich juft as a farmer, and no otherwife. Let
us fuppofe the whole ifland of Portland one farm; and that the
owner, befides what ferves his family, carries to market, to Wey-
mouth and Dorchefter, &c. cattle, corn, butter, cheefe, wool, or

---

* Again it fhould be recalled to the mind of the reader at what time thefe letters
were written. No Board of Agriculture was then inftituted; the labours of my friend,
to whom they are addreffed, laudable and perfevering as thofe labours were in that beft
of national caufes, the improvement of agriculture, had then received no national encouragement.

cloth,

cloth, lead, and tin, all commodities produced within his farm of
Portland, to the value of 1000*l.* yearly; and, for this, brings home
in falt, wine, oil, fpice, linen, and filks, to the value of 900*l.* and
the remaining 100*l.* in money. It is evident he grows every year
100*l.* richer, and fo at the end of ten years will have clearly got
1000*l.*—If the owner be a better hufband, and, contenting himfelf
with his native commodities, buy lefs wine, fpice, and filk at market, and fo bring home 500*l.* in money yearly, inftead of 1000*l.*
at the end of ten years, he will have 5000*l.* by him, and be fo
much richer; he dies, and his fon fucceeds, a fafhionable young
gentleman, that cannot dine without Champaigne and Burgundy,
nor fleep but in a damafk bed, whofe wife muft fpread a long train
of brocade, and his children be always in the neweft French cut
and ftuff; he, being come to the eftate, keeps on a very bufy family,
the markets are weekly frequented, and the commodities of his
farm carried out, and fold as formerly; but the returns are made
fomewhat different; the fafhionable way of eating, drinking, furniture, and clothing for himfelf and family, requires more fugar
and fpice, wine and fruit, filk and ribbons, than in his father's
time; fo that inftead of 900*l.* per annum, he now brings home,
of confumable commodity, 1100*l.* yearly. What comes of this?
— He lives in fplendour it is true; but this unavoidably carries
away the money his father got, and he is every year 100*l.* poorer.
To his expenfes, beyond his income, add debauchery, idlenefs, and
quarrels among his fervants; whereby his bufinefs is difturbed,
his farm neglected, and a general diforder and confufion prevail
through his whole family: this will tumble him down the hill the
fafter, and the ftock, which the induftry, frugality, and good
order, of his father laid up, will be quickly brought to an end,
and he faft in prifon; a farm and a kingdom, in this refpect, differ
no more than as greater and lefs. We may trade, and be bufy,
and grow poor by it, unlefs we regulate our expenfes; if to this
we are idle, negligent, difhoneft, malicious, and difturb the fober
and

and induſtrious in their buſineſs, let it be upon what pretence it it will, we ſhall ruin the faſter."

This compariſon of Mr. Locke's runs on all-fours, as well with the actual ſtate of the property, applied to the uſe of the poor in this kingdom, as with the ſituation of the finances belonging to the ſtate itſelf. The reign of Elizabeth made the maintenance of the poor *compulſive*, with reſpect to the laity, which was in remoter times *voluntary*; what might, in thoſe days of frugality, be taken from the pockets of her ſubjects by poor-rates, we know not; but we know, that, about the middle of the laſt century, the cattle, corn, butter, cheeſe, wool, yarn, conſumed by this large family, coſt about 118,000*l.* more than the produce of their in-duſtry amounted to; fifty years afterwards their expenſes out-ran their income annually 819,000*l.*; in 1785, the ſurplus of their expenſes, above their income, or the produce of their induſtry, gradually had increaſed to the enormous ſum of 2,184,904*l.* annu-ally. Here you ſee plainly the effects of the change of manners and living, ſo forcibly inſtanced in Mr. Locke's compariſon; in the eat-ing, drinking, furniture, clothing, ſugar, ſpice, wine, and fruit, *otherwiſe tea and gin*; to which may be added, the debauchery, idle-neſs, and quarrels of the individuals, which compoſe the bulk of this numerous family: to examine the compariſon, with reſpect to the kingdom at large, is not the buſineſs of this tract.

The reign of Queen Anne is not ſo memorable for any laws regulating the internal police of the kingdom, as for the many blows which the ambitious ſpirit of Louis the Fourteenth received from the arms of the allies: nothing òf material conſequence was done with reſpect to the poor. By the 33d chapter of the fifth parliament, the vagrant-act of the laſt reign was continued, with ſome farther directions; as was, by the following chapter, an act made in the 13th and 14th year of Charles II. for the better relief of the poor, and continued by the legiſlature at different times ſince, and which was ultimately made perpetual by chapter the 18th of the

the 12th year of this reign ; and, by chapter 23d, all the laws relating to rogues, vagabonds, fturdy beggars, and vagrants, were
alfo reduced into one act of parliament.

Neither does the fubject feem, throughout this reign of war and
conqueft, to have occupied the attention of individuals ; no publication of any account having lived to the prefent day, except a
letter to the parliament by the author of Robinfon Crufoe, one of
thofe very few books which the late Dr. Johnfon faid he had been
able to read *without fkipping*. Daniel Defoe, in 1704, chofe to
publifh a declamatory epiftle, addreffed to the parliament, with the
following title, *Giving Alms no Charity, and employing the Poor a
Grievance to the Nation.*

In this publication he informs his readers, that Queen Elizabeth,
in her progrefs through the kingdom, obferving the vaft throngs
of poor flocking to fee and blefs her, being ftruck with the multitude, frequently exclaimed, *Pauper ubique jacet* ; and this truth, fo
terfely expreffed by her, occafioned a continual ftudy in her mind
how to recover her people from poverty, and make their labour
more profitable to themfelves in particular, and the nation in general.

He lays down the following as fundamental maxims :

1. There is in England more labour than hands to perform it,
and confequently a want of people, not of employment.

2. No man in England, of found limbs and fenfes, can be poor
merely from want of work.

3. All our work-houfes, corporations, and charities, for employing the poor, and fetting them to work, as now they are employed; or any acts of parliament to empower overfeers of parifhes,
or parifhes themfelves, to employ the poor, except, as fhall be
hereafter excepted, are and will be public nuifances, mifchiefs to
the nation, which ferve to the ruin of families, and the increafe of
the poor.

4. That

4. That it is a regulation of the poor that is wanted in England, not a fetting them to work.

Thefe maxims he profeffes to demonftrate, but does not entirely fucceed in the attempt, although he makes fome very fenfible obfervations in the courfe of his argument on each of the heads.

Dearnefs of labour he advances as a proof of the firft maxim; and gives due praife to Elizabeth for what fhe did for the poor, particularly by encouraging the French manufactories, when the perfecution under the Duke d'Alva drove them from the Netherlands; and alfo by that excellent act of parliament, in the 43d year of her reign, fo often alluded to.

The ftrefs of his argument lies againft employing the poor in work-houfes, corporations, houfes of correction, and the like; becaufe the method propofed to employ them is by fpinning, weaving, and manufacturing our Englifh wool; manufactures of which are all exercifed in England to their full extent, and rather beyond their vent than under it; he, therefore, is of opinion, that, for every fkein of worfted fpun in one place, there muft be one lefs fpun elfewhere. He fuppofes a manufactory of baize to be erected in Bifhopfgate-ftreet; unlefs a greater confumption can be found for more baize than were made before, for every piece made in London, there muft be one lefs made at Colchefter, and, therefore, this is not increafe, but only tranfpofition of manufacture.

The only thing to be done is, to introduce fome foreign manufactory; fomething which was not made here before.

He confiders the poverty and exigence of the poor in England to be plainly derived from cafualty or crime : by cafualty he means ficknefs, lofs of limbs, or fight, and any natural or accidental impotence.

The crimes of the poor, and whence their poverty is derived, as from vifible and direct fountains, are luxury, pride, floth. The pride of good hufbandry is no Englifh virtue : it

may

may have been imported; and, in some places, it thrives well enough.

The English labouring-people eat and drink; but, especially, drink three times as much in value as any foreigners.

He accufes us of being the moft lazy *diligent nation* in the world. Among our poor there is a general taint of flothfulnefs, which diftemper he conceives to be fo epidemic and deep-rooted, that it is a queftion whether an act of parliament will reach it. The number of the poor is occafioned by the men *who will not work*, not by thofe *who can get no work*; all the work-houfes and overfeers in England will not reach this cafe: but if fuch acts of parliament can be made, as will effectually cure the floth and luxury of the poor; will make drunkards take care of their wives and families; fpendthrifts lay up for a wet day; lazy fellows diligent; and thoughtlefs, fottifh, men careful and provident; if this can be done, they will foon find work enough, and there will be lefs poverty among us: if it cannot be done, fetting the poor to work on woollen manufactures, and thereby encroaching on thofe who now work at them, will ruin our trade, and increafe the number of poor.

A bill, brought into parliament by Sir Humphry Mackworth, for employing the poor, which had paffed the Commons with great approbation, gave rife to this tract. By this bill it was intended, as Mr. Chalmers, in his Life of Defoe, tells us, to fupport workhoufes, in every parifh, with parochial capitals, for carrying on parochial manufactures: but it was thrown out by the Peers; to which, it is probable, this fenfible pamphlet very much conduced; in which he pretends, that he *could* propofe a regulation of the poor, which would *put a ftop to poverty, beggary, parifh-charges, affeffments, and the like*; and promifes to do fo, when he has gone through the proof of his maxims; but waves the performance, for this very inadequate reafon, — becaufe he will not prefume to lead a body fo auguft, fo wife, and fo capable, as the honourable affembly to whom the tract is dedicated.

P

There

There are, in this tract, many excellent obfervations, exprefled
with great dignity. That part, which tends to prove that giving
alms is no charity, lays down fome fenfible maxims, on which he
refts the ftrength of his argument, which tends to prove that parochial work-houfes fhould not be encouraged for the purpofe of
parochial manufactures. After having proved that there is more
work in the kingdom than hands to perform it, he afferts, that
begging is a mere fcandal : in the able, it is a fcandal on their
induftry ; in the impotent, upon their country. The poverty of
England does not lie among craving beggars, but among poor families, where the children are numerous, and where death, or ficknefs, has deprived them of the labour of their father. An alms,
ill-directed, may be charity to a particular perfon, but becomes an
injury to the public.

That Mr. Defoe is right in thefe principles, there furely can be
no doubt ; and the truth, that we have *more work in the kingdom
than hands to perform it*, comes home to, and eftablifhes, another
principle, — that the poor *fhould be trained to do all the work that the
nation can find them*. Early habits of induftry are moft likely to
effect this end ; fchools of induftry muft, therefore, be the means.

It furely is no defpotic or flavifh maxim, that the children of
individuals are, in fome refpect, the children of the ftate. Re-
publics, renowned for the freedom of their government, acted on
this principle : *à fortiori, the children of thofe who receive their maintenance, or any part of it, from the property of their fellow-citizens, by
virtue of the ordinances of the ftate, are the children of the ftate*, which,
confequently, has a right to fuperintend their education.

Apply this principle to every individual who does not maintain
his family, but has relief from the overfeer : his children belong
to the ftate : it is the duty of the ftate to take care that they turn
out induftrious fubjects ; and I am fure intereft here well coa-
lefces with duty : fchools of induftry are the means. The firft
fection of 43d Elizabeth provides for their fupport. The end
                                                                    will

will be an induſtrious, moral, poor: a bleſſed contraſt to the lazineſs and diſſoluteneſs ſo much and ſo univerſally complained of.

L E T T E R   XVI.

IN the fifth year of George the Firſt, the parliament empowered
the church-wardens and overſeers, by warrant from two juſtices, to ſeize ſo much of the goods and chattels, and receive ſo
much of the annual rents and profits of the lands and tenements,
of ſuch huſband, father, or mother, as ſhall run away, leaving
their wives and children a burthen upon the pariſh, as the ſaid two
juſtices ſhall direƈt, towards the diſburſing the pariſh where ſuch
wife and child ſhall be left, and alſo for their future maintenance:
this warrant to be confirmed at the quarter-ſeſſions, where a warrant, alſo, for the ſale of the goods, &c. muſt be obtained, before
they can be diſpoſed of; and to which ſeſſions the officers are to be
accountable for the money raiſed.

Two years after this, it was the opinion of parliament, as declared in the preamble to an aƈt for encouraging the woollen and
ſilk manufaƈtures, and more effeƈtually employing the poor,
" That it is moſt evident, the wearing of printed, painted, ſtained,
and dyed, callicoes, in apparel, houſehold-ſtuff, furniture, and otherwiſe, does manifeſtly tend to the detriment of the woollen and ſilk
manufaƈtures of this kingdom, and to the exceſſive increaſe of the
poor; and, if not effeƈtually prevented, may be the utter ruin and
deſtruƈtion of the ſaid manufaƈtures, and of many thouſands of
his Majeſty's ſubjeƈts, and their families, whoſe livelihoods do entirely depend thereupon." It is therefore enaƈted, in the year
1720, that none ſhall wear any garment of printed callico, or any
ſtuff made of cotton, or mixed therewith, which ſhall be painted,

under the penalty of 5l.; or use it in any houfehold ftuff or furniture, under the penalty of 20l.; and that no tradefman fhall make
up fuch furniture, under the fame penalty.

This act is not taken notice of, on account of any effect it has at
prefent in the management of the poor, but as introductory of an
obfervation, neceffary to be attended to, by thofe who would wifh our
ftatute-book to be a collection of efficient and practical regulations
of police; and not, as it in fact is, an immenfe collection of contra-
dictory, heterogeneous, ordinances, militating, in many inftances,
with each other; in many, with the principles of found policy; and,
in fome, with the actual habit and practice of all his majefty's fubjects, of which this ftatute is a remarkable, but no uncommon,
inftance.

No longer ago than the year 1720, this prohibition of callicoes
and ftuff, made of cotton, or mixed therewith, paffed into a law;
and, in 1790, and many years before, every woman in the kingdom
is clothed in thefe very fabrics; moft of our houfehold-furniture is
made of them; this prohibition ftill remaining the law of the
land.

The woollen manufactures of this kingdom certainly deferve
greater encouragement than either linen or cotton; becaufe wool,
the ftaple-commodity of England, is the produce of our own agriculture; hemp, flax, and cotton, are, at prefent, generally the pro-
duct of *foreign* agriculture; and alfo becaufe the fabric of the
woollen manufacture is ftrong and warm, fuited therefore to the ufe
of the bulk of the people: that of cotton and linen, weak and thin,
improper for labour and a northern climate. Woollen clothing
does not require fo much wafhing as our printed linens and white
ftockings, an article of great expenfe in poor families; but *the
revenue* is thought to be a fufficient reafon for thefe paradoxical
abfurdities; and, that the public treafury may abound, drunkennefs, gaming, luxury, and oftentatious clothing, are encouraged,
in open defiance of the laws of the land. Thofe magiftrates would
be

be very coolly thanked for a confcientious difcharge of their duty, who, to promote fobriety, fhould leffen the number of ale-houfes; to difcourage gaming, fhould authorize the parifh-officers to refufe relief to thofe who fingly, or in clubs, buy lottery-chances; or, to promote the manufacture of wool, fhould encourage informations upon the act of parliament juft alluded to; the prevailing and general maxim of financiers, in all times, is *rem facias*; the means are but a fecondary object of their attention.

In the ninth year of this reign, the poor-laws again were an object of parliamentary attention, and an act for amending the laws relating to their fettlements, employments, and relief, paffed; which enacted, that no poor fhould be relieved, until an oath be made, before *one juftice*, of a reafonable caufe, and that the perfon hath applied to a veftry, or to two of the overfeers, and been refufed relief; a fummons is alfo directed to the overfeers, to fhew caufe why fuch relief fhould not be granted, before it is ordered; and, when ordered, the perfon's name is to be entered in a book to be kept for that purpofe, as one who is to receive relief as long as the caufe continues, and no longer; and no officer of any parifh fhall bring to account (except on fudden and emergent occafions) any money he fhall have given to any poor perfon, who is not regiftered in fuch book, under the penalty of five pounds.

It has been fuggefted that one caufe of the bad execution of the poor-laws is the conftant fuperintending authority that the legiflature has delegated to juftices of the peace. Men eminent for their wifdom, and refpectable for their opinions, have attributed much of the mifchief experienced from this code of laws to the conduct of thofe who are the fupervifors of their execution; nor is the complaint new: the great Sir Francis Bacon, it may be remembered, in the very infancy of the code, threw out an idea to this effect, when he made the diftinction between what *was* done by the *diftracted* government of juftices of the peace, and what *might* be done by a fettled ordinance; yet, whatever of ill may have accrued

in

in general from the fuperintending authority of magiſtrates, it has
rather arifen from the *not uſing* their powers, than from either the
abuſe or *miſuſe* of them.　In this particular inſtance, which refpeĉts
the pecuniary affiſtance the poor are entitled to receive from the
overfeers, the interference of a magiſtrate appears peculiarly proper,
when called to aĉtion by the complaint of the poor themfelves;
becaufe the neareſt magiſtrate has it in his power to inform himfelf of the real circumſtances of the cafe, and, from his fituation in
life, is a proper check to any partiality, or improper, although natural, bias, the overfeer who lives more immediately in the midſt of
the poor, and being frequently conneĉted with them, by the different degrees of relationſhip, and generally as their immediate employer, may be influenced by; which motives operate to a greater
degree in the diſtribution of affiſtance to the poor, than at firſt
fight might be imagined, and which gave rife to objeĉtions of the
moſt ferious nature to Mr. Gilbert's Bill, and would have caufed an
oppofition of the moſt obſtinate kind from the yeomanry of this
kingdom, had that bill paffed into a law; which ſtruck at the root
of this power, to give away the money taken, in a great meafure,
immediately from the pockets of this large and valuable clafs of
our countrymen.

　　Befides, it will be found, on inquiry, that the money diſtributed
in the weekly liſt forms no very material proportion of the expenfes
of a parifh;* and in the diſtribution of money there is no room
for lucrative jobs, no knavifh contraĉts for furnifhing the various
articles of confumption; and the overfeer keeping a fair account
can have no profit; and poffibly as money is the common repre-
fentative of all neceffaries of life, fo it is the greateſt, moſt convenient, and beſt appropriated, relief to the individual.　It fomewhat,

---

* This obfervation, I fear, ceafes, from the preffure of the times, to be in general true
at prefent, although it might be fo in 1791.

in its univerfality of ufe, refembles Boniface's ale, — " A poor man and his family may eat it, drink it, and fleep upon it."

Church-wardens and overfeers, with the confent of the major part of the parifhioners in veftry affembled, are alfo, by this act, empowered to purchafe or hire houfes to lodge and employ the poor in, and there to keep, maintain, and employ, them: and fuch poor as refufe to be lodged, maintained, and employed, there, fhall not be entitled to relief; parifhes are alfo empowered to join in fuch purchafe, and the officers of one parifh may, for that purpofe, contract with thofe of another; but the *fettlement* of the poor is not to be affected by their removal to another parifh, in confequence of this act.

The acquifition of fettlement by purchafe is regulated by another fection of the act, which directs, that the purchafe-money muft not be lefs than thirty pounds *bona fide* paid for the eftate, by which a perfon fhall gain a fettlement; and that no perfon, paying to the fcavengers or highway rates, fhall, on that account, be deemed to gain a fettlement: the other fections regulate the notices neceffary on appeals, and the relief the appellant fhall receive on undue removals.

I have not been able to obtain any tract on the fubject written during this reign; nor have I feen any referred to, or quoted, by thofe which have been fince written; the conclufion which follows is, that none of fufficient merit, to efcape oblivion, were publifhed; and indeed the little that was done by the legiflature is a proof that the fubject did not much attract the attention of the nation; that venerable fabric, the 43d of Elizabeth, received a little addition and repairs only, but no material alteration was made.

LETTER XVII.

IT is with great satisfaction, that the opinion of Mr. Locke on this subject, alluded to a few pages back, has been perufed; by which it appears, that about the year 1696, the clamour, with regard to the poor, and the burthen of the poor's rate, having attracted the notice of the Commons, they referred it to the Board of Trade to confider the fact, and to report the remedy: on which occafion Mr. Locke, who was one of the commiffioners, delivers the following opinion in the report made by the board: * — " The multiplicity of the poor, and the increafe of the tax for their maintenance, is fo general an obfervation and complaint, that it cannot be doubted of; nor has it been only fince the laft war that this evil has come upon us, it has been a growing burthen on the kingdom thefe many years, and the two laft reigns felt the increafe of it as well as the prefent. If the caufes of this evil be looked into, we humbly conceive it will be found to have proceeded, *not from the fcarcity of provifions,*† *nor want of employment for the poor* ; fince the goodnefs of God has bleffed thefe times with plenty no lefs than the former, and a long peace, during three reigns, gave us as plentiful a trade as ever. The growth of the poor muft therefore have fome other caufe; and it can be nothing elfe but *the relaxation of difcipline and corruption; virtue and induftry* being as conftant companions on the one fide, as *vice and idlenefs* are on the other. On this firft principle, thus clearly expreffed by Mr. Locke, whofe ftrong intellectual faculties were employed in the exact fituation, to obtain ample intelligence, on the fubject he

---

* Mr. Chalmers's Eftimate, &c.

† By the Windfor-table, the price of wheat, in the years 1696, 1697, 1698, was 3l. 3s. 1d. — 2l. 13s. 4d. — 3l. 9s.

has

has thrown fuch a blaze of light over, one muft reft with confi-- dence; in fact, this truth has often difcovered itfelf to us, in faint glimmerings, during the inveftigation of this fubject; and the reader may have perceived how often this fentiment has obtruded itfelf on the pen. That it meets with fuch honourable confirmation from Mr. Locke's authority, near a hundred years ago, ftamps a fignal mark of propriety on the ideas which have been hitherto fug- gefted; and firmly eftablifhes the following affertion, that, unlefs vice and idlenefs among our poor are *decreafed* fince this opinion was given, the multiplicity of the poor, and the ftill increafing burthen of tax for their maintenance, arifes at the end of the eighteenth century, not from fcarcity of provifions, and want of employment for the poor, but from relaxation of difcipline and corruption of morals.

As it is poffible that the remedy for the difeafe may be difcovered by purfuing the inquiry, with equal clearnefs, as the caufe has been pointed out; we fhall proceed in the fame manner to relate what the legiflature has done, and individuals have written, on the fubject to the clofe of the laft parliament.

The law, with refpect to natural children, remained on the foot- ing the acts of the 18th of Elizabeth and the 7th of James the Firft had left the fubject; until the fixth year of the reign of George the Second, when, it having been found by long experience that the fecurity of parifhes was not fufficiently provided for, the legiflature, by a ftatute then paffed, in the 31ft chapter, enacted, that the perfon charged on oath of being the father of a baftard- child, by any fingle woman who fhall be delivered, or fhall de- clare herfelf to be pregnant, and that the child is likely to become chargeable to the parifh, fhall be immediately apprehended and committed to prifon, unlefs he gives fecurity to indemnify the parifh; but that he fhall be difcharged on the mifcarriage of the woman, or if no order be made in purfuance of the 18th of Eliza- beth within fix weeks after the woman's delivery; and that no

Q woman

woman fhall *involuntarily* be obliged to filiate the child of which
fhe is pregnant, before delivery.

It feems alfo to have been a doubt, whether juftices of the peace
could legally act in any cafe relating to parifhes where fuch juftices
have property; from this, fome inconvenience arofe in the adminiftration of the common bufinefs of a magiftrate : the 18th chapter
of the 16th ftatute of this reign, therefore, clears up the fubject,
and empowers them to enforce the laws, with refpect to the maintenance, relief, and fettlement, of poor perfons; thofe alfo with
refpect to paffing vagrants, repairs of highways, and any other
laws concerning parochial taxes or rates; notwithftanding they
themfelves may be chargeable to fuch rates.

The following year produces an inftance of the attention the legiflature paid to the conduct of the overfeers of the poor; who, according to the preamble of the act of the 17th Geo. II. cap. 3.
" on frivolous pretences, and private ends, frequently make unjuft
and illegal rates, in a fecret and clandeftine manner:" and the preamble to the 38th chapter of the fame ftatute ftates, " that the
money raifed for the relief of the poor is liable to be mifapplied,
after it is, with great difficulty and delay, raifed." To obviate
thefe inconveniences, the firft act directs, that public notice fhall be
given in the church of every rate, for the relief of the poor, the
next Sunday after the fame fhall be allowed by the juftices; and
that the overfeers fhall permit fuch rates to be infpected at all fea-
fonable times, on payment of 1s. for the fame, and copies fhall, on
demand, be given, allowing 6d. for every twenty-four names; the
rate to be void if no fuch notice be given, and a penalty of 20s. on
refufal of fuch infpection, or copy; and the 38th chapter directs
" that the church-wardens and overfeers of the poor fhall yearly,
within fourteen days after other overfeers fhall be appointed, deliver a juft, true, and perfect account, in writing, fairly entered in
a book to be kept for that purpofe, and figned by the faid church-
wardens and overfeers, of all the fums of money received, or rated

                                                                    and

and not received; and alfo of all goods, chattels, ftock, and materials, that fhall be in their hands, or in the hands of the poor, in order to be wrought; and of all moneys paid by fuch churchwardens and overfeers, and of all other things concerning the faid office; and fhall pay and deliver over all fums of money, goods and chattels, and other things, as fhall be in their hands, unto the fucceeding overfeers; and that this account fhall be verified on oath before one or more magiftrates, who fhall alfo fign the faid account, without fee; and this book fhall be carefully preferved; and all perfons liable to be affeffed fhall be permitted to infpeȼt it, on payment of 6d. and copies fhall be given alfo on demand, on payment of 6d. for every 300 words. In cafe of the death of an overfeer, two juftices are to choofe another; if an overfeer remove from the parifh, his account, teftified as above, fhall be delivered to the remaining overfeer or church-warden; and the reprefentatives of an overfeer fhall account within forty days after his deceafe. Appeals to any rates or affeffments, reafonable notice being given, lie to the next general or quarter feffions of the peace; where, if the whole rate be appealed to, the juftices may quafh it, and order the church-wardens and overfeers to make a new one; but, where juft caufe is feen, to give relief only, by altering the rate, the juftices are empowered to amend the rate, in fuch a manner as fhall be neceffary to fuch relief only.

As great care is taken by this aȼt, that the rates fhall be fair and equal, and that the parifh-officers fhall difcharge their refpeȼtive offices honeftly; fo does it provide againft any vexatious aȼtions being brought againft them, by declaring that no want of form, either in the appointment of overfeers, the rate or affeffment, or in the diftrefs, fhall render them unlawful; nor fhall the parties diftraining be accounted trefpaffers, *ab initio*, on account of any irregularity in their proceedings, but the parties aggrieved fhall recover for the fpecial damage fuftained by fuch irregularity.

Succeeding overfeers are alfo enabled to levy any arrears due to former overfeers; and, in cafe of perfons removing out of parifhes, and others coming in, they fhall pay their rates in proportion to the time they have refpectively occupied; the proportion to be af-certained by two or more magiftrates, and recovered by diftrefs.

Copies of the affeffments are alfo directed to be entered in a book, to be kept for public perufal; the entry to be made within fourteen days after the appeal is determined; and all the regula-tions in the act are enforced by a penalty not exceeding 5l.; and the power of overfeers, in places where there are no church-wardens, is declared to be the fame, as where they are both church-wardens and overfeers; and they are fubjected to the fame penalties.

The fection of this act, which directs the overfeers account to be verified on oath before a magiftrate, feems not fufficiently to have explained, whether the magiftrate is to examine the accounts, article by article; or whether the overfeer is to fwear to the whole account only, by the lump, and is not obliged to go through an ex-amination, with refpect to the articles of his account, on an oath *voir dire*: if this is the cafe, the magiftrate acts officially only, and the oath is but of little fervice, as an appeal lies to the quarter-feffions.

The 11th chapter of the 31ft ftatute of this reign makes fome regulations in the fettlement of apprentices; and enacts, that a perfon bound apprentice, by any deed, writing, or contract, duly ftamped, fhall be entitled to a fettlement where he is fo bound and has ferved: the other fection of the act relates to the power given to juftices, in fettling difputes between mafter and fervants, and confequently comes not under the fcope of our prefent difquifition.

The laft act of parliament in this reign, which refpects the poor, is ftatute 32, chapter 22, which provides for the maintenance of the wives and families of militia-men, when in actual fervice, by directing that the overfeers fhall pay from the poor's rate, by order of one juftice of the peace, a weekly allowance to the diftreffed

families

families of militia-men, embodied, and called out into actual fervice, according to the ufual price of labour in hufbandry within the county or diftrict, by the following rule : for one child, under ten years, one day's labour; for two, under the fame age, two days labour; for three children, three days labour ; for five, or more, four days labour ; and for the wife, one day's labour : but that the families of thofe, only, chofen by *lot*, and not *fubftitutes*, fhall be entitled to this allowance; for which payment the overfeers are to be reimburfed out of the county-ftock.

To pafs over the ftatute-book of this reign, without mentioning the vagrant-act, the 17th Geo. II. cap. 5. would appear an inftance of inattention to the general defign of thefe papers ; although much the greateft part of it affords no infight to the fubject, becaufe it in general refpects the treatment of thofe who have *forfeited the protection of fociety*, and are to be confidered as its *outcafts :* but if, through the fault of an improper fyftem of legiflation, or through the mal-adminiftration of the laws which are in force refpecting the poor, the number of thofe, who come under the defcription of vagrants, is increafed ; the laws themfelves, or the execution of them, have thrown out of the protection of fociety a number of people who are not vagrants from their own fault ; and, fo far, the laws themfelves are accountable for the mifchief which they have occafioned ; while the punifhment, fevere to excefs, falls on unoffending individuals. In enumerating the particular offences which occafion perfons to be claffed under the defcription of *idle* and *diforderly* perfons, whom one juftice may commit to the houfe of correction, to hard labour, for a month, are thofe who *threaten* to run away, and leave their wives and children to the parifh. This is a *curious* offence, certainly not a *heinous* one, for it may confift in words only, unaccompanied with acts or intentions ; but for this they may be committed ; and, if they refift the commitment, or efcape, are inftantly to be claffed among rogues and vagabonds.

All

All perfons who return to the parifh whence they have been removed, without a certificate, ftand in the fame predicament: the law of fettlements, therefore, tends to increafe the number of rogues and vagabonds.

All perfons who have not wherewithal to live idle, without employment, and refufe to work at the common ufual wages given to other labourers, in the like work, in the parifh wherein they then live, are alfo liable to the fame punifhments, and to become vagrants.

An induftrious handicraftfman, who has maintained his wife and family creditably and honeftly, by his induftry, if removed, from the town where his trade is carried on, to his place of fettlement, a village, where there is no employment but in hufbandry, muft, of neceffity, fall under this defcription ; becaufe, not being able, from different habits to thofe of a labourer, to do a fair day's work, he will not eafily find employment. A man does not give up a portion of his natural liberty, and his only property, his abi- lity to earn his bread, for this kind of protection from the focial compact. This alfo arifes, in a great meafure, from the law of fettlements.

All perfons who run away, and leave their wives and families, whereby they become chargeable to any parifh, are, *ipfo facto*, to be deemed rogues and vagabonds ; whofe punifhment is immediate commitment, until the quarter-feffions : then they are liable to be committed to hard labour, for a time not exceeding fix months ; and, during their confinement, to be corrected by whipping.

In this inftance, alfo, the crime againft fociety may not be fufficiently ferious to deferve fo fevere a punifhment. Until a poor perfon, his wife, or family, has become chargeable to a parifh, the reftraining him from leaving his home, by the fear of fo rigorous a fentence, does not arife abfolutely from neceffity, and therefore the reftraint is not juftifiable, on principles of common juftice.

The

The *poſſible* event, which may come to paſs from his leaving them, ſhould not, therefore, in the firſt inſtance, claſs him among rogues and vagabonds. He ſhould not be deemed an outcaſt of ſociety, by anticipation of evil : he ſhould have firſt been a *penſioner* on the public fund of charity, before he ſhould, by ſo ſevere a law, be reſtrained of his liberty. This deſcription of the crime, therefore, is too comprehenſive, and occaſions many innocent ſubjects to be claſſed with, and be ſubjected to, the puniſhment appropriated to rogues and vagabonds.

With but a ſuperficial knowledge of the ſubject, were theſe ſtrictures, on the ſituation of our poor, at firſt undertaken. The purpoſe was, to inveſtigate, and point out, the cauſe of that vaſt expenſe, which every rank of ſociety, with reaſon, complains of, in maintaining this numerous claſs of our fellow-ſubjects; and to explain the true foundation of that very wretched ſituation in which we ſee too many of them; in fact, to account for this ſtriking paradox, — that, while millions ſterling are expended in their relief, millions of the poor ſtill ſtand in need of more relief than they receive. A diſtant gleam of hope occurred, alſo, to the mind, that, by inveſtigating the cauſe of the evil, poſſibly the remedy might alſo be diſcovered. The method choſen was that of fixing a foundation, in the firſt principles of ſociety, and proceeding by an hiſtorical analyſis: this has laid me open to ſome apparent contradictions and miſtakes; theſe letters being ſent to the preſs, as freſh information gave freſh matter, and enabled the writer to proceed in developing the hiſtory of the poor, the laws reſpecting them, and the opinions of thoſe who have turned their attention to the ſubject; which miſtakes might have been avoided by a different mode of proceeding: but then the communication could not have been prepared for that very uſeful periodical magazine of agricultural intelligence in which it firſt appeared: beſides, probably, by this means of treating the ſubject, dogmatic principles or preconceived opinions are avoided; they, at leaſt, have leſs time to eſtabliſh themſelves.

themfelves. The mind, which confefles itfelf to be employed in obtaining information, is not likely to deal in dogmas; and, when the profeffed purpofe is to digeft annals, as a means of arriving at a truth, it would be an aberration, indeed, to attempt the eftablifhment of a fyftem.

LETTER XVIII.

UNTIL the eftablifhment of literary reviews, the writer of the fugitive piece of the day poffeffed but little chance of pofthumous reputation. His fame refembled the life of the ephemeron in duration, as did the production of his ingenuity that infect by infignificance; both foon perifhed, and were alike forgotten: unlefs extraordinary merit, or chance, preferved the one, in the libraries of the learned; and fcarcity, or beauty, the other, in the collections of the naturalift.

But few treatifes on this fubject, written in the early part of the late reign, are now to be found in the fhops of the bookfellers. Mr. Hay,* a member of the Houfe of Commons, publifhed, in 1735, fome remarks on the laws relating to the poor, with propofals for their better relief and employment. Thefe propofals were reduced into the form of an act, and brought into the Houfe the fame year the pamphlet appeared, but did not pafs into a law. Among other remarks may be found, in his publication, the following judicious obfervations:

" It is certain, that the obligation on each parifh to maintain its own poor, and the confequence of that, a diftinct intereft, are the roots from which every evil relating to the poor hath fprung, and

---

* Of Glynd, in Suffex, author of an agreeable Effay on Deformity.

which

which ever muſt grow up until they are eradicated. Every pariſh is in a ſtate of expenſive war with all the reſt of the nation, regards the poor of all other places as aliens, and cares not what becomes of them, if it can but baniſh them from its own ſociety. No good, therefore, is ever to be expected till parochial intereſt is deſtroyed, till the poor are taken out of the hands of the overſeers, and put under the management of perſons wiſer and more diſintereſted, and until they be ſet to work on a *national*, or at leaſt a *provincial*, fund, to ariſe from benefactions, and the labour of the poor, as far as they will go; and what more is wanting to be levied by an equal tax."

On this principle, he propoſes, that every perſon be deemed legally ſettled in the pariſh where he has continued a year, without being chargeable; and, if he has gained no ſuch ſettlement, then at the place of his birth; and, if not born in the kingdom, then where he ſhould want relief.

The heads of the bill, which was rejected, proceeded principally on this idea, and conſiſted chiefly of a plan for a county or diſtrict work-houſe, if the county ſhould be too large; to be maintained by an equal rate throughout the county, to be governed by twelve perſons reſiding in each diſtrict, poſſeſſed of a certain eſtate in land, to be drawn by lot at the quarter-ſeſſions, and incorporated by the name of the guardians of the poor within the diſtrict; ſix of them annually to go out, and ſix new ones to be choſen in the ſame manner; benefactors to be guardians for the time being, in proportion to the ſum given. They ſhould be enabled to purchaſe lands, in fee, near the middle of the county or diſtrict, thereon to erect buildings for the uſe of the poor; to furniſh and provide ſtock to ſet the poor at work. To this plan many regulations are annexed, which, as it never paſſed into a law, it is unneceſſary to tranſcribe them, or any of his reaſons for them.

From this period until 1751, no other publication on this ſubject has come to hand; and, in that year, Mr. Henry Fielding, as

R   well

well known to us in thefe days for his excellent novels, replete with nature, mirth, and pathos, as he was in thofe for his excellence as a magiftrate, publifhed " An Inquiry into the Caufe of the late Increafe of Robbers, &c. with fome Propofals for remedying the growing Evil." This treatife is full of obfervations, worthy a man of his abilities and intimate knowledge, from extenfive experience, as a Middlefex magiftrate, of this important fubject; a few of his leading principles, as far as they relate to our prefent inquiry, fhall be given.

After having inveftigated the nature of the *conftitution* of his country, as far it relates to the fubject-matter, and explained what he intends by the word *conftitution*, he divides the fubjects of the realm into three orders, — the nobility, the gentry, and the commonalty: the laft divifion he afferts to be vaftly changed from what they were in the days of vaffalage, and conceives this change to have arifen chiefly from commerce, which has fuperinduced an almoft unbounded liberty or licentioufnefs, and a vaft addition of power, to that clafs of people; while, in the mean time, the civil power having decreafed in the fame proportion, the *laws, as at prefent adminiftered*, are not able to govern them.

The fubject of the firft fection is, the too frequent and expenfive diverfions of which the lower clafs of people partake; this, he fays, is one caufe of thefts and robberies.

In the fecond fection, he confiders drunkennefs as a vice which the legiflature has been particularly careful to fupprefs, and that the only blame in this cafe refts in the remiffnefs with which thefe wholefome laws have been executed; and adds, " Although I will not undertake to defend the magiftrates of former days, who have furely been guilty of fome neglect of their duty, yet, in behalf of the prefent commiffioners of the peace, the cafe is different; they are very different offices, to execute a new or a well-known law, or to revive one which is obfolete. In the cafe of a known law, cuftom brings men to fubmiffion; and, in all new provifions, the

ill-will,

ill-will, if any, is levelled at the legiflature, who are much more able to fupport it than a few magiftrates." He then expatiates on the terrible confequences arifing from drunkennefs, acquired by drinking the ftrongeft intoxicating liquors, and particularly gin; and, in a fine fpirit of prophecy, foretels the fatal confequences flowing to pofterity from this pernicious practice. " Doth not this polluted fource, inftead of producing fervants for the hufbandman and artificer, inftead of providing recruits for the fea or the field, promife only to fill alms-houfes and hofpitals, and to infect the ftreets with ftench and difeafes?"

The third fection is on gaming, but as this vice has not, at prefent, been fo directly the caufe of the increafe of the poor's rates, as it has of thefts and robberies, and is not, except in the fhape of an annual lottery, fo likely to tempt the inhabitants of the country as of crowded cities, our author's obfervations on this vice need not be recapitulated.

The fourth.fection contains a review of the laws relating to the poor; and, having before run over the confequences of luxury among the lower claffes of people, in the inftances of diverfions, drunkennefs, and gaming, as tending to promote their diftreffes, he confiders the improper regulation of the poor as a fecond caufe of thefts and robberies; this, he thinks, proceeds from three fources, — the abufe of fome laws, the total neglect of others, and fomewhat from a defect in the laws themfelves. He adds, that it muft be matter of aftonifhment to any man to reflect, that, in a country where the poor are, beyond all comparifon, more liberally provided for than in any other part of the world, there fhould be found more beggars, more miferable diftreffed objects, than are to be feen throughout all the ftates of Europe.

The other fections in this tract relating only to the fubject immediately under his confideration, and not affecting our prefent inquiry, no farther extracts fhall be given of the publication.

R 2 We

We now proceed to a name known to all the civilized world, and the particular boaft of this ifland; not as a legiflator, not as a magiftrate, but as a poet and a pleafant moralift.

A pamphlet, entitled, " A compendicus or briefe Examination of certaine ordinary Complaints of diverfe of our Countrymen in thefe our Dayes, by William Shakefpeare, Gentleman," imprinted in 1581, was reprinted in 1751 in London.

The Monthly Review, a valuable collection of criticifm on and repofitory of moft that is worth notice in the literary productions of the laft forty years, preferved the republication of this pamphlet to my notice, which certainly, with refpect to the remote date of its original publication, fhould have ftood foremoft in the lift of tracts on the poor; it being written anterior to the great corner-ftone of the poor-laws, the 43d of Elizabeth, and to the principle of which it might have afforded a valuable hint.

Although in 1751, when this tract was reprinted, the fame of Shakefpeare had not rifen to that ftupendous height in the opinion of mankind it now poffeffes; nor had the anecdotes of his life, and criticifm on his beauties and defects, fwelled to fuch a bulk as they have fince arrived at, through the ingenious comments of Johnfon, Farmer, Stephens, Malone, and others; yet one fhould have ima-gined that enough had been known of the poet, from Rowe's life of him, to have precluded a poffibility of miftaking William Shakefpeare, the author of this tract, for our renowned poet: this pamphlet being printed in 1581, when, by the parifh-regifter of Stratford, Shakefpeare was not above feventeen years of age, and more probably engaged in the truant pleafures of youth than in writing a ferious dialogue between a doctor of divinity, a merchant, a hufbandman, and a capper;* in the handling of which, the re-viewers fay, the author difcovers a much greater knowledge of trade and commerce than people would be apt to expect from a

* Capper, one who makes and fell caps.   Johnson.

poet.

poet. The depth of obfervation and knowledge of mankind, as well as of trade and commerce, which was poffeffed by the writer of this tract, whoever he may have been, may be conceived from the following quotation from it, which appears to ftrike deeper at the principle of the poor-laws, as far as it refpects *compulfive* induftry, than any other argument which has fallen under my recollection.

" It is an old faying in Latin, *bonos alit artes,* that is to fay, profit or advancement nourifheth every faculty; which faying is fo true, that it is allowed by the common judgement of all men. We muft underftand alfo, that all things that fhould be done in a commonwealth be not to be conftrayned by the ftraight penalties of the law; but fome fo, and fome either by allurement, and rewardes rather. For what law can compel men to be induf-trious in travayle, or labour of body; or ftudious to learne any fcience or knowledge of the minde: to thefe things they may well be provoked, encouraged, and allured, if they that be induftrious and painful be rewarded well for their paines, and be fuffered to take gaynes and wealth as rewardes of their labours, and fo, like-wife, they, that be learned, be advanced, and honoured, according to their forwardnefs in learning; every body will then ftudy to be induftrious in bodily labour, or ftudious in things that pertayne to knowledge. Take thefe rewardes away from them, and go about to compel them by laws thereto, what man will plough or dig the ground, or exercife any manual arte, wherein is any paine ?"

As every act of parliament, refpecting the poor, proceeds on a principle of compulfion *only,* and is not intermixed with rewards or encouragement incitive to induftry, the prefent fyftem of laws militates with this humane and fenfible obfervation of Mr. William Shakefpeare; and it may be the price of our labour, in a future part of this inquiry, to confider whether the principle of the poor-laws would not be meliorated by intermixing allurements to induftry with compulfion; but, as the chief.fcope in this pamphlet

was

was to recommend the manufacturing our own wearing-apparel, inftead of going to a foreign market, for our own materials worked up by foreigners; a queftion which feems to have excited the attention of the fenfible part of the nation, a few years after the Duke d'Alva's feverities had driven manufactures and commerce from the Spanifh Netherlands into this ifland; the tract itfelf contains little more on our fubject worth tranfcribing.

Towards the end of 1751, an anonymous publication made its appearance, entitled, "Confiderations on feveral Propofals for the better Maintenance of the Poor:" the author's defign is, to prove that the prefent fyftem is fufficient, if properly executed; and with great reafon is he averfe to leaving the poor to be maintained by voluntary contribution, or accidental charity only; becaufe they, having now, for near two hundred years, been maintained by a regular fyftem of laws, enforcing contribution, thoufands would perifh, trade would greatly fuffer, and much confufion would arife from fuch a total change of fyftem; he thinks, that the divifion into parifhes is fufficiently large; becaufe a multitude can be beft governed by a divifion into fubordinate parts; and conceives, that the internal police was better regulated when the counties were divided into hundreds, thefe hundreds into decennaries, and each man of the decennary was anfwerable for the reft; he propofes a more ftrict infpection into the conduct of the poor, and of ale-houfes, by the conftables of the diftrict, who fhould make regular weekly returns to the high-conftables, and thefe to make monthly returns to the juftices at their petty feffions: on the whole, there appears to be much good fenfe, knowledge of, and attention to, the principles of the conftitution in this tract.

EARLY in the year 1752, Thomas Alcock, A. M. gives his opinion on the fubject, and profeffes himfelf highly diffatif-fied with the manner of providing for the poor : he diflikes *compul-five relief*, and thinks it hath a tendency to hurt induftry, care, and frugality; the fluggard, on the prefumption that he hath a right to relief, is tempted to continue in floth; and the glutton as he receives his gains eats them, and the drunkard drinks them; in fhort, men labour lefs, and fpend more; and the very law that provides for the poor increafes the number of the poor : compul-fion to relieve, he fays, is contrary to the principle of charity, and deftroys gratitude in the receivers, creates ill blood, murmuring, and indignation, on the fide of the contributor: " it muft be allow-ed, therefore, that the poor-law tends to deftroy charity, efpecially when the legal exaction is fo very high, that no lefs a fum than *three millions yearly*, at a medium, is levied for this purpofe, which is equal to a land-tax at fix fhillings in the pound; add to this, that the fhamelefs, the impudent, the idle, and leaft deferving, run away with this vaft fum; while the modeft, the bafhful, and really indigent, are fuffered to languifh in the moft diftrefsful circum-ftances imaginable."

It is impoffible in this place to avoid obferving upon the fact ftated, that *three millions were raifed by legal exaction yearly, about the year* 1751, for the poor; or, in other words, that the poor's rate at that time amounted to three millions yearly; the fact appears to be queftionable; but, as the account of the poor's rates, returned by the different parifhes throughout the kingdom, does not go back to this period, and no other proof to the contrary can be at prefent advanced, Mr. Alcock muft be allowed credit for the affer-tion, that three millions were raifed by the poor's rate annually,

about

about the year 1751; becaufe, the nature of his argument, as well as the pointed expreffion, *legal exaction*, preclude the idea of his mixing the numerous charitable funds and contributions throughout the kingdom to fwell the produce to that enormous fum.

Now, the Windfor-table of the prices of wheat, which has been once before referred to, ftates the price, in 1750, at 1*l.* 8*s.* 10*d.* a quarter; and, in 1751, at 1*l.* 14*s.* 2*d.*; in 1785, at 1*l.* 16*s.* 11*d.*: but, by the overfeers' returns to the Houfe of Commons, the poor's rate, in 1785, amounted only to 2,184,904*l.*: the expenfes of the poor were, therefore, lefs in that year, than in 1750, above 800,000*l.* and wheat 8*s.* a quarter more; another proof that the price of bread increafing has not been the caufe of an increafe in the poor's rate. *

It would extend this inquiry to a tedious length, if every fcheme which has been offered in print, on the maintenance and employment of the poor, were to be detailed. Mr. Alcock, whofe language is rather declamatory than argumentative, likewife offers his plan; the intent of which is, to relieve the indigent, without oppreffing the public in fuch an intolerable manner. He is not for *repealing* the poor-laws, but only for *amending* them; and, among other matters, propofes a plan of hundred work-houfes, to confift of three parts; one for the impotent, the able, and the induftrious poor; the fecond for the fick; and the third for the vagrant and idle poor; to be built and furnifhed at the expenfe of the feveral parifhes, in proportion to what they paid, at a medium, for maintaining the poor, the laft four years. The overfeers of the parifhes to be governors thereof, annually, by rotation; and all perfons that

---

* In 1680, a regular eftimate was made of the poor's rate, and it amounted to 665,362*l.*; and, in 1772, it amounted to 3,000,000*l.*: in 1680, wheat was 2*l.* a quarter; in 1772, it was 2*l.* 15*s.* 1*d.*: here the price of wheat is increafed little more than one-third, and the rates more than quadrupled. ANNUAL REGISTER, 1773.

beg,

beg, or afk relief, to be fent to this houfe, and immediately ad nit-
ted, on an order figned by the overfeers of the refpective parifhes ;
and no money, .but what paffed through this houfe, to be charged
to the parifh .by the overfeers.

The fubject feems now to have attracted the attention of fome
enlightened minds among the higher orders in the ftate. The Earl
of Hilfborough and Sir Richard Lloyd drew up two feparate plans
into the form of an act of parliament, but neither of them paffed
into a law.

The Earl, by his plan, printed in 1753, propofes to repeal all
the poor-laws, and to deftroy every idea of fettlements and removals ; and to re-enact, with fome alterations, the claufes appointing
overfeers, the mode of levying a rate, the laws refpecting baftard-
children, binding apprentices, rendering parents and children mu-
tually liable to maintain each other; and propofes, that, in every
county, there fhall be one corporation, confifting of fuch perfons
who fhall fubfcribe, and pay, annually, not lefs than 5l. towards
the relief of the poor of the county, who fhall be called governors
of the poor, and who may purchafe lands, make bye-laws, appoint
officers, &c. with falaries.

That one or two hofpitals be erected in every county: in thefe
hofpitals to be three diftinct apartments, for the children, the aged,
the difeafed. The charges of the building, furniture, and materials, to be paid out of the contributions, and out of fuch money
as may be granted for that purpofe by parliament, and out of an
affeffment, for two years, of 3d. in the pound, annually, and an
affeffment of 6d. in the pound for maintaining the poor admitted
into thefe hofpitals : the profits of any work done in them, alfo, to
be added to the revenue of the hofpital.

Many good rules are alfo given by the Earl for the internal regulation of thefe hofpitals, but of too minute a nature to render a
tranfcription of them neceffary.

S   Sir

Sir Richard Lloyd's plan principally confifts of a houfe of induftry for the education of the children of the poor.* It is aftonifhing that nearly forty years fhould have elapfed fince a name of
fome eminence has recommended fuch an inftitution, and, except
part of Lincolnfhire, no other confiderable divifion of the ifland
has carried the idea into execution, although many individuals have
fhewn that the plan is feafible ; and experience has now feconded
the ftrongeft convictions of its excellence which human reafon
alone was able to give. Sunday-fchools, which fhould be, as it
were, the apex of the ftructure, the laft finifh of the plan, will, it
is to be hoped, now be made ufe of as the ground-work : and,
while charity, uniting with religion, influences us to take care of
the religious fentiment of the rifing generation of the poor, by
inftructing them in learning and the duties they owe to God and
man on a *Sunday*, let the good principles, the patrons of thefe
inftitutions are actuated by, influence them to attend to the induftrious habits of their young pupils through the other days of
the week.

This fcheme of Sir Richard's recites, that, whereas the education of the children of the poor cannot be fo well effected, nor the
poor be fo comfortably, nor at fo eafy a price, maintained in fmall
numbers, and in diftinct families, as in large and well-ordered
houfes fet apart for that purpofe, therefore the juftices, in feffions,
fhall divide the county into as many diftricts as they fhall think
proper ; and that they, and alfo other perfons of confiderable
eftate fhall be chofen as jurors, are, and fhall be, guardians of
the poor within each diftrict ; and perfons contributing a certain

---

* The Memoir of the Board of Trade, drawn up by Mr. Locke, had not, at this
time, fallen into my hands ; and, when this was written, it was not generally known that
the Memoir exifted entire ; only detached parts of it had been quoted. The laft edition of
an Account of the Society for promoting Induftry in the County of Lincoln has, by the
permiffion of John Pownal, Efq. been the means of making the whole of this important
paper public.

fum

sum shall be also guardians : they shall be a body-corporate, shall make bye-laws, appoint officers and servants, and form themselves into committees; shall purchase land, on which to build a house of industry, and other convenient buildings, for lodging and employing the poor within the district: the expense to be defrayed by a lottery, by voluntary contributors, and by an assessment: the charges, for the relief and employment of the poor, afterwards, to be raised by an assessment on the several parishes, in proportion to the number of poor they send to the house.

No other alteration is proposed to be made in the poor-laws, nor does this plan provide any compulsive means to oblige the poor to send their children to the house of industry : on the whole, it appears a very crude and indigested scheme.

Mr. Fielding, in a pamphlet, entitled, " A Proposal for making an effectual Provision for the Poor," printed in 1753, again offers his advice on the subject, and proposes a scheme, which seems, in Dr. Burn's opinion, as supplementary to the two last-mentioned.

Speaking of the necessity of some regulations, he says, that " the poor are a very great burthen, and even a nuisance, to the kingdom; that the laws for relieving their distresses, and restraining their vices, have not answered their purposes, and, at present, that they are very ill provided for, and worse governed, are truths which every man will acknowledge ; and that every man who hath any property must feel the weight of that tax, which is levied for the use of the poor; and every person, who hath any understanding, must see how absurdly it is applied. So very useless, indeed, is this heavy tax, and so wretched its disposition, that it is a question whether the poor or the rich are actually more dissatisfied, or have indeed greatest reason to be so, since the plunder of the one serves so little to the real advantage of the other. The *sufferings* of the poor are, indeed, less known than their *misdeeds*, and therefore we are less apt to pity them! They starve, and

S 2

freeze,

freeze, and rot, among themfelves; but they beg, and fteal, and rob, among their betters."

He then propofes a plan for the county of Middlefex, which, if fuccefsful, may be followed in other counties; but gives it, as his opinion, that no divifion, lefs than a whole county, will anfwer the intention. The heads of which are:

That there be a large building erected, confifting of three courts. The two outermoft of the courts to be called the *county-houfe*, and the innermoft to be called the *county-houfe of correction*, with a chapel, and offices.

That, in thefe houfes, the men and women be kept entirely feparate from each other.

That the county-houfe fhall confift of lodgings for the officers; of lodging-rooms, and of working-rooms, for the labourers; of an infirmary; of a chapel; of feveral large ftore-rooms, with cellarage.

That the county-houfe of correction confift of lodging-rooms for the officers; of lodging-rooms, and working-rooms, for the prifoners; of an infirmary; of a *fafting-room*; of feveral cells, or dungeons; of a large room, with iron grates, which fhall be contiguous to, and look into, the chapel.

That there fhall be a houfe for the governor, one for the deputy-governor, one for the chaplain, one for the treafurer, and one for the receiver-general of the houfe; and that likewife there be built, on each fide of the county-houfe, nine houfes, for providing the labourers and prifoners with the neceffaries of life.

..Thefe, with many other lefs important, regulations are the whole of Mr. Fielding's plan; on which, and alfo on his ideas on the fubject of the poor, the following obfervations fhall be ventured:

.That they are collected from an intimate knowledge of the wretchednefs and villany which prevail among the loweft clafs of our fellow-creatures, in the purlieus of an overgrown metropolis.

polis. That the picture which he draws of them is too over-charged; the outline too hard; and, it is to be hoped, it is rather a caricature of the fink of wretchednefs in London, than a natural reprefentation of country-manners, even in thofe families where lazinefs and debauchery are in league with poverty, to render human mifery complete. His plan is alfo of a piece with his picture; therefore, we read of dungeons, cells, iron grates, and fafting-rooms; although he, indeed, apologizes for the laft, on the experience of their good effect in bridewells, and other houfes of correction; but, befides all this, the expenfe attending building fuch large offices, together with houfes for about half-a-dozen offi-cers, and confequently falaries, that they may be able to live in their houfes, is fuch an expenfe as would ftartle any county, although Middlefex fhould have fet a fuccefsful example.

It does not appear that the legiflature, in confequence of the reafoning and plans detailed in thefe ingenious tracts, made any alterations in the ftatute-law of the kingdom. The arguments, as well as the plan, fell to the ground, not having made a fuf-ficient impreffion on the mind of parliament to occafion any of them to pafs into a law, although feconded by the weight of no mean ability and by the influence of men of confiderable confe-quence, the vagrant-act, and that which refpects the regulation of the poor's rate, being the only acts, on this head of internal police, which paffed until towards the clofe of the reign of our late king; and the date of thefe acts is anterior to the pamphlets which have juft been noticed.

The multitude of inftances, affecting to humanity and decency, which arofe from the depravity and wretchednefs of the numerous proftitutes who haunt the ftreets of the metropolis, occafioned, about the year 1758, fome gentlemen, of equal generofity as huma-nity, to enter into a fubfcription, which laid the foundation of the Magdalen-Houfe. The fubject becoming a fafhionable topic of con-verfation, many arguments on the good which might be expected

to

to arife from fuch an inftitution were held, and many plans were offered; among others, a plan for eftablifhing charity-houfes for expofed and deferted women and girls, and for penitent proftitutes; together with confiderations, relating to the poor and poor-laws of England, were written, in 1758, by J. Maffee, who appears to have been, on other fubjects as well as this, a well-meaning and en-lightened projector. The principal part of this publication was occupied on thefe inftitutions, and confequently not in point with our inquiry; but he alfo threw out fome fenfible hints on the fub-ject of the poor and the poor-laws: of thefe it will be proper to take fome notice.

He afferts, that the great increafe of unemployed poor is owing to parochial fettlements, and that the increafe of thieves, beggars, and proftitutes, is immediately caufed by want of employment, and, in fome meafure, by want of proper provifion for diftreffed working-people, when out of the parifhes to which they belong; and partly to the feverity of our poor-laws, in affixing the fame punifhment to begging as to ftealing.

He apprehends, that monopolizing farms and the inclofure of common lands are among the caufes of an increafe of the poor.

He attempts alfo to prove, by authorities, that fubftantial people have decreafed in number; and afferts, that our interior weaknefs, the precarious ftate of our trade, and the great increafe of the poor, are primarily, or principally, caufed by removing multitudes, from our *natural and fixed bafis-land,* to the *artificial and fluctuating bafis-trade.*

A new fyftem is alfo propofed by him, for relieving, employing, and ordering, the poor, which he divides into ten propofitions; of thefe only the firft three fhall be noticed, becaufe thefe only are properly fundamental, and the reft in the nature of auxiliary regu-lations.

Firft, That the charge of maintaining the poor fhall be equally borne by the wealthy and fubftantial inhabitants; that the fame

fhall

shall be assessed by the rents of houses and lands, and that each person's quota be determined by a pound-rate on the full annual value or rent. .

Secondly, That every poor person, wanting relief, shall be equally entitled thereto, in any city, town, parish, or extra-parochial place, without regarding where such person was born or had lived.

Thirdly, That a competent number of houses of maintenance and employ be established for the reception of all poor persons, within each county respectively.

With respect to these three propositions, the first leaves the principle of the poor's rate exactly as it is at present; the second is impracticable in the full extent intended; and the third lays a foundation for an immense expense in buildings.

In 1759, a short anonymous tract appeared, in which the writer gives it as his opinion, that the principles are false on which the poor-laws are founded; particularly this, that it is reasonable *every place* in the kingdom should maintain *its own poor*; and asserts, that they ought to be relieved where they are in want of relief, and be employed where they are most useful; and, to effect this, that the fund to support them be *national*, not *parochial*. This writer offers his plan also, and proposes, that all charities, hospitals, work-houses, &c. be ingrafted into a general plan for the relief of the poor; and the several members thereof be united into a corporate body, to take the appellation Sir Josiah Child gave them, and be called fathers of the poor.

There also were published, about this time, some well-intended tracts, which recommend decreasing the number and regulating the conduct of ale-houses; a very proper, nay a necessary, step towards a well-ordered internal police: ale-houses are undoubtedly at present a principal origin of the evil complained of; but it surely might be possible to restrain their bad tendency, and make them in one respect a convenience to the laborious poor; instead of putting it into the power of licensed ale-houses to draw every

sixpence

fixpence from their pockets and every good principle from their breafts; if, under the authority of the prefent fubfifting laws, the magiftrates would be more ftrict in reftraining them from permitting *tippling*, and not licenfe any ale-houfe where there was not kept a ftock of beer conftantly on fale to thofe, only, who carry it home, of a ftrength equal to common table-beer, and at a price which would allow of a moderate profit only. The authority of magiftrates, over the conduct of thofe they licenfe to keep ale-houfes, is great indeed; and every exertion of their authority to preferve fobriety and regularity among the lower claffes of the people, who are the principal cuftomers to thefe fhops of drunkennefs, is in the ftrict line of their duty. The leading principle in the Court of King's Bench, which fuperintends the conduct of the magiftracy of the kingdom, is favourable to fuch a ftrict difcharge of office; and were they, in that difcharge, rather to exceed, than fall fhort, of their legal authority, while the intention was right, that court would hold them blamelefs. It is only when interefted views or felfifh principles influence their conduct, that the Court of King's Bench reprimands and punifhes magiftrates.

LETTER XX.

WE are now arrived at an æra, when the arms of Great Britain were carrying its fame and dominion to the remoteft parts of the globe: an æra, when this ifland, in profperity, political confequence, and reputation, was, by many of its moft fanguine patriots, conceived to have arifen to its acme: and when, by many, alfo, whofe opinions carried weight with them, it was believed to have ftretched its credit almoft to its deftruction; and, while it was rifing in fame, to be finking, in

fact,

fact, under the immenfe load of its national debt: experience has now proved to us, that both thefe conceptions of our fituation, formed at the commencement of the prefent reign, were equally removed from truth; our profperity and political confequence, now that above thirty years of his prefent Majefty's reign has paffed over, continue to increafe; and above a hundred million has alfo been added to the national debt.

This is a paradox, which politicians may attempt to explain; it refpects our fubject no farther, than as the internal happinefs of the mafs of individuals, who form the population of the kingdom, may be interefted. Has *their* profperity increafed progreffively with that of the ftate? is a queftion of fome importance; if it has, our wars, our treaties, our taxes, the high political fituation this kingdom now fills, have operated to general good; they have increafed the general ftock of profperity and happinefs: but, if the reverfe is fact; if, among the mafs of our fellow-fubjects, more idlenefs, more dif-fipation, worfe principles, worfe habits, and their confequences, greater poverty and diftrefs, prevail among them; what is all our boafted greatnefs, our high name for wealth, profperity, and poli-tical confequence, but a fplendid pall, to conceal from view the hideous appearance of mortal wretchednefs?

That this is the cafe; that the aggregate of mifery is greater among the poor than it was; that the axiom, *it has increafed, is in-creafing, and ought to be diminifhed*, is to the full as true as ever was the fame axiom when applied to the influence of the crown, no one who fees their prefent wretchednefs, and knows the amount of the rates raifed for their relief, will hefitate to allow; and, while this remarkable fentence is applied to their *miferable fituation*, with equal force will it apply to the *revenue* raifed for their relief. — But what has the legiflature done throughout this period to diminifh their diftrefs or our expenfes? Nothing, or next to nothing: the legiflature has treated the fubject as the phyfician, whofe hu-manity exceeds his fkill, treats his patient, whofe cafe he defpairs

T   of:

of : he prefcribes narcotic palliatives, and exerts his knowledge to render lefs painful that cataftrophe which he cannot prevent.

That this apathy or inattention of parliament, to the fituation of the poor, has not been exaggerated, will clearly appear by the following notices of the ftatutes which refpect them, culled from a farrago of fourteen volumes of public legiflative acts, containing above one thoufand chapters, paffed in thirty-one years of the prefent reign; among which, the firft fourteen years contain not a fyllable upon the fubject, except an act paffed in the fecond year, cap. 22, which refpects the metropolis only; being an act for the keeping regular, uniform, and annual, regifters of all parifh-poor infants under a certain age, within the bills of mortality; as a means of preferving the lives of infants under the age of four years.

But local inconvenience and diftrefs have neverthelefs, during this period, occafioned many diftricts, hundreds, and parifhes, to apply to parliament for affiftance, and to be petitioners for acts for the better relief and employment of the poor within the diftricts refpectively applying : among a number of thefe, we fhall find, in the year 1764, acts for the better relief and employment of the poor, within the hundreds of Blything, Bofmere, and Claydon, Samford, Mutford, Lothingland, and Wangford, in the county of Suffolk; the conveniences and inconveniences, arifing from the carrying into execution the acts of parliament, in the feveral hundreds thus incorporated, at their own requeft, by parliament, fhall be attended to in another place, by a digeft of the beft information that can be obtained from the incorporated parifhes ; but, at prefent, a detail of what the legiflature has done on the general fubject fhall be purfued.

In 1775, parliament repealed an act of Elizabeth, againft erecting and maintaining cottages ; which had reftrained the building them, unlefs four acres of land was laid to each cottage ; and had alfo reftrained the owners from placing more families than one in any cottage, or receiving any inmates ; becaufe it appeared, as

ftated

ſtated by the preamble to the act repealing, that it laid the induſtrious poor under great difficulties, and tended very much to leſſen population.

The 16th of Geo. III. cap. 40. in its preamble, ſtates, that the great and increaſing expenſe of maintaining and providing for the poor, and their continual diſtreſſes notwithſtanding, make it highly expedient for the legiſlature to take this great ſubject into their ſerious conſideration. And that information of the *ſtate of the poor* and the nature of thoſe expenſes are neceſſary to be procured, to enable the two houſes of parliament to judge of proper remedies to redreſs thoſe grievances; and that ſuch information cannot be effectually obtained, without the aid and authority of parliament.

Therefore it is enacted, that the overſeers of the poor throughout that part of Great Britain, called England and Wales, ſhall make returns upon oath to certain queſtions ſpecified in the act, relative to the ſtate of the poor; and that the juſtices of peace, within their reſpective diviſions, be authorized and requeſted to take ſuch returns on oath, and to cauſe them to be tranſmitted to the clerk in parliament. Then follow the ſeveral clauſes preſcribing the means to effect this end, and alſo a ſchedule of the queſtions to which anſwers are to be returned.

There now ſeemed to be a ſerious intent in the legiſlature to inveſtigate this important queſtion; and a preamble better adapted to the purpoſe, and more expreſſive of the ſerious magnitude of the ſubject, the neceſſity of inveſtigating it, and remedying the evils complained of, could not have been prefixed to the enacting clauſes; and theſe clauſes are in general well calculated to obtain the end required; but ſurely an omiſſion appears in the ſchedule of queſtions annexed.

I. What was the amount of the aſſeſſments for the relief of the poor in the year ending at Eaſter, 1776?

II. How much of thoſe aſſeſſments was applied for the relief or on account of the poor, and how much for the payment of county-

rates,

rates, or any other purpofes ? diftinguifhing, alfo, the amount of
what was paid for the rent -of work-houfes, or paid or allowed
for habitations for the poor; and if any poor refide in houfes built
at the expenfe of the parifh, townfhip, or place, ftate the total
annual value of fuch houfes.

III. What number of poor have received conftant relief during
that year, and what has been the expenfe thereof, as near as the
fame can be eftimated ?

IV. Is there a work-houfe in the parifh ? if fo, what number of
poor will it accommodate ?

V. What was expended in litigations about fettlements, removals, appeals, or other difputes, concerning the poor within that
year, diftinguifhing how much of fuch expenfes arofe from difputes with parifhes, townfhips, or places, not within the county,
riding, divifion, precinct, foke, franchife, liberty, city, or county
corporate, wherein fuch parifh, townfhip, or place, lay ?

The return made from the poor-rates to parliament, ftated to be
from Eafter, 1775, to Eafter, 1776, in anfwer to the preceding
queftions, amounted, as appears in the Annual Regifter for 1777,
to the following total refult :

	Money raifed. £. s. d.	County-Rates. £. s. d.
England - - -	1,679,585 0 0 —	131,387 18 11
Wales - - - -	40,731 14 7 —	6,268 11 9
	1,720,316 14 7 —	137,656 10 8

	Expended on the Poor. £. s. d.	Rents. £. s. d.	Ligitation. £. s. d.
England,	1,523,163 12 7 —	78,176 4 0 —	33,935 18 0
Wales -	33,640 13 8 —	2,120 10 7 —	1,136 2 8
	1,556,804 6 3 —	80,296 14 7 —	35,072 0 8

The

The continual diftreffes of the poor are mentioned, in the *pre--amble* to the act, as one of the ftrong inducements to the inquiry; and, alfo, that information of the *ftate* of the poor. is neceffary to be procured.   Does any one of thefe queftions in the fchedule reach this point?   Does any of the queftions afk, what are the pre--vailing diftreffes among the poor in your parifh?   Do they arife from their own extravagance, or from the price of labour?   Are the neceffaries of life rifen in price?   Has the earnings of the poor rifen proportionably?   What is the ftate of their morals?   Are they greater drunkards, more lazy, than heretofore?   Is the num-ber of ale-houfes increafed within the laft fifty years?   Is the pro-duce of excife in your parifh more than formerly, and to what amount?   Thefe or fome fimilar queftions would have expofed the caufe of the diftreffes of the poor, and their *real ftate*; which, if the overfeers could not have anfwered, the refiding clergyman'o knowledge of the fubject might have been called in aid, and the information, ftated as neceffary in the preamble, would have been obtained.   But all this part of the inveftigation is forgotten in the act itfelf; and the inquiry goes folely to the quantum of the rate, and the mode of expenditure.

And what great leading regulation followed from this important inquiry?   What was the happy refult from this great body of in-formation obtained by all the force and energy of the conftitu-tional legiflature?   Alas!

Parturiunt montes!

But nothing was brought forth.   This mafs of information, thus conftitutionally obtained, has ferved for nothing but wafte-paper: and a neceffary folemn inquiry, anfwered on oath, which coft the nation thoufands of pounds, and the magiftrates and overfeers of the poor, throughout the kingdom, not a little trouble and atten--tion, tended to no one good end whatever.   Surely, when thefe great phyficians of the ftate had felt the pulfe of the patient, and weighed,

weighed, with due folemnity, every fymptom of internal decay, they found themfelves unequal to attempt the cure, and gave up the cafe as loft.

Two years after the return of the overfeers had been received by the clerk in parliament, inftead of any code of police, affecting this very important fubject, we find a trivial, yet very proper, alteration in one of the fections of the 43d of Eliz. changing the period, to which parifh-apprentices fhall be bound by indenture, to the age of twenty-one years, inftead of twenty-four. This is effected by 17 Geo. III. cap. 48.

Many applications, from particular parifhes, diftricts, and hundreds, ftill continued to be made to parliament, for acts to relieve, regulate, and maintain, the poor, within their refpective local fituations; and many acts accordingly paffed, much, it is to be hoped, to the general good of the places applying. Amongft others, paffed in the 19th of this reign, are two, incorporating the hundreds of Hartfmere, Hoxne, and Thredling, the hundred of Cofford, (except the parifh of Hadleigh,) and alfo the parifh of Polfted, in Suffolk. The fair conclufion to be drawn from thefe inftances is, that, as the legiflature felt the fubject at large of too great a magnitude for their attention, thofe diftricts, moft preffed by the urgency of neceffity, found themfelves obliged, at their own expenfe, to apply for leave to take care of themfelves.

By ftat. 20. Geo. III. cap. 46. it is directed, that *all perfons* to whom any children fhall be appointed to be bound, in purfuance of any act for the relief of the poor in any particular diftrict in England, *fhall* be obliged to provide for them; but that no perfon fhall be compellable to take a poor child apprentice, except he be an inhabitant and occupier of lands, &c. in the parifh to which fuch child fhall belong; and that baftards born in houfes of induftry fhall belong to the mother's parifh.

In the 22d year of this reign a long act paffed, entitled, " An Act for the better Relief and Employment of the Poor ;" which, although

though not fo exprefled in the preamble, appears to be an aggregate of all the beft regulations which had been brought before parliament by the multitude of acts which had of late years pafled for incorporating parifhes, particular diftricts, and hundreds, and maintaining and employing the poor therein.

The confiderable length this act is extended to, comprehending in it all the neceffary directions for the proceeding of parifhes, where two-thirds of the owners and occupiers of land agree to unite, the mode of appointing the different neceffary officers and their duties, the qualification of the voters at their meetings, the application of the poor's rate raifed in the different parifhes uniting, together with the multifarious directions refpecting the internal police of an united houfe of induftry, would render the moft concife abridgement of this act too long for the attention of thofe who may run the eye over thefe curfory obfervations. Befides that it would be of no real fervice, as any parifhes wifhing to unite, on the power and principles of the act, muft have recourfe to the act itfelf, which appears to have thus much ufe in it, that it renders the expenfe of obtaining an act of parliament unneceffary, provided the parties agreeing to unite are fatisfied with this code of regulations, and can make them coincide well with their own views and intentions.

It is not in my power to affert, pofitively, but it is believed, that very few parifhes have taken the advantage this act has given, and have united for the purpofe of relieving and employing their poor, by virtue of the powers, and fubject to the regulations, of this ftatute.

What can have been the reafon, that, fince the legiflature has opened the means to an union of parifhes, without the expenfe of an act of parliament, for thofe *very purpofes*, to obtain which many applications had been made to parliament, at an expenfe of fome hundreds of pounds, in the outfet of the fcheme, fo very few inftances

ftances fhould have appeared of parifhes uniting by virtue of the powers in this act?

If we fuppofe experience to have proved, that general good has arifen in thofe parifhes which have been incorporated by different acts of parliament, this is a queftion which will not foon be re-folved; becaufe, it is not eafy to fuggeft a reafon for thofe advan-tages to be refufed, when offered *gratis*, which have, in a great many inftances, been obtained at a confiderable expenfe: and, in the *united* parifhes in the county of Suffolk, the fact, that the poor--rates have greatly decreafed, is generally allowed. Why, then, is not the greateft part of the kingdom incorporated into convenient diftricts, for the purpofe of relieving and maintaining their poor by means of the powers and regulations of this act? Why have we *very* few, if *any*, inftances of this act being enforced?

We cannot fuppofe that the claufes in the act militate, in gene-ral, with the regulations thofe parifhes which wifh to unite would choofe to embrace, becaufe they are a felection of the beft general regulations from all the acts applied for by the parifhes incorpo-rated. But, does it not arife from the want of a centre of union, a man of confequence and ability, whofe influence could render the fluctuating confents of a number of interefted people fteady, and fix them to the plan they have in agitation, but cannot abfolutely refolve on? The attorney who was applied to when a bill in par-liament was to be paffed is this *kind of perfon*; he was interefted in bringing the determination of the leading men in the different parifhes to a point, and fixing them in their refolves. But now no one man takes any more intereft in the matter than as an indi-vidual among equals; and moft men underftand, and feel them-felves inclined to fupport, in all its purity, the maxim, — *inter pares, equalis eft poteftas.*

In the 26th year of this reign, cap. 56. another act paffed to oblige the overfeers of the poor to make a return, on oath, to certain queftions relative to the ftate of the poor. The preamble

to

to this act is the fame; and the act itself proceeded on much the fame plan, and principle, as that which has been mentioned to have paffed in the 16th of the king, except that a penalty of 50*l*. for making falfe returns, is added; and, alfo, a claufe, fubjecting perfons taking falfe oaths to the pains and penalties of thofe convicted of wilful and corrupt perjury: the queftons afked are alfo fomewhat different.

And, in the fame year, by cap. 58, an act paffed, for procuring, on oath, returns of all charitable donations, for the benefit of poor perfons, throughout that part of Great Britain called England and Wales. The returns are to be made in writing, on oath, by the minifter and church-wardens of each parifh. This act gives fimilar powers, and is armed with fimilar penalties, as the other.

LETTER XXI.

THE following queftions were referred, by the act of parliament which paffed in the 26th year of the prefent reign, to the overfeers of the poor, to which they were obliged to make returns upon oath.

Queftion I. What money was raifed, by affeffments, for the relief of the poor, in the refpective years, ending at Eafter, 1783, 1784, and 1785?

II. What number of poor received conftant, and what number occafional, relief, during each of the faid years, as near as you can afcertain the fame?

III. How much was paid out of the faid money, in each of the faid years, for expenfes of overfeers in journeys, and attendance on magiftrates and others; and how much for entertainments at meetings of the inhabitants on affairs relative to the poor?

IV. What payments were made out of the faid money for law-bufinefs, and for orders, examinations, certificates, and other proceedings, refpecting the poor, in each of the faid three years?

V. How much of the money collected, under thefe affeffments, was applied for the payment of county-rates, or any other, and what, purpofes that did not concern the poor?

VI. How much of the money fo raifed has been expended in providing materials and utenfils for fetting the poor to work?

The returns made by the overfeers to thefe queftions, in purfuance of the act alluded to, were digefted into form, and an abftract printed, containing every parifh in England and Wales, reduced, alphabetically, under their refpective counties and hundreds, giving an account, under fourteen diftinct columns, of the name of the hundred within which the parifh is fituated; the money raifed by affeffment for the years 1783, 1784, and 1785, and the medium of thofe three years; expenfes not applicable to the poor; the medium of net-money annually paid for the poor; net-money paid for the poor in 1776, taken from the returns then made to parliament; and heads of particular expenfes: the general totals of which, for England and Wales, are as follow:

Money raifed by Affeffment.

				£.	s.	d.
For the year 1783.——England	-	-		2,068,585	7	1
Wales	-	-		63,901	5	1
				2,132,486	12	2

For

	£.	s.	d.
For the year 1784.——England - -	2,117,432	11	0
Wales - -	68,456	16	8
	2,185,889	7	8
For the year 1785.——England - -	2,115,775	2	5
Wales - -	69,129	16	6
	2,184,904	18	11
Medium of thofe years.——England -	2,100,587	16	11
Wales - -	67,161	16	9
	2,167,749	13	8

Expenfes not applicable to the Poor.

	£.	s.	d.
Medium of money applied for county-purpofes, vagrants, militia, bridges, gaols, &c.			
England - -	113,714	15	6
Wales - - -	5,565	11	4
	119,280	6	10
Medium of expenfes not concerning the poor, re-pairing churches, roads, falaries to minifters, &c.			
England - -	43,223	5	7
Wales - -	1,007	15	4
	44,231	0	11

Medium

$£.$ $s.$ $d.$

Medium of net-money annually paid for the poor.

England - -	1,943,649	15	10
Wales - -	60,588	10	1

	2,004,238	5	11
Net-expenfes in 1776 '- -	1,529,780	0	1

Increafe - - - -	474,458	5	10

Net-expenfes for the poor in 1776, taken from the returns then made to parliament.

England - -	1,496,129	6	3
Wales - -	33,650	13	10

	1,529,780	0	1

Heads of particular Expenfes.

$£.$ $s.$ $d.$

Medium-expenfes of overfeers in journeys, attendances on magiftrates, &c.——England -

England -	23,545	0	10
Wales -	948	17	8

	24,493	18	6

Medium-expenfes of entertainments at meetings relative to the poor.——England - -

England - -	11,329	15	11
Wales - - -	383	4	10

	11,713	0	9

Medium-

	£.	s.	d.
Medium-expenfes of law, orders, examinations, and other proceedings, relative to the poor.			
England - -	53,757	11	0
Wales - - -	2,033	11	6
	55,791	2	6
Medium of money expended in fetting the poor to work. England - -	15,680	14	9
Wales - - -	211	14	1
	15,892	8	10

The mafs of information thus obtained from that part of the nation, fubject to the operation of the poor-laws, digefted, with great labour, by the committee of the Houfe of Commons, which fat for the purpofe, and printed at no inconfiderable expenfe, muft furely have given rife to many ufeful reflections and obfervations in the minds of thofe gentlemen who were on the committee, although their country has not, as yet, reaped any benefit from their very important labours. They muft furely have been ftruck with the alarming increafe of the annual net-expenfes of the poor fince 1776, when they were 1,529,780l. to the medium of the years 1783, 1784, and 1785, which is ftated to be 2,167,749l. a yearly increafe of expenfe amounting to near 500,000l. If they, at firft fight, might conceive this vaft difference to have arifen from any extraordinary fcarcity prevailing through the laft three years, and examined into the fact, they would have found the average-price of wheat, through this period, to have been 2l. 3s. 7d. and that the average-price, for 1776, was 2l. 2s. 8d. being an excefs only of 11d. per quarter, or not 2l. 10s. per cent. which will,

by

by no means, account for a rife in the expenfes of the poor equal
to above forty-one per cent. : to other caufes, therefore, muft they
attribute this amazing increafed expenfe, than thofe which arife
from the dearnefs of provifion; affuming it as a faƈt, that the price
of bread-corn may be taken, with fome degree of accuracy, as a
fign of the price of moft of the neceffary viands which feed our
numerous poor ; and thofe, who know how the poor live, know,
alfo, that bread, in faƈt, conftitutes near two-thirds of the expenfe of a poor family for provifions : the increafed expenfe of the
years 1783, 1784, and 1785, does not, therefore, arife from the
increment of neceffary expenfes in provifions.

Neither does it arife, in any great degree, from a deficiency of
work, or decreafe of the price of labour ; — the price of labour
remained much the fame as in 1776 ; and, in this period, the
American war had begun to drain the nation of its population and
money, but no great effeƈts had then been felt from it : in the laft
period, the nation was recovering from its loffes ; manufaƈtures
were again thriving, and the fenfible part of our countrymen were
looking up to agriculture, as a means of recruiting thofe fources
which the wafte of war had diminifhed.

Although, that an increafe of expenfe, rather more than proportional, took place in the great manufaƈturing-towns, is plainly
proved from this abftraƈt, in which Birmingham, Sheffield, Man-
chefter, certainly more than keep pace with other towns, where
the poor are not employed by manufaƈtures ; yet to be certain how
this faƈt will apply, and what principle may be colleƈted from it,
the returns from the fame manufaƈturing-towns, of the expenfes
of the poor, fhould be feen, for the laft two or three years, during
which, our manufaƈtures have flourifhed exceedingly : from many
inftances within the county of Suffolk, the poor-rates continue
increafing, although the poor are, or might be, in full employ ;
for inftance, Glemsford, rifing gradually from 404*l.* 5*s.* 8*d.* in 1774,
to 456*l.* 7*s.* 4*d.* in 1776, to 551*l.* the average of the three years,
1783,

1783, 1784, and 1785, to 1062*l.* 6*s.* 4*d.* in 1790, as appears by Mr. Butt's account, in vol. xvii. p. 497, of the Annals of Agriculture; and a fimilar rife, but in a lefs proportion, takes place at Melford, Clare, &c.; if this is the cafe in general, other caufes than want of work muft be fought for.

Another obfervation muft alfo have ftruck thefe gentlemen, or, at leaft, thofe among them who act as magiftrates in the counties where their refpective qualifications, as members of parliament, lie; that the money expended in *fetting the poor to work throughout the kingdom* is but little more than what is fpent in *entertainments at meetings* relative to the management of their affairs; not *two-thirds*, of what comes under the article of *overfeers journeys, and attendance on magiftrates*; and about *one-fourth* of the fum which is the total under the column *of law-expenfes:* they muft alfo recollect, that the firft fection of the 43d of Elizabeth gives authority to the overfeers to raife weekly, or otherwife, by taxation of every inhabitant, a convenient *ftock of flax, hemp, wool, thread, iron,* and other neceffary ware and ftuff to *fet the poor to work*; and that this application of the money, raifed by affeffment, is the *primary object* in view of the legiflature, in that act of parliament, under the authority of which, they perceive, by their printed abftract, above two millions to be annually raifed on his Majefty's fubjects, through that part of the kingdom fubject to the operation of the act; they muft alfo know that the application of competent fums of money, toward the neceffary relief of the lame, impotent, old, blind, and fuch other of them being poor and not able to work, and alfo for putting out children to be apprentices, was a fecondary confideration of the legiflature, and by no means comes into the foreground of the piece; and that law-expenfes, expenfes of overfeers in attendance on magiftrates, expenfes of entertainments, &c. were not in view, or, at leaft, like all objects in the back-ground, where the perfpective is well preferved, were but dimly and indiftinctly feen; but that prefent practice has fo reverfed all regularity and

order

order in the prefent fyftem of the poor-laws, as exhibited to the committee, that the great object of Elizabeth's legiflature is now thrown into the back-ground, and the whole order of the picture reverfed : the conclufion, that muft be obvious to every one, is, that the 43d of Elizabeth, like Mr. Gamon's Act, refpecting outfide paffengers in ftage-coaches, although the law of the land, is not the practice of the land.

The total fum falling under the column of expenfes of entertainments, 11,713*l.* certainly is not much for the number of parifhes in England and Wales; but it leads to the expenfes contained under the heads of law-bufinefs, attendances on magiftrates, journeys, &c. Thefe two columns form no inconfiderable total, 80,285*l.*; when a veftry, which ought to meet and conclude the bufinefs of their meeting in a part of the church appropriated for that purpofe, adjourns to the neighbouring ale-houfe, the trifle which they expend of the poor's rates is not all; parifh-bufinefs is the object ; at a meeting of parifhioners, having a common topic to converfe about, fome foon become interefted in defending their opinions ; more talk requires more liquor, and their determinations are made, not like thofe of their German anceftors, *deliberant dum fingere nefciunt : conftituunt dum errare non poffunt* ; but they reverfe the order, they deliberate, while they are fober, and determine when they are drunk ; hence journeys to magiftrates, orders of removal on doubtful fettlements, appeals to feffions ; thence to the King's Bench ; hence attorney's bills, and enormous affeffments. Was no order of veftry good, or no parifh-officer to be indemnified in expending the parifh-money in law-contefts, unlefs by an order of veftry, figned before noon, in the parifh-church, after regular notice given, and no adjournment allowed, much of the article of expenfe would difappear.

Another ufe may alfo be made of this abftract : there are fome very able, although not accurate, obfervers of what refpects the poor, who have imagined, that the great increafe of our expenfes,

relating

relating to them, has arifen from temporary want of work. It may be recollected, that this cannot happen where the employment is agriculture, becaufe this occupation always requires nearly the fame number of hands all years, and is independent of any defultory call for work; which may, as all manufactures do, the demand of which is uncertain, give full employment to the poor fome years, and leave them to fubfift on the poor's rates when the demand for the manufacture ceafes ; a comparifon being made of the medium of net-expenfes of the poor, from the returns made to parliament in 1776, and the medium of 1783, 1784, and 1785, taking the total of five or fix of thofe parifhes, which may be known, by the per-fon making the comparifon, to depend principally, or entirely, on agriculture ; the increafe on the laft medium will be found to rife from thirty to above forty per cent. more than the expenfe was in 1776, a rife by no means to be accounted for on the principle of the advanced price of the neceffaries of life during this interval ; and the idea of want of work in thefe parifhes, which are thus felected, as being employed in agriculture, muft be thrown out of the cafe ; the effect then muft have arifen from fome other caufe ; a caufe, I fear, neither tending to the comfort of the poor, nor the credit of the overfeer.

That column which contains the medium of expenfes not con-cerning the poor, viz. repairing churches, roads, &c. falaries to minifters, &c. amounting to 44,231l. certainly ought not have made its appearance in this abftract, becaufe no part of the money collected by affeffments for the relief of the poor ought to have been applied to purpofes fpecifically different from thofe to which the rate is appropriated by the 43d of Elizabeth, and which pur-pofes have their different funds provided for them by other autho-rities : the church-wardens rate repairs the church ; the furveyors rate repairs the roads ; and the ecclefiaftical eftates are amply fuffi-cient for providing and paying falaries to minifters : it is, there-fore, fome matter of furprife, why the poor's rate is clogged with

X   fuch

fuch a confiderable fum, which is foreign to its proper application : in well-regulated parifhes fuch charges on the poor's rate are not admitted; and many blanks, confequently, appear againft individual parifhes under this column.

No abftract of the returns made to the fecond queftion appears, which inquires what number of poor received conftant, and what number received occafional, relief ? A queftion of, at leaft, equal importance to any of the others, as the aggregate would have been nearly, if not fully, a return of all the poor throughout England and Wales; or, at the leaft, it would have informed us of the number of thofe who have been at any time, within the three years, a burthen on the public. Why the committee did not inform themfelves of this fact, it is no eafy matter to guefs ; — poffibly, the returns were too incomplete to afford any certain information ; but, if that were the cafe, the queftion fhould have been repeated from year to year, until the returns had been accurate and full ; becaufe this fact muft be known before any radical cure can be attempted, as it leads to a certain knowledge of the extent of the difeafe.

The report from the committee, appointed to infpect and con-fider the returns made by the minifters and church-wardens, re-lative to charitable donations, for the benefit of poor perfons, in purfuance of the 58th chapter of the fame year, ftates, that it appears by a former report, made under the faid act, the 23d day of May, 1787, that, out of near thirteen thoufand parifhes, from which returns of charitable donations have been required, there were only fourteen parifhes that had made no fuch returns.

That the committee directed an abftract to be made of the re-turns ; but finding, on infpection of the abftract, that a great number of the parifhes had made defective returns ; fome by not naming the perfons who gave the charities ; others by not naming the truftees ; others by not defcribing whether the donations were in land or money; others by not defcribing the produce of the

money,

money, lands, or rent-charges, fo given; the committee directed their chairman to write circular letters to the minifters and church-wardens of all the parifhes, &c. where fuch omiffions appeared, requiring them to fend more perfect returns.

The committee then reports, that about 4065 letters had been fent, that anfwers had been received to about 3376 of them, many of which had given the explanation required; and many others had ftated that they could give no farther information.

That the committee have caufed the produce of the faid charities, in land and money, as far as they can be collected from the faid returns, to be caft up in each county; by which the annual amount of the produce of the money and land, through England and Wales, appears to be:

MONEY.

England,	£ 46,173	9	9
Wales,	2,070	0	8
	48,243	10	5

LAND.

England,	£ 206,301	8	8
Wales,	4,166	0	2
	210,467	8	10

Making together a total of £ 258,710 19 3

And that the committee had reafon to believe very confiderable farther fums will appear to have been given for the like charitable purpofes; whenever *proper means* can be found for inveftigating and completing thofe difcoveries, by extending the inquiries to corporations, companies, and focieties of men, as well as feoffees, truftees, and other perfons.

The committee alfo obferves, that, upon the face of the faid return, many of the charitable donations appear to have been loft, and many others are in danger of being loft, and that the matter

X 2

feems

feems to be of *fuch magnitude* as to call for the *ferious* and *fpeedy* attention of parliament, to amend and explain the act, by fpecify-ing, with certainty and precifion, the objects to which they may think fit to direct their inquiries, in order to procure full and fatisfactory returns, and *the eftablifhment of fuch meafures as may be effectual for the relief of the poor perfons who were the objects of the faid donations*; and for carrying the charitable purpofes of the donors into execution.

The committee appears to have been ftrongly impreffed with the idea, that much information on the fubject was intentionally with-held, and that a more minute inveftigation was neceffary to acquire a fufficient infight into this important branch of the revenue be-longing to the poor. When it is recollected, that the inquiry on this head was made with a view to the beft of purpofes, that of re-gulating the application of thefe eftates, which had, from moft diftant times, been left by charitable donors to the ufe of the poor; and that the information is required from *thofe who are the proper guardians of thefe eftates*; and the queftions are accordingly applied to the minifters of parifhes and the church-wardens; it is a matter of furprife that fuch faulty or deficient returns were made; but is it not matter of greater furprife, that the committee fhould ftand in need of more full and fatisfactory returns, in order to *eftablifh fuch meafures as may be effectual* for the relief of the objects of the faid donation, while the ftatute of charitable ufes, paffed in the 43d of Elizabeth, is the law of the land? and which was paffed with a view of fnatching thefe eftates from the hands of thofe harpies, who would *then*, as they will *now*, if they can, divert their produce from the poor into their own pockets. This ftatute paffed in the fame year as the leading ftatute which refpects the poor, and forms part of a plan, at the time in contemplation ; and a very prudent part it is, to make as productive as poffible that revenue which the poor could claim as their *right*; at the fame time as they took from the pockets of their richer fellow-citizens, what that revenue might, when

when applied according to the intention of the donors, fall fhort of fupplying their abfolute neceffities.

This ftatute empowers the chancellor or keeper of the great feal, and the chancellor of the dutchy of Lancafter, for the time being, within the dutchy of Lancafter, to award commiffions to the bifhops of every diocefe, and to other perfons of good and found behaviour, or any four or more of them, authorizing them to inquire, as well by the oaths of twelve men or more of the county, as by all other good and lawful means, of all and fingular fuch eftates, and gifts, &c. and of all abufes and breaches of truft refpecting them; an ufeful and neceffary commiffion, which, if iffued in thofe inftances where the committee fufpects information to be held back, would be equal to every good effect, and preclude all neceffity for more acts of parliament on this head, either to compel a difcovery or to enforce an application of the rents and profits of thofe eftates, to the purpofes for which they were originally granted.

LETTER XXII.

THE Hiftory of the Poor-Laws, with obfervations, is the firft publication of any confequence on this fubject, which appeared in his prefent Majefty's reign; and the fame author's name being in the title-page as in that well-known book, Burn's Juftice, the reader has reafon to expect much information on the fubject, nor will he be difappointed. Burn lays the foundation of his inquiry in remote antiquity, informing us how the poor were maintained in this country as foon as we began to enjoy the firft dawn of civilization, and proves that the ecclefiaftic revenue was fubject to the burthen as far as one-fourth of the produce at firft, and one-third afterwards. To this purpofe he quotes Kennet's Impropr.

14, 15, and fays, that the poor alfo received fome portion of their maintenance from the alms of the people and from the monafteries.

He then recites, rather fully, all the ftatutes relative to the poor, dividing them into three heads; fervants, &c. vagrants, and impotent poor.

Obfervations on the ftatutes form the fifth chapter; and here I muft exprefs my difappointment, in not receiving any information from this able writer, at what time, and by what means, the poor in particular, and the nation at large, loft their hold on that portion of the ecclefiaftic revenue, which he ftates them originally to have enjoyed. The author of Burn's Ecclefiaftical Law was affuredly able to give full information on this important fubject; and it was a necefſary part of his plan, becaufe he is obliged to lay the foundation of the compulfory maintenance, which they now partake of, *in the cuftom of begging*; a practice which, in his chapter on farther regulations, he very ftrongly deprecates, and is of opinion it fhould be utterly abolifhed: whereas, the cuftom of begging has its moft natural foundation in the want of necefſary relief; an exigency, urgent in proportion as they were deprived of their fhare of this eleemofynary revenue; which being withdrawn gradually by the ecclefiaftics, the poor were encouraged from the pulpits to beg that maintenance of the people at large, which they had been accuftomed to receive from the eftates of the church in a certain proportion, and which being exhaufted, they then might reafonably have been permitted to afk alms from the people, and not before. On this topic he is filent, and tells us, " That the minifter *was to take* all opportunities to exhort the *people* to be bountiful: — houfes were to be provided for them by the devotion of *good people*, and materials to fet them on fuch work as they were able to perform: — then the minifter, after the Gofpel, every Sunday, was fpecially to exhort the *parifhioners* to a liberal contribution: — next, the collectors for the poor, on a certain Sunday in every year, immediately after divine-fervice, were to take down, in

writing,

writing, what every perfon was willing to give weekly for the enfuing year; and, if any fhould be obftinate and refufe to give, the minifter *was gently to exhort him*; if he ftill refufed, the minifter was to certify fuch refufal to the bifhop of the diocefe, who was to fend for and exhort him in like manner; if he ftill ftood out, the bifhop was to certify the fame to the juftices in feffions, and bind him over to appear there; and the juftices, at the feffions, were again gently to move and perfuade him; and, finally, if he would not be perfuaded, then they were to affefs him what they thought reafonable towards the relief of the poor: and this brought on the affeffment in the fourteenth year of Queen Elizabeth." Such is Dr. Burn's deduction of the compulfory maintenance. Now, it is obfervable, that whatever of compulfion there might be in this duty of the minifter, who, it is ftated, *was to take all opportunities to exhort*, it did not receive its fanction from the law of the land, until the 27th year of Henry the Eighth; therefore, many centuries before that period, it was a voluntary act on the part of the ecclefiaftics, who gradually withdrew that portion of their tithes, belonging to the poor, from their ufe, as they were able, by their influence, to perfuade the parifhioners to reinftate by their alms; and hence arofe the neceffity of our prefent poor-rates.

That the poor were, during the times of popery, maintained chiefly by the religious houfes, is ftated as a vulgar error: "Their hofpitality was to the rich; they were great inns; they entertained thofe bountifully who could be bountiful to them again." With this obfervation the former part of our inquiries perfectly agrees.

Another fact this treatife ftates as remarkable, is, "That every propofal which hath been made for the reformation of the poor-law hath been tried in former ages, and found ineffectual."

The antiquity of fettlements is deduced from the more antient ftatutes, and proved not to have originated from the ftatute paffed in the reign of Charles the Second: the doctrine of removals is alfo traced from the fame fources. But thus much is clear; that, from

whatever

whatever fource the idea of them originally fprung, they are themfelves an abundant fource of expenfive litigations.

The origin and progrefs of the office of overfeer is ingenioufly
traced from the church-wardens, who were the orignal overfeers,
and ftill by ftatute-law continue fo; becaufe the management of
the poor, Dr. Burn fays, was, at firft, *folely an ecclefiaftical matter*,
" in aid of the church-wardens, collectors were appointed, and afterwards the overfeer."

Begging is traced from the firft ftatute in the 23d of Edward
the Third, " when none under the colour of pity and alms were to
give any thing to fuch as might labour, under pain of imprifonment;" to the laft act of parliament in the 17th of George the Second, which makes it the firft ftep towards vagrancy, " perfons
begging within their own parifh, being deemed idle and diforderly
perfons, and to be fent to the houfe of correction."

Badging of the poor, which is directed by the 8th and 9th of
William the Third, is fuppofed to have fprung from the military
inftitution, when the nobility diftinguifhed their followers with
peculiar enfigns.

What obfervations there are in Burn's tract, refpecting the
vagrant-laws, relate chiefly to their extreme feverity; it is a matter
of felf-gratulation to the writer of thefe pages, that, in a former
part of them, he fhould have fallen into a train of fimilar fentiments on this head. Rating the wages of fervants by ftatute has
alfo fallen under our confideration; no additional information is to
be found in his obfervations on thefe ftatutes, except the affertion,
that, by the experience of four hundred years, it appears, that the
regulating the prices of work leaves no room for induftry and ingenuity; " for, if all perfons, in the fame kind of work, were to receive equal wages, there would be no emulation."

The clothing of the poor, in antient times, is difcuffed; and,
from the argument, it appears, that the ftatutable clothing, in the
reign of Edward the Third, for handicrafts and yeomen, was not to
exceed

exceed 4*s.* 6*d.* a yard, or thereabout, eſtimating by the money of the preſent times; for which price a ſtrong and warm clothing might ſtill be purchaſed.

This tract then gives an account of the different ſchemes for reforming the poor-laws, and goes at ſome length into Lord Hales's, Sir Joſiah Child's, Mr. Cary's, Mr. Hay's, Mr. Alcock's, Anonymous, Lord Hilſborough's, Sir Richard Lloyd's, Mr. Fielding's, and Mr. Cooper's, plan; all which have been already explained in the former pages of our ſtrictures on this ſubject. We then come to the ſeventh chapter, in which the author propoſes farther regulations:

" Thus," he ſaith, " hath the wiſdom of the nation in parliament, and of individuals, been employed in providing properly for the poor; and yet they are not properly provided for." The fact is true; but it ought not to induce an opinion, that it is impoſſible to meliorate their ſituation and lighten our burthens.

Two particulars, he ſays, ſhould be rectified, until time and experience ſuggeſt farther alteration: firſt, to prevent the nuiſance of common begging:—the means he propoſes are, give them nothing: " if none were to give, none would beg, and the whole myſtery and craft would end in a fortnight:" and, in order to bring this about, he would have all who relieve a common beggar be ſubject to a penalty. Surely the principles of liberty, policy, and humanity, all equally militate againſt ſuch a regulation; experience alſo has proved its inſufficiency for the purpoſe: in times of ignorance the experiment was made, and found ineffectual. By the 23d of Edward the Third, none was permitted, under colour of alms, to give any thing to ſuch which may labour, under the pain of impriſonment. This ſtatute was repealed by Edward the Sixth.

The other fundamental defect is, according to this writer, in leaving the whole management to thoſe annual officers, called overſeers of the poor; and the practical duty of ſuch an officer is ironically pointed out with ſome humour: " He is to keep an extraor-

Y   dinary

dinary look out, to prevent perfons coming to inhabit without certificates, and to fly to the juftices to remove them ; and, if a man
brings a certificate, then to caution all the inhabitants not to let
him a farm of 10l. a year, and to take care to keep him out of all
parifh-offices; to warn them, if they will hire fervants, to hire
them half-yearly, or by the month, by the week, or by the day;
rather than by any way which fhall give them a fettlement; or, if
they do hire them by the year, then to pick a quarrel with them
before the year's end, and fo to get rid of them : to maintain the
poor as cheap as poffible they can at all events; not to lay out
two-pence in profpect of any future good, but only to ferve the
prefent neceffity ; to bargain with fome fturdy perfon to take them
by the lump, who yet is not intended to *take* them, but to hang
over them *in terrorem*; if they fhall complain to the juftices for
want of maintenance, to fend them into the country a begging ; to
bind out poor children apprentices, no matter to whom or to what
trade, only take care that the mafter lives in another parifh; to
move heaven and earth if any difpute happens about a fettlement,
and in that particular to invert the general rule, and ftick at no
expenfe; to pull down cottages, to drive out as many inhabitants
and admit as few as poffibly they can ;" with many other ironical
directions, reminding the reader of Swift's Advice to Servants; by
which it is apparent, that this our great luminary in the duty of
magiftrates knew well that the office of an overfeer was fometimes
neglected, fometimes perverted, and but feldom properly executed.

He, therefore, is of opinion, that the office fhould not be entirely
abolifhed, but that a general fuperintendant over a certain number
of parifhes, as the juftices in feffions fhall find moft convenient,
fhould be appointed ; and that the overfeer fhould collect the
rate, and it fhould be applied under the direction of the fuperintendant, whofe bufinefs he more particularly points out.

To affift this purpofe, he recommends monthly feffions to the
juftices, at which the church-wardens, overfeers, and fuperintendant,

dant, fhould attend, give in their report, and receive farther orders: and thofe who think themfelves aggrieved at thefe diftrict-feffions fhould have a right of appeal to the quarter-feffions.

To infure attendance, he propofes that the juftices fhould be allowed half-a-guinea a day out of the county-ftock; and fays, that thefe monthly feffions might alfo be ufeful to carry into execution the acts of parliament, refpecting the highways, then in force, together with that variety of bufinefs, which is now the employment of juftices at their common meetings or fpecial feffions.

A curious inftance is mentioned from a book of " the Police of France," written about 1753, which proves, that at the fame time the French were anxious that their police, refpecting the poor, fhould be put on the fame footing as our Englifh poor-laws, feveral propofals were publifhed in London, recommending fuch a method of maintaining our poor as was then practifed in France ; viz. by general hofpitals in provincial towns ; exemplifying, in a very ftrong light, the truth of Horace's maxim,

———— Laudet diverfa fequentes.

The French mode, he very properly obferves, will annihilate all family-connections, and will create a *populus virorum* and a *populus mulierum*, which, at the fame time that it leffens the number of the poor, will tend to depopulate a kingdom.

A county, inftead of a parifh, fettlement, provided the poor could be maintained on a county-plan, he thinks might be advifeable; but that the idea of fettlement fhould not be abolifhed, " only reftrained, to the place of birth, or of inhabitancy for one or more years, and that fuch a reftriction would tend to abolifh certificates, by deftroying the caufe of requiring, granting, or denying, them." How this would be effected by reftraining fettlements to the place of birth or inhabitancy, for one or more years, I confefs myfelf not able to fee; that the number of law-fuits, to afcertain the

Y 2   fettlement,

fettlement, might be diminifhed, is plain, but that certificates, to authorize the pauper to live elfewhere, would be as neceffary as at prefent, is alfo equally obvious.

A reduction of all the poor-laws into one is recommended ; as is alfo a reduction of the highway-laws into one. The laft alteration has been effected by the 13th of the prefent king, chap. 58, and has undoubtedly much fimplified their ufe and operation, and rendered them, in moft inftances, a practicable and ufeful code : — equally good effects would arife from a fimplification of the poor-laws. A code of acts of the legiflature, militating in fome inftances with each other, whofe feveral dependencies and connections are not eafy to be difcovered by a fuperficial obferver or temporary officer, who muft pick his duty out of the Statutes at Large, forms no bad apology for ignorance ; and ignorance, at the fame time that it excufes neglect, becomes alfo a cloak to interefted miftakes.

Thefe are the chief notices which the author of the Hiftory of the Poor-Laws has made on the fubject ; there are fome other obfervations on the defects of the law, under the adminiftration of juftices of the peace, which do not immediately relate to the poor, and, therefore, may very properly be paffed over, more efpecially, as it is apparent from the fmall fale of the book, although fanctioned by his well-known name, that it is by no means a fubject which has excited much attention, or is generally ftudied, although it very intimately concerns all claffes of people.

In 1764, a pamphlet, publifhed by Becket, Obfervations on the Number of the Poor, and on the heavy Rates levied for their Benefit, ftarts an idea on the fubject, that, whether true or not, proves fome theoretic principles in the fecond part of Paine's Rights of Man to have no claim to originality.

But this writer fo entirely lofes the avowed purpofe of his pamphlet in the title-page ; fo neglects the interefts of the *real* poor, in attending to the political confequences refulting from the number

ber of *genteel* poor, that it is futile to follow him in a fubject which opens a field of argument vaftly too extenfive for this publication, foreign to its intention, and mifchievous in its difcuffion.

LETTER XXIII.

IN 1767, the Farmer's Letters to the People of England appeared, which, among a variety of topics treated with much fpirit and ftrength of argument, afford a few ftrictures on the poor, and the laws refpecting them : the prevailing ideas fhall be fhortly mentioned, although the propriety and juftnefs of them cannot be fully admitted.

The author confiders the poor-laws of England as univerfally encouragers of idlenefs, drunkennefs, and tea-drinking : he wifhes for a total abolition of them, and for a new code, on the principle that thofe only fhould be maintained at the public expenfe who cannot maintain themfelves, and that fuch maintenance fhould be in hundred-houfes of induftry.

Is it not the principle of the exifting code that thofe only who cannot maintain themfelves fhould be maintained at the public expenfe ? And, if the parifhes agree in thinking them advifeable, may not hundred-houfes of induftry be now the means ? Why then abolifh the old laws to make new ones on the fame principle ? Would a man of fenfe pull down a family-manfion, in good repair, to build a new one on the fame principle ? Surely not.

A prevailing idea in this publication feems to be, that the poor fhould have no certainty of provifion except from their own induftry. But is not fuch the theoretic principle of the exifting poor-laws, as far as is confiftent with humanity ? If practice has departed ed from the principle, blame the execution of the laws, and not the principle.

Dr. Price's Obfervations on Reverfionary Payments, Annuities, &c. were publifhed in 1772. The principle of fome of thofe ufeful focieties called box-clubs originated from a plan intended for the benefit of the labouring-poor in this very excellent publication. The following is the calculation alluded to :

" Let the fociety, at its firft inftitution, confift of a hundred per-fons, all between the age of thirty and forty, whofe mean age may, therefore, be reckoned at thirty-fix ; and let it be fuppofed to be al-ways kept up to this number by the admiffion of new members, be-tween the ages of thirty and forty, as old ones die off: let the con-tribution of each member be 4d. a week, making, from the whole body, an annual contribution of 85l. 17s.: let it be fuppofed that feven of them will fall every year into diforders that fhall incapaci-tate them for feven weeks ; 30l. 12s. of the annual contribution will be juft fufficient to enable the fociety to grant to each of them 12s. a week during their illnefs, and the remaining 55l. per annum laid out, and carefully improved, at the rate of three and a half per cent. will increafe to a capital that fhall be fufficient, according to the chances of life in the tables three, four, five, to enable the fo-ciety to pay to every member, after attaining to fixty-feven years of age, or upon his entering into his fixty-eighth year, an annuity, beginning with 5l. and increafing, at the rate of 1l. every year, for feven years, until, at the age of feventy-five, it will be a ftand-ing annuity of 12l. for the remainder of life. Were fuch a fociety to make its contribution 7d. a week, an allowance of 15s. might be made, on the fame fuppofition, to every member during ficknefs, befides the payment of an annuity, beginning with 5l. when a member entered his fixty-fourth year, and increafing for fifteen years, until, at feventy-nine, it became fixed for the remainder of his life at 20l."

If

If fociety has a right to expect from its conftituent parts every exertion in their power to maintain themfelves, before any individual has a claim for any part of their maintenance on fociety in the aggregate, an univerfal plan, obliging thofe members, who have nothing to fubfift on but their labour, to lay up a fmall part of its produce, while in health, againft the day of ficknefs and want, would be no unjuft obligation, but would, on the contrary, be founded on a ftrictly equitable principle; and, if the foregoing calculation is right, it would be no inconfiderable affiftance in ficknefs, and through the declining years of age: befides, the plan is eafy of execution, and is at prefent, in many places through the kingdom, executed voluntarily by the poor, being encouraged by the fubfcription of men of fubftance; and very good effects arife from it, not only in relief of the poor fubfcribers themfelves, and in relief of the poor's rates, but alfo in the prefervation of good order among the lower claffes of fociety, who, having men of principle for their charitable fubfcribers, truftees, and directors, are lefs likely to be incited to infurrections and difturbances than thofe who, having no communication with any claffes of men fuperior to themfelves, are eafily led on to thofe riotous proceedings which are a fcandal to good government.

Mr. Hanway, in his ftrictures on the caufes of diffolutenefs which prevail among the lower claffes of people, laments that the number of country-gentlemen is fo much reduced that they can no longer form a body of referve to defend the caufe of virtue, or furnifh the means of its defence. He afks, what is the fituation of a free- people, when a gentleman of education, of five hundred or one thoufand a year, who fhould be one of their chief guardians, brings himfelf and family into an expenfe which requires three times his income? He who might be a fovereign in his own demefne, and look down on what the world calls greatnefs, is now loft in the mafs of fplendid vanity, and bewildered in trifles.

With

With reafon might this worthy philanthropift make the foregoing remark. From this caufe no inconfiderable degree of the
diffolutenefs which prevails in the country arifes. Good examples
are of great force, and fuch the country ftands in need of. Were
the examples which the clergy fet in private life equally moral as
their exhortations to their parifhioners from the pulpit, even in that
cafe the inftances of moral conduct among that clafs of fociety, to
which the labourer looks up with refpect, would not be fufficient :
they want ftronger incitements, and a greater number of refpectable
examples ; their immediate pay-mafters and employers are not fufficiently raifed above them, and too much mix with them in concerns of intereft, to be refpected as patrons; it is the hofpitable
country-gentleman, the refpected magiftrate, who underftands, and
is attentive to, their real interefts, that are wanted, as conftant
houfe-keepers, in the country : but the prefence of fuch at their
country-refidences cannot be commanded, and will not be voluntarily accorded, unlefs our huge overgrown metropolis, refembling
the poet's greatnefs, void of wifdom, fhould meet with the fame
fate, and

Fall by its own weight.

In the fame year as the two laft publications which have been
noticed made their appearance, there came alfo from the prefs an
anonymous treatife, called, A View of real Grievances, &c. in
which are a few juft and pointed remarks, founded on truth and
actual obfervation. " Many fmall country-villages can date the
commencement of poor-rates from the introduction of public-
houfes, which corrupt the morals, impair the health, impoverifh
and reduce the poor to the greateft penury and diftrefs." But the
expenfes of government are fo enormous, that the excife is too confiderable an object not to be encouraged at all events, and no tax
that fwells it will be taken off, to fave the lower clafs of people
from deftruction. This writer is alfo of opinion, that the laws

relative

relative to parifh-fettlements are a very confiderable caufe of the increafe of the poor-rates.

Mr. Kent, in his Hints to Gentlemen of Landed Property, is of
opinion, that the great increafe in the poor-rates arifes from the
rife in the value of the produce of land, which, he fays, is full
fixty per cent. and that the rife in the price of labour is not above
twenty. Another caufe is, the difadvantage the poor labour under
in carrying their penny to market : formerly they could buy their
butter and cheefe of the farmer; now they are driven to the fhop-
keeper: they could formerly have their wheat ground; they are
now driven to the miller and baker. The remedy he propofes is,
that gentlemen of fortune take on themfelves the fuperintendence
of country-bufinefs : let them act as guardians for the poor, reduce
the fize of farms, increafe the price of labour, and the induftrious
poor will find a fupport by fuch encouragement : but he profeffes
he knows no law which can force people to be induftrious.

This affertion of Mr. Kent's, refpecting the advanced price of
the produce of the land, compared with the advance of wages, demands proof before it ought to be reafoned from as a principle;
and at prefent it ftands a mere *gratis dictum*, as advanced by him.
Adam Smith goes more minutely into the queftion, which requires
a decided judgement before confequences are deduced from it.
The difadvantages the poor lie under in going with their penny
to market are great; but it is much to be doubted whether, at any
time, they could buy the produce of land immediately of the farmer, unlefs from their mafter: the quantity wanted by each individual is too fmall, to fuppofe that the farmer could allow that
lofs of time which would be neceffary to deal to each one his
trifling dole ; and, if they lay in a ftock, wafte will make a greater
confumption in their earnings than the advanced price of the fhop-
keeper.

The firft edition of An Inquiry into the Nature and Caufes
of the Wealth of Nations appeared about this time; a book uni-

Z   verfally

verfally commended for the folidity of its principle, the clearnefs
and accuracy of reafoning it contains, and the fair inveftigation of
the fubject which the learned author treats of. Some opinions
which refpect the poor, in this treatife, may, therefore, with propriety, be taken as fo many aphorifms, and quoted as fuch,, leaving
the reader to trace the deductions this great writer has made in
his own volumes, if he doubts the principles of his judgement.
As the axioms, on the fubject of the poor, which can be collected from thefe volumes, are fcattered throughout the whole
work, they fhall be inferted, as they occur, in turning over the
pages of Adam Smith's moft luminous tract on the Wealth of
Nations.

" A man muft always live by his work, and his wages, muft
be, at leaft, fufficient to maintain him ; they muft even, upon
moft occafions, be fomething more, otherwife it would be impoffible for him to bring up a family, and the race of fuch
workmen would not laft beyond the firft generation."   B. i. c. 8.

" In Great Britain the wages of labour feem to be evidently
more than what is precifely neceffary to bring up a family."
B. i. c. 8.

" Lord-Chief-Juftice Hale, who wrote in the time of Charles the
Second, computes the neceffary expenfe of a labourer's family, confifting of fix perfons, (the father and mother, two children able to
do fomething, and two not able,) at ten fhillings a week, or twenty-fix pounds a year."   B. i. c. 8.

" In 1668, Mr. Gregory King, whofe fkill in political arith-
metic is fo much extolled by Dr. Davenant, computed the ordinary income of labourers and out-fervants to be fifteen pounds
a year to a family, which he fuppofed to confift, one with another, of three and a half perfons : both fuppofe the weekly
expenfe of fuch families to be about twenty-pence a head."
B. i. c. 8.

" The

" The real recompenfe of labour, the real quantity of the neceffaries and conveniencies of life, which it can procure to the labourer, has, during the courfe of the prefent century, increafed,
perhaps, in a ftill greater proportion than its money-price." The
foregoing maxims, with refpect to the wages of labour, are ad-
mirably elucidated in chapter the 8th, book the 1ft, of this excellent work.

" Since the time of Henry the Eighth, the wealth and revenue of
the country have been continually advancing ; and, in the courfe of
their progrefs, their pace feems rather to have been gradually acce-
lerated than retarded. The wages of labour have been continually
increafing during the fame period ; and, in the greater part of the
different branches of trade and manufactures, the profits of ftock
have been diminifhing." B. i. c. 9.

" A little grocer will make forty or fifty per cent. upon a ftock
of a fingle hundred pounds, while a confiderable merchant, in the
fame place, will fcarce make eight or ten per cent. on a ftock of ten
thoufand. The greater part of the apparent profit on a little ftock
is wages." B. i. c. 10.*

" The produce of labour, which arifes from the leifure particular
employments allow of, comes frequently cheaper to market than
would otherwife be fuitable to its nature." B. i. c. 10.

" The property which every man has in his own labour, as it is
the original foundation of all other property, fo it is the moft facred
and inviolable." B. i. c. 10.

" In Great Britain, the wages of country-labour approach nearer
to thofe of manufacturing-labour, than they are faid to have done
in the laft century, or in the beginning of the prefent." B. i. c. 10.

" The very unequal price of labour which we frequently find in
England, in places at no great diftance from one another, is pro-

* By this is meant, payment to the little grocer for lofs of time in retailing his commodities in fmall quantities.

bably

bably owing to the obftruction which the law of fetlements gives to a poor man, who would carry his induftry from one parifh to another, without a certificate."   B. i. c. 10.

" To remove a man who has committed no mifdemeanor from the parifh where he choofes to refide, is an evident violation of natural liberty and juftice. The common people of England, however, fo jealous of their liberty, but, like the common people of other countries, never rightly underftand in what it confifts, have now, for more than a century, fuffered themfelves to be expofed to this oppreffion, without a remedy. Though men of reflection alfo have fometimes complained of the law of fettlements, as a public grievance, yet it has never been the object of any general popular clamour, fuch as that againft general warrants; an abufive practice, undoubtedly, but fuch an one as was not likely to occafion any general oppreffion."   B. i. c. 10.

" The obftruction, which corporation-laws give to the free circulation of labour, is common to every part of Europe. That, which is given to it by the poor-laws, is, fo far as I know, peculiar to England; it confifts in the difficulty in which a poor man finds in obtaining a fettlement, or even in being allowed to exercife his induftry in any parifh but that to which he belongs." B. i. c. 10.

" The complaint of workmen, that rating of wages by act of parliament puts the ableft and moft induftrious upon the fame footing with an ordinary workman, feems perfectly well-founded." B. i. c. 10.

" The money-price of coarfe cloth in the fifteenth century, compared with the money-price at prefent, cloth is cheaper now than formerly, and probably much better."   B. i. c. 11.

" The fame comparifon is made with refpect to ftockings, and to the fame effect: — a pair of ftockings for a poor fervant did then coft as much as a bufhel and a half of wheat." B. i. c. 11.

" Neither

" Neither wind nor water mills of any kind were known in England fo early as the beginning of the fixteenth century." B. 1. c. 11.

This affertion cannot be intended to extend to corn-mills; and yet, by the wording of the fentence, it extends to wind and water mills of all kinds; it fhould, therefore, be qualified in a future edition : water-mills moft certainly were in ufe before the conqueft, although the firft inftance of the writ *fecta ad molendinum* appears, by Fitzherbert's *Natura Brevium*, to have iffued in the 29th of Edward the Third.

" All thofe improvements in the productive powers of labour, which tend directly to reduce the real price of manufactures, tend indirectly to raife the real rent of land." B. i. c. 11.

" The whole annual produce of the land and labour of a country, or, what comes to the fame thing, the whole price of that annual produce, naturally divides itfelf into three parts, the rent of land, the wages of labour, and the profits of ftock, and conftitutes a revenue to three different orders of people; to thofe who live by rent, to thofe who live by wages, and to thofe who live by profit." B. i. c. 11.

" The intereft of thofe who live by wages is as ftrictly connected with the intereft of the fociety as thofe who live by rent." B. i. c. 11.

" The wages of the labourer are never fo high as when the demand for labour is continually rifing, or when the quantity employed is every year increafing confiderably; when this real wealth of the fociety becomes ftationary, his wages are foon reduced to what is barely enough to enable him to bring up a family, or to continue the race of labourers; when the fociety declines, they fall even below this." B. i. conclufion of c. 1.1.

" The proportion between the price of provifions in Scotland and England is the fame now as before the great multiplication of banking-companies in Scotland; and corn is, upon moft occafions,

full

full as cheap in England as in France, although there is a great deal of paper-money in England, and fcarce any in France." B. ii. c. 2.

" It is not the number of ale-houfes which occafions a general difpofition to drunkennefs among the common people; but that difpofition, arifing from other caufes, neceffarily gives employment to a number of ale-houfes." B. ii. c. 5.

" The money-price of corn regulates that of all other home-made commodities ; it regulates the money-price of labour, which muft always be fuch as to enable the labourer to purchafe a quantity of corn fufficient to maintain him and his family, either in the liberal, moderate, or fcanty, manner, in which the advancing, ftationary, or declining, circumftances of the fociety oblige his employers to maintain him." B. iv. c. 5.

" The real value of every other commodity is finally meafured and determined by the proportion which its average money-price bears to the average money-price of corn." B. 4. c. 5.

" A tax on the neceffaries of life operates exactly as a direct tax on the wages of labour." B. v. c. 2.

" But it is different with taxes on luxuries, even on thofe of the poor; although thefe might fomewhat increafe the diftrefs of diforderly families, and thereby diminifh fomewhat of their ability to bring up children, they would not, probably, diminifh much the population of the country." B. v. c. 2.

" Under neceffaries, the author comprehends not only thofe things which nature, but thofe alfo which the eftablifhed rules of decency, have made neceffary to the poor ; as linen, foap, leather fhoes, in England: all other things he calls luxuries, without meaning to throw the fmalleft reproach on the temperate ufe of them, fuch as beer, ale, tobacco, tea, fugar, fpirituous liquors." B. v. c. 2.

LETTER

FROM the date of thefe laft-mentioned publications, no other tract of any notice appeared, until Mr. Gilbert's exertions in the Houfe of Commons again roufed the public attention to this important object. The fchedule of inquiries tranfmitted by the Houfe to all the magiftrates, the clergy, church-wardens, and overfeers of the poor, throughout England and Wales, compelled a fcrutiny into that fubject; which, having been the concern of every one, had become the care of no one. The refult of the inquiry alarmed the public, and their minds were agitated on two very important confiderations : the firft was, the extent of the evil; a fact eftablifhed by the returns required by the legiflature to the queftions afked; it appearing, that a fum exceeding two millions was expended annually for the relief of the poor; and that this fum had increafed by hafty ftrides, being an excefs of nearly one-third of the total expended on the fame account eight years before. The other point, on which the public attention refted, was the plan propofed by Mr. Gilbert to remedy this alarming evil. Several publications appeared on this topic, which, in general, condemned the means propofed, allowing, at the fame time, every merit of good intention to the propofer. Thofe tracts which paffed the prefs, for the purpofe only of criticifing Mr. Gilbert's plan, may be paffed over in filence, unlefs they elucidate fome principle on the fubject of the laws or management of the poor. But, before thefe publications are noticed, it may be proper to give a fummary abftract of the bill which Mr. Gilbert offered to the legiflature of his country, to be paffed into a law, and which he introduced to the attention of the public by a pertinent and fenfible pamphlet, well calculated to explain the evils he

wifhed

wifhed principally to regulate, and the means by which he intended to correct them.

The bill, by its preamble, ftated the fact that gives rife to the regulations propofed : " That the rates and affeffments for the employment and relief of the poor have, for many years, been greatly increafing ; notwithftanding which, many fick and impotent perfons are left to perifh, or endure great neceffities, for want of timely and effectual affiftance ; and others, who are healthy and able to work, are not properly employed, but are permitted to contract habits of idlenefs, and at length to become vagrants and thieves."

It then proceeds to ftate the remedy, intended to be paffed into a law by the legiflature, viz. the uniting and incorporating feveral parifhes, for the purpofe of maintaining and employing their poor, upon one common fund, under the direction and fuperintendence of gentlemen of character and fortune, refiding in or near fuch parifhes, and employing permanent and able officers and agents for the purpofe.

This method the preamble ftates to have been found, by experience, better to anfwer the purpofe than any other mode.*

The enacting-claufes contain the means propofed to carry this fyftem into execution. The following are the heads of thofe claufes very briefly ftated :

Juftices at quarter-feffions to appoint a day for choofing commiffioners, who are to take an oath prefcribed, and choofe a chairman, and appoint a clerk and two agents, and receive information on oath from high-conftables, church-wardens, overfeers, &c. and fhall unite the parifhes into diftinct diftricts, not exceeding thirteen parifhes in a diftrict, nor lefs than three ; but their powers

---

* The *experience* alluded to, moft probably, was collected from the inftances of the incorporated houfes of induftry in Suffolk, Norfolk, and elfewhere, throughout the kingdom.

fhall

fhall not extend into any diftrict whofe poor are provided for under any fpecial act of parliament.

Thefe commiffioners fhall appoint not more than forty, nor lefs than twenty, committee-men in each diftrict; .fhall limit their qualification by eftate; and fhall fix the falary to be paid to the diftrict-agent; and the committee-men fhall be chofen by fuch as are qualified in a manner required by the commiffioners, who fhall alfo make a report of what they have done, in this refpect, to the juftices of the peace of their refpective'counties; and fhall deliver fuch reports to the clerk of the peace, which fhall be printed, and a copy fent to every acting-juftice of the peace, and to every high-conftable; and the magiftrates, at their quarter-feffions, fhall pay, out of the county-money, the commiffioners their reafonable expenfes.

If two-thirds of the perfons, qualified to be diftrict-committee-men, are of opinion to adopt the provifions of the act for incorporating the diftrict, that diftrict fhall then be declared incorporated, and fhall proceed to ballot for a committee, and elect overfeers.

The overfeers are to return, on oath, the names of fuch as are qualified to be balloted for as committee-men. The mode of balloting is defcribed, and fubjected to certain regulations. The committee-men, when elected, are to take an oath to execute the truft repofed in them impartially.

When the major part of the diftricts have adopted the provifions of the act, it fhall be declared eftablifhed throughout the whole county or riding.

The diftrict-committee-men are empowered to appoint a diftrict-agent: they are to forfeit for non-attendance; and each diftrict is to be a corporation.

All the clergy are qualified to be chofen committee-men for the diftrict in which they do duty, for the time being, although not poffeffed of the qualification by eftate.

A a

New

New committee-men to be elected every year.

Parifhes are to choofe three overfeers, in the manner prefcribed by the bill, from whom the committee are to fix on one, who is to be allowed a falary ; and, from the time of the appointment of fuch new overfeers, the duty of the old ones is to ceafe.

The duty of the new overfeers is to inquire into the condition of the work-houfes, and of the poor, within their refpective parifhes; and to make a report thereof to the diftrict-agent, and alfo of all alterations that may happen in any particular ; and to obey the orders and commands of the diftrict-agent or the diftrict-committee.

The diftrict-agent is to lay fuch reports before the diftrict-committee ; and to inform himfelf of all particulars with refpect to the condition of the poor, as to their maintenance, employment, &c. which he fhall alfo report to the diftrict-committee at every meeting.

The property of all work-houfes fhall be vefted in the diftrict-committee, with all the furniture, ftock, and inftruments of trade, which have been bought and fupported by the poor's rates and affeffments:—which work-houfes, &c. they may fell and difpofe of, and the money arifing from the fale to be applied in aid of the poor's rates.

And the diftrict-committee are empowered to erect houfes of induftry where they cannot purchafe or hire convenient buildings for that purpofe ; and alfo to purchafe or hire land, and to contract for wafte or common grounds, with the confent of the lord of the manor.

The diftrict-committee to become additional truftees of any fums of money, left in truft, to be laid out in the purchafe of lands for any infants, lunatics, idiots, &c. in cafe the fame fhall exceed the fum of 20l. until fuch fums of money are laid out in the purchafe of lands ; and the money, in the mean time, fhall be laid out in the public funds, in the names of two or more per-

fons,

fons, one to be named by the perfons interefted, and the other by the diftrict-committee, or any ten of them; and the intereft, in the mean time, to be applied to the ufe of the perfons interefted.

As foon as the houfe of induftry fhall be fitted up, and furnifhed, for the reception of the poor, in the manner directed by the act, no poor perfon is to receive any pay, penfion, or relief, except in cafes of violent ficknefs or fudden accidents.

Where, by the laws now in force, magiftrates are empowered to proceed, on the complaint of the overfeers of the poor, with refpect to any baftard-child, they are then to proceed on the complaint of the diftrict-committee.

The diftrict-committee is empowered to apply what fums of money they may occafionally think proper towards paying the weekly contributions of fuch of the poor as are engaged in clubs and friendly focieties, for eftablifhing funds, by weekly contributions, to their relief and fupport when difabled by ficknefs or accidents, and alfo for the purpofe of paying teachers, and providing books, for the inftruction of children at Sunday-fchools. The diftrict-committee is alfo required to provide a fchool for the education of poor children.

Every diftrict-agent fhall, with the affiftance of the clerk of the diftrict, keep, in a book, an exact account of all expenfes attending building, furnifhing, and providing ftores and utenfils for the houfe of induftry, and of the maintenance of the people refiding therein, and of all other expenfes refpecting the poor, and fhall lay a ftate of fuch expenfes every month before the committee; and fhall, in order to fix a proper meafure of diftribution from the parifhes within the diftrict, procure an account of the medium-expenfes of the poor of every parifh, within the years 1783, 1784, and 1785, for which returns have been made to parliament, and lay the fame before the committee, who are to infpect and examine fuch returns, and make them as perfect as poffible : and, to that

purpofe, they fhall be empowered to fummon before them fuch
perfons as have been parifh-officers for thofe years, and all other
perfons who can give them information on the fubject, who are to
attend, and anfwer all queftions relative to the fubject, on oath,
under pain of commitment for non-attendance, and of indictment
for perjury if they fpeak falfely.

After the provifions of the act are adopted within any diftrict, the
fums to be annually raifed for the relief and maintenance of the
poor fhall not, in any parifh, exceed the annual fum fo raifed
therein upon the medium of the faid three years. The diftrict-
agent fhall alfo, at the end of every quarter of a year, a week at
leaft before the meeting of the next monthly committee, make an
accurate account of the expenditure within the faid quarter, and
lay it before the faid committee, that they may be enabled to make
an order for the levying the poor's rates; and the diftrict-agent
fhall alfo fettle the quota of each parifh, and lay the fame before
the committee for their allowance, which fhall be notified to the
overfeers of the parifh, who are to affefs and collect the fame, and
pay it to the diftrict-agent.

And, to raife money for buildings, &c. the committee may borrow a fum not exceeding four years poor-rates, and affign over the
buildings, &c. and all or any part of the poor-rates, as fecurity for
the principal borrowed and intereft.

No fees or perquifites fhall be received for any bufinefs done, by
virtue of this act, by any agent, overfeer, clerk, or others. The
appeal to the poor's rates to be to the quarter-feffions.

If any diftrict-agent, or overfeer, on requifition from the diftrict-
committee to come to account, fhall refufe fo to do, he fhall be
committed to the common gaol for a fpace not exceeding fix calendar-months, or until he complies. All penalties inflicted by the
act fhall be recoverable before one juftice of the peace.

Thefe are the heads of all the material claufes in Mr. Gilbert's
bill; there are fome others which relate to the interior regulation

of

of the houfes of induftry, and alfo two fchedules of the rules, orders, by-laws, and regulations, which are referred to by the act; but the whole plan itfelf, a plan of that magnitude, as to involve in it confequences, immediately affecting the liberty and comforts of not lefs than fix millions of our fellow-fubjects, and a confiderable part of the property of the remainder of our countrymen, was overturned, on a motion for the fecond reading of the bill, by a divifion of the Houfe of Commons, of thirty-four members who were againft the bill, to ten who were for it; only forty-four members being prefent.

Mr. Acland's plan, for rendering the poor independent on public contribution, ftands next in order of time, having made its appearance in 1786.

The mode, after Mr. Gilbert's bill failed, he offers to fecure that independence to the poor, which, he profeffes to hold out to them, is the eftablifhment, throughout that part of the kingdom fubject to the poor-laws, of a general fociety, on the principle of the box-clubs; by which the members become entitled to a certain weekly falary, during ficknefs or incapacity to work, through accident or old age, on the payment of a certain fum of money weekly.

Another part of the plan he offers, is to fecure to the poor their natural right of earning their bread where they are beft able to do it, by abrogating the laws refpecting fettlements.

The only obfervation I fhall at prefent venture on this fubject is, that box-clubs have been in many places voluntarily inftituted by the poor themfelves; and experience has proved fuch inftitutions beneficial; and that what has in many places been done voluntarily might, without injuftice, become obligatory to all; more efpecially if fuch obligation was counter-balanced by their recovering the liberty they have by nature, and which ought not to be taken from them by the laws of fociety, — of getting their bread where they beft are able.

An

An anonymous pamphlet, introducing a sketch of a bill for the relief and employment of the poor, appeared the same year Mr. Gilbert's introductory plan was published.

The writer reduces the complaints to two heads ; first, the great misapplication of the parish-money ; secondly, the general neglect of the parish-officers in employing the poor. He also affirms, that an increase of the impotent poor, beyond a certain proportion, is an impossibility, except in case of a pestilential disease : therefore he is of opinion, that the increase of the poor, which is so much talked of, is mere sound, and signifies nothing. He also says, that the only proper objects of charity among the poor are those who would work, but are not able.

The act he proposes is revisionary of the forty-third statute of Elizabeth ; the spirit of which is to be the main object of the act proposed ; and only such of the regulations in the other statutes are to be adopted as have a manifest tendency to the same principles ; but the act he proposes is, at the same time, undoubtedly *visionary*, for it is to *execute itself*; that is, it must leave nothing to the discretion of those who are empowered to execute it.

Thoughts on the Cause of the Increase of the Poor, 1787. This pamphlet asserts, that the increasing burthen of the poor's rate arises from the absorption of smaller farms in greater, and by depriving the poor labourer of a portion of land round his cottage. Whether such an effect could arise from such causes, if they *universally* took place, shall not now be agitated, because it is apprehended the facts are by no means *general*; but the increment of the poor's rate is *universal*; and as considerable in those parishes where the smaller farms have *not* been absorbed by the greater, and where the cottager has *not* been deprived of his *garden*, as where these circumstances *have* taken place.

Mr. Godschall, in his general plan of parochial and provincial police, complains, and with much reason, of the negligent execution of the poor-laws, and with great truth and propriety inveighs
against

againſt the ſwarm of ale-houſes that infeſt all our towns, and deprave and impoveriſh the labouring poor. This pamphlet was publiſhed in 1787.

The Rev. Joſeph Townſend, of Pewſey, in Wiltſhire, tells us that the poor-laws, ſo beautiful in theory, promote the evils they mean to remedy, and aggravate the diſtreſs they were meant to relieve.

" They are not only unjuſt, oppreſſive, and impolitic, but proceed on principles which border on abſurdity; becauſe they ſay, that in England no man, even by his indolence, improvidence, prodigality, and vice, ſhall ſuffer want."

He ſays alſo, that the diſtreſs of the poor does not ariſe from the high price of corn, ſoap, leather, candles, ſalt, &c, as will appear from the high price of labour, which has advanced in the proportion of ſix to four within a century; and, for this aſſertion, refers to Sir William Petty.

That, under the preſent ſyſtem, the maſter muſt either connive at the neglects of his ſervants, or maintain them without work; that the laws diſcourage improvements in agriculture; waſte-lands would otherwiſe be tilled, as they are exempted from the claims of the church ſeven years, but not from the demands of the poor; that a fixed and certain proviſion for the poor weakens the ſpring of induſtry.

The law of ſettlements has reſtrained the poor to their own pariſhes, where they are regarded with an evil eye, and has prevented them going elſewhere, where they would be received with joy; pariſh-workhouſes diſarm the magiſtrate, and intimidate the poor; badging the poor is alſo ſtrongly reprobated; county-workhouſes are liable to ſtill ſtronger objections; and farming the poor is the top of the climax of oppreſſion and abſurdity.

Such is Mr. Townſend's Philippic on the preſent ſyſtem of the poor-laws, contained in a publication which made its appearance in 1787, in which are many very ſenſible obſervations on the ſubject;

ject; although it is conceived, that very few of thofe, who are in the
practice of experiencing the execution of the fyftem, will join in
fuch an unqualified invective.

The reform propofed is, to abolifh the whole fyftem of compulfive charity; to promote voluntary contributions, as in the early
days of Chriftianity; to encourage induftry, economy, and fub-
ordination ; and to regulate population, by the demand for labour ;
to eftablifh work-fhops in every parifh, to train children to ufeful
labour ; to caufe friendly focieties to be eftablifhed and regulated by
the legiflature; and, as long as it fhall be expedient, to retain a
given proportion of the poor's rates, the difpofal of which fhould be
wholly at the difcretion of the minifter, church-wardens, and overfeers, fubject only to the orders of a veftry; to lay a tax on horfes,
to drive farmers to ufe oxen, which will increafe the quantity of
food for the poor; to inclofe commons, and relieve the poor by
voluntary contributions.

The Rev. T. Haweis, rector of Aldwinkle, All-Saints, in 1788,
offered a plan to the public, under the title of " Hints refpecting
the Poor, fubmitted to the Confideration of the Humane and Intelligent." He recommends box-clubs, to which the poor fhall all be
obliged to contribute, not lefs than one thirty-fixth, nor more than
one twenty-fourth, of their earnings; all menial fervants and young
unmarried people, to pay one eighteenth of their wages and earnings; and every occupier of lands and tenements, to pay one twen-
tieth of his rent; the minifter, church-wardens, and overfeers, to
be a body-corporate for the management of the fund, and to have
affociated with them a perfon chofen by the poor, who contribute
to the fund; the payments to be made by weekly contributions, and
mafters to be refponfible for the quota of their fervants and labourers ; and each parifh to be diftinct from any other, and no
affociation of counties, hundreds, or diftricts. From this fund the
poor are to be relieved, with a fum not above four fhillings a week,
at the difcretion of the body-corporate, without interference of a

magiftrate;

magiftrate; but, in particular cafes, where the eftablifhed rate of relief is not fufficient, the minifter, during divine-fervice, is to mention the particular cafe to the congregation, and the church-wardens to collect for that particular cafe a free benevolence.

Begging to be reftrained by a penalty on the *giver* to thofe who beg, and fettlements to be abolifhed; but whoever migrates muft give to the parifh-officers an account of what parifh he removed from, and where he paid his laft contribution; and, if the officers of the parifh do not choofe to admit him as a parifhioner, they muft give to the officers of the parifh, where he laft contributed to the parifh-fund, a memorandum or note, promifing to pay them the portion of his earnings; and, in fuch cafe, he fhall continue a parifhioner of the parifh whence he migrated.

All baftard-children to be deemed parifhioners where their mo-thers are fettled; but the fathers liable, as at prefent, to maintain them.

Such are the general heads of this plan, the minute organiza-tions of which are not neceffary to be noticed in the curfory view which is meant to be taken of thefe publications; the author alfo compares the fum of the proportion of contributions, propofed to be raifed by his plan, with the amount now levied by the poor's rate in his parifh, to fhew the advantage and facility of the fcheme pro-pofed; and adds fome well-founded remarks and fenfible reafons in fupport of his propofals.

L E T T E R   XXV.

SOON after the fecond reading of Mr. Gilbert's bill was put off, *fine die*, in the Houfe of Commons, William Young, Efq. now Sir William Young, Bart. member of parliament for St. Mawe's,

B b   brought

brought in a bill, which he had previoufly introduced to the notice of the public, by a pamphlet, entitled " Obfervations Preliminary to a propofed Amendment of the Poor-Laws ;" which publication was corrected and enlarged in a fecond edition, whence a fhort fummary of the principal heads of the act he propofed fhall be taken.

The preamble ftates, that many poor perfons become chargeable for want of employment where they are fettled ; who, if permitted to inhabit elfewhere, would not be chargeable.

Therefore be it enacted, that no perfon be removed to his place of fettlement, until he be actually chargeable.

Provided that fuch perfon attends the fummons of two ma-giftrates, and makes oath of his laft legal fettlement ; otherwife he fhall be removed to his fettlement, it being afcertained by other means ; and attefted copies of fuch examination fhall be given to the parifh-officers of the parifh into which fuch pauper is come to refide, and to the pauper himfelf, which fhall be admitted as evidence of his laft legal fettlement in all courts, &c.

Refidence ten years in any parifh, without being chargeable either to the parifh in which they refide or to that where their legal fettlement was, fhall obtain a fettlement in fuch parifh for a pauper and his children.

No perfon, from the date of the act, to gain a fettlement by pay-ing taxes, by fervice, nor by apprenticefhip, unlefs with confent of the parifh-officers, fignified in writing ; but this act to have no retrofpective view.

Baftards are to be fettled with their mother.

Overfeers removing a pauper are to be reimburfed by the parifh to which he belongs : reafonable charges of maintenance and re-moval to be fettled by one magiftrate.

All contracts for maintaining the poor, allowed by the 9th of George II. to be void, and fo much of that act to be repealed ; but contracts for the maintenance of poor children above the age of of feven to the age of feventeen, with the confent of the veftry and the parents of the children, fhall be valid.

No publican fhall be a parifh-officer.

The overfeers, &c. fhall give a true account to two juftices every fix months, at ftated times, of all ware, implements, tools, &c. for fetting the poor to work; and alfo of all materials and ftuff manufactured; and fuch juftices are empowered to order the over-feers to purchafe other ware, implements, and tools, out of the money collected by the poor's rates; which order they muft obey under a penalty not exceeding ten pounds.

The overfeers are to regifter in a book, the names, fex, age, if married or not, — and children, their names, fex, and age, — of all poor perfons receiving relief; and fhall produce this book twice a year, at ftated times, to two juftices, at their petty-feffions, under the fame penalty.

Two juftices, at fuch fpecial feffions, are to be empowered to order the overfeers to bind out any poor children they think proper; but no perfon, unlefs living in the place of his legal fettlement, is compelled to take fuch apprentice.

A veftry fhall be empowered to fix a rate of wages, from the 30th of November to the 28th of February, which a majority of them fhall agree on, to be paid to fuch poor people as cannot find work, and to fend them round in rotation to the parifhioners, pro-portionally as they pay to the rates; to be employed and paid, in the proportion of two-thirds by the perfon employing, and one-third by the parifh-officers, out of the rates; which proportion, if any parifhioner refufe to pay, a juftice of the peace fhall levy treble the amount.

A fuperintending-overfeer, with a falary, may be appointed for a parifh, hundred, or divifion, by two juftices, at their petty-feffions; the falary to be paid by the overfeers of the refpective parifhes out of the money collected by the rates; the duty of fuch overfeers is defcribed at large in the bill; and power is alfo given to the ma-

B b 2   giftrates

giftrates to remove him for mifbehaviour, and he fhall alfo be liable to a penalty not exceeding ten pounds for every offence; and no perfon is to obftruct him in his office under a fimilar penalty.

The penalties levied, by virtue of this bill, to be paid one half to the informant, and one half to the overfeers of the parifh where the offence fhall be committed.

An appeal to the feflions given to perfons aggrieved.

Sir William Young's preliminary obfervations to this bill contain much inftructive matter, and prove, that the mover of the bill well underftood the fubject he brought forward to the confideration of the Houfe; the attention his pamphlet, at the time of its publication, attracted, was fuch a teft of its merits, as to occafion a wifh that the limits of this tract would permit a recital of the greateft part of its contents; but, as the fincerity of unqualified praife is always fufpicious, it will therefore better become the writer of thefe pages to mention an inftance or two in which it is prefumed Sir William Young has drawn a conclufion that the premifes ftated by him will not warrant.

He fays, in page 23, that an avidity to increafe income has introduced the inclofure of commons and waftes, which has tended to increafe the poor's rates; and inftances fix parifhes in Buckinghamfhire, which were not inclofed in 1776, when the aggregate of the poor's rates in thofe parifhes was 756l. 16s. 1d. but were inclofed in 1786, when the aggregate amounted to 1485l. 3s.; therefore he concludes, that inclofing waftes increafes the poor-rates.

By the abftract of the returns made by the overfeers, prefented by order of the committee, the expenfes of a great number of parifhes have increafed in a fimilar ratio between the two periods of 1776 and 1785, where there has been no inclofure of wafte, equally as in thefe fix parifhes where inclofures have been made; therefore one fact oppofes and deftroys the other, confequently no fuch conclufion can be drawn.

The

The confolidation of farms, which this enlightened fenator ftates to have arifen from the neceffity that part of the landed intereft, who fpend their time in our luxurious metropolis, feel to increafe their incomes, is alleged as another caufe of our increafed expenfes with refpect to the poor; but the inftance brought to elucidate the affertion is not in point; nor is it the practice, when one farm is increafed to five hundred pounds a year by the confolidation of ten fmall ones of fifty, to pull down nine farm-houfes; but, on the contrary, to put labourers into them; and the ftock of the ten farms, which, when in the hands of ten little farmers, probably did not amount to two thoufand pounds, increafes in the hands of a capital farmer, of five hundred a year, to at leaft double the amount; and, where there is the greateft ftock, there will be, *cæteris paribus*, the greateft employment: but this argument has been fo ably handled by other pens, as to require no affiftance I can give it; thus much, however, is certain, that where a confolidation of fmall farms proceeds to that excefs, as to preclude the labourer's expectation of raifing himfelf in the world, — honeft ambition, the belt fpur to induftry, is nipped in the bud.

The public had already received, from the pen of the Rev. Mr. Howlett, vicar of Great Dunmow, Effex, feveral tracts on the regulation of the internal police of the kingdom; more particularly on the fubject which has juft been mentioned, as glanced at by Sir William Young, viz. the effects arifing from inclofures; which this very accurate inveftigator, and minute inquirer into facts, ftates to have been, improved agriculture, plenty and cheapnefs of provifion, population, private and national wealth. In 1788, he turned his attention to the caufes of the increafe of the poor, and produced a pamphlet, entitled, " The Infufficiency of the Caufes to which the Increafe of the Poor, and of the Poor's Rates, have been commonly afcribed: the true one ftated, with an Inquiry into the Mortality of Country-Houfes of Induftry, and a flight View of Mr. Acland's Plan, for rendering the Poor independent."

Four

Four principal caufes, Mr. Howlett fays, have been affigned for the increafe of the poor, and of the expenfes for maintaining them: 1ft, Our injudicious fyftem of poor's laws, and their defective execution; 2d, the great number of ale-houfes; 3d, the growing wickednefs and profligacy of the poor; 4th, the ingroffing of farms. — The firft caufe has been affigned by Mr. Townfend and Mr. Gilbert, whofe arguments and conclufions Mr. Howlett attacks, and then draws an inference; that, " upon the whole, though our poor-laws may be imperfect, and their execution defective; we have yet been prefented with no fatisfactory proof that any of thefe deficiences are fo great as to have caufed that rapid increafe of our poor and of our poor-rates, which have taken place;" and he is of opinion, before we afcribe thefe evils to the fpirit of our laws, or their execution, we fhould inquire how the matter ftands in other kingdoms of Europe, where no fuch laws exift ; — he gives an inftance of a parifh in Edinburgh; another in Glafgow; where the expenfes for the maintenance of the poor have increafed very confiderably; and concludes this head of his inquiry with extracts from fome letters of Monf. Pataud, vicar of the parifh of Paterne, in the city of Orleans, which ftate the population of that city at fifty thoufand perfons, of whom one-third receive charitable affiftance; and that there is collected, by various means, and expended for their maintenance, about fifteen thoufand pounds a year, and many, neverthelefs, perifh for want. From information contained in thefe letters, Mr. Howlett alfo concludes that five millions fterling are raifed for the poor throughout the kingdom of France; and then afks if England cannot raife two millions better than France can five ?

In the fecond fection, he expreffes his doubts of Mr. Godfchall's opinion of the fact, that ale-houfes are much increafed in number throughout the kingdom; and conceives, on the contrary, that the number is confiderably decreafed; at leaft they are fo in the hundred of Hinckford, in the county of Effex; therefore he concludes,

as

as far as ale-houfes are concerned, if the reafoning alluded to be juft, our poor's rates ought to have been gradually diminifhed.

In the third feétion, the wickednefs and profligacy of the poor are confidered : the increment of which the author does not, upon the whole, confider as equal to the increment of their expenfes or aétual diftrefs; although he acknowledges that there are fome confiderations which incline him to think, that there is really a greater degree of moral depravity and a greater frequency of vice among our poor than there were formerly; but this increafe he, with great humanity, argues to have been the *confequence* of their poverty, not the *caufe* of it. In the purfuit of this inveftigation he takes notice of, and treats with no great refpeét, the opinions of Mr. Firmin, Mr. Locke, Lord-Chief-Juftice Hale, Sir Jofiah Child, Mr. Defoe, Mr. Godfchall, and others, who, refpeétively, at different times, from 1678 to the prefent period, have declared themfelves of opinion, that the relaxation of difcipline and corruption of manners have occafioned a general averfion to honeft employment.

The queftion, whether the abforption of fmaller farms in larger has tended to increafe the number of poor and their expenfes? occupies the fourth feétion. Mr. Howlett enters fully into the fubjeét; and proves, by fair deduétion of argument, that, allowing the number of labouring-families to be increafed, by the fmall farmers being reduced to labourers, to the amount of even forty or fifty thoufand, yet, as the call for labour in hufbandry has, by the fame means, been increafed, and the number of poor added to the total being not a hundredth part, it will, at the moft, allow for an increment of expenfe amounting to ten thoufand pounds a year. To prove this, thefe faéts are ftated : — 1ft, that the number of labourers, forty years ago, was five millions; 2d, that the poor coft the kingdom, at that time, a million fterling; and that the praétice of engroffing farms may have converted farmers' families into labourers to the amount of forty

or

or fifty thoufand. Mr. Howlett gives every commendation to the ingenious manner in which the Editor of the Annals of Agriculture has treated this fubjeft, in vol. vii. p. 516. — Having, in the firft part, offered his objeftion to the caufes affigned by many eminent men, who have given their opinion on this fubjeft, as being inadequate to the effeft attributed to them; he proceeds; in the fecond feftion, to ftate what appears to him *alone* fufficient to have raifed the expenfes of the poor much higher than they have rifen, to place them in a fituation equally comfortable with what they poffeffed forty or fifty years ago, " *This is none other than, that the price of labour has not advanced in proportion to the advance in the price of provifions.*"

To detail the train of arguments followed by our well-informed and ingenious inveftigator, would extend this part of the prefent inquiry to too great a length; and, to mutilate arguments, where one doubts of their folidity, would not be candid: let it fuffice, therefore, to drop the fubjeft at prefent, ftating only the refult of the author's opinion, in his own words : — " Upon the whole, there is a long and uniform chain of evidence to eftablifh *our main point*, that the increafing miferies and expenfes of the poor have been owing to the greater advance in the price of provifions, either gradual, or fudden and temporary, than in the price of labour."

In the next feftion, Mr. Howlett conceives it neceffary to obviate a very natural conclufion from the doftrine he has attempted to eftablifh, *viz.* that, if the price of labour has not increafed in an equal proportion with the price of provifions, it is an evidence of the declining profperity of the kingdom, and a certain indication of ruin : this he by no means admits to be the cafe, and accounts for the exception to the rule by collateral circumftances, as the increafe of people and the fimplification of labour by the ufe of machines, and concludes with this obfervation : — either raife

.the

the wages of the poor, or give them provifions as they had them forty years ago.

The remaining part of this publication, which relates principally to an examination of the plans that have been offered, particularly Mr. Gilbert's, and the invalidation of thofe reafons which that gentleman has advanced for conceiving a good opinion of houfes of induftry, as to the object of a diminution of the expenfe, by pointing out the precarioufnefs of fuch a diminution continuing, and by meeting the good effect which they have occafioned in leffening expenfe, with inftances of increafed mortality, efpecially among children, cannot be now dwelt on; as it is the purport of this tract to weigh the general fentiments of the kingdom, on the leading points of the police refpecting the poor, in a balance compounded of the fenfe of the legiflature, as collected at different periods, and the opinions of individuals, who have given us their fentiments in print, on this important topic, rather than to cavil at any of thofe opinions that militate with the writer's ideas; which, until the fubject is fully inveftigated, have not the fanction of folid judgement, nor the light of clear information.

That many more tracts than thofe which have paffed, as it were, in review on this fubject may have been written, and that more rays of light might have been collected on a topic which is fo much the concern of every man, and appears to be the immediate care of no man, cannot be denied. Many pamphlets have furvived by name only, but not a fingle copy of them can be found: poffibly, had they contained any matter worthy of notice, they would, by fome means or other, have been preferved to us, either in the volumes of the reviewers, or by fubfequent editions: but it appears abfurd to regret the want of that information which the age, cotemporary with the writer, did not think worth handing to pofterity; and the only apology to be made is for that inattention, if fuch be the fault, which has ne

C c glected

glected to take notice of what would afford folid information; which, it is hoped, will not be found to be very confiderable, more efpecially when the plan of thefe letters is confidered, which is calculated to bring to the mind what the legiflature has done, and fenfible men have written, on the fubjeft, from the time that the police of the poor firft claimed the attention of the community.

Some ftrefs has been laid on the increafing population of the kingdom as a caufe of the increafing expenfe in maintaining thofe who clafs under the title of labouring poor: the progreffion of that increafe in our number fhall now be fhortly ftated, as it will be at leaft fatisfactory to know the degree : we may afterwards reafon on the effect.

Lord-Chief-Juftice Hale and Mr. Gregory King agree in afferting, that the population of England, on the arrival of the Normans, in the year 1077, might be about 2,000,000.

From a computation which appears accurate, or as nearly fo as the nature of the cafe requires, or can be expected to be, the population of England and Wales was, in the year 1327, about 2,092,978.

In 1583, the number of people amounted to about 4,688,000.

In 1662, Mr. Graunt calculated the population at 6,440,000.

In 1690, Mr. Gregory King calculated them at 5,500,000 ; but he eftimated four and a half to a houfe, whereas it is fuppofed that the number of inhabitants were, to the number of houfes, as about five two-fifths to one, which would increafe the number to about feven millions. — Mr. Chalmers's eftimate.

Mr. Howlett calculated them, a few years ago, at 8,691,597 : — the Editor of the Annals of Agriculture, 8,500,000 : —Dr. Price, about the fame time, at only 5,000,000 : but the concurrent opinions of political arithmeticians agree, that the higher numbers are neareft the truth; and that Mr. Howlett's proportion of five and two-fifths to a houfe is as exact a *ratio* of inhabitants to dwellings

lings as can eafily be pointed out.   In the parifh of Clare it was, in 1786, very near the truth, the dwellings being 201, — the inhabitants 1077.

The following deviation from the propofed line of this inquiry fhall clofe this paper:

Mr. Howlett having appeared, in the laft number of the Annals, to doubt the validity of an obfervation, which has fallen from me, with refpect to the call for labour being of a more conftant nature, and lefs defultory, in agriculture than in manufactures; the obfervation fhall be repeated in the expreffion made ufe of on the occafion: and, to prevent the effect which might arife in the minds of thofe who pay any attention to the fubject, from the refpect due to the opinion of the gentleman who doubts the propriety of the idea alluded to, the affertion fhall be re-examined by the teft propofed by himfelf. — The paffage alluded to is as follows:

" Some have imagined that the great increafe of our expenfes, relating to the poor, has arifen from temporary want of work: it may be recollected, that this cannot happen where the employment is agriculture, becaufe this occupation always requires nearly the fame number of hands all years, and is independent of any defultory call for work, which may, as all manufactures do, the demand of which is uncertain, give full employment to the poor fome years, and leave them to fubfift on the poor's rates when the demand for the manufacture ceafes."

Mr. Howlett fays, and it muft be allowed as a fact, that, near the commencement of a leafe, a greater quantity of work is done in a farm than towards the conclufion: but this corroborates the affertion alluded to, which refpects the kingdom at large; for innumerable leafes are conftantly commencing and expiring: the whole quantity of work done in agriculture, one year with another, muft therefore be nearly the fame; and, though individual parifhes may find fome difference, the aggregate of work throughout the kingdom muſt be at all times equal; and this is not only *poſſible* or *pro-bable*, but *inevitable*; but the univerſality of the cauſe, both in reſpect to time and place, producing an effect directly oppoſite to that which would ariſe from a cauſe affecting time and place par-tially only. If, throughout England, all leaſes were to commence at the ſame time, and expire at the ſame time, the effect Mr. How-lett contends for would happen, and the difference in the demand for labour might at times be great; but the fact is different, ſo is the effect.

Mr. Howlett ſays, ſeaſons occaſion a difference in the demand for labour. — So they do. But the *quantum* of earnings remains the ſame at the end of a year: for inſtance, in a wet ſummer, during the actual falling of the rain, the application of induſtry to the works of the field is ſuſpended; but the call for labour is propor-tionably greater when the earth is fitted to receive again the labour of the huſbandman; and probably the demand increaſes in a greater *ratio* than the time loſt: we know how difficult it is to keep land clean in a wet ſeaſon; we know that a greater burthen of ſtraw is grown, which occaſions a greater demand of labour to harveſt, and alſo to threſh; a greater demand for work brings a greater price; hence the advance of price in the harveſt and the barn repays the loſs of time, and the quantity of labour done throughout the year remains the ſame.

The idea of " the earth being faſt bound in chains of froſt for three or four months in the year, which defy the mattock, the ſpade, and the plough," cannot be allowed, in all its latitude of aſſertion, to take place in England : few farmers diſcharge their la-bourers for a froſt ; and in that time of the year, when we have reaſon to expect ſuch chains of froſt, the plough ſuffers no im-priſonment, for it would not otherwiſe be at work; the mattock and the team can ſtill find work; a *ſnow only* can prevent *them* being employed, and that but for a few days; the ſpring of induſtry will, when affected by ſuch a mere temporary ceſſation, immediately

afterwards

afterwards re-act with greater force, being excited by a brifker demand.

Difference of produce, except in the cafe of hops, which are too confined and local a culture to reafon from generally, can very little affect the quantity of labour throughout the year; a wet feafon generally produces worfe crops throughout the kingdom at large than a dry one, although not in quite fo great a difproportion as Mr. Howlett afferts; but a wet feafon produces a greater demand for labour to keep the land clean, and alfo in hay-time, in harveft, in threfhing, although the produce of corn is lefs; therefore, fpeaking generally throughout the kingdom, the lefs productive the crop, the more the labour.

In fhort, Sir, had not the cavil fallen from fo able a critic and fo refpectable a man, I fhould not have thought my obfervation required a defence; it is to vindicate the general rectitude of the fentiments which have efcaped from me on this fubject in his and your readers' minds, that I have revifed what I had advanced, and remain of opinion, that reafon is on the fide of my obfervation, and believe that experience will not contradict it.

LETTER XXVI.

FROM the information contained in the preceding pages of thefe letters, and from the evidence which they have opened to our knowledge of what has been done by our legiflators, and written by the enlightened part of our countrymen on this fubject; although that information cannot claim the merit of minute detail, nor the evidence that fpecification of particulars which would have difgufted the many, although it might have been approved of by a few; it is conceived feveral ufeful principles may be deduced, that

may

may ferve as a ground for maxims, which, if called into action, by the energetic power of the legiflature, may probably produce an improvement in the moral habits of the poor, lead them on to the enjoyment of a greater fhare of the comforts of life, and diminifh, at the fame time, the expenfes of their maintenance.

That thofe, who are in fuch a ftate, with refpect to the riches of this world, as to have no other property than that which their labour can produce them, claim as a right, in all civilized nations, however the laws which refpect property may be modified, protection from perfonal injury, is a pofition which cannot be doubted; no focial compact can otherwife be fuppofed to exift between man and man.

This claim leads on to another, flowing from it as a natural and inevitable confequence; a claim to maintenance; when, by the lofs of health, accidental debility, or age, their power to maintain themfelves ceafes; becaufe, in this cafe, they would otherwife fuftain a perfonal injury, from the modification of property by the laws of fociety; and in a fimilar proportion is their claim, as through any of thefe caufes that power is diminifhed.

Thefe are principles implanted on our minds; they are anterior to and vaftly above all human laws; they form an impulfive duty as ftrong in its operations, and as lovely in its effects, as the στοργη in the animal creation: it is upon this bafis, as upon an immoveable rock, that Chrift builds his ftrongeft moral exhortations, and calls this duty *charity*; tells us that it will cover a multitude of defects, that it binds us by a ftronger obligation than any other moral or religious duty.

In all climes, through all ages, wherever civilization has fpread a fingle ray of light, has this principle been inculcated; and that not as an optional fervice, to be done or neglected, at the will of the free agent, but as a bounden duty; one, the omiffion of which, is an affirmative offence; and thus preached the Apoftles, thus the fathers of the church, and thus their fucceffors.

The

The fruit of their doctrines has been great, it has been worthy of the caufe; it was the caufe of human nature, of religion confined to no fect, fworn to no mafter; it was alike the caufe of the Chriftian, the Jew, the followers of Mahomet, and Confufius; it was the caufe of univerfal humanity.

But we will confine our view to the effect of the doctrine of charity in this ifland: and here reference muft be had to our public archives, as well thofe which are ftill in the poffeffion of the chapters in the different diocefes throughout the kingdom, thofe which are in the cuftody of the public in their feveral repofitories, as thofe alfo in the poffeffion of private individuals; recourfe muft alfo be had to printed books, to writers in paft ages, whofe labours have collected the gleanings of antiquity, and, by the means of the prefs, have preferved them for the perufal of ages then unborn; a kind of teftimony, to which our laws, and the practice of our courts of law, give fanction; it being not unfrequently the beft evidence the nature of the thing is capable of.

Do not all thefe, taken feparately and together, inform us, that all the tithes in the kingdom, every acre of church-land, every thing moving from the produce of the land, affifted and cultivated by the labour of man, which is claimed by the church as tithe, whether prædial, mixed, or perfonal, takes its origin from this fource; were they not all feparately, and in the aggregate, the fruit of thefe doctrines; obtained from our rude and unlettered forefathers as acts of religious duty and moral obligation? If they were not, whence flowed they? From what law of fociety? From what human precept? A divine right cannot be claimed for them in any Chriftian country; our conftitutional lawyers have uniformly afferted, that a divine right to tithes, certainly ceafed with the Jewifh theocracy, and they have not proved that it in fact ever exifted.

Thefe, therefore, muft be taken as facts; that the law of God and of Chrift have eftablifhed the duty of charity in the breaft of man; and, that the labourers in the Chriftian vineyard, have in

this

this country cultivated this principle to a productive purpose; and that, in elder times, a diftribution was made to the poor, of part of that eftate thus obtained and invefted in the ecclefiaftics, by the donations of thofe who had landed pofleffions, in difcharge of their religious and moral duties ;— but thofe days have long fince paffed away ;— and, in proportion as the refrefhing ftreams were diverted from their proper current, the principle of charity, ever fruitful in means to accomplifh its godlike purpofes, has ftruck, like Mofes, from the rock, other fruitful ftreams to refrefh thofe who ftand in need of refrefhment ; and, on the bafis of fluctuating compaffion, has founded a firm municipal right.

In remoter times, when the feudal tenures fubfifted in this king-dom, which made no other confideration of man, than as an agent of defence or deftruction; when the maxim, *detur fortiori* was paramount, every claim which the rights of nature or the con-ftitution of the country held facred ; the voice of the laws or the claims of equity could be heard but feldom, amidft the din of arms ; which the contentions among the defcendants of William, the Norman, for the fovereignty of that kingdom, that he had wrefted from its old pofleffors, occafioned ; no wonder if, in fuch times, the more filent claims of the poor, for that dole which they had been accuftomed to receive the diftribution of, from the in-cumbent clergy, were of no avail ; and that, when the immediate defcendant of the alliance between the houfes of York and Lancaf-ter broke all bounds with the court of Rome, fpurned the fource whence he had perfonally received the title of *fidei defenfor*, and divided the fpoils of the monafteries among his unprincipled cour-tiers ; no wonder that thefe claims fhould have remained dormant; and, having remained through fo long a period in a ftate of reft, it fhould be. held in thefe times ufelefs, if not imprudent, to revive them.

Hence, therefore, may be dated the origin of the compulfory maintenance ; hence, as from a channel whofe fources have in paft

ages

ages been diverted from their natural and proper current, may be deduced that steril appearance, which would have clofed in fcenes of blood or famine, and all its horrid accompaniments; if the legiflature, in the age of Elizabeth, awakened from a long apathy to the fufferings of poverty, by thofe fcenes of woe which the Queen's progreffes through her kingdom offered to her view, and which occafioned that feeling exclamation, *Pauper ubique jacet!* had not opened, by the compulfion of legal authority, new fources to feed the wretched.

But the diftribution of charity was not the total of the lofs fuftained by the poor; they were, during the earlier ages of this kingdom, ufed to receive advice, and the direction of their moral conduct, from the exhortations of the clergy; and that not from their pulpits only, but they were the private friends, the patrons, the counfellors, the confeffors, of the poor; they held an amazing fway over their minds; a fway, I fear, ill exchanged, both here and in a neighbouring country, for that unhallowed indifference for every thing facred which now prevails: but here, as there, while the clergy guarded the moral conduct, watched over the induftry, the health, the economy, of the parifh-poor, they protected their own eftates from incumbrance; and, in proportion as their parifhioners poffeffed the moral and economic virtues, in that proportion were the ecclefiatic eftates productive to the refpective incumbents; becaufe the wants of the poor were lefs; and a probability of increafing the voluntary contributions of the more opulent parifhioners was greater, as the refpect the parifh held the clergy in increafed.

It was with a view to this influence, and to preferve the decaying authority and practice of the clergy in this refpect, that thofe admonitions to charity from the pulpit were enjoined by the ecclefiaftic courts, which Dr. Burn mentions; and which prove, that thofe courts, however *now* they may have fallen into difrepute, felt *then* ftrongly the obligation upon their fuitors, to provide a fund for the poor, not merely to relieve the temporary neceffities of

D d   hunger,

hunger, thirft, or nakednefs, but to pour the balm of comfort into their minds, to inftruct them in their duties to God and their neighbour, to fix in their hearts a confidence, that although they be poor, and negatived in every comfort of life, yet they may, by a pious and virtuous conduct, diminifh the fum of their afflictions here, and lay up a certain treafure of happinefs for the life which is to come.

LETTER XXVII.

ASSUMING therefore, at prefent, the foregoing ftate of the matter as fact; would it not tend in every refpect to the advantage of the poor, and, confequently, of the kingdom, (for, alas, the neceffitous are the million !) if the refident clergy, be they rectors, vicars, or curates, fhould have an active and directing control over the management of the poor in their refpective parifhes; that they may again, as they did formerly, by their precepts, their exhortations, and their examples, introduce fuch moral, economic, and induftrious, habits among the poor, as may tend to make them more comfortable as men, and more refpectable as citizens ? at the fame time, fuch a control would place the clergy in a much more refpectable fituation than they at prefent poffefs; and it would be a refpect flowing from a proper caufe; as it would engraft authority upon precept, united with example; and enable them to enforce, in practice, thofe moral duties, which many of them fo eloquently inculcate from the pulpit.

Advertifements of affociations, for the commutation of tithes, appear frequently in our public prints: whether a general commutation is practicable, or, if practicable, would be relifhed by the clergy throughout the kingdom, it is difficult to determine; but, if a commutation fhould take place, it certainly is worthy the con-

fideration

fideration of the landed intereft, whether they fhould choofe to
convey any portion of their eftates in mortmain as a compofition
for tithes, free and difcharged of *thofe fervices*, for which the *tithes
themfelves* were, by the pofleffors of thofe eftates, *originally* granted ;
which fervices were, amongft other confiderations, *that advice, that
counfel,* that authoritative injunction, coupled with *example*, which
would effect more, by means of good morals, to increafe the comforts of the poor, diminifh their expenfes and the rate collected for
their relief, than the whole of the ecclefiaftic revenue, applied to
the fame purpofe, under the prefent execution of the laws.* Thefe
fentiments, on the neceffity of a national provifion for the poor,
flow from my pen, in direct oppofition to the opinion, fo warmly
expreffed on this topic by you, my friend, in your excellent publication on French agriculture, internal economy, and politics ; and
in oppofition, alfo, to your idea, fo frequently ftarted in converfation, that the poor originally had no right to pecuniary affiftance from the ftate; that they fhould be left to private charity.
The reflection, *Mais cette exemple eft un grand et important leçon
pour nous; car, indépendamment des vices qu'elle nous préfente, et d'une
dépenfe monftrueufe, et d'un encouragement néceffaire à la fainéantife, elle
nous découvre la plaie politique de l'Angleterre la plus dévorante, qu'il
eft également dangereux, pour fa tranquillité et fon bonheur, de détruire
ou de laiffer fubfifter,* which the Committee of Mendicity, in the
Conftitutional Affembly of France, threw out with refpect to the
mifchiefs of the Englifh fyftem, arofe, from their miftaking the
effect of the faulty execution of that fyftem, for the code of laws
itfelf; which remains in a great meafure a dead letter. And it is

---

* I cannot conceal my opinion, that any general commutation for tithes, either in
land, corn, or money, or any other valuable confideration, to be extended by force of
law throughout the kingdom, would be prejudicial to the *laity*, fhould it meet, which is
not very probable, the approbation of the pofleffors of tithes ; and that the moral and
religious duties of life would be lefs in practice, after fuch change had taken place, than
they are now.

no improbable prefumption, that, feeling, as they did, the facred duty, to provide relief for the poor, they adopted the principle of the Englifh fyftem with their eyes open to the evils of it, becaufe they knew of none better; although moft certainly the fame facred duty which requires the expenditure of thirty millions of livres a year, would extend the expenfe to fifty millions, to one hundred, or to any indefinite fum, if neceffity required it : and it was with *them* a facred duty ; for, having poffeffed themfelves of the clerical eftates, they could not, in juftice to the body of their country-men, take them to the ufe of the ftate, otherwife than as the clergy held them, fubject, in fome degree, to the maintenance of the poor.

In the mean time, it is the duty, as well as the intereft, of thofe from whom this revenue is collected, there as well as here, to watch over the execution of the laws, and the expenditure of the revenue raifed for the poor ; which conduct will prevent fuch a neceffity : but if, by negligence, extravagance, or peculation, the urgency of the cafe fhould require a larger fum to be raifed ; it will arife *there*, as it does *here*, from the pockets of thofe, by whofe negligence, or mifconduct, fuch urgency was occafioned.

As to leaving the poor to private contributions, it would, in our prefent ftate of civilization, refinement, and general apathy to reli-gious matters, be a cruel and unjuft dereliction. Were they to be fupported by thofe alone who are the beft members of the fociety, the compaffionate, the religious, and thofe who live in retirement, would then witnefs fuch fcenes of diftrefs as would wring every penny from their pockets, or they muft become immoveable to every feeling of compaffion ; while the gay, the joyous, the unfeeling, — thofe who live in crowds, and in the buftle of the world, — would contribute not a farthing to thofe fcenes of diftrefs from which they are fo far removed.

In anfwer to the fuppofition, that dire neceffity will compel ex-ertions of induftry, it is much to be doubted whether extremity of

diftrefs

diftrefs generally roufes the human mind, or the faculties of the body, to great active exertions. From amidft thofe fcenes which have required vaft exertions to preferve human life, very few have been faved, in proportion to thofe who have perifhed. Difaftrous voyages, fhipwrecks, retreats of armies before a conquering enemy, all prove how few have magnanimity of foul to bear up againft extremity of diftrefs: and, of all thofe circumftances which drive the human mind to apathy or defpair, poverty, and its lowering concomitants, cold, hunger, and thirft, are the moft formidable; becaufe, in proportion as thefe debilitate both the body and the mind, does the urgency of the cafe require the greater activity of exertion: it may, therefore, with great reafon, be afferted, that an increafe of diftrefs will not occafion an increafe of induftry.

. If the cafe of the poor in Scotland and Ireland be produced as a proof, that leaving them to private charity would have a better effect than the rates of England, the anfwer is obvious; that, in Scotland, they are not left to private charity, in their principal cities, but are admitted to a provifion out of the funds of the general-feffion of thofe cities: and that they emigrate from the Highlands, and the country where agriculture and manufactures do not find them fufficient employment, to thofe countries where there is employment: and the emigration of the ufeful fubjects of a country has never yet been produced as a proof of the excellence of its internal economy.

Ireland prefents, in your accurate and particular account of its internal police, no very flattering profpect of the fituation of the poor, either with refpect to their modes of life, their moral habits, or their induftry. In the firft inftance, they are, in general, what the Englifh peafantry were five hundred years ago: the cottage, which affords neither window or chimney, where cows, calves, pigs, children, men, and women, all lie on ftraw together, on the fame floor; their raggednefs, which approaches to nakednefs,

and

and the general difuſe of ſhoes and ſtockings, give one no refined
ideas either of their cleanlineſs or their comforts : and a country
where pilfering is carried to that exceſs, that turnips are ſtolen by
the poor in cart-loads, and acres of wheat carried away in a night,
is not a country of well-regulated police or good moral principles :
neither will the dance in the evening, or the laſt poliſh which they
receive from the dancing-maſter, who is eſſential to their ſyſtem of
education, compound for that exceſs of lazineſs, and that weak-
neſs in their exertions, when *encouraged* to work, which has occaſioned you to doubt of the heartineſs of their food, — potatoes,
oatmeal, and milk ; although the athletic forms of the men, and
the ſwarms of children in their miſerable cottages, beſpeak vigour
and health. I muſt conclude, therefore, that, were the Iriſh to
take the forty-third of Elizabeth, together with the conſequence
flowing from a ſtrict execution of it, the poor, as well as the rich,
would find their ſcale of comfort and proſperity riſing from the
change : and were we, in this kingdom, to call the parochial clergy
to our aſſiſtance, in preſerving an execution of the laws reſpecting
the poor, more conſiſtent with the original intention and obvious
meaning of thoſe laws ; which are calculated to encourage a ſpirit
of induſtry, not of idleneſs ; of economy, not of profuſion ; a ſpirit of honeſty, not of theft ; of religion, not of atheiſm ; of ſubordination, not of riot ; and if the legiſlature of this country
ſhould ordain ſuch to be their line of duty, which certainly is their
line of conſcientious and honourable intereſt ; the ſcale of proſperity
and comfort among *our* poor would alſo riſe, and that of the expenſe attending their maintenance and relief would gradually
ſubſide.

THE laws and ordinances of all countries, towards the firſt periods of their civilization, partake of the rough and ferocious nature of the times and of the inhabitants ; who, being lately emerged from a wild and ſavage ſtate, although they may be awake to ſome of the advantages ariſing from ſubordination, are not ſufficiently refined to be bound by ſilken chains. But, as ſociety advances, and the ſocial bleſſings of civilization by degrees unfold themſelves, thoſe laws which regulate the multitude take a milder tone, and obedience to them is ſecured by inclination, as well as duty, until luxury and diſſipation, ſure prognoſtics of a falling ſtate, occaſion the legiſlator again to ſtain the pages of the penal code with blood.

Such has, in part, been the progreſſive temper of the ſtatute-laws of this country. We find, in paſt ages, the lower claſſes of people reſtrained by a variety of ordinances, which breathe but little of the ſpirit of humanity ; while they ſtrongly prove, that *here* no portion of thoſe abſurd ideas, which have involved France in a ſcene of horrid anarchy, at any time prevailed. The earlieſt regulations of written law, which affect the maſs of the people, compelled " thoſe who rank in the claſs of labourers and artificers, who were able in body, and within the age of threeſcore years, not living in merchandize, exerciſing any craft, or having of their own whereon to live, to work, at regulated prices, on pain of impriſonment, and of being burnt with a hot iron."

Vagabonds, or valiant beggars, as the old acts of parliament call them, were treated with greater rigour : they were to be inſtantly committed to gaol, to be fed with bread and water, to be ſet in the ſtocks, beaten with whips through the towns where they were taken,.

and

and then fent to the place where they laft lived; and this for the firft offence.

For the fecond offence; to be fcourged two days, to be fet in the pillory, and one ear to be cut off.

In fhort, the category of punifhments inflicted, by authority of law, on this defcription of perfons, is too irkfome to be dwelt on: but it is fuch as plainly proves, that our anceftors had no idea of the Gallic principle of equality, of weighing number in the balance againft property; for, we perceive, the multitude is to be reftrained by thefe laws refpecting labour, and to be punifhed for a breach of them: property is exempted.

With refpect to thofe poor who, from age, ficknefs, or accident, had become impotent, and were compelled, by neceffity, to afk alms, they were to fubfift on fuch as they could obtain by begging within certain limits, which feem to have been the hundreds, or towns, where they were born, and, in fucceeding times, where they had lived the laft three years; and, if thefe real objects of compaf-fion wandered beyond thofe limits, or fuch as the juftices of the peace, within the diftrict, fhould allot to them, they were to be punifhed by imprifonment and the ftocks, and their children, under the age of five years, might be taken from them, by any perfon, to be brought up to any honeft labour.

Such were the reftraints and difabilities under which the lower claffes of our fellow-creatures lived in the days of our forefathers; and fuch were the punifhments to which they were fubject for a breach of thofe laws; which laws lean to oppreffion, not to huma-nity; to fervitude, rather than to freedom.

The lenient fpirit of more polifhed times tacitly relieved them, by degrees, from a great portion of thefe reftraints, by ceafing to inflict the punifhment annexed to a breach of the law; and, by fo doing, the fpirit of the times outftripped the attention of the le-giflature, to the happinefs and eafe of the people.

No

No law ought to remain unrepealed, which is not intended generally to be enforced; a partiality in this refpect has not in view the welfare of the governed, and may defcend to that *mifera fervitus ubi lex eft aut vaga aut inconcinna.* The volumes of the Statutes at Large are, on that account, in fome meafure a grievance; becaufe, in a code of pofitive inftitutions, many of them highly penal, which has fwelled within this century to fo enormous a bulk* thofe acts of parliament that, from their long difufe, as well as from the remote antiquity of their original formation, not being adapted to the fpirit of the prefent times, may be called obfolete; and thofe alfo which are not commonly put in practice, but may, at the fame time, be ufed as concealed arms by the malicious, to annoy their unwary and incautious fellow-fubjects, as well as thofe which ftill remain the written law of the land, although not the practical municipal rule of the day, fhould not remain in our law-books; increafing the number of pages, which are, without them, too numerous.

Such are the reflections which have occurred to me, on the evidence before us, with refpect to the ftate of the poor, as far as it relates to confining them to certain parifhes, which we, in thefe days, call their places of fettlement. But it is time to recollect, that, as the judgement fhould not fuffer itfelf to be led captive by the imagination, fo neither fhould the difcurfive refearches of the antiquary lead the pen away from the more immediate purpofe of this letter; which is intended to point out the prefent fituation of the poor, both with refpect to the law of fettlements and certificates, as far as their fituation may be affected, not only by the

---

* Pickering's edition of the Statutes at Large is comprifed in thirty-eight volumes octavo; the laft fix volumes of which are remarkably thick, and in bulk near twice the quantity of paper in the firft fix volumes; and only the firft nine volumes and about half the tenth include the acts of parliament to the end of the laft century; the remaining twenty-eight volumes are filled with the acts of the prefent century, and fifteen of them with the acts of the prefent reign.

E e   law

law of the land, but alfo by the practice of the magiftrates ; together with fuch alterations as may tend to increafe the general ftock
of induftry : permit me, therefore, after a quick retreat from this
fhort digreffion upon the temper of former times, to re-enter on my
fubject, which regards thofe days in which we live, and alfo thofe
which are to come, and may pafs away before the view of our
pofterity,

Although the antiquity of reftraints on the liberty of the poor
to go from place to place, as they imagine they may beft be able to
find provifion and employment, is of a date prior to the days of
Elizabeth, yet the idea of a parifh-fettlement certainly arofe from
the parifh-rate, enacted in the forty-third year of her reign ; nor
does it feem a remarkable circumftance, that fome diftinct rules
fhould be drawn by the legiflature how each parifh might know its
own poor, and be able to confine the expenditure of the rate to its
parifhioners only.

But this was not all: each parifh being obliged to maintain its
own poor, it was prudent to do it by their own officers, and under
their own infpection: hence arofe a reftriction, that, however juft
it might be with refpect to the interefts of parifhes one with
another, is injuftice with refpect to the poor themfelves, and a confiderable obftacle to the encouragement of general labour and induftry throughout the kingdom.

Confinement of the poor within their refpective parifhes, which
is the principal object in the ftatutes 13th and 14th Charles II.
cap. 12, is the reftriction alluded to; becaufe every perfon, whatever may be his ingenuity, induftry, or abilities, falls under the fcope
of this law, if the parifh-officers choofe to complain to a magiftrate
that he is likely to become chargeable; unlefs fuch perfon occupies
a tenement of ten pounds yearly value, or lives on property in
houfe or land of his own.

Adam Smith attributes the very unequal price of labour in
England, in places of no great diftance from each other, to this
                                                              caufe ;

caufe; and he alfo fays, that, to remove a man from the parifh where he choofes to refide, is an abridgement of natural liberty.

Mr. Hay, in his plan, publifhed in 1735, would have all notion of parochial fettlement abolifhed, as being the root from which every evil relating to the poor fprung; every parifh being in a ftate of expenfive war with the reft of the nation, regarding the poor of all other places as aliens, and caring not what becomes of them; Mr. Acland, Mr. Townfhend, Sir William Young, have alfo profeffed an unfavourable opinion of the law of fettlements; and the laft gentleman has offered to the Houfe of Commons the heads of a bill, that would, in a great meafure, have removed the objectionable reftraints on fo large a portion of our fellow-fubjects, and would have fimplified the law on this point; the expenfes arifing from which coft the occupiers of houfes and land, throughout England and Wales, above fifty-five thoufand pounds annually, in the years 1783, 1784, 1785; and it is much to be feared that thefe expenfes are an increafing, not a decreafing, evil.

Neither the law nor the equity of this cafe feems to have been clearly underftood by parliament, when the reftrictive acts paffed; they proceeded on this principle, that the object of expenfe between parifhes was the only point of confequence to be confidered; whereas, in fact, it ought not to have come into queftion at all: the 43d of Elizabeth, fection the third, providing for any cafe where the inhabitants of a parifh might *not be able* to maintain the poor, by calling in aid other parifhes within the hundred; and the parifh in which I am now writing is an inftance in point, that this fection has been frequently carried into execution; other parifhes, within the hundred, having been called in aid to relieve the poor of Clare, the expreffion *not able* muft be allowed to be of great latitude; the meaning annexed to the expreffion by the legiflature cannot be eafily defined; according to the common acceptation of the word, no fuch a cafe can well exift, every parifh in the kingdom may be *able* to maintain its own poor; and, if *ability* is to be explained by *choice*,

E e 2   few

few will be found *willing :* the word muft therefore have fome relation to moral convenience, and then it would depend on the quantum, or reafonable proportion, of his means of living, which
moral obligations would induce a man to part with towards the
maintenance of his poor neighbour; it muft then be meafured by
the principle of charity. Poffibly, was this undefined expreffion
to be precifely explained by fome rule of proportion to occupations
in a parifh, the contefts between parifhes would be at an end,
and they would arife only between hundreds. Even this would
greatly diminifh the fource of litigations; more efpecially if incorporations of hundreds, for the maintenance of the poor, fhould
become general.

Therefore, as the law formerly ftood, although not as it is now
executed, the conteft, if any, ought to lie between hundreds, and
not between parifhes. This alone would be a great relief, not
only to the poor, with refpect to general convenience, by increafing
the market for work, but by the confequential diminution of the
expenfes of maintaining them ; fuppofing it to be true, that, the
more a poor family *earns,* the lefs parochial affiftance it requires.
If the conteft lay between counties it would be better.

But there ought to be no litigations at all about the fettlements
of the poor; " *le jeu ne vaut pas la chandelle* ;" there fhould be no
attorneys bills in overfeers accounts : it is cheaper to relieve, than
to remove, a family by a fuit at the feffions ; which, if the overfeers are peculiarly aftute in watching over the interefts of their
parifhes, or, in other words, are tenacious of their opinions, will
go into the King's Bench, and the fuccefsful parifh may find
an honeft family removed, to their utter ruin, at double the
expenfe that would have maintained them and their pofterity
for ever.

If a man of property has half a fcore contiguous farms in his
occupation, it would be extreme folly to ftation a certain portion
of his farming-ftock at each individual farm, and not allow that
ftock

ftock to migrate to his other farms, as food, utility, or the general convenience, and attention to profit, might give occafion. To fix, irrevocably, three fcore fheep in this farm, fix fcore in that, fo many bullocks in one, fo many in another, would be a remarkable inftance of bad management. A good manager certainly would rather form a calculation of what ftock the whole number of acres in his occupation might fupport, with the greateft probability of the greateft profit; and, with that view, would remove them from one part of his eftate to the other, without having any refpect to the divifion of his farms. — So ftands the intereft of the nation with refpect to the poor; it is one large domain, and the ftock, or people, ought to be farmed *quoad hoc* in the fame manner; and fimilar means would produce correfponding effects: the proprietor of land would turn *his acres* to the greateft poffible profit; *the nation* would produce the greateft poffible quantity of induftry; and the poor would be maintained at the leaft poffible expenfe.

LETTER XXIX.

A TOTAL repeal of the law of fettlements might, in the prefent ftate of things, promote vagrancy, which is a diforder, both in morals and induftry, tending to the worft confequences that can arife from population: the abolition of fettlements, therefore, cannot be recommended; a modification of them, on principles more confiftent with the general advantage of fociety, is the whole that fhould be attempted.

The preamble to the act of parliament, confining the poor to their refpective parifhes, ftates, that the people endeavour to fettle themfelves where there is the beft ftock, the largeft commons or waftes to build cottages, and the moft woods for them to burn and deftroy;

deftroy; and, when they have confumed them, that they go to another parifh, and at laft become rogues and vagabonds.

The ftatute-law was, in the reign of Charles the Second, fufficiently fevere to protect the woods from being burnt or deftroyed, if feverity of punifhment operated to that effect; and the laws refpecting vagrancy were, at that time, not lefs penal: if any additional feverity might have been neceffary, the vagrant-act, of recent memory, is not deficient in that refpect. If feverity of ftatute-law will not protect our woods from burning and deftruction by the poor, will the law of fettlements do it? Certainly it is not the probable effect arifing from the confinement of the poor to parifhes where they cannot obtain a fair market-price for their labour, that they fhould pay refpect to thofe waftes, and woody tracks, which produce no call for agricultural induftry. The reafons adduced in the preamble to the act of fettlements muft, therefore, fall to the ground, and the inducement to the enacting claufes will then remain: that the poor will put themfelves into a fituation to live at the leaft poffible expenfe to their neighbours, by going where they can find employment, and where they are moft likely to maintain themfelves. And ought they not to be permitted fo to do, unlefs other confequences than thofe ftated in the preamble to the act reftraining them, or, at the leaft, thofe confequences themfelves, are to.be apprehended?

The effect moft to be apprehended is; that fuch liberty might tend to the encouragement of vagrancy, or fuch a wandering plan of life, as would not permit parifh-officers, if fortunately they fhould be fo inclined, to introduce any fettled induftrious mode of education among their children; as fuch an education is one of the moft defirable objects to be obtained in the difcipline of the poor; it may be proper to modify that reftraint which is thought neceffary to be retained over them, fo as to be moft conducive to this end; for, although the prefent execution of the poor-laws proves, in general, either that the overfeers are ignorant of their power in this

refpect,

refpect, or, which is more probable, diflike the trouble of attending to youthful induftry; yet it requires no extraordinary prophetic forefight to aflert, that this muft become, and fhortly, a ferious part of their office; or we fhall find what the French Committee of Mendicity have afferted to be too true; that the fyftem of our poor-laws, as at prefent executed, " is the moft deftructive political gangrene in the Englifh conftitution."

If the poor were permitted to remove from place to place, as beft fuited the interefts of induftry, it would be reafonable,. that the fame authority which granted them the liberty fhould connect it with fuch regulations as are neceffary to the fafety and advantage of the ftate; which might probably be effected by preventing that liberty, which was intended for the encouragement of induftry, degenerating into vagrancy; by making it of immediate ufe, in diminifhing the expenfes of their maintenance, and by offering a profpect of advantage to pofterity, from the certain good tendency of an induftrious education.

To effect the firft end, box-clubs fhould be the means; which fhould be obligatory on all the poor while in health, and without a family of children; or, poffibly, the *lex trium liberorum* might with propriety be the point of exemption; but thofe who migrate, as the only good reafon for their migration muft be larger wages, fhould contribute a larger proportion of their earnings; if one-thirtyfixth were the general proportion, one-twenty-fourth might be a proper proportion of the earnings of thofe who leave their parifhes.

Government has an undoubted right, on every principle of natural juftice, to direct, in fome meafure, the education of thofe children whofe parents are chargeable to fociety; and this arifes from the reciprocity on the part of government, to preferve all the governed from perifhing by want.

Where there are feminaries inftituted for educating children in habits of induftry, the poor fhould be compelled to fend their children to them in thofe parifhes where they refide; the migrated families,

families, by the alternative of the attendance of their children at the fchool of induftry, or an order of removal of themfelves to their place of fettlement.

Thefe terms being complied with, the poor might, without fear of their becoming vagrants, or neglect of induftrious habits in the rifing generation, be permitted to feek their bread, by means of labour and induftry, wherever good wages will enable them beft to find it; and a foundation of a fund would be laid for their main-tenance when in diftrefs, which would be productive in proportion as the number of the migrants increafed, or in other words, as the total fum earned by the induftry of the nation increafed.

Taking one of the heads of Sir William Young's bill as the ground-work of our propofed regulation, the general idea would ftand thus.

No perfon fhall be removed to his place of fettlement until actu-ally chargeable to the parifh where he refides, provided that he has made oath, before two neighbouring magiftrates, of the place of his legal fettlement; and that, from the time of his firft refidence in the parifh, he has contributed, according to the rules of the fociety, one-twenty-fourth part of his earnings to the box-club of that parifh; and hath alfo, from the fame time, fent his children, above the age of fix years, and under the age of eleven, to the fchool of induftry in the faid parifh; and having fo refided ten years in any parifh, without receiving any parochial relief whatever, he fhall obtain a fettlement where he hath fo refided.

It would farther tend to prevent vagrancy, if the pauper fhould be obliged to obtain the approbation of two magiftrates, refiding near the parifh whence he removes, teftified by their figning their confent, and fpecifying the place to which they allow the pauper to go, prior to his actual migration; which confent fhould be imme-diately delivered to the overfeers of the parifh where he intends to refide. But no evidence that thefe conditions were not complied with fhould be allowed to be given in any conteft at law as to his

place

place of fettlement; becaufe it would tend to create litigation, and could be of no other fervice, the magiftrates having the power to punifh the omiffion by fending the pauper back to his place of fettlement.

Thefe regulations would certainly diminifh the fources of legal contefts, on the variety of cafes refpecting fettlements and certificates; and would tend to bring thofe difputes, which are fo very inimical to the pockets of the parifhioners and the peace of the parifh, into a very narrow compafs; they would alfo open to the poor the means of carrying their induftry to the beft market; at the fame time that the obligation to contribute to a box-club, in a greater proportion than if they had remained where they were fettled, might tend to keep them from migrating, unlefs the profpect of advantage was confiderable; the being obliged to fend their children to a fchool of induftry would alfo check that fpirit of vagrancy, which idlenefs, during infancy and youth, is apt to promote. But thefe obligations proceed on the idea that box-clubs and fchools of induftry were eftablifhed by authority of parliament throughout that part of the kingdom fubject to the poor-laws; for, vain would be the regulations, if, for want of thefe inftitutions, they could not be complied with; and it is much to be feared, that, whatever may be the excellence of them, they will not inftitute themfelves throughout the kingdom in general, without the affiftance of the legiflature, although the good arifing from them is already experienced in many parifhes.

There feems uniformly one falfe principle, that is inconfiftent with that degree of freedom which is the beft inheritance of all of us, conftantly pervading this head of the laws refpecting the poor, exclufive of the reftraint which the law of certificates occafions. The principle alluded to, is the right claimed by the officers of a parifh to remove thofe whom they may deem *likely* to become chargeable; the undefined idea, of what *may poffibly happen in future*, fhould not be permitted to operate in the latitude it does; for, it is not neceffary

to

to the interest of the parish, but in a moft infignificant degree; and
even that trifling intereft would difappear inftantly, on the principle being exploded, and a general practice diametrically oppofite
prevailing; all men are liable, as the law at prefent ftands, to be
taken by a warrant before a magiftrate, if a parifh-officer thinks
proper to declare his belief that the individual is *likely* to become
chargeable; and this affertion may fometimes be founded on pique,
intereft, or private refentment; confequently we are all liable to
this impertinent intrufion, and, what is worfe, to an examination
into our circumftances and fituation in life; the knowledge of
which fhould be in the power of every man to preferve in his own
breaft, unlefs he be fo fufpicious a character that the fafety of fociety or of individuals requires a public inveftigation of his fituation
and circumftances; but, in this cafe, the expofition of the private
concerns of an individual is founded folely on this trifling plea of
intereft, — that a parifh may not expend a trifle by *once* relieving
him.

Therefore, the paltry confideration of a few pence, in the expenditure of an individual parifh, expofes all his Majefty's fubjects to
the poffibility of this difagreeable fcrutiny into their private affairs;
and this on the unfounded affertion of a parifh-officer, that a re-
fiant *may* become chargeable; a very difagreeable confequence, flowing from a very infignificant caufe. Actual relief received from a
parifh ought to be the only cafe where fuch an intrufion fhould
take place; and that rule, if univerfal, would produce no general or
even partial inconvenience; and it would, at the fame time, relieve
all from the poffibility of being placed in a humiliating, vexatious, and difagreeable, fituation, without fufficient reafon.

L E T T E R

THE natural right of the poor to the affiftance of fociety, when, by misfortune, ill health, or age, their labour is not equal to their fupport; and alfo the propriety of allowing them the liberty of removal from one place to another, for the purpofe of rendering their labour more equal to their fupport, having been dif-cuffed, this paper fhall be dedicated to the purpofe of examining the expediency of raifing the price of labour; defiring that the reader will recollect agricultural labour is principally adverted to; and that the data, from which the conclufions will be drawn, may be found among the evidence which has been collected in fome of the former papers on this fubject.

It has already been afferted as a truth, in a manner felf-evident, that the price of labour fhould be equal to maintain the labourer in that fituation of life he occupies in fociety, whether as a hufband, a father, or a fon; confequently, that it fhould enable him, while in health, to fupport a wife, children, or aged parents; and the evidence produced has tended to prove that it was fo in former times; before the eftablifhment of a compulfive maintenance, and before thofe adfcititious and enervating luxuries of life, fpirits and tea, impaired the ftrength of the parent, debilitated his progeny, and wafted the produce of his labour.

The rating of wages, by authority of parliament, might alfo, in thofe days, have tended to preferve a juft proportion between the price of labour and the neceffaries of life; for, if the practice had not that good effect, it operated to the difadvantage of the labourer; becaufe, by limiting the price, it reftrained the fpirit of competi-tion; all the ftatutes, from the reign of Edward the Third to that of James the Firft, on that head, being reftrictive againft giving *more*, and not compulfive to give the price rated by the juftices;

confe-

confequently, they tended rather to reduce than to raife the price of labour.

But let us examine how the proportion was preferved in times antecedent to the eftablifhment of a poor's rate, and how it is preferved now, and let us make a comparifon of the facts: the means are in our hands, and the refult may eftablifh a ferviceable truth.

In the twenty-third of Edward the Third, the price of agricultural labour was regulated, in many inftances, by parliament. — Two of thefe fhall be taken; harveft-wages, reaping corn by the day, three-pence; threfhing wheat, by the quarter, two-pence half-penny: in that year, 1338, the price of wheat, by the quarter, was three fhillings and four-pence; therefore, a day's work in harveft would not produce quite one-thirteenth of a quarter of wheat, and the price of threfhing a quarter was one-fixteenth of its value. In 1792, the price of a day's harveft-work, in the cheapeft counties, was, at the leaft, half-a-crown, and the price of threfhing wheat was alfo about half-a-crown a quarter : the average-price of wheat, throughout the year, might be about two guineas a quarter : the labour of threfhing, therefore, was, to the price of the wheat, as one to fixteen or feventeen; and a day's harveft-wages bore the fame proportion to the fame quantity of wheat. In the years 1387, 1389, wheat was threfhed at four-pence a quarter, and reaped at feven-pence an acre. In 1388, the price of wheat was four fhillings a quarter : in this inftance, the price of threfhing fhall be taken, becaufe the price of reaping an acre of wheat muft then, as now, depend on many circumftances, and rife or fall accordingly : threfhing then produced one-twelfth of the value of the wheat. In 1446, a reaper received five-pence a day ; the price of wheat was, in 1445, four fhillings and fix-pence a quarter ; and, in 1447, eight fhillings; therefore, a day's harveft-work, at that time, produced one-tenth of a quarter of wheat: in 1445, the year preceding the price of reaping, and the year fucceeding it, it, one-nineteenth yearly; the *Chronicon Pretiosum* giving no instance of the price of wheat in 1446: the average of thefe prices of labour is one-fourteenth of a quarter of wheat; and the price of the fame articles of labour, in the year 1792, having been taken at one-fixteenth of the value of a quarter of wheat, it is manifeft that the price of agricultural labour was then fomewhat higher, in proportion to the price of wheat, than at prefent; that is to fay, as a fourteenth is to a fixteenth; which would increafe harveft-wages to about three fhillings a day, and threfhing wheat to three fhillings a quarter, fuppofing the average-price of wheat to be two guineas a quarter.

So few inftances occur when the price of wheat and the price of agricultural labour can be obtained in the fame year, before any regular regifters of the price of wheat were kept, that the exactnefs of the average cannot be depended on; nor is the calculation pretended to be correctly exact; but it is apprehended that both the average and the calculation are fufficiently fo, to warrant the conclufion that is inferred from them: and it fhould alfo be recollected, that no compulfory maintenance for the poor was eftablifhed during the period in which thefe averages have been taken.

In 1661, the juftices of Effex, in their Eafter-feffions, fixed the rates of agricultural labour for that year: the reaper, one fhilling and ten-pence a day harveft-wages; the threfher, exactly the fame price per quarter: the price of wheat was, by the Windfor-table, 3*l*. 2*s*. 2*d*.; by which it is manifeft, that a day's harveft-wages, and the threfhing a quarter of wheat, would not either of them purchafe one-thirty-fifth part of the quarter. At this period the compulfory maintenance had been eftablifhed near forty years.

In 1682, among the wages of fervants and labourers in hufbandry, rated by the juftices at their quarter-feffions, holden at Bury, in Suffolk, and recorded in Sir John Cullum's Hiftory of Hawftead, we find that a man-reaper's wages, in harveft, was one fhilling

ling and eight-pence; a common labourer, in fummer, one fhilling; in winter, ten-pence: the average-price of wheat we find, by the Windfor-table, to have been, that year, 1*l.* 19*s.* 1*d.*; a day's harveft-wages would, therefore, in 1682, purchafe one-twenty-third part of a quarter of wheat; a day's common wages, in fummer, about a thirty-ninth part; a day's common wages, in winter, about a forty-feventh part. It fhould be mentioned that thefe prices are all without meat and drink.

In 1668, Mr. Gregory King computed the ordinary income of labourers and out-fervants at fifteen pounds a year, to a family which he fuppofed to confift of three and a half perfons; and he computed the weekly expenfe of fuch families to be about twenty-pence a head. About the fame time, Lord-Chief-Juftice Hale computed the neceffary expenfes of a labourer's family, confifting of fix perfons, the father, mother, two children able to do fomething, and two not able, at ten fhillings a week, or twenty-fix pounds a year: the average-price of wheat was, by the Windfor-table, that year, 1*l.* 15*s.* 6*d.*; and the average-price for twenty-five years, taken annually, from 1655 to 1680, during which period of time the Chief-Juftice muft have made his calculation, was generally above 2*l.* 5*s.* never under 2*l.* 2*s.* a quarter. We have feen the rates of wages at the Effex quarter-feffions in Eafter 1661, and at the Suffolk quarter-feffions in 1682; the inference, with refpect to the ratio which agricultural labour bore, when wages were rated, to the neceffaries of life, can eafily be drawn; and, when drawn, will prove that the practice was not favourable to the labourer.

The difficulty of obtaining inftances of the prices of labour, in years fo long paffed away, prevent me from felecting a fufficient number of facts to form a very exact average; but it is prefumed that fufficient has been done to lay a foundation for the following affertions:

Firft.

Firſt. — That, before the rate operated to the relief of the poor, their wages were larger, in proportion to the price of wheat, than at preſent.

Secondly. — That ſince the operation of the 43d of Elizabeth, by raiſing a ſum in every pariſh for their relief, their wages have been leſs, in proportion to the price of wheat, during the *laſt century*, than at *preſent*, as the ſame quantity of work will now purchaſe a ſixteenth of a quarter of wheat, which, in 1661, would purchaſe only a thirty-ninth part, and, in 1682, a twenty-third part of a quarter of wheat only. To judge how ſuch a price for labour, ſo diſproportioned to the price of wheat, affected the poor's rate in thoſe days, is not at this diſtance of time in our power, except in thoſe pariſhes where accident may have preſerved the account of the rate raiſed in thoſe years; and, in ſuch a caſe, ſome idea might be formed by comparing the then rate with the preſent, ſuppoſing the ſtate of population and of the manufactures to be alſo known.

Thirdly. — It appears, not only that the rating of wages tended to depreſs the price of labour; but that, before the poor partook of a revenue raiſed from the pockets of their fellow-ſubjects; the un-feeling hand of legiſlation having precluded miſery from its laſt reſource, — the compaſſion of the wealthy, by reſtraining them from begging, and their opulent neighbours from giving them relief, through fear of impriſonment; the poor muſt have been in a moſt deplorable ſituation, and muſt have continued ſo until the beginning of the reign of Henry the Eighth, when juſtices of the peace were empowered to licence aged and impotent perſons, to beg within certain diſtricts. This alſo will, in ſome meaſure, account for the deficiency of our population in thoſe times, it being, in the fourteenth century, not one-fourth of what it is at preſent.

Therefore, although the price of labour might be, through the thirteenth, fourteenth, and fifteenth, centuries, higher, in proportion to the price of wheat, than at preſent; the rough temper of the times, inſtanced by the concurrent acts of legiſlation, left the

poor

poor without any refource in the hour of diftrefs, except from the
ecclefiaftical eftates; and, with refpect to the time paffed fince the
43d of Elizabeth, it has been feen, that the price of labour was
much lower, in proportion to the price of wheat, during the laft
century, than at prefent.

The conclufion which follows, from the few facts that apply to
the queftion, is, that, in the three centuries preceding the poor's
rate, they were in a worfe fituation that at prefent, although their
wages were more proportionate to the neceffaries of life; becaufe
there was no refource left to them from private charity, and a compulfive maintenance was not eftablifhed, to which they might apply
in the hour of diftrefs; and through the feventeenth century, after
a compulfive maintenance had been eftablifhed, they appear to have
received wages lefs proportionate to the neceffaries of life than they
do at prefent; confequently, their prefent fituation, with their
wages, is preferable to their former.

————————

L E T T E R   XXXI.

BUT it may be objected, that the inftances produced, having
mentioned the concurrent price of only one material article of
life, wheat; the others, as clothing, fire, houfe-rent, butcher's meat,
and a long train of et cæteras, have not been glanced at.

This difficulty may be folved by a fhorter, and probably a more
fatisfactory, proof, than a detail of the concurrent prices of a long
category of articles, at the feveral periods when the foregoing notices were taken, were fuch an accurate detail in our power; the
proof alluded to is the opinion of Adam Smith on this fubject,
who fays, " The money-price of corn regulates that of all other
home-made commodities; the real value of every other commodity
being

being meafured and determined by the proportion which its average money-price bears to the money-price of corn."

The detail of the facts and arguments, from which this principle is eftablifhed by Dr. Smith, would probably be thought tedious and unneceffary, having his name as authority for the opinion ; a fhorter proof may be thought a better proof; and a plain and intelligible *forites* may effect as much in a few words as a long argument in many pages. — For inftance :

The labour of man fhould be equal to his fuftenance, the principal article of which is corn. — By the labour of our poor are home-made commodities produced and manufactured ; what produces or manufactures commodities is the meafure of their value; what fuftains the poor is the efficient means of their labour. Corn principally is the fuftenance of the poor; therefore, corn is the meafure of the value of home-made commodities ; or, in other words, the money-price of corn regulates the money-price of thofe articles, which are neceffary to the fuftenance of the poor.

Another point to be fettled before we proceed, is to afcertain the articles which common confent will agree to call the *neceffaries of life* ; becaufe no wages of labour will provide for a confumption, *ad libitum*, of every article of food and clothing ; which a poor family may *choofe* to make ufe of; and, at the fame time, a deduction of every article, not abfolutely neceffary to the fuftentation of human life, would leave fo little to be purchafed by the labour of man, as to admit of no doubt on the queftion.

No writer has delivered his fentiments on this topic with that precifion of idea, that appropriate happinefs of expreffion, and, what is beft, with that full knowledge of the fubject, as the fame writer we have before referred to : his opinion therefore will, with no fmall degree of propriety, ftand in the place of any fluctuating defultory notions, which humanity, mifled by luxury, might throw out ; this one idea being granted, that the comforts of life and the neceffaries are different things; the firft are properly within the

G g   reach

reach of thofe whofe property, ingenuity, or induftry, puts them beyond the probability of feeking relief from the rate levied for the poor; the laft comprehend only thofe articles which are neceffary to the prefervation of human life in health, and the perfon in fuch clothing as not to offend the eye of decency and propriety.

By neceffaries, Adam Smith fays, he underftands not only the commodities which are indifpenfably neceffary for the fupport of life, but whatever the cuftom of the country renders it indecent for creditable people to be without; and explains himfelf, by admitting, that a linen fhirt and leather fhoes are among thofe things which the pooreft creditable perfon of either fex in this country would be afhamed to appear in public without; falt, candles, leather, foap, and fuel, he admits as neceffaries, to a certain degree of confumption.

Grain, and other vegetables, with the help of milk, cheefe, and butter, or oil where no butter is to be had, he affirms, are known from experience, without any affiftance from butcher's meat, to afford the moft nourifhing and invigorating diet;* and therefore he doubts whether butcher's meat be a neceffary of life any where; but, not determining that point, he calls all other things luxuries, fpeaking of articles of diet, without meaning, by this appellation, to throw the fmalleft degree of reproach on a temperate ufe of them; he fays, " Beer and ale in Great Britain, and wine even in wine-countries, I call luxuries: a man of any rank may, without any reproach, abftain totally from fuch liquors; nature does not render them neceffary for the fupport of life, and cuftom no where renders it indecent to live without them."

Many names, and fome of eminence in the political as well as in the literary world, have given fanction to ftrictures on our police refpecting the poor, from the time of Lord Verulam to the

* See page 287, of the 19th volume of the Annals of Agriculture, where an extract from the Editor's Tour in Ireland is quoted, much in point with Adam Smith's. opinion.

prefent

prefent day; but this particular topic, the wages of labour, has not been glanced at until lately; hence we may collect, that it was not thought a ftriking object; and may alfo venture to affert, that no material, no glaring, difproportion fubfifted between wages and the neceffaries of life, during thofe times, when Bacon, Lord Hale, King, Davenant, Firmin, Defoe, Locke, Sir Jofiah Child, Cary, Hay, Alcock, Lord Hilfborough, Sir Richard Lloyd, Fielding, and Burn, turned their attention to this fubject; for, had any material difproportion prevailed in the opinions of thefe writers, or any of them, that difproportion would have been fuggefted as a caufe of the mifchief complained of, have been adverted to, and a remedy propofed; but we can collect no arguments from their writings, either for or againft a rife of wages; and, as great a difproportion fubfifted in their times between the price of corn and the price of labour as at prefent, their filence may therefore be conftrued into an acquiefcence, that no foundation of complaint exifted.

Indeed, no hints of any weight, no affertions of ferious authority, can be found in the writings of our forefathers, on which we may reafon, as on a folid foundation; building our argument on the refpect due to a great name; which, when fact, experience, ftrict demonftration, and analogical inference, fail us, may ferve as a reafonable caufe of belief, though by no means of implicit conviction.

But the fame excellent, moral, and political, cafuift, whofe treatife on the Wealth of Nations we have juft had recourfe to, gives his decided opinion on this topic, which fell directly under his attention.

He informs us, that, " in Great Britain, the wages of labour feem to be evidently more than what is precifely neceffary to bring up a family.

" The real recompenfe of labour, the real quantity of the neceffaries and conveniences of life, which it can procure to the la-

bourer,

bourer, has, during the courfe of the prefent century, increafed
perhaps in a ftill greater proportion than its money-price.

" The wages of labour have been continually increafing fince
the time of Henry the Eighth, and in the greater part of the
branches of trade, the profit of ftock has been diminifhing.

" In Great Britain, the wages of country-labour approach nearer
to thofe of manufacturing-labour, than they are faid to have done
in the laft century or in the beginning of the prefent."

Thefe extracts plainly declare the opinion that this author held
on this fubject : thofe, who wifh to fee the ground-work of his reafoning, will find full caufe to be fatisfied with the folidity of his
obfervations and the precifion of his arguments, by perufing books
the firft, the fecond, the fourth, and fifth, of this valuable work.

Mr. Townfhend concurs in the fame opinion ; he fays, in his
Diflertation on the Poor-Laws, " if we take the average of fixty
years, which terminated at the commencement of the prefent century, we fhall find the price of wheat to have been fix fhillings and
four-pence halfpenny per bufhel, whereas for the fubfequent fixty
years it was only five fhillings ; and for the laft twenty years, ending with the year 1782, not more than fix fhillings and fixpence;
yet, during that long period, in which provifions were the cheapeft,
the poor's rates were continually advancing ; that this diftrefs does
not arife from the high price of foap, leather, candles, falt, and
other fmall articles, needful in a family, will appear not only from
the fuperior advance in the price of labour, in the proportion of fix
to four within a century, but from hence, that where the price of
labour is the higheft, and provifions cheapeft, there the poor-rates
have been moft exorbitant."

Mr. Howlett is the only writer of reputation who has advanced
an opinion different from that which has been generally received, or
filently acquiefced in, by all who have, in paft times, left us their
thoughts on the ftate of the poor, and diametrically oppofite to the
fentiments

fentiments of Adam Smith and Mr. Townfhend, who have very lately had the fubject under their confideration.

Mr. Howlett fays, in his pamphlet, which has been already noticed, part the fecond, fection the firft, " the great and real caufe of the increafed proportion of the poor, as well as of the increafed expenfe of maintaining them, is, that the price of labour has *not* advanced fo much as the price of provifions." And he concludes with this obfervation, " either raife the wages of the poor, or give them provifions as they had them forty years ago."

Laying afide, for a time, all the refpect that is due to the authority of great names; leaving at prefent out of the queftion the uniform affertions of many eminent writers on this fubject, from the age of Queen Elizabeth to the prefent, who have one and all complained of the profligacy of the poor; a profligacy which feems to have gathered ftrength, in proportion as relief at a veftry, or by the order of a magiftrate, fupplied the place of the wages of induftry; and who have attributed the increafe of this poverty and expenfe in their maintenance to that caufe principally; let us meet this affertion, and examine it by teft of fact, adduced by Mr. Howlett himfelf.

The average-expenfe of the poor, the three years preceding 1776, is produced; and the average of the expenfe, in the years 1783, 1784, 1785, is alfo produced; the firft amounts to 1,529,780*l*. 0*s*. 1*d*. per annum; the laft to 2,004,238*l*. 5*s*. 11*d*.; the difference between them is 474,458*l*. 5*s*. 10*d*. If the price of the neceffaries of life increafed in the laft period in an equal proportion with the expenfes of the poor, that is to fay, between a third and a fourth more than their price at the firft period, the affertion might be warranted by the confequence in its fulleft extent; for, the price of labour certainly has not rifen a third, or even a fourth: but let us examine the fact.

During the years of the firft period, the average-price of wheat was, in 1773, 2*l*. 19*s*. 1*d*.; in 1774, 2*l*. 15*s*. 1*d*.; in 1775, 2*l*. 11*s*. 3*d*.; the average of the three years is 2*l*. 15*s*. 1¼*d*.

During

During the years of the fecond period, the average-price of wheat was, in 1783, 2*l.* 7*s.* 1*d.*; in 1784, 2*l.* 7*s.* 2*d.*; in 1785, 1*l.* 16*s.* 11*d.*; the average of the three years is 2*l.* 3*s.* 8¼*d.*

Therefore the price of the neceffaries of life, or, in other words, the money-price of corn, which regulates the price of the neceffaries of life, *i. e.* home-made commodities, was in the laft period cheaper than in the firft, in the proportion of between a fourth and a fifth; and the expenfes of the poor in the laft period were greater than their expenfes in the firft, between a third and a fourth.

L E T T E R   XXXII.

MR. Howlett fuppofes that each individual confumes at leaft a quarter of wheat a year; a family of fix therefore confumes fix quarters annually; corn, therefore, cofts fuch a family annually, on the average above-mentioned, the three years preceding 1776 inclufively, 16*l.* 10*s.* 9*d.*; and 13*l.* 2*s.* 3*d.* the three years preceding 1785 inclufively; confequently, the difference between thofe fums, 3*l.* 8*s.* 6*d.* remains in the pocket of the family, to expend in other neceffaries, in the laft period more than in the firft; and, taking the number of labouring poor individuals in England and Wales to be at fix millions and a quarter, as Mr. Howlett ftates them, during both the periods, the whole of their expenditure for wheat would, in the laft period, be lefs than in the former 3,567,708*l.*; and we have feen that their expenfes in the laft period have exceeded their expenfes in the firft near half a million.

Having fubftantiated this fact, we will now examine the articles which the *taxes*, during the American war, had increafed in price in 1785 beyond that in 1776. It has been proved, that the price of corn regulates the price of the other articles of neceffary confump-

tion;

tion; therefore, as corn was cheaper, they could not be materially dearer, but by the operation of fome tax.

Had the American war, in 1785, occafioned any additional duty on any article which may be called a neceffary of life? Was any duty laid on milk, cheefe, butter, foap, leather, candles, but- cher's meat, linen, cloth, firing, to which they were not equally fubject in 1776, if fubject to any tax at all? The anfwer is a nega- tive: therefore how the price of all, or any of them, could be in- creafed one-fifth, by the means of taxation, I cannot difcover; neither can it be granted as a fact, that leather, foap, candles, butter, cheefe, coft one-fifth more in 1785 than in the years imme- diately preceding the American war: that thefe articles might fome of them be fomewhat dearer, may be fact; but, although the exact proportion cannot eafily be afcertained, the affertion may be fafely ventured, that they had not increafed a fifth in price. Beer, fpirits, tea, fugar, fnuff, tobacco, were increafed in price during this war; but as thefe cannot be numbered among the neceffaries of life; and the firft, the only article, the ufe of which can be approved of, is generally found the labourer in agriculture by his mafter; it can- not form a general article of unavoidable expenfe.

We have feen that the average-price of wheat, during the firft period, was fo much more than during the laft, as to make a difference of 3l. 8s. 6d. annually, in the expenditure of a family of fix people; and the fum it cofts fuch a family for corn, in the laft period, is more than half the probable earnings of a labourer's family; therefore the expenfes of that family, in all other articles of confumption, could not be increafed more than it had faved in the proportional price of wheat, had the price of thofe articles in- creafed one-fifth, as Mr. Howlett has afferted.

Where then refts the proof, that the number of poor, and the increafed expenfe of maintaining them, arifes from the price of la- bour not having rifen in proportion to the price of the neceffaries of life? And where do we perceive the caufe for an increafe of

agricultural

agricultural wages, which are known to have rifen two-pence in the fhilling in daily labour fince the laft century, and in tafk-work much more? The price of corn has not rifen in any fuch a proportion, and the price of corn regulates the price of home-made commoditics. If greater wages are given, they will be given for expenfes in articles widely different from the neceffaries of life; they will be given for the encouragement of idlenefs, by the increafe of the excife-revenue. Idlenefs is the root of all evil;—articles of excife are the moifture which nourifhes that root.

But, while our reafon can find no caufe for a rife of wages, both that and our humanity plead ftrongly for fome encouragement to induftry; becaufe it is apprehended, that a profpect of reward is a more active and honourable inducement than a fear of punifhment. So thought and fo wrote William Shakefpeare, in 1581. The human mind is fooner roufed to action by a hope of rifing, than by a fear of falling: that apprehenfion cannot pervade the mafs of labouring-people;

So fafely low the poor, they cannot fall.

But no fituation in this country fhould be beneath a probability of advancement. Hope fhould be permitted to travel through life with all of us. When that pleafing companion, that chearful ray of untried felicity, is excluded from our fight, our journey is gloomy indeed: defpondence and apathy then are affociated with us; and mifery, as Trincalo fays, acquaints a man with ftrange bed-fellows.

The confolidation of fmall farms, where the practice prevails to that extent as to leave no fmall occupation for the labourer who might have faved money fufficient, or, by a courfe of honeft and induftrious conduct, have obtained credit fufficient, to ftock and farm a few acres of land, moft certainly operates to a great difcouragement of induftry.

In

In parishes where this practice so generally prevails, there is no other chance for him, whose manual labour *tills* the land, to *reap* the produce of it, than by occupying the glebe of the parish, or those lands which have been left in trust for the uses of particular charities. The proper tenants of such lands, and also of the glebe, if the incumbent does not occupy it himself, are the industrious poor; and, in such cases, the parish-rates should become the security for the rent.

If box-clubs were generally established, such of the subscribers as have continued their payments a given number of years, who might be thought by the parish-officers worthy to be trusted with a small occupation of land, should be permitted to draw out of the stock the amount of their subscriptions, deducting such sums as they may have received from the club, whenever such an opportunity of occupying land might offer. In that case, those who have migrated from their parishes to obtain greater wages, and have paid a larger proportion of their earnings to the stock, as was proposed, would have a proportional greater chance of rising in their situations.

To appropriate any part of the compulsory maintenance to the encouragement of youthful industry, might possibly be thought an unwarrantable perversion; but it certainly would not be an illegal application of part of the poor's rate; for, it should be in our recollection, that to set the poor at work was one great cause which induced the legislature to institute a poor's rate: and it must be acknowledged, that this rate can be diminished by no means so proper, and beneficial to the public, as by the promotion of general industry: and we should also bear in our minds, that industrious habits grow by encouragement more thriftily than by compulsion.

Every encouragement given by agricultural societies tends to this end: rewards for good and skilful operations in husbandry, — for long and honest services, — for bringing up, without parish-assistance, a family of children, — fchools of induftry, with prizes to the moft deferving, — all tend to excite and preferve a fpirit of induftrious emulation, productive of the beft effects; a fpirit well exchanged for that idle thievifh difpofition, too prevalent, at prefent, among the rifing generation of the poor.

The overfeers of the poor, in their refpective parifhes, poffefs numberlefs opportunities of encouraging induftry. The application that a poor perfon is obliged, by the ftatute, to make to them for relief, before he is authorized to be relieved by the next magiftrate, gives them ample opportunities to obtain information of the induftry, the economy, the earnings, the expenditure, of the perfon applying. When the overfeers perceive one family in want of parifh-relief, and the adjoining family, in a fimilar fituation with refpect to number, age, and capability of maintaining themfelves, not only not in want, but poffeffing a vifible property, they muft feel that the duty of their office requires fome inveftigation of this apparent paradox; and if, on inquiry, they find, that honeft induftry and rigid economy place the one family above want, and that idlenefs and wafte reduce the other to diftrefs; if they dole to the one neceffary relief, which is more than they deferve, they fhould, by every encouragement, hold the other out as an example to be imitated. The natural claims of the one on fociety are equivocal; the merits of the other are certain.

LETTER   XXXIII.

IT appears illiberal to refufe affent to the only reafonable excufe that can be alleged, in behalf of the poor, for the miferable degree of poverty in which they are plunged, and for the increafing burthen

burthen of expenfe to the public in their maintenance: an excufe which, if it exifted, would throw the blame from *their* fhoulders to *thofe* of their employers.

It would alfo ill become any man occupying a confiderable portion of landed property, and refiding in a country where the general appearance of his labouring neighbours indicates fuch diftrefs as, when it meets the eye, muft affect the heart, and which diftrefs arifes either from their wages not being fufficient to purchafe the neceffaries of life, or from a deficiency of economy and induftry in the poor themfelves, to deny the firft caufe, and affert the laft to be a fact. Such conduct would be inexcufable in any man, unlefs, from candid inveftigation, he was firmly perfuaded of the fact, and was confcious that fuch a reprefentation was the language of truth; and, in that cafe, it becomes, in an inquiry of this nature, his duty to make his opinion public, and to affert, that the neceffaries of life are not rifen in price more than agricultural wages.

Such is the opinion that the laft pages of this inquiry have attempted to eftablifh as truth; and, if they have fucceeded, the following confequence, which refults from it, is apparent, and cannot be contradicted: — That economy and prudence are neceffary to make what the poor earn go as far towards the fupport of life as poffible; and induftry alfo is neceffary to make their time as productive as poffible: for, if it be true that agricultural labour is as well paid, all things being confidered, as it ought to be, there is no way to increafe the earnings of the poor but by increafing the general quantity of induftry. This is therefore the point to which our attention fhould be directed.

Mr. Locke's opinion has been mentioned, with refpect to the relaxation of difcipline among the poor. To this he attributed, in 1697, their mifery and our expenfes. This opinion was extracted from a collection of pamphlets concerning the poor, publifhed at

Edinburgh

Edinburgh in 1787, which referred to Mr. Chalmers's Eſtimate of the comparative State of Great Britain.

The whole of Mr. Locke's memorial, as one of the Commiſſioners of the Board of Trade, was not then in print; nor was any other ſtreſs laid on it than ſuch as the opinion of a man of his abilities and ſolid judgement demanded: but the laſt edition of the pamphlet, publiſhed for the benefit, and giving an account of the inſtitution and management, of the ſchools of induſtry in the county of Lincoln, has thrown a much ſtronger light on this memorial; has placed the whole of it before our view; and, by ſo doing, has connected the practice and experience of a moſt excellent regulation for the encouragement of youthful induſtry, with the ſentiments of a vigorous and highly-cultivated mind.

This Report from the Board of Trade, drawn up by Mr. Locke, contains not *his* opinion only, but that alſo of *other commiſſioners*, founded on a full and mature examination both of facts and arguments, produced from a multiplicity of proofs which they had full power to call for. It originated at the inſtigation of William the Third, who had the regular employment of the poor much at heart, and mentioned the ſubject to his parliament, on opening the ſeſſion in 1699, as a meaſure he very much intereſted himſelf in; and there was, accordingly, an act of parliament drawn up, that ſtill exiſts, although, owing to the altercations between him and his parliament, which took place about this time, it was never paſſed into a law.

One capital feature in this excellent memorial is, the recommendation of ſchools of induſtry; and ſurely ſuch an inſtitution, if *ever* adviſable, is *now* adviſable; if it was *ever* neceſſary, by a regular education, to increaſe the honeſt means of maintenance among the labouring poor, it is *now* neceſſary; if *ever* there was reaſon to fear that the poor's rate may anticipate the ſources of our national expenditure, we have *now* reaſon to fear it; and ſurely if

we

we *ever* had caufe to dread the confequences of fuch an anticipation to the interefts of the kingdom at large, to the internal peace of its inhabitants, and to the fafety of our much-admired conftitution, we have *now* every reafon to dread the confequences of a poor's rate, which has rifen upon us in times of peace and profperity, and which will continue to rife in a greater proportion, and with increafed celerity, as war, with its concomitant evils and expenfes, reduces our trade, impoverifhes our manufactures, and increafes the demands upon us for money, the finews of war, in an inverfe proportion with our ability to contribute it.

Fas eft ab hofte doceri.—Shall we then be inattentive to the opinions of thofe with whom we are now at war? An opinion delivered in times of peace, and then conceived, by thofe who formed the firft conftitution after the deftruction of defpotifm in France, as particularly applicable to the intention of inftituting a poor's rate throughout that kingdom fimilar to that of England. Shall we pay no attention to that remarkable expreffion made ufe of by the French Committee of Mendicity which points out our poor's rate as the moft deftructive gangrene of our conftitution? And if that man, whofe effigy, in many places within the kingdom, has been burnt, a ceremony that has thrown out a blaze to the reputation of his abilities, which his intentions by no means deferve from thofe who are friends to the conftitution of this country; if that man has ever, either in his writings or his converfation, declared his opinion, " that the prefent adminiftration of our code of poor-laws will, if continued, in time effect, with certainty, that deftruction of our conftitution," which himfelf, and other enemies to this country, have attempted to bring about in a quicker manner; if fuch is the opinion of Thomas Paine, fhall we not be taught to ftrenghten ourfelves in that weak part which an enemy inadvertently has pointed out; to repair that breach in our citadel; to probe and cleanfe that wound which an enemy knows has been too much neglected, and now, through that neglect, gleƈt, threatens us with deſtruƈtion? * Surely the objeƈt is of importance ſufficient to demand all our attention ; and the attempt of an individual to excite that attention cannot be called preſumptuous, although it may be vain; cannot deſerve reproof, although it may not meet with ſuccefs.

Mr. Locke has reported, that, if the caufe of this evil be looked into, the commiffioners humbly conceive it will be found to have proceeded neither from ſcarcity of proviſions, nor from want of employment for the poor, " ſince the goodneſs of God," he ſays, " has bleſſed theſe times with plenty no leſs than the former."

Has not the goodneſs of God alſo bleſſed this kingdom with plenty fince the determination of the American war ? If, in 1697, this was the language of truth, and the voice of gratitude, is it not ſo, at leaft in an equal degree, at preſent ? Has not the horn of plenty been poured of late years over this country, replete with all the fruits of the earth, in every produƈtion of art and induſtry ? Have not our ſhips conveyed the overflowings of Great Britain, whoſe conſumption borders upon waſte, to all parts of the globe ? And have they not returned home laden with the produce

---

* Early in the ſpring of 179*, ſoon after the Rights of Man was publiſhed, I was invited by a gentleman, to whom I had ſhewn ſome civilities in the county, to dine with him in town. Thomas Paine was one of the company : it was my lot to be placed next to him. The company being large, the converſation ſoon became more divided than general, each perſon talking to his neighbour. Mr. Paine told me he was informed I had paid great attention to the ſituation of the poor in this county, and the laws reſpeƈting them, and aſked me what I thought of the poor's rate. I told him I thought it an increaſing evil. He then made me this reply : — " I am juſt returned from Thetford, where my grandfather was overſeer about half a century ago. I have juſt ſeen the rates for his half-year ; they were under £40. — I think he ſaid £34. — What do you think they are now this preſent half-year ? Sir, they are between £300 and £400. In a ſhort time, if this evil is not ſtopped, the friends of liberty will, with the greateſt eaſe, walk over the ruins of the boaſted Conſtitution : its fall wants no acceleration from the friends of Gallic freedom." — To this a gentleman preſent inſtantly replied, " Thomas, thy wiſh is father to that thought."

of

of all climes? Whatever fruits the earth has produced from the north to the fouth, from the eaft to the weft; whatever commodities the art and induftry of all nations manufactured; have they not been imported in barter for our productions? and has not a vaft balance of trade been ftill in our favour? Surely, then, our profperity, in 1792, was full as remarkable as in 1697.

But let us attend to the fhades of the two pictures, and confider the obfcure as well as the clear. What does Mr. Locke complain of in 1697? The number of the poor, and the increafe of the rate for their maintenance. — In 1697, the Board of Trade reprefented to the king, that the number of infolvent inhabitant houfes was feven hundred and fifty thoufand; which, at five inhabitants to a houfe, a calculation fuperior to what the political arithmeticians of 1690 allow, make a total of three millions feven hundred and fifty thoufand poor; and that the fupport of all the poor muft be four hundred thoufand pounds yearly.*

In 1787, Mr. Howlett calculates the poor at fix millions, and the return of the poor's rates amounted, on the average of three years, ending in 1785, to above two millions, and there is reafon to believe that thefe rates are ftill increafing. If the management of the poor in 1697 wanted regulation, does it not in 1793?

In 1697, Mr. Locke fuggefted that fchools of induftry were the means to increafe the quantity of labour throughout the kingdom, and to decreafe the expenfe in maintaining the poor. Sir Richard Lloyd, between fifty and fixty years afterwards, ftarted the fame idea; but it remained for a part of the county of Lincoln to reduce theory to practice, in the year 1783, and to prove that thofe advantages, of which others had only conceived the probability, were capable, by experiment, of being proved certain. It appears that thofe gentlemen, who formed the plan of inftituting fchools of induftry,

* Collection of pamphlets, concerning the poor, London and Edinburgh, 1787, p. 104. Chalmers's Eftimate, p. 47.

within

within the diftrict of Lindfey, in the county of Lincoln, had not, at that time, nor indeed until very lately, feen the heads of Mr. Locke's plan: other counties in the kingdom may therefore now profit by uniting Mr. Locke's theoretic regulations with the practical experience of the inftitution in Lincolnfhire.

Nor can that experience be flightly eftimated, or its good effects lightly valued, which, upon a general average of the earnings of the children, in thofe fchools, prove clearly, that one hundred and thirty-five, between the age of eleven and twelve years, have, in ten months, taking in the depth of the five winters, ending in 1789, earned the fum of 680*l.* 3*s.* 3*d.* or half-a-crown a week each, " exclufive of all their work, during the other ten months of each of thofe years; exclufive of the work of fuch fpinners as do not feel themfelves, or are not thought by their friends, forward enough to become candidates ; and exclufive of thofe who, having their fettlement in non-fubfcribing parifhes, and being thereby deprived of any chance for thefe encouragements, have yet availed themfelves fo far of the introduction of the Jerfey fpinning, as to earn fome part of their fubfiftence by their own unaffifted efforts, in fpight of the difficulties arifing from the fmallnefs of their cottages, &c.

" Of the two laft defcriptions, the number is very great, but far greater ftill is the multitude of thofe, who, by the obftinacy of parents, the neglect of overfeers, or the general prejudices arifing from old habits, are ftill trained up in floth, vice, and mifery."

The worthy and able patron of thefe fchools, and editor of this publication, continues his exhortations to the public, in the following words :

" Would to God that the eyes of the nation could be opened upon this greateft of all evils ; this fatal fource of national profligacy and misfortune ! — If the reader joins in this fincere and anxious wifh, let him, after he has perufed the following work of the great Mr. Locke, compare it with the many crude attempts that have been made, fince the date of that report, to patch, to alter, or to

abrogate,

abrogate, the wife and beneficial ftatute of Queen Elizabeth ; and,
if he fhall then be of opinion, that parifh-working-fchools deferve
a fair and full trial, let him exert his abilities and his intereft,
whatever they are, in procuring that trial to be fuftained, by the
only authority that can prevail over fuch obftacles, as will ever refift all private endeavours.

<hr/>

LETTER XXXIV.

OF the fame opinion with this worthy magiftrate is the writer
of thefe ftrictures; an opinion formed from an attention to
the habits of the rifing generation; from a knowledge of the real
good thefe fchools of induftry have effected, where they have been
inftituted; and, from an impreffion, indelibly received by precept
and education in early life, that *idlenefs is the root of all evil*, and
now confirmed by obfervation and experience: and moft earneftly
does he join in this exhortation to thofe who have the power, that
they may alfo have the will, to procure a trial of fchools of induftry, by the authority of the ftatute of Elizabeth, affifted by the
contributions of individuals.

It is in this report of Mr. Locke's, here alluded to, that he fug-
gefts the idea of thefe fchools of induftry, and produces the following heads of regulations refpecting them.

" The children of labouring-people are an ordinary burthen to
the parifh, and are ufually maintained in idlenefs; fo that their
labour alfo is generally loft to the public, till they are twelve or
fourteen years old.

" The moft effectual remedy for this, that we are able to conceive, and which we therefore humbly propofe, is, that working-
fchools be fet up in each parifh, to which the children of all fuch

as demand relief of the parifh, above three and under fourteen years of age, whilft they live at home with their parents, and are not otherwife employed for their livelihood, by the allowance of the overfeers of the poor, fhall be obliged to come.

" By this means the mother will be eafed of a great part of her trouble in looking after and providing for them at home, and fo be at more liberty to work ; the children will be kept in much better order ; be better provided for; and, from their infancy, be inured to work, which is of no fmall confequence to the making of them fober and induftrious all their lives after ; and the parifh will be either eafed of this burthen, or at leaft of the mifufe in the prefent management of it : for a great number of children giving a poor man a title to an allowance from the parifh, this allowance is given once a week, or once a month, to the father, in money; which he, not feldom, fpends on himfelf at the ale-houfe, whilft his children (for whofe fake he had it) are left to fuffer, or perifh under the want of neceffaries, unlefs the charity of neighbours relieve them.

" We humbly conceive, that a man and his wife, in health, may be able, by their ordinary labour, to maintain themfelves and two children : more than two children at one time, under the age of three years, will feldom happen in one family ; if, therefore, all the children, above three years old, be taken off their hands, thofe who have never fo many, whilft they remain themfelves in health, will not need any allowance for them.

" We do not fuppofe that children at three years old will be able, at that age, to get their livelihoods at the working-fchool ; but we are fure, that what is neceffary for their relief will more effectually have that ufe, if it be diftributed to them in bread at that fchool, than if it be given to their fathers in money. What they have at home from their parents is feldom more than bread and water, and that, many of them, very fcantily too ; if, therefore, care be taken that they have each of them their belly-full of bread daily at fchool,

they

they will be in no danger of famiſhing; but, on the contrary, they will be healthier and ſtronger than thoſe who are bred otherwiſe. Nor will this practice coſt the overſeer any trouble; for a baker may be agreed with to furniſh and bring into the ſchool-houſe, every day, the allowance of bread neceſſary for all the ſcholars that are there. And to this may be added alſo, without any trouble, in cold weather, if it be thought needful, a little warm water-gruel; for the ſame fire that warms the room may be made uſe of to boil a pot of it.

" From this method the children will not only reap the fore-mentioned advantages, with far leſs charge to the pariſh than what is now done for them, but they will be alſo thereby the more obliged to come to ſchool and apply themſelves to work, becauſe otherwiſe they will have no victuals: and alſo the benefit thereby, both to themſelves and the pariſh, will daily increaſe; for the earnings of their labour at ſchool every day increaſing, it may reaſonably be concluded that, computing all the earnings of a child, from three to fourteen years of age, the nouriſhment and teaching of ſuch a child, during that whole time, will coſt the pariſh nothing: whereas there is no child now, which, from its birth, is maintained by the pariſh, but, before the age of fourteen, coſts the pariſh fifty or ſixty pounds.

Another advantage alſo of bringing poor children thus to a working-ſchool is, that by this means they may be obliged to come conſtantly to church every Sunday along with their ſchool-maſters or dames, whereby they may be brought into ſome ſenſe of religion; whereas ordinarily now, in their looſe and idle way of breeding up, they are as utter ſtrangers both to religion and morality, as they are to induſtry.

" In order, therefore, to the more effectually carrying on of this work to the advantage of this kingdom, we further humbly propoſe, that theſe ſchools be generally for ſpinning or knitting, or ſome other part of the woollen-manufacture, unleſs in countries

where

where the place fhall furnifh fome other materials fitter for the employment of fuch poor children ; in which places the choice of thofe
materials, for their employment, may be left to the prudence and
direction of the guardians of the poor of that hundred ; and that
the teachers, in thefe fchools, be paid out of the poor-rates, as can
be agreed.

" This, though at firft fetting up it may coft the parifh a little,
yet we humbly conceive, that (the earnings of the children abating
the charge of their maintenance, and as much work being required
of each of them as they are reafonably to perform) it will quickly
pay its own charges with an overplus.

" That, where the number of the poor children of any parifh
is greater than for them all to be employed in one fchool, they be
there divided into two; and the boys and girls, if thought convenient, taught and kept to work feparately.

" That the handicraftfmen, in each hundred, be bound to take
every other of their refpective apprentices from amongft the boys in
fome one of the fchools in the faid hundred, without any money :
which boys they may fo take, at what age they pleafe, to be bound
to them till the age of twenty-three years, that fo the length of
time may more than make amends for the ufual fums that are given
to handicraftfmen with fuch apprentices.

" That thofe alfo in the hundred who keep in their hands land
of their own to the value of 25*l.* per annum, or upwards, or who
rent 50*l.* per annum, or upwards, may choofe, out of the fchools
of the faid hundred, what boy each of them pleafes, to be his apprentice in hufbandry, upon the fame condition.

" That whatever boys are not, by this means, bound out apprentices before they are full fourteen, fhall, at the Eafter-meeting
of the *guardians of each hundred* every year, be bound to fuch gentlemen, yeomen, or farmers, within the faid hundred, as have the
greateft number of acres of land in their hands, who fhall be
obliged to take them for their apprentices till the age of twenty-
three,

three, or bind them out, at their own coft, to fome handicraftf-men; provided always, that no fuch gentleman, yeoman, or far-mer, fhall be bound to have two fuch apprentices at a time.

" That grown people, alfo, (to take away their pretence of want of work,) may come to the faid working-fchools to learn, where work fhall accordingly be provided for them.

" That the materials to be employed in thefe fchools, and among other the poor people of the parifh, be provided by a common ftock in each hundred, to be raifed out of a certain portion of the poor's rate of each parifh as requifite ; which ftock, we humbly conceive, need be raifed but once ; for, if rightly managed, it will increafe."

The expreffion, *guardians of the hundred*, refers to a part of Mr. Locke's general plan, which is not neceffarily connected with fchools of induftry : but it would not be difficult to put in practice this re-gulation, with refpect to binding the children apprentice at a proper age, without an appointment of guardians of hundreds. The laft claufe proceeds on the idea, that the application of the poor's rate to this purpofe, or as much of it as is neceffary, is a legal applica-tion of the parifh-money; and that it is fo is certain, as appears by the following extract from the 43d of Elizabeth :

" The overfeers, or the greateft part of them, fhall take order, from time to time, by and with the confent of two or more fuch juftices of the peace, as is aforefaid, for fetting to work the children of fuch whofe parents fhall not, by the faid church-wardens and overfeers, or the greater part of them, be thought able to keep and maintain their children." Sect. 1.

" And alfo to raife weekly, or otherwife, &c. a convenient ftock of flax, hemp, wool, thread, iron, and other neceffary ftuff, to fet the poor at work." Sect. 1.

The firft ftep towards the eftablifhment of fchools of induftry fhould therefore originate from the authority of the magiftrates;

and

and the quarter-feffions might, with great propriety, promote the undertaking, by orders to the following purport:

1. The overfeers of every parifh are, by order of feffions, required, by virtue of the act of parliament paffed in the 43d year of Queen Elizabeth, chapter the fecond, and in obedience thereto, to purchafe ftock and materials, and to provide proper places and proper inftructions to teach the children to knit and fpin of all fuch whofe parents fhall not be thought able to keep and maintain their children.

2. They are alfo required not to grant any relief in money to fuch parents who fhall refufe to fend their children, between the age of three years and nine, to the places appointed them for their inftruction, and fuffer them to continue there as many hours each day, as, by the faid overfeers, fhall be thought fit and proper, and not to ceafe their attendance until difcharged from the faid fchools with confent of the overfeers.

3. That thefe orders be printed, and copies of them difperfed in all parifhes throughout the diftrict.

Orders of feffions fimilar to thefe were iffued by the quarter-feffions at Louth, in Lincolnfhire, in 1783, which were followed by propofals for the encouragement of the working-poor within thofe diftricts, throughout which fchools of induftry have been inftituted.

The following are the propofals for an annual fubfcription for the working-poor, within certain diftricts in the county of Lincoln, which laid the foundations of the fchools of induftry in that county:

1. That every parifh, within the diftrict above-mentioned, be requefted to fubfcribe a fum amounting to the proportion of 1 per cent. upon the poor's rates of the laft year.

2. That individuals, within the faid diftrict, be folicited to fubfcribe the fum of five fhillings each annually.

3. That

3. That a meeting of the fubfcribers be called as foon as conveniently may be, to choofe a committee for the management of the bufinefs of the fubfcription.

4. That premiums be given from the faid fubfcription to fuch children, of certain ages and defcriptions, within the faid diftrict, as in a given time fhall have produced the greateft quantity of work, of different kinds, and of the beft quality.

5. That thefe premiums fhall confift in different articles of clothing, and the higheft premium in complete clothing. The faid clothing to be made handfome and uniform.

6. That, whenever any young perfon fhall go out to apprenticefhip or fervice, or be married, with the approbation of the committee, fuch young perfon fhall receive from the committee a reward not lefs than five pounds, nor exceeding ten pounds, if he or fhe fhall, in the courfe of his or her education, have received three or more of the annual premiums given by the commitee. A reward not lefs than two pounds, and not exceeding three pounds, if he or fhe fhall have received two of the faid premiums. And a reward not lefs than one pound ten fhillings, nor exceeding two pounds, if he or fhe fhall have received one of the faid annual premiums. If the fubfcriptions fhall not be found fufficient for the above rewards, then the value of each to be leffened in proportion to the ftate of the fubfcription.

7. That premiums be alfo given, at the difcretion of the committee, to fuch overfeers of the poor as fhall diftinguifh themfelves in the due execution of the orders of laft quarter-feffions, relative to the employment of the poor.

8. That the fixing the number of annual premiums, and the value of each, fhall be left to the difcretion of the committee.

It fhould be obferved, that, in thofe parts of Lincolnfhire where thefe fchools have been eftablifhed, the working-poor had not been accuftomed to any manufactory; and, except the labour that agriculture demanded, which (in a country where the tract of land,

cultivated

cultivated by the plough, being fmall in proportion to that ufed for
grazing) could not be fufficient, at all times of the year, to find
employment for their hufbandmen; the poor, confequently, were not
trained to regular habits of induftry; the women and children
efpecially had no means of increafing the income of their family,
had they, in fact, been poffeffed of the will, which, unfortunately,
they were not; but, on the contrary, the parents of children who
were at thefe fchools made ufe of every means in their power to
ftifle, in the cradle, an inftitution which had youthful induftry for
its object; although the fruits of that induftry were an increafe of
income to themfelves, clothing to their children, regular manners,
moral habits, honorary rewards, good characters, and a profpect of
more material advantages in future.   To fuch a degree of inveteracy was the oppofition of the poor to this excellent inftitution arrived, that many parents have been known to beat and otherwife
ill-treat their children, for having deferved and received rewards
from thofe appointed to diftribute the prizes.

The habits of the working-poor, in Suffolk and Effex, are materially different, as it is to be hoped they alfo are in moft counties
in England; the manufactures which have been eftablifhed among
us, in this part of the kingdom, for feveral centuries, have been
carried on with fuch reputation and fuccefs, as to give names, from
the towns in which they are made, to feveral kinds of highly valuable cloths, by which names they are known in the moft diftant
countries on the globe : at the fame time they have raifed many
worthy families to opulence and refpect; and, although it muft be
allowed, that the poor's rates have not always diminifhed in proportion as the manufactures have been fuccefsful, and have generally increafed as the demand for goods decreafed ; yet, as the poor
have been exercifed in habits of induftry, there is no fear that prejudices, fimilar to thofe in Lincolnfhire, fhould prevail here: the
temptation held forth to the children to be induftrious, by rewards, public exhibitions, and fhowy proceffions, which fo con-
                                                              fiderably

fiderably increafed the expenfes of the inftitutions in Lincolnfhire, will not be fo neceffary with us, nor in general throughout the kingdom; confequently a fmaller fubfcription, and lefs encouragement from the pockets of individuals, will infure fuccefs in other counties, than was found neceffary in Lincolnfhire; and probably an application of a proportion of the poor's rate may no longer be neceffary, than what is warranted by the letter and fpirit of the claufe in the forty-third of Elizabeth, authorizing the overfeers to take order for fetting the children of the poor to work, and to raife weekly, or otherwife by taxation, &c. a convenient ftock of hemp, wool, flax, &c. for that purpofe.

But fome fubfcription, fimilar to that propofed and carried into execution in Lincolnfhire, is certainly neceffary, to provide a falary for inftructors, and alfo prizes for the moft deferving. The working-rooms, the materials to manufacture, and the utenfils for the purpofe, may undoubtedly be purchafed by the poor's rate; but no act of parliament authorizes the overfeers to raife a fum to reward and encourage the poor, to incite them to induftry, and to ftir up a fpirit of emulation among that moft numerous clafs of our fellow-subjects, in the moft laudable exertions which can occupy the hours of human life.

There is no doubt but that the inhabitants in every county in the kingdom, by a laudable patriotic fpirit, which is conftantly manifefting itfelf in fo many fplendid inftances, to the honour of the country and of the age, would be induced to ftand forward with a fubfcription to this purpofe, were they impreffed with a conviction of the expediency, the utility, and practicability, of the meafure : to attempt fuch an impreffion fhall be the aim of the next Letter on this fubject.

LETTER

LETTER XXXV.

NO reliance fhall be placed on a train of inferences, which might, in this cafe, follow each other with all the authority of felf-evident propofitions; we will not at prefent rely on thofe de-duftions, which plain reafon and common fenfe muft make from fo univerfally acknowledged a principle, as that the riches of a nation are in proportion to its induftry, and its induftry depends on the habits imbibed by its young people; but we will, for a time, fup-pofe, that it is become the bufinefs of the writer to weaken and di-minifh, in the mind of his readers, their refpeft for and reliance on thofe arguments in favour of fchools of induftry, which he is not able to confute.

The propriety of the plan fhall firft be fuppofed to be attacked on this ground; that, allowing it to be no *illegal* appropriation of part of the poor's rates, to apply a fmall fum towards raifing a ftock for poor children to work out, and to teach them to earn a livelihood; yet it would be improper, becaufe common experience, as inftanced by the returns of the overfeers in the three years ending in 1785, has proved, that it has been their general praftice to apply a very fmall portion of the poor's rate in the purchafe of ftock for the poor to work up; not above a hundred and thirty-third part of the total raifed, or about fifteen thoufand pounds of the whole fum; and that this has been principally for the ufe of *grown people*, who are lefs likely to wafte and fpoil the ftock than *children*.

That, where the wants of the poor are fo prefling, as to occa-fion the fum raifed for their relief to be inadequate to the purpofe, the appropriating a larger portion to a precarious advantage would be improper.

That the attempt, to raife a fum by a general voluntary fubfcrip-tion, would, if it fucceeded, have the effeft of an additional rate:

if

if it did not fucceed, the money applied from the poor's rate would
be thrown away by the failure of the plan; therefore, in both
cafes, the attempt is improper.

That the fame objections, which apply to the propriety of the
plan, would equally apply to its expediency; and there are feveral
other obfervations which may be brought to prove it not expedient.

The only means of employing the children, and the only kind of
handicraft they are intended to learn, is knitting and fpinning;
thefe employments, however proper for girls, cannot be thought fo
for boys; a more active habit being neceffary to bring up men to
a life of agricultural labour, than the almoft fedentary employment
of the wheel; and it has been experienced, that habits of life, obtained by confinement, unnerve the man, and render him lefs fit
for thofe occupations for which the poor fhould be educated: for
inftance, a tailor or fhoemaker feldom becomes active and laborious, even though he may be induftrious; the foldiers and failors,
that come from the fpinning-wheel or the loom, are not fo likely
to be equal to a difcharge of their military duties, and to the hard-
fhips of their profeffion, as thofe from the plough or the faw;
nor is a fpinning-fchool fo likely to teach boys to go aloft as the
mafon's fcaffold.

Befides, what will be done with the produce of the fchools of
induftry? where will you find a fale for the yarn and the ftockings?
and, unlefs a market can be found, we fhall lofe both ftock and
block; and fhall confequently expend no inconfiderable portion of
the poor's rate, in teaching our poor children an art, which neither
ourfelves can, at prefent, or they, in future, turn to a profitable
account.

The fchools which are alluded to, as having been eftablifhed in
Lincolnfhire, have an advantage over fimilar fchools of fpinning
and knitting, in moft other counties: they were eftablifhed for the
exprefs purpofe of encouraging a manufacture, for which the *long
wool of Lincolnfhire* is particularly proper; the fale of the ftaple-

commodity of their county was the principal object that the promoters of thefe fchools had in view : — in other counties, if Jerfey or worfted fpinning is to be the employment, the manufacture of the ftaple-commodity of two or three counties alone will be the object ; and, in proportion as the diftance increafes, where thefe fchools are encouraged, from the counties where the long wool is produced, in the fame proportion will the expenfe of the carriage of the raw commodity be increafed ; and, as the diftance increafes from the northern counties, fo will the price upon the fpot, of the yarn manufactured, decreafe.

How, and where, can teachers be procured in every village ? The expenfe will be too great, where the number of the fcholars is fmall ; and, where large, not only teachers will be wanting, but fchool-rooms, which will add very confiderably to the expenfe.

Thefe, very probably, are the principal reafons that may be alleged againft this inftitution ; as thefe appear at firft fight fufficient to raife a doubt in the minds of thofe, whofe encouragement would be neceffary, not only in word but deed ; whofe good report of the meafure is not the only act required in its favour, but whofe activity and fupervifion are wanted, after their liberality has been experienced by a public fubfcription : it is therefore proper not to rely on the effect of panegyric only ; but to obviate thefe objections, which may appear to fome of confiderable importance.

With refpect to the firft objection, it fhall be anfwered ; that a vicious or bad practice fhould be abolifhed, and that the univerfality of it ought by no means to be produced as an argument in its favour, but as a proof to the contrary ; if an individual parifh lofes ten pounds a year, becaufe the overfeers do not provide a ftock for the poor to work up, as, by the ftatute of Elizabeth, it is their duty to do, fuch conduct of the officers is blameable and detrimental to that parifh ; and it will not become lefs fo if a fimilar conduct prevails in ten thoufand parifhes ; but, on the contrary, the lofs will be co-extenfive with the univerfality of the neglect, and the bad

bad effect of fuch conduct will prove itfelf by the fum-total of the lofs.

Now, let us reverfe the object, and fuppofe an oppofite caufe producing an effect diametrically oppofite: if ten pounds per annum would be the gains of a fingle parifh, from the employment of children, two hundred thoufand pounds would be the profit, if the practice were univerfal.

But let us fee the good confequence in the light of habit only; and let us confider youthful induftry as being calculated, by raifing an induftrious generation, to increafe the wealth of the kingdom, which muft bear a proportion with the work done within it. We will take it for granted that this fifteen thoufand pounds, which has been returned to the committee of the Houfe of Commons as the fum expended in providing materials and utenfils for fetting the poor to work throughout England and Wales, could have been only fufficient to provide work for the impotent and aged poor, and a few children in the work-houfes, what would, by this time, have been the happy effect throughout the kingdom, if twenty times that fum had been employed in teaching, and fetting to work, all the children of the poor through the three years when this average was taken, even if no profit had arifen from the work itfelf?

Thofe happy effects are beyond our calculation: we can only have a faint notion of them, by forming an idea of the reverfe of their prefent miferable fituation; by placing before our eyes the happy profpect an induftrious generation forms, when placed in contraft with an idle race of people: we fhould fee cleanlinefs inftead of filth, clothing inftead of nakednefs, comfort and content inftead of mifery and diffatisfaction.

This advantage is not precarious, but certain, independent of immediate profit from the materials worked up. Suppofing no market for their yarn, no fale for their ftockings; even fuppofing the lofs of materials and of time certain; the habits of induftry

try obtained, alone, would be worth ten times the amount of the whole expense.

But there is no reason to suppose the produce of youthful ingenuity unsaleable or unprofitable : has it been so in Lincolnshire? If not, why must it be so in Suffolk, in Essex, or in any other county? That yarn which is fit for market may have a longer carriage upon it, if no sale can be found at home, it is true : it certainly is farther from Suffolk and Essex to Yorkshire, than from Lincolnshire : but why must the schools of industry in these counties be employed only in spinning of Jersey? Why could not they be employed about such yarn as would find a market with the neighbouring manufacturers? If it be answered, that the neighbouring manufacturers do not keep the *parents* in constant work, and consequently the *children's yarn* would not find a sale, the difficulty is easily removed : let it be proposed to increase the consumption of coarse woollen cloths, by clothing our numerous poor in warm and comfortable apparel, manufactured by their own children. We are constrained, by act of parliament, for the encouragement of the woollen-manufacture, to bury people of all ranks and conditions in a shroud made of sheep's wool only. Why should not our poor (all those who are in such a situation of life as to be relieved by the poor's rate) be clothed by the manufactory arising from the ingenuity and industry of their children? This would be a real encouragement of youthful industry. The obligation, when once become the law of the land, would, it is believed, by general consent, become the practice: and this, at least, is certain, that the poor would experience the comforts of such clothing ; they would experience, also, other great benefits, arising from the habit of industry, imbibed by their young family.

LETTER

LETTER XXXVI.

WITH refpect to the impropriety of employing any part of the poor's rates, in a plan, the fuccefs of which may be doubtful, and of collecting, from the pockets of the benevolent and charitable, a kind of additional poor's rate, the anfwer is obvious : — the benevolent and charitable may be difappointed, if the plan fhould not be fuccefsful, but will receive an equivalent for their money fubfcribed in their intention to do good : and, if the plan fucceeds, the good effect itfelf will infure a chearful continuance of their fubfcription : in the mean time, a portion of the poor's rate will be applied according to the fpirit, as well as the letter, of the law : and, fhould it fail of the fuccefs expected, one truth will be eftablifhed; a melancholy one indeed, but fuch as we ought not to be ignorant of, if it be a truth : — that youthful induftry cannot be made productive of advantage to fociety, except in the *habit itfelf*, which will not leave them in maturer life, when it *will be of fervice*; and, in that cafe, we have gained the habit of induftry in return for the expenfe.

But the employment, being confined to fpinning and knitting, has been ftated as an objection.   Let us fuppofe thefe to be the fole employments; although, if the plan fucceeds, and their work is profitable, other handicrafts might be introduced: the objection may be anfwered in the words of that gentleman * to whom the county of Lincoln has been fo much obliged for thefe inftitutions.

* See an Account of the Society for the Promotion of Induftry in Lincolnfhire, by the Rev. R. G. Bower, one of his Majefty's juftices of the peace for the county of Lincoln.

" Now

" Now I would afk, which parifhes will hereafter ftock the country with the moft laborious, honeft, and intelligent, fervants or labourers? Will they be thofe where children, until they become thirteen or fourteen years old, *at leaſt*, continue to be nurtured in idlenefs (whether at the public expenfe or that of their parents); where they fee nothing but patterns of diffolutenefs and immorality; hear nothing but oaths, blafphemies, and flander; learn nothing but to plunder hen-roofts, orchards, and hedges; and, for thefe and fimilar purpofes, keep the moft irregular hours, and are accuftomed to prowl about at night like fo many beafts of prey? It is faid, *the children, under the care recommended above, will, at thirteen or fourteen years of age, know nothing but fpinning.* Yes, they will know much more; unlefs regularity of hours, decency of behaviour, a habit of perfevering induftry, and a fenfe of duty to God and man, with the means of perpetuating it, are nothing. But will fuch objectors lay their hands on their hearts, and fay, that *one* in *twenty* of the pauper's children, at prefent, when thirteen or fourteen years old, knows *any thing at all*, unlefs it be fome of the wicked accomplifhments above alluded to? If they *do not*, it is mere cavilling, and not worth a ferious anfwer, to fay, that we muft not teach them what we propofe, only becaufe it is not, perhaps, in our power to teach them more; at leaft, not without fuch funds as we can have no reafon to expect. Would not, then, any confiderate man, about to hire a lad or a girl of the age above-mentioned, give a decided preference to thofe who fhall have been educated in a parifh, where, in conformity to the plans of our fociety, children from five or fix years of age are affembled, under the fame roof, at an early and regular hour of the morning; kept fteadily to the purfuit of bufinefs; taught that, even fo early in life, they are *able to maintain themfelves*; made to take a pride in nothing but what they obtain by merit; and to difpute about no other object, than who, by being forwardeft in the performance of

duty,

duty, fhall be entitled to the higheft of thofe rewards which the liberality of the fociety of induftry fhall, from time to time, hold up to their view?

" Can it be fuppofed that fuch an education will make no diffe- rence either in the morality of the country or the incumbrance of parifhes? Will all this care and trouble be thrown away upon them? Will they remember none of the good leffons they have heard and will hear? Will they at once caft off all the regularity they fhall have been inured to, during thofe fix or feven years of human life, wherein habits, either good or bad, are eafieft planted, and take the deepeft root? Will they be as much inclined to pick- ing and ftealing as if they had never tafted the fweet produce of ho- neft labour? Will they, exclufive of principle, be as *dexterous* in the trade of iniquity as if they had never been exercifed at any other? Will they, when decorated with the honourable marks of our fociety's approbation, care as little about *their character, thus eftablifhed*, as thofe who never knew how great a treafure a good name is? Laftly, will they eafily be induced to raife a clamo- rous tongue, or extend an idle hand, for parifh-relief, at thirty or forty years of age, when they were taught to fcorn it at nine or ten?"

As to the want of activity in the employment, if the knitting- pin is to be handled, or the fpinning-wheel is to be turned, the ob- fervation is futile. The chief time of girls and boys, in all fchools, is paffed in a fedentary pofture; but they have their hours of relaxa- tion, during which they unbend their minds, and train, by youth- ful fports, the body to exercife and health. Have not all our large fchools produced excellent foldiers and failors? Where can we, with reafon, expect our commanders by fea and land to be edu- cated, if not in thofe feminaries, where the improvement of the mind confines them many hours in the day to a fedentary pofture, pleafureably exchanged, in the hours of relaxation, for the native vigorous fports of youth?

L l

Say, Father Thames, for thou haft feen
Full many a fprightly race,
Difporting on thy margent green,
The paths of pleafure trace.

But, allowing it to be expedient that the rifing generation of
the poor ought to be brought up in more active employments than
the knitting-needle or the wheel only, might they not intermix
the labours of the field with the employments of manufacture? If
ftones are to be picked for the furveyor, wheat to be drilled, pulfe
to be hoed, corn to be weeded, grafs to be made into hay, wheat to
be reaped, and all other various employments of hufbandry to be
learned, could not the fuperintendant of the fchools go with his
pupils into the fields, and fee that they do their work properly?
Very little inftruction would be neceffary; the only object would be
to keep up the habit of induftry, which might be effected with as
much eafe in a field as in a room.

With refpect to the difficulty of finding teachers for every village,
and a falary to pay them, it is apprehended that any village, producing twenty male and female fcholars, will find it the beft economy to pay a perfon fuch a falary as will be worth the acceptance
to keep thefe young people in habits of induftry, and to inftruct
them in the ufe of thofe very common inftruments, the knitting-pin
and the wheel : the farmer who employs them will find it worth his
while that they fhould not remain ignorant of the mode of per-
forming operations in agriculture, when they can be of fervice in
that line.

Where the number of fcholars is fmall, one fchool-room would
be fufficient, which might be eafily found in any village; and, where
the number is large, it is better to have different rooms than to
croud many in one, both in regard to health and to convenience :
the fame teacher could fuperintend two rooms, half-a-mile from
each

each other, with equal, if not greater, convenience, than if the whole number of scholars were in one.

It would be premature to offer, at this time, any specific plan for the establishment of these schools, either throughout the kingdom at large, or in that small proportion of it to which these letters are more particularly addressed; it may, nevertheless, be proper to observe, that Mr. Locke's theory, united with the experiments already made in the county of Lincoln, would together form a good outline, which might be filled up according to the disposition and situation of the inhabitants in any village, or town, which might choose to make the experiment, and in which the local convenience of the particular places might be consulted and attended to.

In an excursion which I made into Lincolnshire, in the summer of 1787, to view the state of agriculture in that county, and also to inspect the regulation, and to be able to form some idea of the use, of these institutions, some notes of which journey are in the eighth volume of the Annals of Agriculture, I became acquainted with a gentleman who took an active part, as a trustee, in the direction of them; and, wishing to introduce a similar institution in Suffolk, I wrote to him requesting some information as to some particular points which were stated to him. I cannot conceive this gentleman will be offended with me for making public so much of his answer as respected this subject of our correspondence, it reflecting much credit on himself for the obliging and instructive manner in which he gives his information. A copy of that part of his letter shall, therefore, be subjoined, as it will point out the means the gentlemen in the southern district of the parts of Lindsay, where these schools were first established, took to insure success in their attempt.

Dec. 8, 1787.

DEAR SIR,

———— " It was entirely through the recommendation of the quarter-feffions, held at Louth, that the poor were fet to fpinning through this part of the county of Lincoln; and by the great affiduity, &c. of our worthy magiftrate, Mr. Bowyer, the plan has been carried fo very far into execution. The materials were at firft procured by the overfeers of the poor of each parifh, and the wheels and reels, &c. bought by them, at the parifh's expenfe ; and, as foon as the children can fpin tolerably well, the wool-comber delivers out the wool to the fpinners, and pays them for the fpinning per pound, and overhanks; and the children earn foon from 18*d.* to 3*s.* per week, from feven years old.

" The children in fchools were and are taught by a woman procured for that purpofe, at the expenfe of the parifh at firft, but are afterwards paid out of the earnings of the children fo taught, in proportion to their earnings ; and deductions are alfo made for fire and candle.

" Before any fchool-rooms were built, the children were taught in fome convenient room in each parifh, or in fome old uninhabited houfe, as beft fuited. The fchool-hours are generally from fix in the morning, in fummer, until fix or feven in the evening; and, in winter, from feven in the morning till feven or eight at night.

" No fchool-rooms have been built fo large as to contain a hundred children ; nor do we think it would be eligible to have them fo large as to contain fo many; but, on the contrary, we think the beft fize are thofe which will *properly* hold about twenty wheels, or fewer, according to the children in each parifh ; and, where there is a great number of children, *I think* different fchools fhould be erected in fuch parts of the parifh as may beft fuit the convenience of the children coming to and going from fchool; which fchools may be built of flight and cheap materials; but *that* as parifhes choofe;

choofe; for fome have been made for the purpofe *alfo* of the teacher's refiding in. A fchool for twenty fhould be 36 feet long by 15 or 16 feet wide, with windows on *both* fides, as may be beft for light; and, for warmth, we ufe ftoves generally, which are not expenfive at *the firft*, and fave a great deal in coals, &c.

" The teachers are *always* fuch as can teach the children to read, one hour *at the leaft* each day, and take good care of their morals; and alfo inftruct them how to behave themfelves to *all forts* of people, as far as in their power.

" Where Sunday-fchools are already eftablifhed, the children are attended *generally* by the teacher, and others appointed."

Such an inftitution would, wherever it is carried into effect, tend to every defirable confequence, as well with refpect to the pecuniary interefts of the occupiers in the place, by diminifhing the poor's rates, as to the comfort of the poor themfelves, by introducing among their children regular habits of induftry and orderly behaviour, and would, confequently, tend to the happinefs of thofe alfo, who, although elevated above the apprehenfion of poverty, are not above the feelings of humanity, and therefore muft lament thofe diftreffes of their neighbours, which they cannot help feeing, and are not able to remove. Next to the defire of poffeffing a competency ourfelves, it is a natural wifh, that all thofe with whom we are connected, by any intercourfe of vicinity or employment, fhould alfo betray no figns of mifery or diftrefs, arifing from poverty. The vifions of the philofopher or poet, who fancies happinefs lies in rural independence, can never be realized in fituations where much is feen, heard, or felt, of his neighbour's mifery; nor can a well-difpofed mind tafte *the fweet oblivion of the cares of life*, while in the midft of fcenes of diftrefs.

Some men of tafte have fuppofed, that, in a landfcape, the pleafing effect upon the mind, of fmoke arifing from the chimney of a neat cottage, flows from a felfifh comparifon of one's own fituation with that of the cottager: — it is pleafant *procul alterius.*

fpectare

fpeĉlare laborem: — but they muft excufe me if I differ with them in opinion; it is a matter of feeling only, the cottage-fmoke awakens an idea of comfort; the imagination rufhes to the chimney-corner, and fees honeft labour recompenfed by its proper rewards; and the pleafure which is then tafted is of a purer nature; it is pleafant *propè alterius fpeĉlare folamen:* — but if the hideous appearance of mifery and diftrefs, arifing from chilling poverty, mixes with the idea, every pleafing effeĉt is inftantly changed to its oppofite; and we turn with anguifh from thofe objeĉts which recal to the mind fcenes of mifery we are not able to relieve.

Thofe, who are advocates for, or patrons of, Sunday-fchools, would be more certain of their good effeĉt, and the caufe of religion and morality would receive a greater advantage from their very laudable endeavours, were the foundation of thofe fchools to be laid in fchools of induftry: a fuperftruĉture of religious fentiment would be fubftantially built on the folid foundation of habitual induftry. A poor man *cannot be religious who is not induftrious;* becaufe, having no property himfelf, he cannot honeftly command the comforts, or even the neceffaries, of life, but by induftry: every church-going habit in that clafs of fociety, not accompanied by habitual induftry, is hypocritical; becaufe honefty cannot be the moral fentiment which influences the habit.

That the poor fhould be inftruĉted in their duties of religion is certainly neceffary; but we fhould remember that thofe are divided into two heads, our duty towards God and towards our neighbour; the one cannot be difcharged without the other; that induftry, which is a neceffary duty towards your neighbour, is equally neceffary to render your religious duties towards God acceptable.

But the art of writing is not neceffary to a performance of the duties of the poor, either towards God or towards their neighbour, and it may lead towards a breach of their duty towards *both:* there muft be in fociety hewers of wood and drawers of water; if all are good penmen, where are thofe to be found who will contentedly

perform

perform the laborious offices of fociety, and live through a life of toil ? If honefty be not a fixed principle of the mind, the acquifi-tion of writing may offer a temptation that will lead to ruin.

Reading may be confidered nearly in the fame point of light. If we could confine the poor boy to reading his Prayer-book and his Teftament only, nothing but good would arife from teaching poor children to read ; but, the art being acquired, can we be fure whi-ther the ufe of it may lead ? To prognofticate; let us only recollect what books ourfelves, when boys, would read with the greateft avidity ; and, before we have reafon to deplore the confequence of bringing the poor up, in fuch a manner, as may make them lefs fatisfied with their humble and laborious ftation in life, let us, in idea, anticipate the probable mifufe of thefe qualifications, and, by a kind of prophetic forefight, be certain of the effect, before we, by encouragement, fofter the caufe.

While thefe doubts are thrown out, with refpect to the expe-diency of fo much of the inftitution of Sunday-fchools, as refpects the teaching *all* the children of the poor to read and write ; an im-plicit confidence in the good intention of the patrons of them fhould be explicitly declared, coupled with this fuggeftion ; that, probably, the only proper foundation of a Sunday-fchool is upon a fchool of daily induftry.

So thought the patrons of the fchools in Lincolnfhire, and fuch has been their practice ; the refpectable magiftrate, to whom that county has been, and it is hoped all England will be, obliged, for his excellent exemplification of the experiment, as well as for his perfpicuous and well-written recommendation of the inftitution, and the detail of its fuccefs in that county, has finifhed the plan in a moft complete manner, by a Sunday-fchool ; and, in fo doing, has fet us a noble example of training youth in the habit of induftry the fix days, and in the duties of religion the feventh.

LETTER

I HAVE, in purfuance of my plan, now fent you a few pages on ale-houfes and their cuftomers; tracing the rife and progrefs of the baneful and feducing habit of drinking ftrong liquors, from the earlieft days, in this ifland, to the prefent æra; when the revenue receives above five millions annually from the inhabitants of the fouthern part of Great Britain, by their indulging themfelves in this practice.

Julius Cæfar, in defcribing the manners and cuftoms of the inhabitants of England, at the time of his invafion, about 77 years before the Chriftian epoch, fays, that thofe were the moft civilized who inhabited Kent, and that they differed but little from the Gauls; that thofe, who lived in the interior parts, fowed but little corn, and lived on milk and flefh.

In defcribing the inhabitants of Gaul, he fays nearly the fame of them, " *Agriculturæ non ftudent; majorque pars victus corum in lacte et cafeo et carne confiftit."*

Solinus, who wrote about eighty years after the birth of Chrift, fays, that the Britons drank a fermented liquor, made of barley, unknown in former ages, or in any other country in Europe.

Tacitus, who wrote about thirty years afterwards, fpeaks ftrongly of the drunken habits of the Germans, near neighbours to the Gauls; " *Diem noctemque continuare potando, nulli probrum;*" he alfo fays, that they made ufe of a liquor from barley, or wheat, fermented.

We muft conceive, that Cæfar was either a very fuperficial obferver of the habits of thofe people, into whofe country he carried fire and fword; or that, in a few years, habits, deftructive of their health and morals, were introduced among them by their con-

querors,

querors, and had ftruck fuch a root, as to have very foon become a national vice.

The attachment of favages to ftrong liquors is a well-known fact; the excefs in which they indulge themfelves with ardent fpirits, whenever they can get at them, and the inveteracy of the habit, when once indulged in, almoft tend to prove, analogically, that fermented liquors were not known, in Gaul and Britain, in the days of Cæfar, although, about a hundred years afterwards, the drinking them to excefs was become a confirmed habit to the Germans, when Tacitus wrote his terfe and elegant differtation on their manners.

In the firft century of the Chriftian æra, the Britons ufed a fermented liquor from barley : in the latter end of the 18th century, the public revenue arifing from the duties on liquors, principally made from barley, and moft in ufe with the common people, exceed five millions fterling a year.

The habit is become of too ftrong a growth, is too general, and too inveterate, to be eradicated ; and, were it not, the financier of the day would difcourage the attempt ; he would tell us, we fhould act as unfkilful gardeners, plucking up valuable plants with the weeds ; if drunkennefs difappeared from the land, a confiderable part of five millions fterling would difappear from the coffers of the Exchequer ; and, in proportion as we reftrain the habit, we diminifh the revenue arifing from it.

But, however impolitic the eradication of drunkennefs may be, when feen in the light of revenue, were it poffible to effect it, there can no harm arife, either to our finances or our morals, in tracing as well as the very few lights, which can be found on this fubject, will permit us, the habit of Englifh drunkennefs, from its infancy to its maturity : it will be the hiftory of ale-houfes ; will be found to grow with their growth, and to increafe with their number ; and it is poffible that, in the progrefs of the inveftigation, one great and operative caufe of the expenfe in maintaining our poor, and

M m   the

the miferable poverty they fuftain, may appear too plainly to be miftaken; and, having found out the caufe of a difeafe, he is a timid phyfician who does not prefcribe the remedy.

A fermented liquor from barley was the firft intoxicating drink we read of in ufe among the Britons; but probably hydromel, or honey mixed with water and fermented, was nearly a cotemporary indulgence; when the aborigines of the ifland, to avoid the tyranny of the Romans, withdrew to their mountains and *moraffes*, we find that they carried with them the knowledge and ufe of the one, if not of the other; the firft they called *cwrw*, which is the Welch name for ale at prefent.

The vice of drunkennefs does not feem to have been general until the Danes and Saxons came among us; and they brought not only the vice, but alfo the names of the liquors which were in moft general ufe among them, mead and ale, and which have preferved the fame appellations to the prefent times.

Mr. Strutt, in his hiftory of the ancient Britons and Saxons, tells us, that intemperance in drinking was a prevailing vice, both among the Anglo-Saxons and Danes, with people of all ranks, in which they often fpent whole days and nights without intermiffion; all meetings, public and private, terminated in rioting and exceffive drinking, not excepting religious feftivals; at which times it was ufual for them to drink large draughts, in honour of Chrift, the Virgin Mary, the Twelve Apoftles, and other venerated faints. In the reign of Edgar the Peaceable, the vice of immoderate drinking prevailed fo greatly, that laws were thought neceffary to reform it; and that prince, to prevent quarrels that arofe in public-houfes, from any one's drinking more than his fhare, which it feems was very frequent; caufed certain pegs or knobs to be put, at proper diftances, into each drinking-cup; and no man was to drink beyond thofe knobs at one draught, under a fevere penalty; which was alfo to be inflicted upon thofe who would compel others to

drink

drink beyond them: he quotes William of Malmſbury, and Bartholinus, as his authorities.

But it cannot be ſuppoſed, that, by the expreſſion *public-houſes,* ſimilar places of entertainment to thoſe which now bear that general appellation can be intended; becauſe we find, that above a century after the concluſion of the Saxon monarchy, by the death of Edward the Confeſſor, public-houſes were not known, even in the metropolis: Fitzſtephen's Deſcription of the City of London, which is ſuppoſed to be written in 1174, mentioning the cuſtom of ſelling wines by retail, in *ſhips* and *vaults*; and that there was only one public eating-houſe, or cook-ſhop: — " *Præterea eſt in Lundonia ſuper ripam fluminis, inter vina in navibus et cellariis venalia, publica Coquina."*

About ninety-two years afterwards, appears the firſt inſtance of the attention of the legiſlature to our favourite beverage, ale; in a ſtatute paſſed in the 51ſt year of the reign of Henry the Third, called *Aſſiſa Panis et Cereviſæ.* As much of the ſtatute as relates to *cereviſa,* or ale, follows in theſe words:

" When a quarter of wheat is ſold for three ſhillings or three ſhillings and four-pence, and a quarter of barley for twenty-pence or two ſhillings, and a quarter of oats for ſixteen-pence, then brewers in cities ought, and may well afford, to ſell two gallons of beer, or ale, for a penny; and, out of cities, to ſell three or four gallons for a penny; and, when in a town, three gallons are ſold for a penny; out of a town, they ought, and may, ſell four; and this aſſize ought to be holden throughout all England."

But by ſtatute the ſixth of the ſame year, called the Statute of the Pillorie and Tumbril, it is enacted, — " That, when a quarter of barley is ſold for two ſhillings, then four quarts of ale ſhall be ſold for a penny; when for two ſhillings and ſix-pence, then ſeven quarts for two-pence; when for three ſhillings, then three quarts for one penny; when for three ſhillings and ſix-pence, then five quarts for two-pence; when it is ſold for four ſhillings, then two quarts

at one penny; and fo, from henceforth, the prices fhall increafe
and decreafe after the rate of fix-pence."

Mr. Barrington, in his notes on thefe ftatutes, feems to be of
opinion, that women, at this time, principally carried on this
trade; and corroborates that opinion by the term *brachiatrix* being
ufed: and alfo on the authority of Harrifon, who, in his defcription of Britain in Queen Elizabeth's reign, fpeaks of *ale-wifes*
ufing deceits in brewing; and alfo becaufe it is ftill faid in Wales,
that no one hath reafon to expect good ale unlefs he lies with his
brewer.

Although the ftatute proportions the price of ale, by meafure,
to the price of barley, it does not proportion the quantity of barley
to the meafure of ale; we muft therefore fuppofe the quantity of
barley ufed to a certain quantity of ale to be fixed, although we do
not know, with certainty, what it was.

The firft ftatute regulates the price of ale by the prices of wheat,
barley, and oats: we have therefore reafon to imagine that they were
ufed indifferently, or perhaps altogether, in the compofition of ale:
and it appears that, in thofe days, not only wheat and barley, but
alfo honey, was made ufe of for this purpofe, the fheriff of Hamp-
fhire being allowed, in his accounts at the Exchequer, twenty-fix
fhillings and ten-pence for *wheat, barley*, and *honey*, to make ale for
the Duke of Saxony, in the 31ft year of the reign of Henry the
Second.*

L E T T E R   XXXVIII.

DURING a period of feveral centuries, before the exceffes of
the people were made ufe of for the purpofe of raifing a
revenue, it is no eafy matter to find any anecdotes of ale-houfes,

---

* Madox Hift. Excheq. vol. i, p. 369.

or their patrons, the intemperate. If drunkennefs muft ever remain one of the incorrigible vices of fociety, it is but fair that the purfe of the drunkard fhould be drained its full proportion, for the general prefervation of order and decorum, and that thofe who will not, by good example, add any thing to the general ftock of morality, fhould pay for the prefervation of order: it is, at the leaft, ftriking fome fparks of good from a great mafs of evil.

But, while general hiftory and the laws are filent on the fubject, fome few lights are thrown upon it by Fleetwood, in his *Chronicon.*

The firft inftance is in 1302, when malt, ground, was three fhillings and four-pence a quarter: wheat fold, at the fame time, for four fhillings a quarter.

In 1309, at a feaft given by Ralph de Born, prior of St. Auftin's, in Canterbury, on his inftallation-day, malt was fix fhillings a quarter: at the fame feaft, wheat coft feven fhillings and two-pence a quarter.

In 1315 and 1316, malt was thirteen fhillings and four-pence a quarter: wheat, at the fame time, was twenty fhillings; and, by the rains in harveft, wheat came to thirty and forty fhillings a quarter, and good ale to two-pence a gallon; the better fort to three-pence; the beft of all to four-pence. On this a proclamation was iffued, that a gallon of ale fhould be fold for a penny; and that no wheat fhould be malted *(imbrafiatum)*, which the Londoners had ufually done, to the great confumption of corn, and fold it *(i. e.* ale made of it) at three-halfpence a gallon; the viler ale at a penny.

In 1339, wheat and malt bore the fame price, nine fhillings a quarter.

In 1423, malt was five fhillings a quarter; wheat, eight fhillings.

In 1425, ale was from a penny to three-halfpence a gallon.

In

In 1440, malt was thirteen shillings a quarter; wheat, twenty-four shillings.

In 1444, malt, four shillings; wheat, four shillings and four-pence a quarter.

In 1445, ale was one penny halfpenny a gallon.

In 1451, ale was at the same price.

In 1453, ale, one penny farthing a gallon.

In 1455, malt, one shilling and five-pence a quarter; wheat, one shilling and two-pence; ale, one penny a gallon.

In 1457, wheat, seven shillings and eight-pence a quarter; ale, one penny a gallon.

In 1459, wheat, five shillings a quarter; ale, one penny a gallon.

In 1460, wheat, eight shillings a quarter; ale, one penny a gallon.

In 1504, wheat, five shillings and eight-pence a quarter; ale, about three-pence a gallon.

In 1551, wheat, eight shillings a quarter; malt, five shillings and a penny.

In 1553, wheat, the same; malt, five shillings a quarter.

In 1554, 1555, 1556, 1557, wheat and malt remained at the same price as in 1553; but Mr. Stow says, that in 1557, before harvest, wheat rose in London to two pounds thirteen shillings and four-pence a quarter; malt, to two pounds four shillings: and, after harvest, wheat sunk to five shillings; malt, to six shillings and eight-pence a quarter: while, in the country, wheat remained at four shillings a quarter; malt, at four shillings and eight-pence.

In 1561, wheat, the quarter, eight shillings; malt, five shillings.

From these notices, taken, at unequal intervals, through the period of two centuries and a half, very few, if any, certain conclusions can be drawn, either with respect to the quantity

of

of the materials, or of the materials themfelves, of which ale was in thofe. days compofed. Malt feems, in general, to bear a price fomewhat proportional to the value of wheat ; from which it alfo appears to have been fometimes made: but that proportion is fo frequently broken through, efpecially in the year 1504, in the price of ale, that but little reliance can be placed on it.

The price of wheat and malt in 1557, in London, compared with its price in the country, ftrikes one as a remarkable in-ftance of a deficiency of police in regulating the fupply of the metropolis by its confumption ; for, while the country enjoyed plenty, London experienced the advanced prices of a famine; the caufe of which the hiftory of the times does not fufficiently explain.

No price of hops is mentioned in Fleetwood, although the ufe of them had become general, and there had paffed already one act of parliament regulating the importation of them. Mr. Pennant, in his Britifh Zoology, quotes a diftich to prove that carp and hops came into England the fame year, viz. about 1514 :

Turkies, carps, hops, pickerel, and beer,
Came into England all in one year.

And then produces an extract from " The Boke of St. Alban's," printed in 1496, to prove that carp was known here before. The regulations and eftablifhment of the houfeholds of Henry Alger-non Percy, the fifth Earl of Northumberland, at his caftles of Wrefill and Lekinfield, in Yorkfhire, in 1512, will prove, alfo, that hops were in general ufe before the year allotted for their in-troduction into England by the diftich; and will alfo fhew the proportion of hops ufed to the malt.

" Hopps for brewinge. — To make provifion for five hundred and fifty-fix pounds of hopps for brewinge of beere, for the expenfes

of

of my houfe for one whole yeere, after the eftimation of thirteen
fhillings and four-pence the hundred.

" Malte. — To make provifion for two hundred and nine quarters, one bufhel, of malte, after four fhillings the quarter, by eftimation."

This is at the rate of about two pounds eleven ounces of hops
to a quarter of malt; but fome ale was brewed in which the
quantity of hops was much lefs than in beer; confequently, the
proportion of hops to a quarter of malt in beer might be more
confiderable.

Thefe notices are inferted rather as matters of curiofity than as
information tending to throw much light on the progrefs of ale-
houfes and their concomitant ebriety: however, they at leaft tend
to fhew, that neither the vice, nor the confumption of liquor
which it occafioned, had as yet been fufficiently attended to by
the legiflature to occafion them either to regulate the immorality,
or to raife a revenue from licenfing its continuation.

In the mean time, houfes of entertainment increafed in number,
and alfo in licentioufnefs. In the fourteenth century, Chaucer, in
his Canterbury Tales, makes us acquainted with a confiderable inn,
at which the palmers fpent a night, in their pilgrimage to the
fhrine of St. Thomas, at Canterbury:

> " In Southwerke at the Tabberd* as I lay,
> " Redy to wendin on my pilgrimage
> " To Canterbury with devote corage,
>   *   *   *   *   *
> " The chambers and the ftables werin wide,
> " And well we werin efed at the beft."

---

* *Tabberd.* — A jacket, or fleevelefs coat, worn formerly by noblemen, in the wars;
now only by heralds: it was the fign of an inn in Southwark; it is now the fign of the
Talbot. — *Urry's Gloſſary to Chaucer.*

His

His hoft was like a hoft of modern days,

> " Bold of his fpeeche, and wife, and well taught,
> " And of manhode lakkid him right naught:
> " And eke thereto he was a *mery* man."

Shakfpeare, who drew from nature, has alfo left us ftrong traits of charaĉter in his Hoftefs of Eaftcheap : he, in the beginning of the feventeenth century, gives us feveral inftances of the manners of inn-keepers towards the end of the fourteenth : the Firft and Second Parts of his King Henry the Fourth abound with them.

But we want not the inftances; we ftand not in need of the hint; we know that no man can be a vender of any commodity, who is not in his heart an encourager of the confumption of it.

Very early in the fixteenth century, in the nineteenth year of the reign of Henry the Seventh, the bad effeĉts of the common fale of ale and beer were fo fenfibly felt, as to occafion parliament to reftrain the praĉtice, and to authorize two juftices of the peace to rejeĉt fuch ale-houfes, as they fhall think proper. This appears to be the firft inftance of the interference of the legiflature.

The next is about fifty years afterwards, in the reign of Edward the Sixth, the preamble to which has been already noticed in a for- mer part of this traĉt. This firft gives to two juftices the power of licenfing ale-houfes or tippling-houfes, and direĉts them to take bond and recognizance of fuch as fhall be admitted to keep them, as well againft the ufing of unlawful games as for the maintenance of good order; it punifhes the venders of ale without licence, (except in the time of fairs,) by imprifonment, and recognizance with two fureties, not to offend in the fame manner again.

After the lapfe of another fifty years, parliament again, in the firft year of the reign of James the Firft, found it neceffary to in- terfere in the conduĉt of ale-houfes. The preamble to the aĉt recites, with great propriety, their true ufe; " for the receipt, relief, and

N n   lodging,

lodging, of way-faring people, and for the fupply of the wants of fuch people as are not able to make their provifion of victuals, and not for the entertainment of the idle to confume their money and time in a drunken manner."

This act not only punifhes the alehoufe-keeper, by a penalty of ten fhillings to the poor, who fuffers any perfon to remain tippling, " other than fuch as fhall be invited by any traveller, and fhall accompany him during his neceffary abode there; and other than labouring and handicraftfmen in cities and towns corporate, and market-towns, upon the ufual working-days, for one hour at dinner-time, to take their diet in an ale-houfe; and other than labourers and workmen, which, for the following of their work by the day, or by the great, fhall, for the time of continuing their work there, fojourn, lodge, or victual, in any inn, ale-houfe, or other victualling-houfe;" but alfo inflicts a penalty of forty fhillings, to be paid to the ufe of the poor, on the conftables and church-wardens for neglect of duty, in not levying the penalty on the alehoufe-keeper offending; and alfo regulates the price at which ale and beer fhall be fold, viz. one full quart of the beft ale or beer for a penny, and two quarts of the fmall; and, if any alehoufe-keeper fell lefs, he forfeits twenty fhillings. The penalties to be levied by the conftables or church-wardens.

In the 4th year of the fame reign, parliament again was compelled to attend to ale-houfes; — " whereof," the preamble to the act fays, " the multitudes and the abufes are become intolerable, and ftill do and are likely to increafe." To prevent the evil, no perfon fhall fell, utter, or deliver, any beer or ale, to any perfon not having a licenfe to fell ale or beer, except for the convenient ufe and expenfe of his houfehold, under the penalty of fix fhillings and eight-pence for every barrel.

And, by the next chapter, entitled, An Act for repreffing the odious and loathfome Sin of Drunkennefs, after making ufe of the following ftrong language as a preamble:

" Whereas

" Whereas the loathfome and odious fin of drunkennefs is, of late, grown into common ufe within this realm, being the root and foundation of many other enormous fins, as blood-fhed, ftabbing, murder, fwearing, fornication, adultery, and fuch like, to the great difhonour of God and of our nation, the overthrow of many good arts and manual trades, the difabling of divers workmen, and the impoverifhing of many good fubjects, abufively wafting the good creatures of God."

The act inflicts a penalty of five fhillings on every perfon convicted of drunkennefs; three fhillings and four-pence on every perfon who fhall remain drinking and tippling in any ale-houfe in the city, town, village, or hamlet, where he lives. If any perfon fhall be a fecond time convicted of drunkennefs, he fhall be bound, with two fureties, to the king, for his good behaviour, in the penalty of ten pounds.

And thefe offences fhall be inquired of, and prefented before juftices of affize, juftices of the peace in their quarter-feffions, mayors, bailiffs, and other head-officers of cities, towns, &c. by all conftables, church-wardens, headboroughs, tithing-men, ale-conners, and fidefmen : the penalties are to go to the poor of the parifh. The act was farther enforced, and made perpetual, by the 1ft of Car. I. cap. 4.

Three years afterwards, the attention of the legiflature was again called forth, and any alehoufe-keeper, being convicted of any offence committed againft either of thefe two acts, entitled, An Act to reftrain haunting and tippling in Inns, Ale-houfes, and other Victualling-Houfes; and the Act againft the Sin of Drunkennefs; fhall be difabled from keeping an ale-houfe for three years following fuch conviction.

And, by the 21ft ftatute of this reign, chapter the feventh, the two laft acts, which were at firft only temporary, are made perpetual ; and proof, by one witnefs only, is rendered neceffary ; and that one witnefs may be a perfon who has voluntarily confeffed that

himfelf

himfelf has been guilty of the offence; a kind of evidence to which recourfe ought never to be had, except in thofe inftances of enormous crimes, where, for the fafety of fociety, the conviction of an offender is neceffary.

In the 1ft year of Charles the Firft, foreigners, or perfons not inhabiting in the towns or villages within which they fhall be convicted of tippling in any ale-houfe, were made alfo liable to the penalty, which they were not liable to by the acts paffed in the laft parliament; and the alehoufe-keepers, who fhall permit them to tipple, are alfo made liable to the fame penalties as they were by former acts, with refpect to the inhabitants; as are alfo vintners, keepers of taverns, and victuallers; and they are taken to be within the two former acts, and alfo within the ftatute then paffed. Chapter 4.

By the ftatute, the 3d of Charles the Firft, chapter the fourth, reciting, in the preamble, that the act, made in the 5th year of Edward the Sixth, had not wrought fuch reformation as was intended, for that the fines were feldom levied, and many of the offenders are neither able to pay them, nor to bear their own charges of committing to gaol; therefore it is enacted, that he, who keeps an ale-houfe without licenfe, fhall forfeit twenty fhillings, which the conftables or church-wardens fhall levy for the ufe of the poor; which, if the party is not able to pay, he fhall be whipped; and, for the fecond offence, he fhall be committed to the houfe of correction, for the fpace of one month, there to be dealt with as a diforderly perfon; and, if he fhall again offend, and be again convicted, he fhall be committed to the houfe of correction, there to remain until difcharged by order of the juftices in their general feffions.

Throughout the reign of James, and in the beginning of the reign of Charles the Firft, the legiflature appears to have taken every means that penalties, imprifonment, and difgrace, could effect, to prevent the bad confequences arifing from ale-houfes and drunkennefs. In fact, the evil had been feverely felt for feveral

centuries,

centuries, and had been attended to by government from the year
1503 to the date of the laft-mentioned act, 1627, but without
effect: ale-houfes increafed in number, and their frequenters in
drunkennefs, indolence, and licentioufnefs; and, although the laws
refpecting them were fevere, they were deficient, no proper means
having been provided to compel their execution; and were then, as
the laft act ftates, what we at prefent find them to be, — feldom or
never put in force.

This feems to have been the laft attempt of the legiflature to
regulate the moral conduct of ale-houfes, and to prevent the bad
effects. of ebriety: and thefe feveral acts of parliament ftill remain the law, although, unfortunately for the caufe of morality
and economy, not the practice.

LETTER XXXIX.

AS yet the public revenue had not been confiderably benefited
by popular depravity; at leaft the money arifing from the
licenfing ale-houfes had not enriched the coffers of the ftate, but
had filled the pockets of thofe minions of the crown who had fufficient intereft at court to obtain the privilege of granting them, a
remarkable inftance of which occurred in the year 1621, when the
Houfe of Commons received many petitions againft fome grants
which the king had made to certain individuals of the power of
licenfing inns and ale-houfes; and which he declared, in his fpeech
in the Houfe of Lords, it was his intention to recal, having, till
then, been ignorant of the ill effects which fuch patents had occafioned.

Soon after the reftoration of Charles the Second, in the year
1666, parliament granted, among other profits arifing from articles

of

of excife, thofe on beer, ale, mead, cider, perry, and foreign fpirits, in augmentation of the royal revenue.

In the 9th of Queen Anne, a duty of four fhillings was laid on any piece of vellum, parchment, or paper, on which fhall be engrofled a licenfe for retailing of wine; and one fhilling on a fimilar licenfe for retailing of beer and ale, or other excifable liquors.

And, by the 6th of George the Firft, all perfons, whofe office it fhall be to take any recognizances on account of ale-licenfes, fhall be obliged to make out fuch ale-licenfes on paper duly ftamped, before they take the recognizances, under the penalty of ten pounds.

In the beginning of the next reign, parliament took into confideration the inconvenience which had arifen from perfons being licenfed to keep inns and common ale-houfes by juftices of the peace; who, living remote from the places of abode of fuch perfons, might not be truly informed of the want of fuch inns and ale-houfes, or of the characters of perfons applying for licenfes; and therefore enacted, by ftatute 2d, chapter 28, and fection 11, " That no licenfe fhall be granted but at a general meeting of the juftices, acting in the divifion where the perfons applying for licenfes dwell, on the 21ft of September, or twenty days after, or at any other general meeting of the faid juftices, to be holden for the divifion wherein the faid perfon refides; and that all licenfes granted otherwife fhall be void."

And, by the 26th of George the Second, chapter 31ft, the above-mentioned claufe is repealed; and the manner of licenfing ale-houfes, in that part of Great Britain called England, is regulated: and it is ordered, " that no licenfe to keep any ale-houfe, &c. fhall be granted to any perfon not licenfed the year preceding, unlefs fuch perfon fhall produce, at the general meeting of the juftices in September, a certificate under the hands of the parfon, vicar,

vicar, or curate, and the major part of the church-wardens and overfeers, or elfe of three or four reputable and fubftantial houfe-holders and inhabitants of the parifh, or place, where fuch ale-houfe is to be, fetting forth that fuch perfon is of good fame, and fober life and converfation; and it fhall be mentioned, in fuch li-cenfe, that fuch certificate was produced, otherwife the licenfe fhall be void."

It remains to be obferved, that, to prevent any licenfe from being obtained on motives of intereft in the magiftrates, by their being concerned in habits of trade with the perfon licenfed, no juftice of the peace, being a brewer, inn-keeper, or diftiller, or a feller of, or a dealer in, ale or fpirituous liquors, or interefted in any of the faid trades, or being a maltfter or victualler, fhall be capable of granting licenfes to fell ale or beer, by virtue of an act of parlia-ment paffed in the fame year.

By this long category of pains, penalties, and reftrictions, has the legiflature attempted, through the lapfe of near three centuries, to prevent the ill effects of ale-houfes on the morals, the induftry, and the economy, of the people; but they have attempted it in vain; and the government, not having been able to preferve our poor in habits of fobriety, has determined that the revenue fhould feel the good effects of public vice; and, therefore, by a variety of taxes on thefe commodities, the confumption of which is fo gene-ral, and which taxes having increafed nearly *pari paffu* with the ftamp-duties on the ale-licenfes, (viz. from one fhilling, in the reign of Queen Anne, to one-and-thirty fhillings and fix-pence, in the 24th year of the prefent reign, befides the duty on the houfe itfelf, if at a rent above fifteen pounds a year,) have raifed from the public, in the four quarters of the year ending the 10th of October, 1792, the vaft fum of five millions two hundred and nine-teen thoufand feven hundred and fifty-one pounds, as may be feen by the following extract from a ftatement prefented to the Houfe

of

of Commons, purfuant to an act of the 27th year of his Majefty's reign.*

Net-Produce of the Duties of Excife in England.

On beer - - - - - - -	£2,012,373
Hops - - - - - -	82,776
Malt, perpetual duty - - -	612,235
Spirits, Britifh - - -	644,104
Ditto, foreign - - - -	704,392
Licenfes to retailers of fpirituous liquors -	160,704
Duties commenced ⌠ Spirits, Britifh - -	111,307
5th Jan. 1791. ⎨ Ditto, foreign - - -	142,737
⌡ Malt - - - -	118,033
Annual malt, &c. - - - - -	607,200
	5,195,861
Cuftoms on gin - - - - -	23,890
	5,219,751

When it is confidered that none of that immenfe quantity of
gin and malt fpirits, which are fmuggled into this country clear
of all duties, and alfo none of the cuftoms on foreign brandy,
rum, and foreign wines, are taken into this account, which, alone,
amount to upwards of feven hundred and fourteen thoufand pounds;
becaufe thefe are liquors that we may fuppofe are drunk exclufively
by the people of property, and are not generally the beverage of
the common people; and, alfo, becaufe we cannot, in fuch a
general eftimate as is here attempted to be made, ftate accurately
how great a proportion of thefe commodities, which are excifed,

* Annals of Agriculture, vol. xx. p. 100, 97.

is

is exported: we may, therefore, for an inftant fuppofe, that the quantity exported, together with the confideration that foreign wines, brandy, and rum, are not the general drink of the mafs of the people, will leave the fum-total of the duties of excife, together with the cuftoms on gin, amounting to £5,219,751, a fair average annual tax, paid, by the people of England, for the liquor drank by eight millions five hundred thoufand fubjects, men, women, and children. This being allowed to be a probable average, where exactnefs cannot be pretended to, it will then appear, that each individual pays to the revenue for his beer, ale, fpirits, and ftrong liquors, exclufive of the cuftoms on foreign wines, brandy, and rum, above twelve fhillings and three-pence farthing annually.

It can fcarcely be fuppofed, that the fum paid by the confumers for thefe liquors can be fhort of five times the tax which government has laid on them; although the abfolute proof that it is fo (were fuch a proof poffible) would be too tedious an inveftigation for this curfory inquiry: but, if either the article of ale or of fpirits be feparately examined, with refpect to its tax and its retail price, it is imagined the proportion mentioned will be found to be far within the truth. We fhall then perceive, that each individual expends above three pounds one fhilling and four-pence farthing in that indulgence which Adam Smith does not reckon among the neceffaries of life.

Now let us have recourfe to Mr. Howlett's computation of the number of labouring poor individuals in England, — fix millions and a quarter, — thefe forming that clafs of the people for whom the poor's rates are raifed; and it will be found that their expenditure in ale, beer, and fpirituous liquors, will confiderably exceed nineteen millions.

Nor can this be deemed an extravagant computation; when it is remembered, that the confumption of wines, and alfo that confumption of brandy and rum, which may be calculated as attach-

ing

ing itfelf to the cuftoms on thofe fpirits, are, in this calculation, fuppofed to belong exclufively to the remainder of that population; which is calculated to amount, in the whole, to eight millions and a half, or to two millions and one quarter only of our fellow-fub-jects; the fix millions and one quarter of the labouring-poor being deducted.

To compute the yearly earnings of the poor throughout England, is a matter infinitely above my ability; and to guefs at them is taking a leap fo much in the dark, as would be an imputation on the prudence of any man.   Mr. King, in 1668, computed the income of labourers and out-fervants at fifteen pounds a year, to a family confifting of three and a half perfons; Chief-Juftice Hale, about the fame time, computed the expenfes of a labourer's family, of fix perfons, at twenty-fix pounds a year; fuppofing either of thefe computations nearly right at that time; and fuppofing the price of wages to be now double; and the expenfes of a labourer's family, of the fame number of perfons, to be double; and more than that they cannot be; it will be found that the expenfes of the ale-houfe will confume no inconfiderable proportion of a labourer's wages, and bear a large proportion to the total of his expenfes.

Therefore, it muft be apparent, that one great and leading fource of the evil we complain of, in the ftate of the poor of this country, may be traced hence; from the vaft fums which are fpent in thefe licenfed places of ebriety; which are fo many in number, that it is a matter of furprife how the keepers of them can get a livelihood; by honeft and fober conduct they could not; but it muft be by an improper folicitation for drunken cuftomers; by giving them credit for liquor, and encouraging them in bad habits; it appearing that the number of ale, fpirit, and wine, licenfes is, to the number of inhabitants, nearly as one to ninety; therefore, the profit on the expenfes of a number, much fhort of ninety people, for ftrong liquors, enables a man, not only to fupport himfelf,

family,

family, and fervants, but alfo, in many inftances, to acquire a fortune; for, it fhould be mentioned, to the credit of our countrymen,
that of ninety individuals, men, women, and children, probably
half of them fcarcely ever tafte ftrong liquors, and are certainly no
cuftomers to ale-houfe-keepers.

The caufe of a difeafe being known, it has been faid, he muft
be either an ignorant or timid phyfician who knows not what remedy to prefcribe, or, knowing it, is fearful of applying it.

If time loft, and the money fpent, in the indulgence of drinking-
habits, be in any degree the caufe of the diftreffes of the poor, and
of the increafe of the rate for their relief and maintenance; it is
plain that, in proportion as the opportunity of indulging in thefe
habits is diminifhed, the bad effects of them will difappear; and it
is an experimental truth, that, in proportion as you ceafe to indulge a habit, does the habit itfelf difappear.

It is true, a patient, whofe conftitution has been injured by
drinking, may at firft conceive he cannot exift without his ufual
indulgence: — but what will his phyfician prefcribe? Probably not
an immediate and total abftinence from ftrong liquors, but a gradual reduction of the quantity, and of the frequency of the indulgence: the patient, in the mean time, finds health return, his conftitution is ftrengthened, and the bad habit is weakened; and, in
the end, he perceives that health and fobriety are not incompatible.

In the fame manner fhould the phyficians of the ftate proceed
with their patients,—the people; not by encouraging the *means* of
indulgence, and reftraining the *practice* by pains and penalties;
thefe we know, by the experience of fome centuries, have no effect; it is like holding a rod and a cherry to a child; the one will
be eaten, and the other ought not, on fuch an occafion, to be ufed;
neither ought the pains and penalties, in the various ftatutes refpecting ebriety, to be inflicted, until the temptation is farther removed. If a labouring-man has but to ftep over his own threfhold
to the next door to indulge himfelf in drinking, it requires fome

philofophy, while he has either money or credit, to refrain: oblige him to go a confiderable diftance, and he will not fo often yield to the temptation.

If parliament fhould order a *cenfus* of the people to be taken, by an actual numeration of them, by the conftables of each parifh, who might return the number to the high-conftables, and they to the quarter-feffions in each county, and by a fimilar method in cities; the actual population of the kingdom might eafily be known.

The number of ale, fpirit, and wine, licenfes might alfo be known from the excife-office.

Whatever be the proportion that the number of thefe licenfes bears to the amount of the population at prefent; if that proportion fhould be decreafed one-third by an experimental act of parliament for three years, the effect of fuch an experiment upon the morals of the people, the diftreffes of the poor, the poor's rates, and alfo upon the revenue, in refpect to the produce of the duties of excife, would be known; and, if it was on the whole advantageous to the morals, to the poor, and the rate for their maintenance was diminifhed, the experiment fhould be perfifted in by a farther decreafe of the proportion, between the number of people and the number of licenfes, for the next three years, and fo on, until the point be found, beyond which the decreafe would be prejudicial.

In fuch an experiment, undoubtedly the good effect propofed would be oppofed by a diminution of the revenue which arifes from thefe articles of the excife; for, it is plain, that the fmaller the confumption of ftrong liquors, the lefs the revenue arifing from that confumption; and, the fmaller the number of licenfes, the lefs the produce of that branch of the revenue: but, if the end of government be the good of the governed, can this be an objection? Surely not, unlefs revenue is of more confequence to a ftate than the morals, the religion, the happinefs, of its fubjects.

If

If the revenue fhould prove deficient, through the experiment, and it could not, unlefs the experiment fucceeded, would it not gain by other and better means? If the quantity of national drunkennefs, indolence, and expenfivenefs in the articles of liquors, was diminifhed, would not the quantity of national morality, induftry, and economy, be increafed? And, in fuch a cafe, would not agriculture and manufactures reftore that defalcation to the revenue, occafioned by a fuppreffion of the habits of indulgence in drinking?

If a diminution of the number of ale-houfes had no effect upon the habits of our fellow-fubjects, but that the man, who would frequent one at his door, would do the fame at a mile diftance,—ftill fome good will arife from the experiment: being fewer houfes, each houfe will have more cuftom, and will not be tempted to encourage the habit in their cuftomers, by the rifk of trufting them: an ale-houfe-fcore does not increafe in the fimple ratio of the quantity drank, but in the compound proportion of the quantity drank, and the hazard incurred by giving credit.

Another advantage would accrue: the number being lefs, the conduct of thofe which remained might be better attended to, and the haunts of ebriety and diffolutenefs might be brought more directly under the eye of the peace-officers; and, if the experiment was attended with a general revifion of the ftatutes refpecting them, the penalties might be put in a way of being levied without expecting neighbours, companions, or friends, to turn informers.

But the number of ale-houfes being diminifhed, and, by that means, the cuftom at the remaining houfes being increafed, they could afford to pay more for their ale, wine, and fpirit, licenfes; and that not only in proportion to the decreafe of the number, but becaufe the additional cuftom they get will be free of houfe-rent and houfe-keeping; therefore, if this regulation fhould not diminifh the quantity of liquor confumed, it will increafe the revenue; and, if it fhould diminifh the quantity confumed, it will proportionably

increafe

increafe the habits of fobriety, induftry, and economy, which are better for the governed than revenue.

On the whole, it appears to be a truth plainly proved, that the wretched fituation of the poor, and the expenfes of their mainte- nance, are, in a great degree, increafed by their habitual fondnefs of drinking, which induces lazinefs, want of economy, and that apathy or indifference to what may happen, which is the confe- quence of habits of ebriety, as it alfo is fometimes of excefs of diftrefs: it has alfo been proved, that, from the time when ale- houfes were firft licenfed, the legiflature has frequently complained of the bad effects to the morals and habits of the poor, from the encouragement thefe, their favourite haunts, gave to drinking and lazinefs; and it alfo appears, that the legiflature has frequently interfered by penal ftatutes to prevent thefe confequences; but without effect.

It therefore now becomes their wifdom to try fome other means: if the evil fo long and fo often complained of not only ftill exifts, but is increafing; and, as the legiflature of this country has, for near three centuries, found, by experience, that, with refpect to penalties, the acts of the ftate are become a dead letter, and the ftatutes of the realm are difregarded; — that, in the mean time, the number of licenfes, and the quantity of liquor confumed, are amazingly increafed; and the confequential habits among the lower clafs of people have occafioned their maintenance and relief to be- come a ferious burthen to that clafs of his majefty's fubjects, which is next in number, as well as importance, to the ftate; — a diminu- tion of the number of houfes licenfed for the fale of liquors is, therefore, the experiment which fhould now be tried, — an experi- ment which, if it fhould be fomewhat injurious to the revenue immediately, will be mediately advantageous; and, at all events, be- neficial to the community: — and, if the experiment fhould not be beneficial to the community, it cannot injure the revenue.

LETTER

LETTER XL.

THERE are very few human inftitutions, refpecting the propriety of which there do not exift two opinions, the good and the bad: the for and the againft are fo interwoven in all our fchemes and plans, that it is fcarcely poffible to find any exifting eftablifhment, in which, while one man or fet of men fees nothing but good, another will fee nothing but evil. The fair conclufion to be drawn is, that, in all our plans, inftitutions, and eftablifhments, there exift both good and evil; but, as we will fuppofe they are generally eftablifhed with a view to good, that evil which does not naturally, and confequentially, arife from them, but only proceeds from a mifufe, or mifapplication, fhould not be eftimated as neceffarily inherent in the plan. The evil, in this refpect, refembles gluttony and drunkennefs: no one but will allow that meat and drink are a neceffary good, although the mifufe of them produces thofe vices. In a former part of this tract box-clubs, or friendly focieties, have been glanced at, and recommended, as tending to diminifh the poor's rate: that they have that tendency, the very effence of their rules will prove; becaufe their fund is created by a voluntary contribution among the members of the club, while in health, to fupport each other, by a weekly allowance, when difeafed or difabled by accidents or age; without which allowance the majority of the members of moft of them would receive a weekly fupport from the parifh-rates. But it may be faid they encourage drinking; for, in general, their meetings are held at a public-houfe; and, probably, inftances may be produced where individuals have returned from their monthly or quarterly meetings intoxicated: and it alfo may be hinted, that their annual meeting, when they dine together, too frequently

is

is a feaft of intemperance. For my own part, I believe that all feafts are feafts of intemperance, both of the poor and the rich. But it fhould be added to the account, that, at feafts in general, every perfon is left at liberty to drink or not. At thefe focieties, one of the firft ftanding rules is against drunkennefs; therefore that vice is neither the object of thefe clubs, nor of the members; and inftances of it may be claffed under the idea of mifufe.

Another objection may be, and has been, made to them, viz. that they may be applied to bad, feditious, and turbulent, purpofes. It is allowed to be poffible; and, more efpecially, in manufacturing-towns; and there is no doubt but that inftances of the kind have happened; that journeymen to different trades, in populous cities and towns, may have combined againft their mafters; may have refufed to work but at a certain price; that feditious and treafonable toafts may have been drunk at thefe meetings; and that riot and diforder may have proceeded from the door of the public-houfe they frequent. It fhould be recollected that thefe inftances only prove, where they have exifted, an abufe of thefe focieties; and are, by no means, a natural confequence flowing from the right ufe of them.

But be that as it may: the particular purport of thefe fheets refpects the labouring-poor; the day-labourer in hufbandry, not the mechanic, the artizan, or the manufacturing-poor, any farther than as they are involved in the general confideration of thofe who may become a burthen on fociety for their maintenance; and thefe abufes of friendly focieties have not as yet been found prevalent where this defcription of men conftitutes the majority of the club. The country-village, or market-town, whofe inhabitants do not rife to opulence by manufactures, has not produced any other than good effects from friendly focieties: among fuch bodies of men, therefore, they certainly tend to good, as far as their rules tend to good order, and the fund they voluntarily raife tends to relieve them

in

in cafes of illnefs and diftrefs, when otherwife the relief muft proceed from the poor's rate.

And the legiflature has acted from the fame opinion : nay more ;
it has proceeded from an opinion of the *general* good they do to
fociety, throughout the kingdom, in all places, and under all confiderations ; as well in the populous manufacturing-towns as in the deferted villages. The parliament has acted upon a general principle ;
and applaud and encourage when the good is general, influenced
by a fentiment fimilar to that of the candid Critic :

> Verum ubi plura nitent . . . . non ego paucis
> Offendar maculis, quas aut incuria fudit
> Aut humana parùm cavit natura.

The act of parliament, which paffed, in the laft feffion, for the
encouragement of friendly focieties, authorizes me to affert that
parliament approves of them generally, both by the preamble to the
act, and by the folid and confiderable encouragement given to them
in the body of the act, only fubjecting their rules to the infpection
and approbation of the juftices at their quarter-feffions.

The preamble to this wife and humane act of parliament ftates,
that whereas the protection and encouragement of friendly focieties,
in this kingdom, for raifing, by voluntary fubfcription of the members thereof, feparate funds for the mutual relief and maintenance
of the faid members, in ficknefs, old age, and infirmity, is likely to
be attended with very beneficial effects, by promoting the happinefs
of individuals, and, at the fame time, diminifhing the public
burthens. May it, therefore, pleafe your Majefty that it may be
enacted,

Sec. 1. That any number of perfons may form themfelves into a
fociety, and raife among themfelves a fund for their mutual benefit,
and make rules, impofe fines, &c.

Sec. 2 and 3. That fuch rules fhall be exhibited to the juftices, in
quarter-feffions, who may annul or confirm them ; and, if con-

firmed,

firmed, that they shall be signed by the clerk of the peace, and be deposited with him; and, until their rules are so confirmed, no society shall be within the meaning of the act, and no confirmed rule shall be altered but at a general meeting of the society, and the alteration shall be subject to the review of the quarter-sessions.

Sec. 5. Such society may appoint officers; and securities shall be given, if required. The treasurers shall give bond to the clerk of the peace, and other officers to the treasurer; and the bonds shall not be chargeable with stamp-duty.

Sect. 6. Committees may be appointed, whose powers, if standing-committees, shall be declared in the rules of the society; and, if particular ones, shall be entered in a book, and shall be controllable by the society.

Sec. 7, 8, and 9. The treasurers or trustees shall lay out the surplus of contributions, and bring the proceeds to account for the use of the society, shall render accounts, and pay over-balances; and, in case of neglect, application may be made to the Court of Chancery, &c. and no fee shall be taken for such proceedings in any court.

Sec. 10 and 11. Executors shall pay money due to these societies before any other debts; and the effects of these societies shall be vested in the treasurers, or trustees, for the time being, who may bring and defend actions.

Sec. 12. But the societies must declare the purpose of their establishment before the confirmation of their rules by the court of quarter-sessions; and the uses to which the money subscribed shall be applied; and may inflict penalties for misapplication of money; and shall not be dissolved, unless by the consent of five-sixths of the then-existing members, and of all persons receiving, or entitled to receive, relief from the society; and their stock shall not be devisable but for the general purposes of the society.

Sec.

Sec. 13 and 14. Their rules fhall be entered in a book, and received in evidence, and they may receive donations of any perfons out of the fociety, which fhall be applied to the purpofes of the fociety.

Sec. 15 and 16. Where any members think themfelves aggrieved, they may apply on oath to two or more juftices, near to the place where fuch fociety is eftablifhed, who are empowered to act, and make fuch order therein, as they fhall think fit; but if, by the rules of any fociety, any matter fhall be left to arbitration, the award of the arbitrators fhall be final.

Sec. 17, 18, 19, 20. No member of a fociety producing a certificate thereof, fhall be removeable from the parifh where fuch fociety is eftablifhed, until he is actually chargeable to that parifh. Thefe certificates fhall be proved by oath of one of the witneffes attefting them before a magiftrate; and, on complaint of parifh-officers, juftices may fummon perfons bringing certificates to be examined, and to make oath of their fettlement; and copies of thefe examinations fhall be given to the parties, which fhall exempt them from future examination; and juftices may declare, by an order in writing, the place of fettlement of perfons fo examined, without iffuing a warrant for their removal; and copies of fuch orders and of examinations fhall be returned to the parifh-officers of the place of fettlement.

Sec. 21, 22, 23, 24, 25. Perfons, aggrieved by the adjudication of juftices, may appeal to the quarter-feffions, and no perfon refiding in any parifh under this act fhall thereby gain a fettlement, nor by paying of rates, nor any apprentice or fervant to fuch perfon; but baftards fhall have the fame fettlement as the mother, who fhall refide in any parifh, by virtue of this act.

Sec. 26. The charges of maintaining or removing refidents, under this act, to be reimburfed by the parifh to which the parties belong. The act to be deemed a public act.

This

This act of parliament will probably be productive of more good
to the nation in general, than that enlightened and humane member of parliament,* from whom the bill originated, conceived;
unlefs, while he intended to raife a revenue from the poor, in aid
of the poor's rates, and for the fupport of themfelves, he, with the
fpirit of prophecy, foretold, from the effect of this act, the gradual
decline, and, in the end, the downfal, of that fervile and expenfive
fyftem, the law of fettlements.   No one act of the legiflature refpecting the poor fince the firft corner-ftone of the fyftem, the 43d
of Elizabeth, is fo replete with good; it holds out to them every
encouragement, and only reftrains, as focieties or clubs, protected
by the legiflature, ought to be reftrained, from doing mifchief to
that very government which protects, encourages, and rewards,
them. The compliance with the requifition of exhibiting their rules
to the juftices at the quarter-feffions is eafy and free of expenfe;
the preíervers of the peace of the county are, at the fame time, the
natural judges of what rules may be inimical to that peace; the
encouragement is fubftantial; and the members of thefe clubs fee
it; for they crowd to have their rules recorded by the clerk of the
peace; and the poor in general know the advantages; for they are
folicitous to become members of friendly focieties.

---

* At the time this letter was written, the author was ignorant that the poor in particular, and the county in general, were obliged to George Rofe, Efq. M. P. one of
the joint fecretaries to the Treafury, for this moft excellent act of parliament; nor was
he then perfonally known to that gentleman, but has now every reafon to congratulate his
county, that, by the ftrong and comprehenfive abilities of Mr. Pitt, applied to the fubject
of thefe letters, aided by the thorough knowledge and indefatigable attention of Mr. Rofe,
together with thofe other honourable members of the Houfe of Commons, who attended
Mr. Pitt many times through the month of February, 1796, on the fubject of the poor-
laws, it is to be expected, that at length the nation will receive the benefit of an act of
parliament, which may turn the prefent tide of idlenefs and diffipation among the poor
to induftrious habits and a more moral line of conduct.

●

IN the nineteenth volume of the Annals of Agriculture, are the rules of a friendly fociety, inftituted under the patronage of feveral gentlemen, whom the poor of a parifh in Norfolk have the happinefs to call their neighbours and friends; which rules appear to be very well adapted to the purpofes of fuch friendly focieties in general; more efpecially becaufe the control of them is by thefe rules invefted in the gentlemen of opulence in the place, together with the clergyman; and becaufe the times of their meeting at a public-houfe are reftrained to the four quarters of the year, and two feafts, (poffibly that might be better altered to one,) inftead of obliging the members to meet monthly. The only article in which thefe rules appear to be materially deficient is, that the club does not in any form of words declare the purpofes of its eftablifh-ment, although they may certainly be collected from the general body of the rules. A copy of thefe rules and orders fhall be added; as they may tend to affift any perfon, into whofe hands thefe pages may fall, in eftablifhing a fimilar fociety, on a better principle, and with better regulations, than thofe ufually drawn up for fuch occa-fions; and the purpofe of the fociety fhall be properly declared ac-cording to the direction of the act of parliament, called the Friend-ly-Society Act.

Rules and orders agreed upon to be obferved by the members of a friendly fociety, inftituted the   day of   , in the year   , for the purpofe of raifing, by voluntary fubfcription of the members thereof, and other charitable perfons who may be inclined to give contributions thereto, a fund for the mutual relief and maintenance of the faid members in ficknefs, accidents, in-firmity, and old age.

Art. 1. That no perfon, after the firft quarter-day after the eftablifhment of this fociety, exceeding the age of forty-five years;

nor any perfon having any apparent infirmity of mind or diftemper of body, fhall ever be admitted a member.

2. That on the Saturday before the full moon preceding the four principal quarterly days of the year, fhall be held the ordinary meeting, in the evening, from feven to nine in the fummer, and from fix to eight in the winter.

3. That no perfon fhall ever be admitted a member but at one of the quarterly meetings, and by the majority of the truftees prefent, as well as by a majority of the other members.

4. That every member is to be prefent at the faid quarterly meetings, and to pay four-pence towards the reckoning of that evening; or, having fome reafonable excufe which may be tranf-mitted to the fociety by the clerk, and fhall be admitted as fuch by the majority prefent, the clerk fhall tender, for each, four-pence; or, if the excufe be not deemed valid, then the member fo abfent fhall pay one fhilling. The faid penalties to be put into the common ftock.

5. That whoever defires to be admitted into this fociety fhall appear at one of the faid quarterly meetings, and if then and there, as above approved of, he fhall pay down one guinea, (befides the four-pence to be fpent,) towards maintaining the common ftock or fund, and thereby he fhall become a full member: but, if not then capable to pay the whole, he muft pay on each quarterly day, be-fides the four-pence for expenfe, for the months immediately pre-ceding, one fhilling per month to the ftock, and fo to be continued for twenty-one weekly months, and not to receive any benefit from the fund till the whole twenty-one fhillings is paid.

6. That there fhall be two feafts in the year; the one on the quarterly meeting before Chriftmas, and the other on the Saturday before Whit-Sunday; and, in order to abridge the lofs of time as much as poffible, the dinners not to be ready before three o'clock, as by that time, with a little management, the day's work may be finifhed; for which feafts every member fhall, on admittance, pay

one

one fhilling, and clear his club-arrears, if any be due, befides the payment of his wonted fubfcription, or be excluded; by which arrears is hereby explained to be meant, a regular payment of one fhilling for every weekly month during the continuance of this fociety, to be put into the common box or fund.

7. And, for the better regulating the affairs of this fociety, the following truftees are hereby appointed, viz.

or the heirs of the faid gentlemen, as proprietors of their eftates in the faid parifh, and the rector or vicar of the faid parifh, for the time being, upon condition that each of the faid gentlemen, their heirs or fucceffors, fhall pay two guineas towards the common ftock or box, as qualifying themfelves for the truft hereby repofed in them.

8. That the majority of the faid truftees fhall either perfonally act, or choofe two ftewards out of the members of the club, to receive and pay all the money belonging to this fociety, taking receipts for whatever they pay; and if the faid ftewards, or either of them, fhall be found guilty of any breach of truft in their office, or of fraudulently converting to any other ufe than that of the fociety any fum or fums of money, or fhall make any falfe or unjuft account thereof, they the faid ftewards fhall, upon difcovery, be forthwith difcharged of their office, and expelled the fociety; and the aforefaid truftees fhall be accountable for, and fhall make good, every embezzlement or injury the fociety may, through the neglect or fault of themfelves, or their ftewards, have fuftained; and the faid truftees, or their ftewards, fhall attend the fociety before the firft half-hour of each quarterly meeting is expired, or the ftewards fhall each forfeit one fhilling to the box or common ftock.

9. For the fecurity of the cafh or other public ftock of the fociety, there fhall be prepared a convenient box, with three locks and three keys, each of different conftructions from the other, and each of the ftewards to have a key, and the mafter of the houfe where the box is kept fhall be in poffeffion of the third; and there fhall

always

always be kept by the clerk a regular cafh-book, and the copy of each day's receipt or expenfe, to be locked up in the box, which is not to be opened, nor any money to be taken out, but at the faid quarterly meetings; the money in the mean time wanted by the fick members, to be fupplied by the truftees, or their ftewards.

10. Every perfon, become a full member of this fociety, if he falls fick, lame, or blind, fo as to become incapable of following his trade or employ, after feven days notice given to the ftewards and apothecary, or one of them, fhall receive out of the box or common ftock, if confined to his bed, a weekly allowance of five fhillings and fixpence; but, if able to go about, not more than four fhillings, till he fhall be fo far recovered as to follow his trade or employ, provided that his ficknefs or lamenefs does not continue longer than one whole year; but, if it does, then he fhall receive two fhillings and fixpence a week, for as long a time as he fhall be afflicted; but, if any fuch member fhall recover before the feven days notice is expired, he will not be entitled to any weekly allowance.

11. In cafe the ftewards fhall have ficknefs, urgent bufinefs, or be otherwife difabled, with reafonable caufe, the truftees may appoint fome other member (for whom likewife they are to be refponfible) to officiate or act in their ftead.

12. Whereas an apothecary will be conftantly employed for the fervice of this fociety, and is to be paid out of the common ftock, and every other proper cafe recommended to the county-hofpital,* it is hereby farther agreed, that every member (the clerk excepted) fhall pay fixpence, at the firft quarterly meeting after the accident happened, into the fund, towards paying the extraordinary expenfe that may occur upon any one of the members which may break a bone, leg, arm, &c. (except by drunkennefs, wreftling, footballplaying, &c.) or for want of fuch payment be excluded; and during

---

* If there is one in the county.

the

the time any member receives money from the box, he shall be excluded all payments to the box or house, except upon deaths, feasts,
and broken bones.

13. Whenever any member dies, all the members are to attend
his funeral, and all (the clerk excepted, who is to give notice of the
burial) shall contribute, at the first quarterly meeting after the funeral, sixpence each, towards defraying the expenses of his funeral,
&c. and every member, who does not so attend, shall pay on the
subsequent quarterly night one shilling into the box, or, in defect of
either of those payments, to be for the future excluded; except the
case of the small-pox, when no attendance will be required.

14. Whenever any member dies, there shall be allowed out of the
box for his burial one guinea and a half; and, if he has a widow or
children, to them two guineas.

15. And, on the death of every full member's lawful wife, the
husband, giving notice to the stewards, shall receive one guinea and
a half from the box, (if demanded,) the said quarterly meeting-
night after her decease, towards paying the funeral-charges; upon
which occasion every member shall, on the same night, or whenever
they appear, pay three-pence towards it, or be excluded.

16. The stewards shall each go once in seven days to visit each
sick member, and shall be allowed for each visit, at the next meeting, sixpence, if no complaint shall be by the sick preferred against
him or them, at the next general meeting, for want of proper attention and care; and the said stewards shall forfeit to the box one
shilling, to be paid at the next meeting, for every time that he re-
fuses to go; but, if it be found that any member has brought upon
himself sickness, distemper, infirmity, or inability to follow his
trade or employment by debauchery, intercourse with lewd women,
venereal taint, drunkenness, fighting, wrestling, or football-playing,
in such sort of cases, he shall not have any weekly allowance from
the society; or if any member counterfeits himself sick or infirm, as
thereby not able to follow his business or trade, and shall for a time,

Q q   by

by means of fuch impofition, obtain and receive any weekly allowance or fupport, fuch member fhall, for the future, be excluded
from every benefit which might otherwife have accrued to him from
the fociety.   And, when any member is fo far recovered from his
ficknefs or indifpofition as to be able to follow his bufinefs, he fhall,
within three days, give notice to one of the ftewards, or be for ever
excluded, unlefs he pays to the box, at the next general meeting, one
whole week's allowance. And, if any member is known by any other
member to work during the continuance of his allowance, he fhall
be expelled, as fhall alfo that other member who does not inform
the fociety of it; and the fick or infirm are to be regularly paid by
the truftees or their ftewards.

17. And, that every thing may at all times be tranfacted with
regularity, decency, and decorum, in this fociety, no member or
members fhall have any drink of any kind to themfelves feparately
from the reft of the fociety, nor fhall any liquors be admitted into
the room where the fociety meets during the time of their fitting,
but what is ordered in by the ftewards; and, when the appointed
and limited hours for the fitting of this fociety are expired, one of
the ftewards fhall give notice thereof, and every one of the members
fhall depart the room in a civil and peaceable manner, and it fhall
accordingly be cleared by one of the ftewards before he departs the
room.   And if any member, during the time of the fociety's fitting,
*fhall fpeak irreverently of the Almighty, difrepectfully of his Majefty or
his government, or fhall lay wagers, or curfe, fwear, blafpheme, talk
obfcenely, ufe taunting, reviling, or abufive, language, or apparently feeks
to quarrel with any of the members*, he fhall fubmit to a fine, to be put
into the common ftock, fuch as the majority of this fociety fhall
think fit to impofe, according to the nature and circumftances of
the offence, fo that it does not exceed two fhillings, nor be lefs than
fixpence.

18. And if any member, after any meeting of this fociety, fhall
fpeak ill of, or caft any reflections on, any member or members of
the

the fociety, on or for what has been faid or agreed to by the fociety, he fhall forfeit five fhillings to the common ftock, or be excluded.

19. No part of the common ftock of this fociety to be lent out,
but upon lawful intereft, government fecurity, and with the confent of the majority affembled, at one of their quarterly meetings.

20. If the wife of any of the members come into the fociety-
room, or be therein while he is prefent, he fhall forfeit fixpence to
the fund, befides immediately leading her out, under pain of forfeiting his right to any part of the fubfcription or common ftock of
this fociety.

21. If any member be caft into prifon for debt, he fhall not be
allowed to pay any fubfcription or forfeitures, nor receive any part
of the fociety's property while in prifon. When he comes out, he
fhall be received again as a member, without coft or charge.

22. The clerk fhall be allowed the fame benefit from the box as
any other member of this fociety, without being fubject to pay any
money towards it, except for forfeits.

23. The cafh and minute books to be bought out of the common
ftock, and alfo to be renewed as often as fhall be neceffary, and the
minutes of each meeting to be regularly figned by the truftees or
ftewards prefent, and may at any time be infpected by any of the
members, on payment of fixpence to the clerk, and fixpence to the
common fund.

24. Hereby power is alfo invefted in the majority of this fociety,
at the time of each Whitfuntide meeting, to make an annual agreement with a furgeon and apothecary, whofe ftipend may and fhould
be abated, upon apparent neglect.

LETTER XLII.

NOW, that this fubject of the poor, their rights, duties, and the laws refpecting them, draws near to its conclufion, it cannot be judged foreign to the defign of thefe Letters, although not immediately within the profeffed purpofe of it, to throw out fome obfervations, and offer a few ftrictures, on the duties and conduct of the domeftic menial fervants of this kingdom, they being, in general, derived from, and are conftantly adding to, the number of thofe who fall under the fupervifion of our poor-laws.

And here it fhould firft be underftood, that fervants in hufbandry, journeymen, or fervants to any trade or manufactory, although they may properly, in fome inftances, be ftyled menial fervants, are not confidered in the following pages ; becaufe their conduct is regulated by acts of parliament, and they are under the cognizance of the magiftrate; but fuch only as are neceffary in the arrangement of domeftic economy, or are retained for the purpofes of luxury, vanity, or oftentation ; and thofe domeftics are fo intermixed in the various departments of fervice, that it is not eafy to feparate them, as it would be very difficult, in the arrangement of any perfon's houfehold, for a ftranger to determine what fervants are of domeftic ufe and neceffity folely, and what are fupernumerary, or retained for the gratification of vanity or luxury.

But, in whatever department they may be engaged, they, in thefe times, are principally derived from that clafs of our fellow-fubjects which have been the immediate object of our attention; and not from a more refpectable clafs of citizens, whofe children formerly thought it no difparagement to be retained in families of fuperior confideration or opulence.

In

In thofe days, the tenantry of the kingdom thought that a fon or daughter, who was retained, as a menial fervant, in a houfe of wealth and confequence, was placed in a refpectable fituation ; and the beft principles of honefty, fobriety, and civility, were inculcated, that their children might preferve themfelves in thofe fituations, which the good conduct and reputation of their parents had obtained for them.

In thofe days the *kinder* duties of mafter and fervant were reciprocally performed. The fervants, on their part, ftrove for the good-will of thofe they ferved, by diligence, honefty, fobriety, regular behaviour, and attention to the interefts of their immediate retainer, by an economic ufe of fuch property as they were entrufted with; and they were rather humble friends than eye-fervants; and they received, exclufive of their wages, their diet, their lodging, and fuch part of their clothing as they agreed for, the advice, the encouragement, the protection, the friendfhip, of their employer, and feldom changed their place, but when they changed a life of fervitude for a life of independence. This reciprocity of duties and affections is beautifully exemplified by Shakefpear in his Orlando and Adam :.

Adam. Mafter, go on, and I will follow thee
To the laft gafp with truth and loyalty.
* * * * * * * * * *
Orlando. There is an old poor man,
Who after me hath many a weary ftep
Limp'd in pure love ; till he be firft fuffic'd,
Opprefs'd with two weak evils, age and hunger,.
I will not touch a bit.

Thus thefe kinder duties were formerly reciprocally performed,. or our Shakefpear has not followed truth and nature in portraying the character of a faithful fervant and grateful mafter.

But

But does the drama of the prefent ftage hold out fuch examples to our view? Alas, no! Yet the ftage ftill profeffes, and, with equal truth, to hold the mirror up to nature ; to fhew virtue its own image, vice her own likenefs. Let us fee what *perfonæ* the modern ftage gives us for modern fervants. The entertainment called High Life below Stairs is in point: no one has ever difputed the exactnefs of the reprefentation to the reality of a modern fervants hall : and where the public, by their unanimous approbation of a theatric reprefentation, have ftamped it with the reputation of being an exact picture of real life, be it allowed to argue from it as from a fact : it is, at the leaft, a lefs degrading and more cleanly manner of identifying fuch a fact, than ftepping into a kitchen, to be able to affert it as fuch.

And can mafters and miftreffes, be they in whatever ftation of rank and opulence it may have pleafed the Almighty to place them, knowing that fuch things are, fuffer them to be ? They can, and they do, becaufe they are poffeffed with fears and apprehenfions, more alarming than thofe arifing from the diffipation of their property, and which force them tamely to fubmit to the taunts and infolence of their liveried and pampered domeftics.

The evil complained of originates from profufion, and is foftered by vanity; which hourly fubmits to the groffeft indignities in private, to fupport an appearance of magnificence in public, after the fundamental bafis of all real greatnefs, independence of mind, is departed.

And, did the evil ftop among people of this defcription, were only the proud, the vain, the oftentatious, and thofe whofe character correfponds with Salluft's terfe expreffions, the *alieni appetentes, fuorum profufi,* fubject to thefe degrading and vexatious circumftances, the evil ought to be left to correct itfelf; or, in other words, the punifhment flowing from the crime, the fufferers fhould receive no affiftance from the interference of the legiflature : they are pilfered

by,

by, and ftand in awe of, their fervants ; true ; but it is no more than they deferve.

But, unfortunately for all ranks and denominations of people in this kingdom, who are fo far elevated, by circumftances, above the want of the neceffaries of life as to keep a domeftic, they are all involved in the contagion, and fuffer in their private economy and domeftic comfort, from the prevalence of a vice encouraged by the great. Becaufe my lord the nabob, or the commiffary pampers a fwarm of unprincipled wretches in his houfehold, who pilfer him of his property, the moft humble mafter in the vale of private life muft fubmit to fimilar depredations, or clean his own fhoes : this is furely an evil, as it involves the innocent in thofe confequences which only the guilty ought to feel.

But, although we fuffer and labour under the difeafe, it is not an eafy matter to point out the cure ; the legiflature feems either not to have thought it a blot in the police of the country, or it is a blot they have been cautious of hitting ; the only attempts made were in the years 1529 and 1792, in which laft year an act of parliament fubjected thofe who gave a forged character, or ftated in a character of a fervant what was not true, to a penalty of 20l.

This can be but of little fervice as the act is framed ; for, the firft claufe refpects only thofe who perfonate a mafter or miftrefs, &c. and give any falfe, forged, or counterfeited, character to any perfon offering as a fervant.

The fecond claufe goes only to thofe who fhall affert that a fervant has been hired for a period or ftation other than fuch period or ftation as he or fhe has been hired in.

The third, to thofe who fhall affert that a fervant was difcharged at any other time, or had not been hired in any previous fervice, contrary to the fact : and there are no other claufes refpecting giving characters of fervants.

The fourth and fifth claufes refpect only the perfons who offer themfelves as fervants, pretending to have ferved where they have not,

not, or offering themfelves with a falfe certificate, or who fhall alter a certificate, or, having been in fervice before, fhall pretend the contrary : the remaining claufes affix the penalty, point out the mode of conviction, and the diftribution of the penalty when recovered.

Had the legiflature probed the foul wound to the bottom, they would have difcovered that no lenient application can be equal to a cure; nothing fhort of making a breach of truft, in the inftance of menial domeftic fervants, a felony, will ftop the contagion; this was done in 1529; but thofe inftances where the value of the goods embezzled did not exceed forty fhillings, which are at leaft equal to ten pounds of the prefent money, are not fubject to the act; and, it is well known, the depredations of fervants are generally compofed of a mafs of minutiæ, fuch as victuals, wine, beer in fmall quantities; each item being individually of fmall value, and the act of embezzling difficult of proof, but eafy to commit, and that facility of commiffion, arifing from a neceffary confidence repofed in the fervant, to enable him to do the duties of his place, for the performance of which, he is hired at the price of his food, clothing, and confiderable wages; therefore, an act of parliament conftituting a fingle inftance of embezzlement of the property of his employer felony, be the value what it may, would have the fame effect as thofe ftatutes, which make it felony, to fteal a trifling value in property, which, neceffarily from the nature of it, lies expofed to depredations; or, probably, the putting the property of people, with refpect to their fervants, on the fame footing as wood, turnips, cabbages, &c. are placed with refpect to people ftealing them; for the firft offence, on fummary proof before a magiftrate, commitment to the houfe of correction for a limited time, and the fecond offence felony; if followed up, by treating the concealment, by the mafter or miftrefs, of fuch breach of truft, as a mifdemeanor, inditable at the quarter-feffions, of which concealment, a character given for honefty, and proof of the mafter or

miftrefs

miftrefs knowing at the time that the fervant had been guilty of a breach of truft, fhall be held fufficient to convict fuch mafter or miftrefs. Such a regulation would probably have fome effect.

But there ought to be eftablifhed, by univerfal opinion among all thofe who retain any menial fervants, a fenfe of rectitude and point of honour, with refpect to the characters which are given of fervants : the line of truth to be purfued fhould be that plain and comprehenfive one defcribed in the *voir dire* of a witnefs at the bar of a court of juftice ; if the character of a fervant is requefted, and is granted, that character, with refpect to his honefty and fobriety, the material points of his moral conduct, fhould contain *the truth, the whole truth, and nothing but the truth* ; the giver of the character fhould fpeak of the fervant as he is, nothing extenuate, nor fet down aught in malice.

During the halcyon days of peace and profperity, the minifter fhewed his attention to thofe in the middling ranks of fociety, by relieving them from the duty on female fervants : it was well done, both becaufe the tax was not productive, and becaufe it was un- popular : fhould the prefent neceffary war we are engaged in rage throughout another campaign, of which there is but little doubt, furely fomewhat might be raifed for the revenue, from the number of our countrymen and women in fervice, who certainly may be faid to be better fed than taught ; by a per centage upon their wages, to be retained by their mafter or miftrefs, accountable to the collectors of the fervants tax, on any fervants leaving their places within a year : a lefs per centage if within two years ; unlefs the perfons who retained them, either break up houfe-keeping, or actually and *bona fide* reduce the number of their fervants, or are convicted, fummarily before a magiftrate, of perfonal ill-ufage or refufal to pay wages ; and this idea, with refpect to the juftice of it, may be fupported on the following generally-allowed fact ; that no mafter or miftrefs willingly changes fervants ; with refpect to livery-fervants, a change is a real and confiderable expenfe, befides

R r   the

the difagreeable circumftance of introducing ftrangers into a private family; therefore, it in general is the fault of the fervant.

Difputes between mafters and their fervants, in a variety of trades and manufactures, are, by various acts of parliament, referred to a juftice of the peace; and, as thefe acts have increafed in number and in extent of operation from an early part of the reign of Charles the Second to the prefent time, we are at leaft juftified in faying, that they have had the advantage of experience, and have proved ferviceable.

What is the reafon, that an act of parliament, framed on principles fimilar to that for regulating difputes between mafters and fervants in hufbandry, and adapted to the fituation of menial fervants, hired for the purpofe of domeftic arrangement, in private families, fhould not be tried? I confefs myfelf unable to fee the objection.

Were the fervants, who are retained in the families of individuals, of the fame clafs and defcription of people they formerly confifted of; did they proceed from the cadets of the beft families - in the kingdom; were they now, as formerly, in the families of our nobility, the younger children of refpectable houfes; or did they in general proceed from the tenantry of the kingdom; and affifted now, as they did then, by being domefticated in the houfe of their immediate fuperior, to preferve the chain of connection, which, in the time of the feudal tenures, fubfifted from the cottage to the throne; there would then be no occafion to reftrain their conduct by fevere laws of the ftate; their actions would then be under the infpection of their immediate fuperior; to whom, in thofe times, they were accuftomed to look up, as to a patron and protector: but fuch connections and fuch habits have paffed away with the fyftem which familiarized them to our anceftors; and our prefent army of domeftics arifes from a different quarter, is endued with different principles and ideas, and, for the fafety of our property and the peace of our families, requires coertion and correc-

tion

tion with a different hand; it is not principle, but fear, which muft now keep them honeft; it is not affection, but intereft, which can infure their civility; and gratitude will no longer preferve their fidelity.

At the fame time, as thefe ftrictures are thrown out, with refpect to a neceffary interference of the legiflature in the regulation of the conduct of menial fervants; which, in thefe days of liberality and licenfe, may feem to fome as founded on a harfh or illiberal principle; but which, in fact, flow from the neceffity of the cafe, which calls aloud for the licentioufnefs of bad fervants to be reftrained, and their peculations to be repreffed; it is but right to obferve, that good fervants fhould undoubtedly be brought forward, as proper objects of reward and encouragement; the beft proof of their defert is the continuance a length of time in a place, and leaving that place handfomely, and with a good character; a per centage upon all the wages they have received, after the wages of the three firft years are deducted; to be paid them by their mafter or miftrefs, on quitting the fervice, in addition to their wages, might be the general reward, by the fanction of an act of parliament to that purpofe; unlefs fuch a fociety, for the encouragement of good fervants, as is eftablifhed in the metropolis, fhould be generally fubfcribed to; or fimilar focieties, being eftablifhed throughout the kingdom; fhould render fuch an interference of the legiflature unneceffary.

LETTER XLIII.

IT has been afferted, in a former part of this inveftigation, that local inconvenience and diftrefs, arifing from the number of the poor, and the expenfes of maintaining them, had occafioned many

diftricts

diſtricts within the county of Suffolk to apply to parliament for the power of incorporating themſelves, and of regulating the employ-ment and maintenance of the poor, within thoſe reſpective diſtricts, by certain rules agreed upon among themſelves; that, in conſe-quence thereof, ſeveral acts of parliament had paſſed incorporating the diſtricts applying for them ; that the poor have been ſince governed and regulated within thoſe diſtricts, according to the powers given by ſuch acts ; and that the convenience and incon-venience, experienced from the execution of them, ſhould be eluci-dated by the beſt information that can be obtained from the diſ-tricts thus incorporated.

In conſequence of this engagement I determined to viſit the houſes of induſtry which have been erected within the county of Suffolk ; that, from actual inſpection, perſonal inquiry, and ocular demon-ſtration, the facts reſpecting theſe inſtitutions, the conduct of them, and the conſequences which have ariſen to the public from them, might, with ſome certainty, be ſtated ; and that ſome pertinent obſervations might be made on thoſe facts and conſequences.

Such notices as were taken on the ſpot, and the informations received ſince, by letter, from the gentlemen who attend to the management of them, with ſuch alſo as have, by their direction, been communicated by letters from the governors, ſhall be ſtated, according to the priority, in point of time, of the incorporating-acts, and the erection of the different houſes of induſtry.

The middle of the ſummer was the time choſen for the excur-ſion ; and the houſes were inſpected, as ſuited convenience, from eight in the morning until eight at night.

The following queſtions were put to the governors of the houſes of induſtry, and their anſwers to them minuted, when ſatisfactory anſwers could be obtained, and are incorporated with the other in-formation collected.　In ſome inſtances, the governor or attendant

could

could not immediately give an anfwer by word of mouth, but engaged to do it in writing.

1. How many poor men, women, and children, have been admitted, fince the erection of the houfe, annually?

2. How many have died, fince the fame time, annually?

3. Has any, and what, part of the debt contracted by authority of parliament been paid?

4. Have the poor-rates in the diftrict incorporated been increafed or diminifhed?

5. What are the manufactures in which the poor are employed?

6. Is the fale of any of the manufactures, and which of them, diminifhed by the war?

7. Are the poor, or any of them, and how many, employed in agriculture?

8. Is any particular difeafe epidemic, or more prevalent than another, among the poor, and what is the nature of fuch difeafe?

Thefe queftions were calculated for the purpofe, to form fome judgement whether thefe inftitutions tend to increafe the chance of human life, to diminifh the poor's rate, both in times of peace and war, and alfo to form fome idea of the comparative profit arifing in thefe houfes from the manufactures of wool and hemp.

The hundreds of Colneis and Carlford were incorporated, by act of parliament, in the 29th year of his late majefty's reign; and their houfe of induftry in the parifh of Nacton was built in 1757, and firft inhabited in 1758.

The information which could be obtained on the fpot was not much to be depended on, the governor and his wife being from home when the vifit was made, which was about fix o'clock on the evening of the committee-day, and no perfon in the way was able to give any material information. My minutes were as follow:

Manufactures

Manufactures are cordage, facks, plough-lines, and fpinning for Norwich.

Boys, employed in fpinning hemp, earn 6*d.* a day, one with another.

Girls employed in fpinning wool : the great girls ftinted at 6*d.* a day, but receive for their work only half.

The dormitory is too much crowded : three or four boys in a bed, two men : there ought to be no more than two children in a bed, and one man. This number in one bed occafioned the air to be difagreeable to the fmell. The fame was not obferved in any of the other houfes.

The dining-hall is very neat and commodious.

Land, in occupation by the houfe, five acres. Two cows are kept. Only one man at work in agriculture, no boys.

The poor are now allowed more liberty, without the walls of the area on which the houfe and offices ftand, than formerly, and are more healthy than they were.

The following anfwer to the foregoing queftions was tranfmitted to me by Mr. John Enefer, clerk to the guardians of the houfe, by the order of Philip B. Brooke, Efq. one of the directors of that houfe.

NACTON HOUSE OF INDUSTRY.

THE poor are employed in wool-fpinning, twine-fpinning, making facks, &c. ; the neat profits of which, from an average of the laft feven years, amount to 277*l.* 13*s.* 6*d.* a year.

The poor's rates were at firft 1487*l.* 13*s.* 5*d.* a year, but advanced, at Michaelmas, 1790, to 2603*l.* 7*s.* 0*d.* a year.

The expenditure upon an average for the laft feven years, 2367*l.* 8*s.* 8*d.* annually.

The original debt was 4800*l.* is now 4400*l.* and will be reduced to 500*l.* more at Michaelmas next, 1793.

The

The men and women, able to work, earn from twopence to fixpence a day.

The children are ftinted (according to their abilities, and not according to their ages) from one halfpenny to fixpence a day.

Very few hands are employed in agriculture.

The number of poor admitted into the houfe, and the number of deaths in the houfe, for the laft 14 years:

Years.	Admitted.	Deaths.
1779	166	46
1780	177	33
1781	193	68
1782	174	33
1783	168	23
1784	155	24
1785	112	23
1786	112	27
1787	108	13
1788	136	11
1789	133	11
1790	142	35
1791	125	21
1792	116	21
	2017	389

The moft prevalent difeafes in the houfe have been the fmall-pox, meazles, and hooping-cough.

The *hundred of Blything* was incorporated in 1764, and the houfe of induftry built on a rifing ground in the parifh of Bulcamp, about a mile from Bliburgh.

They have two manufactures for the ufe of the houfe, viz. linen and woollen, for ftockings and wearing-apparel. Linen is made in
the

the houfe to the value of three fhillings and fixpence a yard, but they fell nothing.

They fpin for the Norwich woollen-manufactures, and have earned four hundred pounds a year.

Forty-fix parifhes were incorporated.

The average-number of poor admitted the firft five years amounted to about 203.

There are now in fummer about 250, in winter about 300, in the houfe.

Many children are admitted without their parents.

About eight hundred pounds are annually paid to out-penfioners.

The fum borrowed was 12,000l.; half was paid in 1780, the whole in 1791.

The average of the poor's rates annually in the incorporated parifhes, when the hundred was firft incorporated, was not above one fhilling in the pound, which rate was diminifhed one-eighth in 1780, when half the debt was paid.

None of the poor are, at prefent, employed in agriculture.

In 1781, a putrid fever raged in the neighbourhood: the town of Bliburgh loft one-third of its inhabitants; this houfe loft 130 of its poor.

Twenty-five acres of land belong to the houfe; thirty acres are hired, fome for the plough, fome lies in pafture, fome in garden.

Sir John Rous, Bart. was fo obliging as to fend me a lift of admiffions and deaths in this houfe fince the inftitution, by which it appears, that, from October 13th, 1766, to Auguft 8th, 1793, five thoufand two hundred and feven paupers have been admitted, and one thoufand three hundred and eighty-one have died.

The hundreds of Mutford and Lothingland were incorporated in 1764: their houfe of induftry is in the parifh of Oulton, near Loweftoft, and has been built twenty-feven years.

The

The number of parifhes incorporated is twenty-four; their income about twelve hundred a year; of this nearly two hundred arifes from earnings.

The fum borrowed was 6200*l*. Expenfes in building were about 3000*l*. The houfe is erected on a frugal plan, and will contain 200 poor. For the firft feven years, not above one hundred were admitted annually; but the annual number now amounts to 150, or thereabouts. 1700*l*. of the original debt has been paid, befides 300*l*. a debt contracted when the houfe was under bad management.

The poor's rates were advanced, in 1781, ten per cent. more than the affeffment of the parifhes, when incorporated, and have not been diminifhed; but 300*l*. of the debt continues to be paid annually.

The regifter of deaths has not been regularly kept during the firft years of the inftitution; but the average-number, during the laft fix years, has been eleven in a year.

The prevailing manufacture is, making nets for the herring-fifhery. The merchants furnifh the twine, and it is braided by the yard.

Hemp: what they grow is manufactured in the houfe; but, lately, the weaving has been put out.

Woollen yarn is alfo fpun; but the trade is at prefent bad; therefore, only fuch are employed in fpinning wool who can do nothing elfe.

A child's ftint, either for braiding nets, fpinning yarn or hemp, is fourpence a day. Several children, not above feven years of age, were braiding.

Sometimes fome of the poor are let out to work in hufbandry at fixpence a day: their employment is chiefly weeding.

Weekly earnings of the houfe, on an average, four pounds.

Out-allowances were, laft year, 55*l*. and are rather increafing, but fuppofed to be bad management, and that they ought to be diminifhed.

S f

Land,

Land, in occupation, twelve acres, all arable; two, yearly, fown with hemp. No cows kept.

The hundred of Wangford incorporated 1764.

The houfe of induftry at Shipmeadow, between Harleftown and Beccles, has been built twenty-fix years. Twenty-feven parifhes are incorporated. The annual income from their rates is 1750*l*. The general number of poor in the houfe about two hundred; of deaths about twenty in a year: amount of labour, about three pounds a week: their employment fpinning for the Norwich manufacturers: there is no manufactory in the houfe.

Out-allowances, about eighty pounds a year.

Children are taken from large families.

Original debt, 8500*l*. of which 4000*l*. is paid.

Land, forty-five acres; twenty-feven of them arable. Five cows are kept.

There is no chapel; they attend the parifh-church.*

The hundreds of Loes and Wilford were incorporated in 1765.

The houfe of induftry, which is in the parifh of Melton, was erected the fame year, and is on a more extended and expenfive fcale than any yet examined. Their dining-hall is very fpacious and neat, as are the dormitories. There are apartments appropriated to the furgeon; and thofe belonging to the governor are large and convenient. The cellars and offices are excellent. The boys fchool and the girls fchool are both of them good rooms. There are alfo rooms which are made ufe of as a penitentiary lodging for refractory people, and thofe guilty of offences which require folitary reftraint, by virtue of the act of parliament, enabling thefe hundreds to borrow an additional fum of money, which act paffed in 1790.

---

* Oulton and Shipmeadow houfes of induftry were vifited, and the notices of them taken, by Samuel Brife, Efq. of Clare, a near relation and worthy friend, who accompanied me to all the other houfes of induftry in the county.

Their

Their manufactures are linen and woollen: the firft for their
own ufe; the profits on the laft are confiderably diminifhed by
the war.

The number of poor in the houfe is between 230 and 240.

Their out-allowances are large; by the laft rules and orders,
drawn up for regulating the proceedings of the directors and acting guardians, printed in 1792, although they feem to have limited
the fums to be allowed with prudence: they do not feem to have
taken care that the number of poor, who fhall receive out-allowances, fhall be fufficiently reduced, by obliging them to come into
the houfe.

Thefe out-allowances are the caufe of the increafe of expenfe,
as far as they tend to the old fyftem, to avoid which was the occafion of erecting thefe houfes.

By a letter which I was favoured with from a gentleman of this
diftrict,* it appears that the original debt of thefe hundreds was

9200l.

---

* Having received from this gentleman an anfwer to a letter I lately fent him, requefting him to ftate the average-rate of affeffments, in the pound, in the hundreds of Lees
and Wilford, and to inform me whether the population of the hundreds was increafed or
decreafed; in which, after faying he is forry it is not in his power to anfwer either of my
queftions, his letter proceeds thus:

" The account you have given, in your Hiftory of the Poor, as received from me, is
notorioufly contrary to fact, and equally impoffible *that I* could have given any fuch information. I have no copy of my letter, and therefore cannot attempt to correct the error,
but truft you will do me the juftice to leave my name out entirely in your intended new
edition."

I have, accordingly, done this gentleman the juftice to leave his name out entirely in
this edition; and now I muft do *myfelf the juftice* to print that part of his letter, dated
Dec. 8, 1793, which refers to the information in queftion, that the public may judge
whether or not the information contained therein juftifies the abftract given in the firft
edition of this work, which abftract is here re-printed without any alteration.

(C O P Y.)
1. Our original debt was £9200.
2. Our prefent debt is £10050.

3 and

9200*l.* the prefent debt is 10,050*l.*; that the maximum of the poor's rates, in thefe hundreds, was not more, including the Marfhal-fea-money, &c. than 15*d.* in the pound annually, eftimating at rack-rent when the hundreds were incorporated; and that they remain the fame.

The average-number of deaths, the laft three years, was about fixteen annually : the governor could give me no information in this refpect farther back, he not having been in that office longer than that period.

A furgeon, fchool-mafter, and fchool-miftrefs, refide in the houfe.

There were between thirty and forty infirm and difeafed poor in the fick-wards; but the greateft number of them complaining of the infirmities of age only, and fore legs, which appears to be a prevailing difeafe.

The poor children are taught different trades in the houfe befides manufactures, fuch as tailors, fhoe-makers; and are employed in thofe trades for the ufe of the houfe.

Three poor men are employed in agriculture.

The quantity of land, about thirty acres. They raife about three acres of hemp, and manufacture it. There is about an acre and a half of garden; the reft pafture. Six cows are kept.

The late governor, as I was informed, had confiderably injured the revenue of the houfe by the conduct of the manufactures.

---

3 and 4. I cannot anfwer with any degree of certainty. The feveral parifhes within the two hundreds were ordered to deliver up their books to committees appointed for the purpofe, who took the feven years next preceding the laft feven years, and, adding the amount together, divided it by feven, and thus formed an average for each refpective parifh, without paying any attention to pound-rates : hence the average in the pound for the hundreds is unknown.

In this parifh our poor-rates, including Marfhalfea-money, which, of late, has been very high, do not exceed 15*d.* in the pound, rack-rent; and, were other parifhes as fully rated, I am of opinion that 15*d.* would be the ultimum.

BEING now, as it were, in imagination, brought back to that part of the county which produced the objects of my inquiries, by the recapitulation of the information I received, no place. can be more proper than the prefent to return my thanks to thofe gentlemen who feconded my views, by their influence in the feveral houfes of induftry, at the time and fince, by communication, by letter, of their knowledge as to the particular points refpecting which their information was requefted; and alfo to teftify, that the excellent order, neatnefs, and regularity, preferved in all the houfes then vifited, prove that their officers and fervants, who produced every where, and at all hours, fuch inftances of attention to their duty, merit great praife.

The hundred of Samford was incorporated in 1765: the houfe of induftry was erected, in 1766, in the parifh of Tattingftone,. and opened for the reception of the poor, at Michaelmas, the fame year.

The original fum borrowed was 8250 l. of which 2450 l. has been paid.

The number of parifhes incorporated is 25; yearly affeffments, 2262 l. 18 s. 6 d.

The rates were fettled, in 1766, at 2 s. 8 d. in the pound, by the year, and remain the fame.

Average-number of poor, in the houfe, during four years, beginning in 1786, and ending in 1789, is 1055; and of deaths, for the fame time, is 117:

The average-number of poor admitted, from 1766, annually, could not be exactly afcertained, but is about 260: the average of deaths, from the fame year, is 37 9-13ths annually: but the fmall-pox, followed by a putrid fever, has been in the houfe three times,

viz.

viz. in the years 1780, 1781, 1791, when the number of deaths was 76, 81, 56.

The poor are principally employed in fpinning for Norwich; the pro-
fit of which was, for the four years ending with 1789, £ 1833 5 8
The out-allowances for the fame years amounted to . .   1042 8 8
The income for the fame years amounted to 11154 3 3
The expenditure for the fame years amounted to . . . 11144 8 5

There are at prefent eleven packs of top-work, valued at above 300l. left unfold, by reafon of the ftagnation of the Norwich trade.

Only two men and three boys are at prefent employed in hufbandry.

The officers of the houfe are a furgeon, chaplain, governor, ma-
tron.

Land belonging to the houfe, 36 acres.

No fick in the infirmary.

In the dormitories, which were large, there were two or three windows oppofite to the general range, which have great effeсt in keeping the rooms airy and fweet.

Moft of the particulars of this houfe of induftry, and alfo of the following houfe at Barham, were communicated to me by the Rev. Mr. Grant, the clergyman of Tattingftone, who very laudably interefted himfelf in putting the Tattingftone-houfe into a fimilar train of management as Barham, about the year 1790, when the management of the former appeared to be unprofitable.

The hundreds of Bofmere and Claydon were incorporated in 1765, the houfe of induftry was erected in 1766, in the parifh of Barham, and opened for the reception of the poor in October the fame year.

The original fum borrowed was 9994l. of which 7294l. has been paid.

The

The number of parishes incorporated is thirty-five; the yearly affessments 2561*l*. 4*s*. 10*d*.; the rates remain the same.

The number of poor in the house for six years, ending in 1792, was 1332; the number of deaths, during the same period, amounted to 253.

The number of deaths was increased considerably in the years 1790 and 1791 by the small-pox, one hundred and twenty-seven having died in those two years. The information received on this head was, that the poor were averse to inoculation ; therefore, when the pest-house, one of which each house of industry has, was full, there were no means left to prevent the natural small-pox going through the house of industry itself: the consequence has been a considerable mortality, but probably not greater than when the same disease has attacked the village-poor, and its fatal effects have not been prevented by inoculation. Barham-house has now two pest-houses at a little distance from it.

The poor are principally employed in spinning for Norwich: their profit has been on an average about 200*l*. annually ; but, for the half-year ending at Midsummer, 1793, only 72*l*. 1*s*. 8*d*.

Their income has amounted for seven years, ending 1792, to . . . . £ 20318 16 11
Their expenditure for the same time 17680 12 9

Profit to the house for that period 2637 4 2

Their average out-allowances for four years, ending 1789, have been annually 341*l*. 9*s*. 4*d*.

Seventeen aged and infirm people are in the sick-wards.

Land belonging to the house, 20 acres ; of which two are garden. Six cows are kept.

There were in this house more women between 20 and 30 years of age than in any other of the houses of industry.

The

The *hundred of Cosford, and the parish of Polsted,* was incorporated, 1779, and the houfe of induftry erected in 1780, in the parifh of Semer.

The original debt was 8000*l.* is now reduced to 180 *l.* and an annuity of 20 *l.* a year granted to a perfon upward of fixty years of age.

The poor's rates have been reduced three-eighths, and a confiderable fund remains in hand.

The poor in the houfe are employed in fpinning wool, which is wafhed and combed in the houfe, and the yarn fold at Norwich by commiffion; the fale of which is confiderably affected by the war, a confiderable quantity now remaining in hand.

The poor, when able, are employed in agriculture, as opportunity offers.

The average-number of paupers in the houfe is generally about one hundred and eighty.

The average-number of burials, fince the inftitution, has been annually about twenty-fix; the much greater proportion died the firft two years after the houfe was inhabited; which was attributed to the paupers, on their firft coming in, having too much meat-diet, after having fuffered extreme poverty. This caufe has been fince guarded againft, and the burials have been much fewer.

The houfe has been free from any epidemic difeafe fince it has been inhabited: when the fmall-pox has prevailed in the country, there has been two general inoculations with great fuccefs each time.

When I vifited this houfe of induftry, the governor was from home; as was the Rev. Mr. Cooke, the fon of that worthy magif-trate, who, from the firft inftitution of the houfe, to the time of his death, regulated the management of it with fo much care, attention, and economy, as to make it productive, in the fhorteft fpace of time, of more beneficial effects than any other in the county of Suffolk. It was from an anfwer to a letter I took the

liberty

liberty of writing to his fon, that the foregoing account has been extracted ; the obfervations made, and information obtained on the fpot, are as follow, from my own notes.

The chief manufactory is fpinning yarn for Norwich ; but fome of the top-work is wove into ferge for the women's jackets at Melford ; coarfe thickfet is bought at Norwich for clothes; linen cloth, for fhirts and fhifts, at Hadleigh.

Paupers in the houfe 25th of July, 1793 ; men 27, women 42 ; children, between the ages of twelve and twenty, 22 ; under the age of twelve, 74; in all, 165.

No men are out at day-labour ; four boys, twelve or thirteen years of age, fearing birds at the wages they can earn by fpinning, which is five-pence a day, none more.

The girls, at the age of thirteen, are put to fervice ; boys, at the age of fourteen.

Twenty-two packs of yarn remain in ftore, value about 600*l*.; land belonging to the houfe, about twelve acres ; of which two are garden, ten meadow and pafture.

Two cows are kept in fummer-time : they make all their butter in fummer, and buy falt butter in the winter.

Only four fick in the infirmary : every thing appeared neat, the poor healthy and comfortable.

The hundred of Stow, incorporated in 1780.

The houfe of induftry, in the parifh of One-houfe, opened for the reception of paupers, Oct. 11, 1781.

The fum firft borrowed was only 8000*l.* but the expenfe of building the houfe fo much exceeded the fum intended to be laid out for that purpofe, that an additional fum of 4150*l.* was afterwards borrowed ; and the rates were increafed one quarter by common confent for three years : they remain now the fame as at firft.

Fifteen hundred pounds have been paid off in the whole, at the proportion of from one hundred and fifty to two hundred pounds per annum.

T t

The

The poor in the houfe are employed in fpinning top-work for Norwich; the wool is bought into the houfe; the clothing for the ufe of the houfe is made from the thrums, ends, and nibbings, and fuch fpinning as is unfit for the Norwich market; their beft rugs are alfo made from thefe materials; no part of their clothing is put out to be made, except ftockings.

The fale of the top-work is confiderably affected by the war: twelve packs are left in the houfe unfold; value about twenty-four pounds each pack.

None are employed in agriculture at prefent; only two men are in the houfe who can do harveft-work; fome children are fometimes employed in weeding; all who are able are employed in hop-picking; but, it is conceived, that nothing is faved by fuch employment.

The average-number of paupers in the houfe is about two hundred.

The number of burials fince Oct. 11, 1780, to Auguft 1, 1793, as follows:

Oct. 11, 1780, to Jan. 1, 1781 -   8
                         1781 - 25
                         1782 - 51 a putrid fever.
                         1783 - 61 a putrid fever.
                         1784 - 51 a putrid fever.
                         1785 - 14
                         1786 -   2
                         1787 - 17
                         1788 - 15
                         1789 - 11
                         1790 - 13
                         1791 - 19
                         1792 - 18
To Auguft 1ft   -   1793 - 17

Thefe

These thirteen years form an average of 24 2-13ths yearly; or, omitting the three years, when the putrid fever prevailed, the average of the remaining ten years is only 15 1-10th.

Annual income from rates, 1987 *l.*; from labour, manufactory, &c. not less than 350 *l.* annually, for the last ten or eleven years; but has amounted to 104 *l.* only the last half-year, owing to the stagnation of the Norwich manufactory.

Out-allowances from 250 *l.* to 300 *l.* annually; but these are increasing, and expected to continue so, from the stagnation of trade.

There has been no fever or epidemic disorder in the house since 1784, although there has been much sickness in the hundred; nor were there in the house, at the time these notices were taken, any of the paupers so sick as to be confined to their beds.

Number of acres 24; of these 3½ are arable, one acre garden, the rest pasture. Four cows are kept, and two horses.

In this house, the spinning-rooms and working-rooms are divided by partitions, in such a manner, as that but few spin or work together; as are also the dormitories. There are not more than seventeen beds in any: this is an improvement not observable in any other of the houses of industry, and tends much to the preservation of health and order.

A tailor and shoemaker are kept in the house.

A schoolmaster to teach the children to read, and a mistress to teach the little children. Relief is given to large families by taking those children into the house which are a burthen to their parents. The same method is in fact practised by all; consequently, the children are taken in very young.

LETTER XLV.

A Neceffary attention to the duties of a magiftrate, together with compaffion for the diftreffes of my poor neighbours, particularly for thofe who were employed in daily labour on my eftate, had occafioned me to vifit, at times, the fick cottager, and the miferable pauper in a parifh work-houfe. The fituation of the firft, whofe narrow tenement forbad the poffibility of feparating the fick from the well, the parent from the children, or the children them- felves from each other; that miferable economy in fitting up the cottage, which too generally has denied the only bed-room either a fire-place or a cafement-window to ventilate the air; the noife of querulous children, the ftench of confined air, rendered epidemic by morbid effluvia; the vermin, too, frequently fwarming on the bo- dies and rags of the wretched inhabitants; all thefe caufes, acting together, procraftinate affliction, prevent a return of health, and in- dicate a depth of mifery, which hard labour and induftry ought not in ficknefs to be liable to endure. Neither did the parifh-work- houfe, the laft fad refuge of miferable indigence, offer a lefs dif- agreeable fpectacle; the want of room, and the bad management of that which they poffefs, occafion fimilar inconveniences: the clothes, or rather the covering, of the inhabitants; the too frequent inftances of infamous debauchery, arifing from the two fexes of all ages and difpofitions kept together; the ignorance and filth the children are brought up in; and the general fpirit of rigid economy which the contracting mafter of the work-houfe practifes, as well in diet as in clothing, lodging, and cleanlinefs, to fcrape from mifery, as foon as poffible, a property which may enable him to retire from his dif- agreeable avocation; give propriety to the opinion and expreffion; that a parifh-work-houfe is too often a parifh-bawdry-houfe, always a bug-bear to frighten modeft diftrefs from applying for relief.

In

In the incorporated hundreds, the houfes of induftry ftrike one in a different light; they are all of them built in as dry, healthy, and pleafant, fituations, as the vicinity affords; the offices, fuch as the kitchen, brew-houfe, bake-houfe, buttery, laundry, larder, cellars, are all large, convenient, and kept exceeding neat: the work-rooms are large, well-aired, and the fexes are kept apart, both in hours of work and recreation.

The dormitories are alfo large, airy, and conveniently difpofed; feparate rooms for children of each fex, adults, and aged; the married have each a feparate apartment to themfelves; mothers with nurfe-children are alfo by themfelves.

The infirmaries are large, convenient, airy, and comfortable; none without fire-places.

All the houfes have a proper room for the neceffary difpenfary; and moft of them a furgeon's room befides.

The halls, in all, are large, convenient, well ventilated, with two or more fire-places in them, and calculated, with refpect to room, for the refection of full as many as the other conveniences of the houfe can contain.

The chapels are all fufficiently large, neat, and plain; feveral of them rather tending to grandeur and elegance. There were two houfes, which had no chapel: one of them made ufe of a room ample enough for the congregation, properly fitted up, and kept very neat: the other houfe attended the parifh-church.

The apartments for the governor were in all the houfes large, and conveniently difpofed : in one or two of the houfes of induftry, thefe apartments were rather more fpacious and elegant than neceffary : there are alfo convenient ftorehoufes and warehoufes, for keeping the manufacture of the houfe, the raw materials, and the clothing, &c. for the ufe of the inhabitants.

The land about the houfes belonging to them, particularly the gardens, are all calculated for producing a fufficient quantity of

vegetable

vegetable diet, so neceffary to the health as well as agreeable to the palate of the inhabitants.

In general, the appearance of all the houfes of induftry, in the approach to them, fomewhat refembles what we may fuppofe of the hofpitable large manfions of our anceftors, in thofe times when the gentry of the country fpent their rents among their neighbours.

The interior of thefe houfes muft occafion a moft agreeable furprife to all thofe who have not before feen poverty, but in its miferable cottage or more miferable work-houfe.

In looking over my notes, I find that the affirmative neatnefs which prevailed from the cellar to the garret, in all the houfes, with very few exceptions in particular departments, occafioned not only a memorandum of the fact, but gave rife to a conception which poffibly lies more in imagination than reality, that, where a deficiency in this refpect is obfervable in any domicile, a concomitant deficiency is alfo obfervable in the healthy looks of the inhabitants.

This neatnefs, which had fo pleafing an effect on the eye, was the caufe alfo that the other fenfes were not difgufted by that conftant attendant on collected filth and foul air, a noifome ftench, as deleterious to human life as it is in general naufeating to thofe who accidentally breathe fuch an atmofphere.

The practice of frequently white-wafhing does much in preferving the air of thefe houfes wholefome and fweet, but the conftant attention of thofe who perform the offices of the houfe is abfolutely neceffary, and even that is infufficient, unlefs the halls, working-rooms, and dormitories, have the external air admitted through the windows, whenever it can be done with fafety to the inhabitants, with refpect to catching cold : this practice of keeping the windows open cannot be trufted to the paupers themfelves; for, ftrange to tell, the general complaint againft them was, that they

would

would not only not attend to keeping them open, but, if the adults and aged had their choice, fuch depravity arifes from habit, they would live in that atmofphere of putrid air, which would undoubtedly produce contagion.

The neatnéfs and *propreté* which prevailed in their halls at the hour of refection were alfo laudably obfervable, moft of thefe houfes of induftry being vifited at the hours of breakfaft, dinner, or fupper. At times I have felt difguft when requefted to take fome refrefhment which has been offered me in a cottage; a difguft arifing from the abfence of that neatnefs which attends the tables of thofe among whom it has been my lot to live: but no want of neatnefs in thefe houfes created difguft; a breakfaft, dinner, or fupper, might have been eaten at their tables with a keen appetite.

Their bread was, in all the houfes, particularly pleafant; it was good brown bread, made from the flour deprived of the coarfeft of its bran: white bread was alfo baked for the infirm, the convalefcent, and young children.

Their cheefe was in general good, although frequently the cheefe of the country: in one houfe they bought Dutch cheefe, which was ftronger in its tafte, and confequently to fome palates not fo pleafant.

The fmall-beer was alfo pleafant: — no wonder; they bought the beft malt and hops, brewed a large quantity at a time, and kept it in excellent cellars: ale was alfo brewed, in inferior quantities, and given to the convalefcent, and to thofe whom the governor thought proper, either as a neceffary refrefhment, or as a reward; and it was alfo diftributed, at ftated times, to the whole houfe.

It did not occur to me to take minutes of the bill of diet in any of the houfes, becaufe *no* doubt has been fuggefted that it is not wholefome and fufficient: that, in fome inftances, it has been too abundant, may be fufpected, as well from the relics which were

feen

feen after their meals, as from the idea thrown out by one of the directors in a letter which has been alluded to. *

The application of thefe facts, which have been ftated, as well upon the credit of perfonal infpection, and information from thofe whofe duty it certainly was, and whofe inclination it appeared to be, to give true and full information upon the fubject, as from thofe gentlemen, alfo, who obligingly communicated any information by letter, now remains to be made to three important queries.

1. Have thefe inftitutions amended the morals of the poor ?

2. Have they tended to diminifh the burthen of expenfe to fociety attending their relief and maintenance ?

3. Have they increafed, or do they tend to decreafe, the chance of human life ?

With refpect to the firft queftion, it may be anfwered in the affirmative without a poffibility of contradiction.

They have amended the morals of the lower orders of people, if the proportional few inftances of indictments, at the quarter-feffions, for actions of inferior criminality, which lead to greater crimes, will prove the fact ; and it does, in this inftance, in a remarkable manner : four inquifitions of murder have been, within this twelve-month, found by the coroner for the county of Suffolk, not one of them in either of the incorporated hundreds. There are twenty-three hundreds in the county ; twelve of them are incorporated, and maintain their poor in houfes of induftry.

If the general good order and regulation the labouring-poor are kept in throughout the incorporated diftricts, which good order is evidenced by their general conduct and converfation, and by their obfervation of thofe laws, the breach of which may tend to endanger the lives, and diminifh the fafety and comfort, of his ma-

* See the extract from Mr. Cook's letter refpecting the Semer houfe of induftry.

jefty's

jefty's fubjects in general; fuch as drivers riding on their waggons; tippling in ale-houfes, and the fmaller immoralities and improprieties' of conduct; if fuch attention to the orders of fociety proves the fact:

If the refpectful and civil behaviour of the poor to their fupcriors, the very rare inftances of children being feduced to fteal wood, turnips, &c. and to the commiffion of other fmall thefts; if thefe and fimilar proofs of good morals, unfortunately not prevalent in thofe diftricts within the county where thefe houfes are not inftituted; if fuch inftances prove the fact, experience tells us thefe inftitutions have tended to reform the morals of the poor.

And the prophetic fpirit of theory had, beforehand, informed thofe, who wifhed to form a judgement on the fubject, that the effect could not be otherwife.

A large building, calculated for the reception of the poor of the diftrict, fituated in the moft healthy fituation, with convenient offices of all kinds, the inhabitants of which are under the regulation of well-chofen officers, fubject to excellent rules, all of them calculated to promote regularity, induftry, morality, and a religious fentiment.

The hours of work, refrefhment, and fleep, uniform and regular.

The children, from the earlieft age, on leaving their mother's arms, are under the care of proper dames, who teach them obedience, and give them the habit of attention.

When more advanced in years, fchool-mafters teach them to read; and the fuperintendants of the working-rooms, fome induftrious employment, and take care that their hours of work fhall not be paffed in idlenefs: here they are generally ftinted, fo that greater induftry is rewarded with greater leifure.

The duties of religion are expected to be regularly attended by all the poor of all ages, no excufe being admitted but illnefs.

It

It required no prophetic fpirit to foretel, that, thefe duties and this fyftem of regularity being perfevered in, the beft effects muft, of confequence, enfue to the morals of the poor of all ages, and to thofe of the rifing generation in particular.

In thefe houfes of induftry, therefore, may be found that plan of education of poor children carried into effect, which has been, in former pages of this tract, fo warmly recommended to be purfued, by the means of fchools of induftry, united with Sunday-fchools.

But it fhould be remembered, that thefe fchools, in the houfes of induftry, are not general for the children of *all* the poor within the incorporated parifhes; only thofe whofe poverty induces their parents to afk parifh-relief are fent here, and, of thofe, only fuch children as are the greateft burthen to their parents : the children of thofe poor who are not petitioners for relief, and thofe children of the poor who are, and whom their parents do not choofe fhould be fent to the houfe of induftry, are kept at home, and have not the benefit of this plan of education ; and it is a circumftance worthy of remark, that parents, in general, from whom to take, for a time, the idle, mifchievous, leaft ufeful, and moft burthenfome, part of their family, to bring them up, without any care or expenfe to themfelves, in habits of induftry and decency, is a very great relief, are very much averfe to fending their children to the houfes of induftry ; from what caufe it is difficult to tell ; but it is plain that no good caufe can give rife to this averfion : fuppofe it to be parental affection and fondnefs, which makes them, with regret, part with their children, the anfwer is obvious ; they are fent but a little way from them, are in the neighbourhood, where they may be feen at all proper times, and, when feen, will be feen in a ftate of cleanlinefs inftead of filth, of employment inftead of idlenefs, with neat clothing and wholefome diet inftead of filthy rags and an empty belly : whereas parents, in higher fituations of life, who feel that fondnefs of affection in, at leaft, an equal degree,

gree, voluntarily, and at a confiderable expenfe, fend their children to feminaries of learning and fchools, for education, at a much greater diftance, and do not fee them for many months toge-ther: much credit cannot, therefore, be given to the fentiment of affection: the only one which can be mentioned as an apo-logy for this averfion, and every other reafon, muft be founded on a bad principle, and confequently ought not to have any weight.

Were thefe inftitutions erected upon a plan which would admit of taking *all* the children of the poor, from the time they are ca-pable of being taught fome employment, and keeping them in the houfe, as in a fchool, until fuch employment is learned, and regu-lar habits of induftry acquired, together with an abhorrence of that life of idlenefs and theft to which the children of the poor are prone, either naturally, or by the encouragement of their parents, every good which can be expected to arife, from fuch an inftitution-as has been recommended, might thus be attained to, in a houfe-of induftry, at a very trifling increafe of expenfe, if at any, and which expenfe would be amply repaid by the general good effect: but fuch a plan, could the houfes of induftry receive them, muft be feconded by the court of quarter-feffions iffuing an order, pro-hibiting relief to be given to fuch parents who fhall refufe to let their children go to thefe fchools, when appointed to them by the overfeers of the refpective parifhes.

- - -

LETTER XLVI.

TO determine the fecond queftion, with certainty, recourfe muft be had to the notices taken, refpecting the fact, in the different incorporations; and it will be found, that, in fome, the

poor's

poor's rates have been diminifhed; in others, they remain the fame as at the time of the inftitution; and, in a few, the rates have been increafed : the different inftances fhall be pointed out, and fome obfervations made on the facts, as they have been ftated.

Blything-hundred; Bulcamp houfe of induftry ; the whole debt, 12000 *l.* has been paid off; the rates were diminifhed one-eighth in 1780; and, as they were not on an average above one fhilling in the pound annually when firft incorporated, they are now inconfiderable.

The hundred of Cosford, and the parifh of Polfted ; the houfe of induftry at Semer ; the whole debt, 8000 *l.* has been paid off, except an annuity of 20 *l.* a year, and 180 *l.*; but they have ftock more than fufficient to difcharge thefe remaining demands ; the poor's rates have been diminifhed three-eighths; and the rates were very moderate when the hundred was incorporated.

Wangford-hundred houfe of induftry, at Shipmeadow ; original debt 8500 *l.* of which 4000 *l.* is paid; rates remain the fame.

The hundred of Samford; the houfe of induftry at Tattingftone; the original fum borrowed 8250 *l.* of which 2450 *l.* have been paid; the rates were fettled at 2 *s.* 8 *d.* in the pound annually, and remain the fame.

Hundreds of Bofmere and Claydon ; the houfe of induftry at Barham ; the original fum borrowed 9994 *l.* of which 7294 *l.* have been paid ; the rates remain the fame.

Stow-hundred ; the houfe of induftry at Onehoufe, near Stowmarket ; the original fum borrowed 12150 *l.* of which 1500 *l.* have been paid ; the rates remain the fame.

Hundreds of Colneis and Carlford ; the houfe of induftry at Nacton ; the original debt was 4800 *l.* is now 3900 *l.* the rates were increafed at Midfummer, 1790, from 1487 *l.* 13 *s.* 4 *d.* annually, to 2367 *l.* 8 *s.* 8 *d.*; but from information it appears, that the rates were not more than fixteen or eighteen pence annually, when the average was fixed ; and the revenue of the houfe has exceeded its expenditure

expenditure on an average of the laft feven years 513 *l.* 11 *s.* 10 *d.* annually.

Hundreds of Mutford and Lothingland; the houfe of induftry at Oulton; the original debt 6500 *l.* of which 2000 *l.* has been paid off; the poor's rates are advanced ten per cent. but 300 *l.* of the debt is annually paid off.

Hundreds of Loes and Wilford; the houfe of induftry at Melton; their original debt was 9200 *l.* their prefent debt is 10050 *l.* their poor-rates, together with their county-rates, do not now exceed 15 *d.* in the pound at rack-rent.

By this recapitulation it appears, that, at two of the houfes of induftry, the rates have been confiderably diminifhed, and the original debt annihilated.

At four, the rates remain; but a confiderable part of the original debt has been paid.

At two, the rates have been increafed, and the debt diminifhed: at the laft houfe of induftry the debt has been increafed, and the rates remain the fame.

The queftion, whether houfes of induftry tend to diminifh the expenfe of the relief and maintenance of the poor, is therefore anfwered in the affirmative, fince in two the rates are diminifhed, the debt is paid; in four, the debt has been confiderably diminifhed, confequently the annual balance in their favour might have been applied to the purpofe of diminifhing the rates, *pari paffu*, with the debt; in two of the others the balances have been applied hitherto to diminifh the debt only, and the rates have increafed; in one, the debt is fomewhat increafed, and the rates remain the fame, at the low average of 15 *d.* in the pound annually.

When the average, at which thefe parifhes fettled their rates, at the time they were incorporated, and the number of years which have elapfed fince that average was fettled, are confidered; in fome, being between thirty and forty years; and in none lefs than twelve or fourteen; and compared with the proportion the rates then bore

to

to a pound, and the proportion they would now bear, had there been no houfe of induftry; taking the advance of the poor's rate in the other parifhes throughout the kingdom in general, and in Suffolk in particular, as they are proved to be, by the returns of the overfeers to the inquiries made by parliament, in the year 1776, and 1783, 4, and 5, as the rule of computation, and no better can be obtained; in which returns it appears, that, in the two contiguous hundreds in Suffolk, not incorporate, Rifbridge and Babergh, the *net expenfes* of the poor alone had advanced from 11,023*l*. 7*s*. 11*d*. to 13,840*l*. 3*s*. 9*d*. being a difference of 2817*l*. or thereabouts, in the courfe of eight years, or above 25*l*. 9*s*. per cent. an advance that brings forward the moft unthrifty management of any of the houfes of induftry into a ftate of pofitive profperity and reduction of expenfe; it will therefore be found, that not only where the rates have been ftationary, but where they have advanced, and in the inftance where the debt has increafed, the poor's rates have been very much decreafed, from what they would have been, had the poor been managed according to the old and the common fyftem; we may therefore with certainty apply the old adage, *non progredi eft regredi*, with refpect to the expenfes of the poor in all the incorporated houfes of induftry.

On the whole, although in an inftance or two, originating from an improvident mode of building the houfes of induftry at firft, more fubfequent expenfes have been incurred than were at that time forefeen, and confequently a larger revenue became neceffary to pay the intereft of the additional fum they were obliged to borrow, and to fupport the expenfes of the houfe than was at firft thought fufficient; and, in another inftance, the difhonefty or profufion of the then governor has fo difarranged the affairs of the houfe, as to render a new loan, and confequently an increafed rate, convenient; yet, on the whole, it is conceived, that not the leaft fhadow of doubt can be raifed, but that even, in thefe inftances, the revenues of the houfes are increafing beyond the difburfements, the debt is

diminifhing,

diminifhing, and the rates will fall even beneath that low medium they have hitherto preferved; and which rates, had there been no houfe of induftry, would probably have rifen twenty-five, or even fifty, per cent. above their prefent amount.

LETTER XLVII.

THE other queftion, whether the houfes of induftry have in-creafed the chance of human life, involves in it fuch com-plicated confiderations, is a queftion of fuch uncertainty of proof, a comparifon with the ftate of population in country-villages, and with the chance of human life of people of particular ages and par-ticular fituations only, and not with human life in general, being to be taken into confideration, and there being no data with which the comparifon of the facts can be made, the tables of the chance of human life being of too general a nature, and the facts them-felves as to deaths, in houfes of induftry, not being fufficiently par-ticularifed as to age and ftate of patients health when admitted to give an exact refult, that fome general obfervations on the deaths which have happened in thefe houfes, compared with the numbers admitted, is all that fhall be attempted, leaving the reader to make up his own mind, as well as he is able, from the imperfect fketch of the queftion it is in my power to offer, to which I fhall very humbly add my opinion, without prefuming to dictate any pofitive conclufion to his judgement.

And, firft, it will be proper to pay fome attention to the fitua-tion of the poor, and their families, before they take refuge from the mifery of extreme poverty in a houfe of induftry. What are, at that time, their expectations of health and life?

They

They are fo reduced by poverty as not to be able to maintain themfelves and their families, and therefore they become inmates of a houfe of induftry; confequently, the conftitution, both of parents and children, muft have been debilitated by want of neceffary food, raiment, and fhelter, that none can be faid to be admitted in found health : no eftimate can, therefore, be made of their chance of life, in comparifon with the inhabitants of villages, towns, or cities, in general.

They are afflicted with difeafe, either parents or children, and therefore they are fent, by the parifh-officers, to a houfe of induftry : the chance of life with fuch is ftill decreafing.

Children are born, and, at the earlieft age at which they can leave their mothers, are received in thefe houfes, and are kept in them through that period when the chance of human life is leaft; and much the greateft number in all the houfes is compofed of children.

The other confiderable clafs is compofed of the aged, and the infirm, either from age or accident. The chance of life, in this clafs, is fmall indeed.

Such are the different fituations of the inmates in a houfe of induftry : very few poor, between the age of fifteen and fifty, are feen there, except difeafes, accidents, infirmities, or particular irregularities of life, have occafioned them to be fent there.

The chance of life, to people in thefe fituations, and of thefe ages, under the preffure of penury, although not abfolutely chilled by the cold hand of extreme poverty, would, in their miferable cottages, be fmall indeed.— Is that chance diminifhed or increafed by going into a houfe of induftry?

Is the chance of human life increafed or diminifhed by being brought from an unwholefome ftarving diet to wholefome moderate plenty; from nakednefs to clothing; from filth to cleanlinefs; from cold to warmth; from the noifome contagion of a filthy cottage,

tage, or parish-work-house, to a healthy air, free from noxious effluvia? Surely, the answer to these questions would, at once, determine the point, did it depend on theory alone.

But it may be said, the question has been tried by the touchstone of experience; one single page of which, honestly recorded, goes farther towards proof positive, than volumes of theoretic reasoning; we must therefore have recourse to this best of demonstrations.

The validity of this observation must be allowed, were the facts produced, of mortality in houses of industry, capable of being compared with the deaths of people under similar circumstances, and of similar ages, at large.

In Nacton house of industry the number of poor admitted the last fourteen years are 2017; the number of deaths, 384; the annual average of inhabitants is therefore 144; of deaths, 27.

In Bulchamp house of industry, the number admitted since the institution, in 1766 to 1793, twenty-seven years, 5207; the number of deaths, in that time, 1381: but, in the years 1781 and 1782, a putrid fever carried off one-third of the inhabitants of Blithburgh, and 217 of the inhabitants of this house; therefore, those two years should be omitted in the comparative statement: the numbers will then stand, of inhabitants, admitted in 25 years, 4725; of deaths, 1064: or, annually, inhabitants, 189, deaths, 42.

Oulton house of industry. Number of inhabitants, on an average, annually, about 150 the last six years; of deaths, for the same period, annually, 11.

Shipmeadow house of industry. Number of poor, about 200 annually; number of deaths, about 20 in a year.

Melton house of industry. Number of poor in the house, from 230 to 240; the number of deaths, for the last three years, about 16 annually.

Tattingstone house of industry. Average-number of poor in the house, annually, for 23 years, 260; average-number of deaths, annually, for the fame time, 33. In this computation, the three years are omitted when the fmall-pox and putrid fever prevailed: the deaths, in the three years when thefe contagious diftempers were fo fatal, bring the average-number of deaths up to 37 9-13ths, as has been ftated in the notices refpecting the houfe.

Barham houfe of induftry. Average-number of poor inhabitants, annually, for five years, as appears by the notices, 222; average-number of deaths, 42. In this houfe, alfo, the fmall-pox prevailed for two years, and deftroyed 127 of the inhabitants; the average of deaths, otherwife, would not have been fo high.

Semer houfe of induftry. Average-number of poor inhabitants in the houfe, annually, from its inftitution, 180; annual number of deaths, 26.

Stow houfe of induftry. Annual average-number of poor inhabitants, in the houfe, about 200; of deaths, annually, 24: but, in this houfe, a putrid fever prevailed three years, and was fatal to 163 people: the average, omitting thefe three years, and taking it for ten years only, is 15 in a year.

In the nine houfes of induftry which have been the objects of our attention, there are, conftantly, one year with another, 1780 poor inhabitants, men, women, and children.

In the fame houfes there happen, annually, two hundred and forty-five deaths, as the number appears by the averages taken.

The number of deaths to the number of inhabitants, annually, in all the houfes of induftry in Suffolk is, therefore, as 1 to 7 one-third, or nearly one-feventh of the number dies every year.

It fhould be recalled to the reader's mind, that the inhabitants are compofed of children, from birth, to the ages of 12, 13, or 14, when they are bound apprentices or get fervices: the chance of life in this early age is fuch as, in the healthieft towns, not half the number is alive at the age of 13, as appears from the tables in Dr. Price's

Supplement

Supplement to his Obfervations on Reverfionary Payments; of old people, whofe work is done; and of poor, of all ages, who, from ficknefs and infirmity, are unable to maintain themfelves. Such being the defcription of paupers admitted into thefe houfes of induftry, it muft again be obferved that no comparifon can be made between the chance of life, of fuch inhabitants, and of thofe inhabiting in cities, towns, or villages, in general; becaufe, in the firft inftance, are comprized only the very young, the very old, and the infirm and difeafed; and thefe are alfo poor, and of impoverifhed blood, and conftitutions weakened by the effects of poverty; whereas the tables in Dr. Price's Supplement to his Reverfionary Payments, and in the publications of other political arithmeticians, comprehend people of all ranks, orders, and fituations, in life, as well the healthy and the robuft as the infirm and the difeafed; as well people of all claffes, at thofe periods when the chance of human life is greateft, as at thofe when it is the leaft.

The queftion of the comparative chance of human life, in thefe houfes, muft, therefore, be left undetermined by any comparifon with fuch chance in general; and, probably, the queftion would be more fairly tried, could a comparifon be made between the mortality in the parifhes incorporated, before fuch incorporation took place, and fuch mortality fince, taking into the account the number of the poor of each parifh who have died in the houfes of induftry.

The effect thefe inftitutions have had, with refpect to population, might alfo, by means of fuch comparative refearches, be more accurately afcertained, were it likely that fuch inquiries would be attended by certain information, which probably might be the cafe, with refpect to the comparative number of deaths, by means of the parifh-regifters, and the books of the refpective houfes; but that part of the queftion, which refpects comparative population, could

not,

not, by any direct inquiry, be afcertained, and can only be computed from the births and burials in the parifhes, which would afford, by no means, an exact refult.

On the whole, this queftion muft be left in doubt, for the prefent. To judge from every appearance attending the interior of the houfes of induftry, no one could hefitate to declare that they muft tend to increafe the chance of human life, and to increafe the population of the diftricts : the fame judgement muft be deduced from all theoretic proofs, reafoning from probable, nay, almoft neceffary, confequences. But when the comparative number of the living to the dead, taken annually, appears to be only as feven one-third to a unit ; or, in other words, that the chance of life, in a houfe of induftry, is not equal to eight years; the fact ftrikes ftrongly, and occafions the judgement upon the queftion to remain fufpended.

But ftill two great points are determined in their favour : they certainly tend to meliorate the morals of the poor, and they alfo tend to diminifh the burthen of the expenfe attending their maintenance : that the other point is not, on experience, determined in their favour alfo, arifes from the difficulty of acquiring every information neceffary to its inveftigation, and from the inability of the writer to apply, with precifion and certainty of proof, fuch facts as he had obtained : he ftill believes that this point will, whenever it falls under the pen of a more accurate inquirer, and an able political arithmetician, conduce alfo to the recommendation of diftrict incorporated houfes of induftry, as tending to increafe the chance of life and population.

I cannot take leave of this fubject, without animadverting upon fome information received refpecting the diffatisfaction of the poor at the firft erection of houfes of induftry, which broke out in riotous proceedings, and, in fome inftances, occafioned a great additional expenfe to the incorporated hundreds; the fpirit of riot having proceeded fo far as to pull down the buildings erected, and

to

to commit other flagrant acts of outrage. It is a well-known fact, proved by long experience, that the clafs of people, conftituting what is called a mob, is never collected and excited to mifchief, but at the inftigation of an individual, or fome few individuals, who poifon the minds of their uninformed but well-meaning neighbours: thefe are men generally of a clafs a little fuperior to the mob itfelf; they are men who mix in converfation with them at the ale-houfes, at the fhop-keepers, and at barbers fhops; are in general interefted cunning people, who, under the mafk of vaft humanity, tender affection, and kind regard, for their poor neighbours, inftigate them to thefe and fimilar acts of outrage. Examine the fituations in life, the habits, the connections, of thefe people, when their fecret machinations are difcovered by the effects of open riot and mifchief, and they ftand the confeffed encouragers of the mob: it muft ftrike every inhabitant upon the fpot, that a trifling degree of attention to the conduct of this defcription of people would have demonftrated before the fact; that thofe very individuals would be guilty of that clandeftine incitement of the mob of the neighbourhood to the very deed of riot which has been committed, and confequently it would be proper in a diftrict, where fuch an incorporation is intended, to be watchful of the conduct and converfation of that defcription of men, whofe interefts will be moft injured by a plan of this nature, and to oppofe the effect of their converfations on the minds of the poor, by every means which prudence can devife and the laws will fanction.

Was any additional inducement wanting to recommend diftrict houfes of induftry, the particular fituation and temper of the times would be that inducement; the lower orders of the kingdom are now preffing on the next, and the toe of the peafant truly galls the kibe of the courtier; that relief which formerly was, and ftill ought to be, petitioned for as a favour, is now frequently demanded as a right; that idlenefs and intemperance, which formerly feared to be obferved, now obtrufively preffes forward to fight; the pauper is no longer

longer fatisfied with his allowance, nor the labourer with his hire; the faint rumour of diftant atrocities, which difgrace human nature, reaches the ear of the multitude cleanfed from the blood and carnage, and affumes to them the pleafing fhape of liberty and property : the only clafs of men who have the power to calm the rifing ftorm are thofe in the middling ranks of life, and they are as much interefted to preferve things as they are as any other rank in the ftate: property is the only folid bulwark of the nation; for, thofe who poffefs it have a natural defire to preferve it, and our laws and our conftitution muft ftand or fall with it; befides, the danger lies immediately beneath this defcription of people: diftrict houfes of induftry confolidate all the men of property, refident in the county, in the fame laudable plan; the prefervation of induftry, good order, and a religious fentiment, among the million; the few gentlemen of fortune, who refide in the county meritorioufly, take an active part in all the incorporated houfes; the beneficed clergy refident there alfo do the fame, and it does them honour, for it is equally their duty as their intereft: fo alfo do the more opulent yeomanry of the county, a body of men of the firft confequence to the prefervation of peace and order: permit, therefore, an individual, who thus freely declares his fentiments on a fubject not generally underftood, to affert, without the imputation of prefumption or arrogance, that equally the duty as the interefts of government call on them to encourage thefe inftitutions by every mode in their power; let every influence be made ufe of by them, and every perfuafion, by men of rank and fortune, to eftablifh houfes of induftry throughout the kingdom; they will prefent, by anticipation of the caufe, a more fure barrier to the infolent attempts of fedition and the prefs of democratic violence, than all the barracks in Europe, and they will prove a more fecure defence of liberty and property, rightly underftood, than the beft-difciplined ftanding army.

LETTER

BEFORE this fubject, of fo much importance to us and our pofterity, is finally clofed; before any recapitulation is attempted of thofe points to which the minifter of this kingdom muft feel himfelf on every principle of duty to his fovereign, and to all ranks of his countrymen, and by every obligation of regard to his own unfullied reputation, bound to attend; it may be proper to fuggeft that the code of poor-laws, which regulates the conduct of upwards of feven millions of his majefty's fubjects, is a vague, unconnected, inconfiftent, piece of patch-work, in which there is no nicety of workmanfhip, no dove-tail exactnefs of joinery: but the original ftatute of the 43d of Eliz. ftands, like fome other elegant pieces of gothic architecture in this kingdom, expofed to the eyes of tafte and criticifm, with a prop in one place, an addition in another; each prop and addition, neceffary, moft probably, to fupport and render ufeful the original building, fomewhat weakened by the flux of time and the alteration of circumftances; but certainly not conducive, in the manner they have been added, to elegant appearance of the whole of that ftructure, whofe foundation, being in times paft bottomed in humanity, juftice, and policy, will reflect to ages yet unborn a credit on that country which laid the foundation, and reared the humane and neceffary, although at prefent expenfive, incompetent, and unfightly, fuperftructure.

Our highways were a few years ago managed and the conduct of them regulated by acts of parliament, collected from different parts of the code of ftatutes, in a manner fomewhat fimilar to our poor-laws; but not fo diffufed over a legiflation of centuries; nor a tenth part fo intricate in their inveftigation and application; nor a thoufandth part fo important in their effects on the happinefs of the multitude: but a fteady light has been thrown on thofe laws,

by

by reducing them under one plain intelligible act; and the roads throughout the greateft part of the kingdom are become good, without the inhabitants feeling any confiderable expenfe; that *lucidus ordo*, which has done fo much on our highways, would alfo do good in the cottages of the poor, in the veftries of our churches, and on the benches of our magiftrates; and it is a felf-evident truth, that a fyftem of legiflation, by which all the fubjects of England and Wales are to be guided, and on which no inconfiderable part of their property, happinefs, and comfort, nay, poffibly, the exiftence of many thoufands of them, depend, fhould be plain and explicit; that thofe who run may read, and that all who read may underftand: this is to be effected in a plain and intelligible manner, in one comprehenfive act, preferving the 43d of Elizabeth as the citadel, and the neceffary additions to, or explanations of, it as outworks.

Another preliminary obfervation is alfo neceffary: — whatever may be the rule laid down by the legiflature for the conduct of the nation with refpect to the poor, it fhould partake of the nature of municipal law; it fhould enforce what is right, and prohibit what is wrong; and, if right muft be enforced, and wrong prohibited by penalties, thofe penalties fhould not appear in the ftatute-book only, but in the revenue raifed for the maintenance of the poor; they arife from nonfeafance or misfeafance; both of them diminifhing the revenue of the poor, or wafting it when raifed: as foon as the fore is felt fhould the falve alfo; this may be done; not by fubjecting the adminiftration of the poor-laws to a new category of penalties, but by making the old the immediate and unavoidable confequence of the offence; by thefe means would the poor-laws be well executed, or the revenue raifed for the poor be increafed by the neglect of its managers: without fome fpecific plan of this kind, every new regulation will only be a new ftumbling-block, and will bring an increafe of expenfe, not of revenue.

A minifter

A miniſter who wiſhes to make uſe of the height of his power and authority, to alleviate the miſeries of the poor, and ſave his country from a long ruin, impending from that very alarming quarter, muſt for a time diveſt himſelf of the thirſt of popular fame; or at leaſt he muſt emulate a famous character of antiquity; muſt be *ſmitten* with the love of that popularity which follows, not that which is followed. The preſent critical ſituation of the kingdom, with reſpect to foreign politics, may be ſuggeſted as a fearful, or at leaſt an imprudent, time, to attempt much regulation at home; but the regulation which is wanted is in favour of the million; in favour of their liberty; in favour of the revenue raiſed for their maintenance; in favour of the general induſtry of the maſs of his majeſty's ſubjects: it is to their eaſe; to their comfort; to the more comfortable maintenance of themſelves, their fire-ſides, and families, this regulation tends. Whom will it affect in a contrary light? not people of rank; not people of property; not the honeſt; not the induſtrious; not the active:— but, if it did, thoſe of this deſcription feel they had rather take the leſſer ill, than run a riſk of undergoing the greater; they had rather part with a trifle than loſe all. But whom would this ſtrictneſs of diſcipline in theſe inſtances affect? the idle, the lazy, or the diſhoneſt, only. And can a miniſter of ſtate either fear the opprobrium of theſe; or care whether he preſerves his popularity among them? No, he will anſwer, with the ſame great character of antiquity juſt alluded to: *ſiqua eſt invidia in conſervanda republica ſuſcepta, lædat invidos, mihi valeat ad gloriam.*

Permit me to dwell a little longer on this topic; permit a few egotiſms to eſcape my pen without tainting the writer with the reputation of arrogance or preſumption. I have acted ſome years as a magiſtrate, and am conſcious, that, from neglect and inattention, I poſſibly may have been the cauſe, either that the revenue belonging to the poor in my neighbourhood has, in ſome inſtances, been neglected in raiſing, or diminiſhed by improper application: theſe are faults, venial undoubtedly; but they are ſuch, as had a penalty

Y y   attached

attached itfelf inevitably to each omiffion of, or inattention to, duty, fomewhat more would have been gained by the poor in increafe of revenue, or decreafe of expenditure; becaufe, either my pride or my parfimony, difliking the record of the inattention, or the payment of the penalty, my duty would have been done with fuperior attention. In a fimilar manner I fhould conceive other magiftrates and overfeers of the poor would feel in fimilar inftances; if fo, undoubtedly would the execution of the poor-laws be enforced by thefe means with greater ftrictnefs of difcipline; and many thoufands of pounds be faved to fuch of his majefty's fubjects as contribute to the maintenance of the poor; and, poffibly, fome thoufands of lives of the poor themfelves might be fnatched from an untimely end.

If flight penal confequences, following inftances of neglect, with the fame unnerring certainty as the night follows the day, would have a good effect on the execution of this code, what fhould prevent fuch regulation taking place? a fear left magiftrates fhould be deterred from taking the *dedimus poteftatem* upon themfelves is the anfwer: but no fuch fear ought to be admitted; there is no occafion for it; the infertion of a name in the commiffion of the peace is now frequently folicited as an honour, and the lord-lieutenants of counties are looked up to as great patrons of provincial confequence and power: but duties are to be performed, and fervices to be exeeuted, by all perfons placed in offices of power and confequence; and it may be depended on, that fuch is the thirft for authority, that the office would be folicited, although the duties of it were to be more rigoroufly exacted.

This idea has, already, been more fully explained, and the heads of an act of parliament, touching the fubject, roughly fketched, in a pamphlet which was fubmitted to the attention of the public when Mr. Gilbert's Bill was before the Houfe of Commons.* To

* Defence of the Statute, paffed in the 43d Year of Elizabeth, concerning the Employment and Relief of the Poor, with Propofals for enforcing it. Sold by Debrett, and B. White and Son.

retail

retail now, in this tract, a plan so little noticed when the topic agitated the country, would be impertinent; because, had the proposition then deserved attention, it may be supposed it would have obtained it; as it did not, the repetition of it here would be serving up a kind of *crambe recocta*, very little palatable to most readers.

But, however, the fact certainly is now as it was then. No act of the legislature can be efficient for the purpose if not executed. We may make laws for ever and for ever; they may swell the pages of the statute-book, and serve to fill up the shelves of our library, but are a mere waste of paper, words, and time, if not enforced: some means should, therefore, be invented, not to multiply our penal sanctions, but to simplify and render unavoidable the execution of our laws. Supposing that to be done, we should proceed, in the poor-laws, just as a prudent man, in his possessions and economy, who is master of a large family: he would, in the first place, make his estates derived from his ancestors as productive as possible; consequently, if he thought that the prodigality, carelessness, or knavery, of those who had been in possession of them in past times, had wasted, neglected, or disposed of, any, without having right so to do, he would attempt all legal means to recover what had been so alienated or disposed of; he would himself occupy, or let to good tenants, at improved rents, what he possessed; he would bring his children up in habits of economy, industry, and sobriety; his servants he would train to regularity, honesty, diligence, and civility; he would excuse a single act of omission of duty, but not a regular inattention to it; he would punish the vicious, and reward the deserving: and surely he would not, if he had the power to prevent it, permit an ale-house to be close at his doors: he would also expect, that the numerous members of his household, or, at least, all of them that could be spared from the necessary domestic duties of the day, (which duties he would reduce into as narrow a

compass

compafs as poffible,) fhould attend divine fervice once a week at leaft, to return thanks to the Almighty for that ftate of regularity and comfortable order they have lived in during the laft week, and to pray him to prolong it to another.

If thofe, who have it in their power, have it alfo in their heart, to do fomewhat efficient in the code of poor-laws, they have only to extend the idea of fuch a family, fo regulated, to the great family of the nation : the plan is plain and practicable ; nay, poffibly the exifting code has done, as far as direction alone can go, nearly the whole bufinefs : little directory is wanting, — but, alas! too much executory.

If the different members of this prudent man's family here alluded to refufe to obey, or are negligent of executing, his orders, and his wifdom is fo lulled afleep, by the eafe of his temper, or the indolence of his habits, that he is averfe to compulfion, the appearance of his houfehold inftantly changes ; the example runs, like wild-fire, through the whole family ; the peaceful fcene of harmony, order, and decorum, vanifhes, and he finds himfelf foon placed in the midft of riot, profufion, intemperance, and ruin.

To proceed to the illuftration of this allufion : — our fellow-fubjects, in that part of the kingdom affected by the poor-laws, are the large family, of which the legiflature is the head or mafter. A large eftate has, by the bounty of our anceftors, been given us for the maintaining our poorer brethren : whether it may be prudent to reclaim that portion of it which has, for many centuries, been diverted from its proper purpofes, or whether, in fact, it is juft fo to do now, is a doubtful point, confidering that the prefent poffeffors, and their immediate predeceffors, for fuch a lapfe of time, have enjoyed the ufufructuary poffeffion of the whole, not divided with thofe who, undoubtedly, at one time, had a right to a confiderable portion of it ; and they have fo enjoyed it, neither by

the

the fraud, covin, or bad faith, of themfelves, or their immediate predeceffors.

But, whatever may be the opinion of the nation at large, or the feelings of that refpectable clafs of our fellow-citizens, as to thefe points, yet, it is taken for granted that they are *ftill* individually, in fome meafure, refponfible for the religious fentiment and moral duties of that portion of his majefty's fubjects, the tenth part of whofe fruits and perfonal induftry they claim as their right; and it is conceived that themfelves would, were the queftion put to them, in general, anfwer, that fuch is their idea of the matter; therefore, would it not be proper that, where a duty arifes, a power fhould be there given adequate to enable the performance of the duty? This might be done by an act, conferring, within their refpective parifhes, on the beneficed clergy, an authority, in the regulation and fupervifion of the poor, concurrent with, and equal to, the authority the ftatutes have given to magiftrates within the pre-cincts of their refpective counties : fuch authority, in all inftances of parifh-relief, and in many other points, where authority confers confequence, would enable the clergyman of the parifh to perfuade, by ftrong arguments, the poor to attend fome place of worfhip con-ftantly, either the church, or the meeting-houfe of fome fect dif-fentient from the church, if fuch fhould be in the parifh, and fuch fhould be their religious tendency; and, by inducements of inte-reft, they would be able alfo to regulate their moral conduct, and allure them to an induftrious life : the confequence would be, bet-ter morals and more induftry, which would meliorate the condi-tion of the poor, and diminifh the expenfe of their maintenance; while the clergy of the eftablifhed church might, by thefe means, honourably to themfelves, in the line of their clerical function, and beneficially to the prefent and future life of their parifhioners, affift to reduce thofe burthenfome expenfes, which now lie fo heavy on the fhoulders of the laity principally. This being the fact, and fuch their duty, if the legiflature fhould think proper to connect
authority

authority with that duty, would not the nation have a juft right to expect a beneficial confequence?

Another eftate has alfo been left by our anceftors for the fame purpofe, in times long fince the former, much of which it is to be apprehended is now perverted to different ufes, by the knavery of fome and the careleffnefs of others, for the recovery of which an Act of Parliament* is ftill in force, but not in ufe; this eftate, therefore, ought not to be loft to the purpofes for which it was left, nor ought the act of parliament to become a dead letter, but rather an active inftrument to wreft thefe eftates from the grafp of the prefent unlawful poffeffors.

The third part of their revenue has been raifed for their fupport and maintenance nearly two hundred years, and has, like the young difeafe of the poet,

        " Grown with our growth, and ftrengthen'd with our ftrength."

This is certainly raifed with ftrictnefs, and expended with careleffnefs. In the increment of this part of their revenue, nothing more ought to be done, too much having been done already; but, in the application of it, much reform may be made. Here then is another point to which the attention fhould be applied.

The laft, but not the leaft, proportion of their revenue arifes from their individual induftry and labour: here again ought the attention to be fixed as to an object of the utmoft importance, involving in itfelf a multitude of confiderations; but they may be reduced under a few general ideas.

A man of fober and regular mode of life, of good moral and religious principles, is more likely to acquire property by hard labour than one of a contrary defcription; and the confequence, which refults to an individual, refults alfo to a million, keeping the quantity

      * Statute of Charitable Ufes, 43d Eliz.

                                           of

of work done, in a progreffive ftate, *pari paffu*, with the number: therefore, if a man, of regular habits of induftry, will earn 20*l*. per annum, twenty millions will be earned by a million: if, on the other hand, the individual lofes five pounds a year by idlenefs, and fpends five pounds in drink, the million will produce towards their maintenance ten millions lefs; the conclufion which follows from the premifes is fo plain, that a recapitulation would be furplufage.

Thus are the moral and religious duties of the mafs of mankind effential objects of attention to the interefts of finance as well as to the public good; and it is not, in many inftances, that fo remarkable a coalition can be pointed out. Suppofing, therefore, this important object to be attended to, we will proceed to the next.

The price at which labour is done follows of courfe; and here the golden maxim fhould be again repeated,—" the labourer is worthy of his hire." When thefe pages were firft entered upon, the prevailing idea of the writer, excited poffibly by a near view of human mifery, was, that the labourer had not his hire; or, in other words, that his hire would not produce him the neceffaries of life, which it ought to do, and fome of the comforts alfo: the fame doubt ftill prevails in fome inftances, but they are exceptions only, not being fufficient in number to form a general rule, and principally are apparent in manufactures, when the demand for the commodity is likely to be, or is actually, diminifhed by war or other unavoidable caufes; although it is certain, that, on a different principle and from a different caufe, have manufacturers diminifhed the prices of labour, viz. to increafe the *quantum* of labour to be performed: this they have done with equal precifion of logical inference, as dereliction of moral principle; reafoning in this manner: — A man muft earn a certain fum to fupport his family a certain time: diminifh his wages in piece-work a given time, and the quantity done in the time will be increafed, or his family will be in want, which he will not fuffer while his induftry can prevent it. By thefe means we kill two birds with a ftone, we gain by fupplying

plying the demand, and we gain by decreafing the price of labour:
fo have reafoned the manufacturers; but the principle on which
they, when reafoning thus, fuppofed the poor man to act, is now
almoft worn out; he will apply to the parifh rather than work
harder to make up his ufual earnings; therefore, in fuch inftances,
when they happen, manufacture literally preys upon agriculture.

On the other hand, in agriculture thefe circumftances cannot
occur; the demand for labour is conftant, and nearly the fame
throughout the year; nothing, therefore, but individual inftances of
avarice in the employer are neceffary to be here guarded againft in
defence of the poor and their rights, as far as the principle " The
labourer is worthy of his hire" extends; for, it has been proved in
thefe pages, that he in general is paid in thefe days by agriculture,
in full conformity to the maxim, " The labourer is worthy of his
hire."

The obfolete laws with refpect to juftices rating the wages of labourers in agriculture, at their quarter-feffions, therefore need not
be revived, at leaft the interefts of the poor do not require their
execution; nor indeed were they ever intended to raife fo much as
to deprefs the price of labour; *whether it may not be neceffary for the
intereft of agriculture, to regulate the* maximum-*price of labour, fo as to
preferve fome proportion between work and price in its extreme, is worth
the confideration of thofe who calculate at what rate corn may be afforded
to be fold, leaving the farmer a fair profit.*

The law of fettlements, and the confequences flowing from it,
occafion an enormous draft on the poor's rate, and diminifh that
part of their revenue which arifes from their labour, by reftraining
them from going where they could make the moft of it. It is probable, if thefe laws were repealed, preferving at the fame time, or
enacting anew, fuch reftraints as tend to prevent vagrancy, the labour of the poor might be confiderably more productive; and they
would enjoy a degree of freedom they have a right to expect from
fociety, if not inimical to peace and good order: but this muft be
touched

touched with a tender hand. The act of parliament refpecting friendly focieties, which paffed the laft feffion, may poffibly be found, by the experience of time, to do all that need be done on the principle of increafing labour, by increafing the facility of choofing a refidence; yet it is a doubt, whether we ought to wait for this probable, but diftant, confequence.

Nothing will do fo much in this point as early induftry. Can it be fuppofed, that a generation of induftrious adults will arife from a race of idle children? Is the adage of the poet fo falfified by experience, as to prove that the tree will be inclined reverfely to the bending of the twig? Unlefs we conceive perfevering induftry and a life of hard labour will be taken up, and the habit continued with equal readinefs and facility as our neceffary repafts and hours of repofe, we act againft our conviction, by expecting the man to be induftrious, who, when a boy, was permitted to live in idlenefs. Schools of induftry would effect much good in this refpect, and an application of fome part of the poor's rate to this purpofe is in union as well with the letter as with the fpirit of our poor-laws.

Houfes of induftry appear from the review which has been had of the general theory refpecting them, and alfo from the infpection of fuch as are fituated within that county which firft made the experiment, to tend to every good end: they, by the means of found morality, religious duties, good order, economy, and fobriety, make the revenue arifing from the induftry of the poor more productive, and expend lefs in their maintenance; at the fame time, that maintenance is the refult of an union of cleanlinefs, decency, and wholefome plenty; the reverfe of what we fee in the cottage; the reverfe of what we fee in the parifh work-houfe. But it is much to be feared thefe houfes of induftry muft be allowed, from the vifibly good effects of them apparent to the fenfible part of the nation, to take their ftations flowly in the land, and cannot, with fafety, be obtruded on our countrymen by the *fiat* of the legiflature.

Z z

· When youth has been trained to labour by habit, and that habit has been encouraged by rewards, the honorary and lucrative spur should not ceafe; nor should young people, so educated, be permitted to remain stationary, possibly to become retrogressive, from the incitement being removed in maturer life, of which they have experienced the effect in earlier days. Much more can be done by rewards than punishment, and the code of poor-laws at present holds out nothing but punishment; departing far from the principles of divine retribution, which, while it threatens with tremendous punishment the bad, offers eternal rewards to the deferving.

The mode and the means of following so excellent an example have been hinted at, and possibly the effect may be greater than the imagination can conceive. To corroborate this idea, something may be collected from amidst the mass of human miseries which now lays waste a neighbouring country : the French troops are undoubtedly brave, perfevering, and determined; ignominy, together with the up-lifted axe, strike their attention on the one hand; rewards, suiting their enthufiaftic ideas, or relieving their extreme poverty, on the other. God forbid that our fellow-subjects should ever feel the impulfe to a difcharge of duty from the uplifted axe! It is equally to be withed that they may experience the incitement from the foftering hand of reward.

But neither punishments will intimidate from wrong, nor will rewards allure to right, while feduction, in the femblance of articles of excife, ftrides, with an unbounded ftep, through this devoted country; while the financier and the moralift, the pulpit and the treafury, are at variance ; and the defalcation of revenue, by a decrement of drunkennefs, is more dreaded by the government than bad morals and a diffolute people. If ale-houfes muft preferve their ubiquity, if the village muft, by means of thefe hot-beds of feduction, partake of the vices of a populous town; the populous town of an overgrown metropolis; becaufe the treafury-coffers require

replenifh-

replenifhing, in vain are all our endeavours to preferve morality; fhe will difappear from among us, and debauchery, with his companions, will take her place : it has been the cafe; it is fo now; and the effects are vifible throughout the land; although the remote, but certain, confequences are not attended to. Here fhould the determined patriot ftrike ; at this he fhould aim the fhafts of his eloquence, not at a change of political party, making an invective on political meafures the means ; all nonfenfe to the million ; who, whatever adminiftration rules, muft live, and ought to live comfortably. Let the true patriot give them the chance of living foberly, by exciting the legiflature to remove, from their too eafy grafp, the temptation to vice : that being done, they will live induftrioufly, and become a benefit, not a burthen, to the community.

Such are the principal objects which ought to ftrike the attention of the patriotic ftatefman as he furveys the vaft horizon which the view of our poor, their rights, duties, and the laws refpecting them, offers to his contemplation. If what has been advanced in thefe pages has the good fortune to point out any leading feature in the landfcape to his notice, and fociety itfelf, or the pooreft individual in it, receives any benefit from fuch an incitement of his attention, the purpofe of the writer has been anfwered, — he has not employed himfelf in vain.

LETTER XLIX.

THE legiflature gave its fanction to no general act refpecting the poor, from the time that Mr. Gilbert's plan met its fate, as has been mentioned, until the feffion of parliament which was held in the year 1793 ; except that, by the laft claufe to an act

paffed,

paffed in 1792, to explain and amend the Vagrant-Act, it was enacted, that, if it fhall be made appear to two juftices of the peace that any poor perfon fhall not ufe proper means to get employment, or, if he is able to work, by his neglect of work, or by fpending his money in ale-houfes, or places of bad repute, &c. he fhall not apply a proper portion of his earnings to the maintenance of his wife and family, and they fhall become chargeable to their parifh, he fhall be deemed an idle and diforderly perfon, and punifhed as fuch.

By 33 Geo. III. c. 35. fome alterations were made in the act paffed, in the twenty-fecond year of his prefent Majefty, for the better relief and employment of the poor; but, in the mean time, many diftricts and parifhes had, individually, applied for, and obtained, acts of parliament for incorporating themfelves, and managing their own poor, in a manner different from that eftablifhed by the ftatute-laws of the realm.

It has been remarked, in a preceding letter, that but few, if any, parifhes had taken the benefit of, and carried into execution, the plan formed by Mr. Gilbert in the ftatute alluded to; and a reafon for that peculiarity has been fuggefted: but, by the bill paffed this feffion, it appears, that all the claufes in that act were not fo perfect as to leave nothing in uncertainty; and that the wording of one or two of them, for want of neceffary technical precifion, might involve the parifhes incorporating themfelves in difputes and lawfuits. It was enacted, " That two-thirds, in number and value, of perfons qualified, according to the recited act, who fhall attend at any public meetings, and fignify their approbation of the provifions of the act, fhall be a fufficient compliance with the recited provifion." This amendment was intended to prevent thofe who did not choofe to attend the meetings afterward coming forward, and oppofing the meafure when the parifhes had incurred an expenfe.

The

The fecond claufe is, to enable the two-thirds of the owners and occupiers of land to recommend two guardians of the poor, if they fhall be of opinion that one will not be equal to the duty.

The third claufe is, to enable all the parifhes uniting to relieve their cafual poor, conjointly, and in the fame proportion as they are directed to contribute for the general purpofes of the faid act.

Thefe were certainly neceflary amendments to the twenty-fecond of Geo. III. c. 83. But the objections pointed out by Sir F. M. Eden, in the firft volume of his Hiftory of the Poor, page 366, are not fo obvious.

He fays, — That few incorporations of parifhes have taken place under the act is not to be wondered at, when it is confidered that, " although it empowers the parifhes uniting to borrow money, on the fecurity of the poor-rates, it directs, that the perfons fent to the poor-houfe fhall be maintained at the general expenfe of the parifhes uniting.

Section 24, of this act, undoubtedly fo directs. And it fays, " according to the terms and in the proportions directed and pre-fcribed by this act."

I muft confefs myfelf unable to fee any objection to this claufe. The poor fent to the houfe are maintained by the confolidated fund formed of the poor's rates of the incorporated parifhes, or for which thofe rates are mortgaged, and, of courfe, the poor in the houfe muft be maintained at the general expenfe of the parifhes uniting, as they muft be maintained out of that fund: and I am more induced to think that no folid objection has appeared to this claufe, becaufe it efcaped the notice of thofe applying for the amendment in 1793: neither can much doubt remain on the minds of magif-trates with refpect to the fending children of the poor to the houfe under the 30th fection of this act.

It fays, that all infant-children of tender years, and who, from accident or misfortune, fhall become chargeable, may be fent, &c.
" But,

" But, if the parents or relations of any poor child fent to fuch houfe fhall defire to receive and provide for fuch poor child, and fignify the fame to the guardians, at their monthly meeting, the guardians fhall, and they are hereby required to, difmifs fuch child from the faid poor-houfe." — " Nothing herein-contained fhall give any power to feparate any child, or children, under the age of feven years, from their parents, without the confent of fuch parents."

I fhould conceive the meaning of this claufe to be, that all in-fant-children who fhall become chargeable may be fent to the poor-houfe; but, if the parents or relations of a child fo fent fhall apply to the guardians, at a monthly meeting, they may take their child out again to provide for it; and that children under the age of feven years fhall not even be *fent* to the poor-houfe without the leave of the parents. The argument, at the feffions at King-fton, the learned baronet rightly obferves, turned on a different point.

Rather later in this feffion, by chapter 54, were the friendly focieties within the kingdom put on a new, fecure, and refpectable, footing; and an inftitution which originated voluntarily among the beft-conditioned of the mafs of his majefty's fubjects, earning their fubfiftence by their daily labour, and which was calculated, as it refpects themfelves, on every principle which can do credit to a human being, whofe fole patrimony is his ability to labour; and, as it refpects their countrymen, from whom the poor-rate is taken, with a laudable intention to relieve them from the burthen which might be laid on them by the infirmities and accidents of life the fubfcribing-members are fubject to, and to fet a good example of economy and prudence to their fellow-labourers; received, by the means of the zealous and unceafing attention of Mr. Rofe to every matter which refpects the interefts of this kingdom, a ftability from the legiflature, which gave, to what was before the paffing of this act, an airy nothing, a local habitation, and a name: but, as the

act

act itfelf has been commented upon at large, in a former letter, the heads of it fhall not be again repeated.

In converfation very lately with a gentleman high in office in the Court of Chancery, on the fubject of the poor, he expreffed his general approbation in ftrong terms of this act ; but obferved, that his-fituation gave him proofs of the inconvenience attending one of the claufes, which enacts that treafurers, &c. fhall render accounts and pay over balances : " And, in cafe of neglect or refufal to deliver fuch account, or to pay over fuch moneys, or to affign, transfer, or deliver, fuch fecurities or funds in manner aforefaid, it fhall and may be lawful for every fuch fociety, in the name of the treafurer or truftees thereof, to exhibit a petition in the High Court of Chancery, or the Court of Exchequer, or the Court of Seffion in Scotland, or the Courts of Great Seffions in Wales, which fhall and may proceed thereon in a fummary way, and make fuch orders thereupon, on hearing all parties concerned, as to fuch court in difcretion fhall feem juft. And, by fec. 9. no fee, reward, emolument, or gratuity, whatfoever, fhall be demanded, taken, or received, by any officer or minifter of that court for any matter or thing done in purfuance of this act." He alfo remarked, that, if this had been left with the quarter-feffions, it would have faved the parties much time and expenfe, which unavoidably were incurred from the application to the higher courts, although no cofts could be given ; and, as that was the cafe, the treafurers, &c. might continue, and had continued, their refufal until attached by the procefs of the court for contempt.*

It appears, from the very able treatife on the police of the metropolis by a magiftrate, that upwards of feventy thoufand

---

* This obfervation has certainly much truth in it; and it is to be lamented, that the matter had not been confidered in time, to have introduced a claufe to that purpofe in the act which paffed 35 Geo. III. c. 111. which extends the powers of the Friendly-Society Act.

families

families are benefited, by the heads of them being members of friendly focieties, within the bills of mortality. Page 166.

The fame very intelligent magiftrate informs us, in a note to page 164, that it is eftimated, in the prefent extended and improved ftate of the metropolis, there are 162,000 inhabited houfes, fuppofed to contain about 240,000 families, including lodgers of every defcription, refiding in nearly 8000 ftreets, lanes, alleys, courts, and fquares.

It is fuppofed, that this number of families is not confined to the bills of mortality; therefore, no exact comparifon can be made between the number of families benefited by the friendly focieties, and the number of families inhabiting within the bills of mortality, by the information derived from this author; but we alfo find in the fame publication, under the article Inftitutions for Charitable Purpofes, 600 friendly focieties in the metropolis and its vicinity now incorporated by act of parliament, compofed of mechanics and labouring-people, who diftribute to fuch as are members, and for funerals, 36,000 l. a year, raifed by monthly payments.

Although no precife comparifon can be drawn from this information between the number of poor inhabitants in the metropolis and its vicinity, and the number benefited by friendly focieties, ftill enough appears, if the information be correct, to convince us that a large proportion of that clafs of inhabitants, who are likely to be at fome time in their lives a burthen on the poor-rates, does already partake of the benefit of thefe focieties in London and its vicinity : probably, nearly as great a proportion is benefited by them in the country. If fuch be the fact, or in proportion with the extent of fuch a fact, any encouragement, compatible with prudence, that may tend to fpread the good arifing from them ftill wider among the mafs of our population, muft be productive of general benefit ; as it will tend to fuperfede, or render needlefs, any meafure to introduce a fimilar effect, under the form of a parochial fund; which, however excellent in its theoretic principle, will, it is feared, if it

arifes

arifes not from a voluntary principle, be attended with too large an expenfe, and too lax an attention of thofe concerned in its exe-cution, to be ultimately effective.

There is undoubtedly a felfifh, but yet a prudent, principle at-tending thefe friendly focieties, which excludes all thofe who are not likely to become profitable members; the aged, the infirm, the maimed, cannot hope to be admitted by ballot; it is not to be expect-ed, that thofe, carrying about with them certain indications of the prefent want of affiftance, fhould willingly be received into a fociety on payment of a fmall periodical fum, which will entitle them to that affiftance of which they apparently, at prefent, ftand in need; while the general appearance and real fituation of the members of thefe focieties indicate found health and ability to labour. The legiflature cannot think of opening the door of thefe focieties wider than the individual rules of them admit, for the purpofe of taking in a defcription of men different from fuch as thofe rules point out; confequently, a certain defcription of poor will never be benefited by them, unlefs fome means could be invented to proportion the price of admiffion, and the *quantum* of periodical payment, to the ap-parent ftate of health, and ability to work, of the perfon propofed, ftill leaving the matter optional on the part of the fociety : in that cafe, it might be a good fpeculation for the parifh to pay the expenfe.

Whether, for the purpofe of giving thefe unhappy men a reft from their labour, and a profpect in the decline of life of fome-thing better than the workhoufe, any other inftitution on fimilar principles fhould be eftablifhed by authority of the legiflature, is a matter of no fmall difficulty to determine : to take from thofe, who, from their difability to do much work, can earn but little, any perio-dic, although fmall, portion of their earnings, with a view to an advan-tageous return of it in the fhape of weekly allowance, when their difeafes increafe and old age preffes on them, and to give them a certain weekly parochial affiftance, whether in proportion to the

A a a number

number of their children, or to the actual preſſure of their prevailing infirmity, that they may be able to pay a certain ſum periodically for this purpoſe, is ſomewhat like taking from Peter to pay Paul, and that, alſo, at the expenſe of conſiderable trouble, ariſing from the neceſſity of keeping accounts of ſome degree of intricacy.

There is, alſo, another claſs of the poor, whoſe comforts are chiefly negative, but whoſe miſery is ſtrikingly affirmative, where the eye of humanity muſt ſee much ought to be done, but where, probably, prudence will allow of but little alteration ; I mean the women, whether wives or widows, of the labouring-poor, and thoſe, alſo, who paſs their lives in celibacy. Their oppreſſed ſituation, particularly of the married women, ſhall be the topic of the next Letter.

LETTER L.

THE farther we recede from civilized ſociety, and the nearer we approach to ſavage life, the more wretched do we find the condition of the females: it ſhould ſeem from this, that, in proportion as men make uſe of that *os ſublime* which induces them to look up to, and attempt, at a humble and infinite diſtance, to imitate the virtues, and render themſelves worthy of the protection, of the Creator, do they ſenſibly feel the bleſſing he has granted them, in giving them, as a companion, not as a ſlave or an inferior, a ſex, whoſe beſt energy conſiſts in modeſt domeſtic virtues, in diſcharging her painful duties with ſubmiſſive patience, in ſoothing the cares, and averting, as much as poſſible, the anxieties, attendant on her more active companion in his journey through human life. But it is civilization, and its concomitant, education, which elicits theſe beſt propenſities, both in man and woman : in proportion

proportion as thefe advance, we more clearly perceive the philofophic maxim of the hiftorian to be founded in nature and truth : — " *Omnis noftra vis in animo et corpore fita eft, animi imperio corporis fervitio magis utimur; alterum nobis cum dis, alterum cum belluis commune eft.*"

Thefe ideas prefs themfelves on my mind by the recollection of that train of difagreeable fenfations which has too often been occafioned by the difcharge of the duties of a magiftrate fituated in this part of the kingdom, and fubject to applications by the poor for an order of relief : frequently have thofe applications been made by females, and happy muft he have felt himfelf when the laws have permitted him to relieve their diftreffing complaints of want of food or clothing. This could not be the cafe when mothers of large families of infant-children, the wives of lazy, depraved, and brutifh, hufbands, have, with all the pathos of truth and diffidence, related the ftarving miferable condition of their children and themfelves, attempting, at the fame time, to conceal, or explain away, the cruel conduct of their lazy or improvident hufband. I will venture to fay, many magiftrates have heard of, and known that there exifted, fuch inftances of diftrefs arifing from the bad conduct of hufbands and fathers of families, as would appear, if in print, to thofe of the rich, who know but little of the miferies of the poor, fcarcely to be within the pale of probability in this kingdom, and have been obliged to difmifs the fuppliants, hopelefs of relief from the poor's rate, by informing them *their hufband* muft apply to the overfeers for relief : if they refufe *him* relief, *he* may then apply to the magiftrate. Alas! their hufbands, confcious of their imprudence, their drunkennefs, or lazinefs; confcious, either that they earned fufficient to fupport their families, but fpent it in an alehoufe, or that they were lazy and had refufed work, would not apply to the overfeers, and all order for relief from the magiftrate was ftopped. In fome inftances, interference has done mifchief, and the overfeer has been *defired*, not *ordered*, to relieve: it has been

complied

complied with : he has then applied for a warrant againft the hufband, as an idle and diforderly perfon, by virtue of 32 Geo. III.
fec. 45. he has been fent to the houfe of correction, as fuch, for a
fhort time; has returned *punifhed*, but not *reformed*; and has added,
to the former neglect of his wife and family, cruelty and ill-ufage,
looking on her complaint as the caufe of his punifhment.

Another bad cuftom has, of late, been in practice among the
clafs of labourers : the appropriating a fmall proportion of his
week's earnings for the maintenance of his wife and family, and
expecting her and his children, who are at home, and probably unemployed, to find the reft. The confequence arifing from this has
been, that every child, from the youngeft that can creep about to
thofe of maturer age, girls efpecially, are lurking about the fields
and farm-yards all day, ftealing whatever they can come at: the
girls foon lofe all fenfe of modefty and propriety of conduct, and
become, at a very early period of life, initiated in all debauchery :
for it is experience that informs us, thofe who, from their bad conduct and character, have not been able to get away from their families into fervice, or fome feparate eftablifhment, but ftill continue to earn a livelihood at home by doubtful means, are aftute and
zealous in feducing their younger neighbours, by information how
themfelves have found means to obtain better fare or more finery.

The laws refpecting property militate greatly with the common
intereft among the loweft orders of fociety : — that principle which
gives the *femme coverte* no right to perfonal property, but vefts the
whole in the *hufband*, not only occafions innumerable inftances of
aggravated diftrefs, but appears to be repugnant to the general
good. How many families might, and would, be faved from deftruction, had the wife but a right to what fhe could acquire ! Induftry and economy ftand in need of this natural incitement : —
that the induftrious and economic fhould poffefs a property in what
their induftry and economy have obtained or faved.

Another

Another circumftance would originate, from this propofition, favourable to individual comfort and to the general good : we might then fee friendly focieties of females which would affift them in the time of labour and ficknefs, and, while they are fuffering under the painful lot the fex is heir to, fome drops of comfort might then be mixed in their cup of afflicﬕion. While this affertion is ventured, let it not be imagined that any material alteration in the general law of property, as it may affeﬅ married women, is recommended, or that, indeed, any change is hinted at, any farther than what tends to fecure, in the loweﬅ ranks of fociety, to the woman and her infant-children, a right to fome proportion of the earnings of her partner and her own, which may enfure them from ﬅarving while the hufband is at the ale-houfe. In a former part of this work, the infinite mifchief done to morality, to economy, to induﬅry, to the health, and, of courfe, to the political profperity, of the kingdom, by thefe licenfed promoters and receptacles of every vice difgraceful to human nature, has been fufficiently dwelt on : if they muﬅ ﬅill remain the glaring opprobrium of our religious and moral government, we muﬅ be fatisfied to pay back, in the fhape of relief, to the mothers and children of ﬅarving families, out of our pockets, fome portion of that revenue which is colleﬅed by means of this miﬅaken policy of the ﬅate.

Sir F. M. Eden, among the mafs of information colleﬅed in the fecond and third volume of his Hiﬅory of the Poor, has given, under the title " Parochial Reports, Carlifle," an inﬅance of a female friendly fociety, and fpecified fome of their rules ; and, at Lancaﬅer, has briefly given an account of five focieties of a fimilar kind, but has not made fuch deduﬅions, from the information he has colleﬅed, as might have proved the quantum of good, fociety in general, or the members themfelves individually, may be likely to receive from thefe female inﬅitutions, while man remains the lord and maﬅer of whatever property his wife may po﬍efs.

Was

Was the legiflature to encourage thefe inftitutions, by giving the wife a right to fuch property as may accrue to her as a member of one of thefe focieties, ftill the hufband, by withdrawing his affif-tance, and expecting that the allowance received from thefe focieties fhould fave a proportion of his earnings, which muft, otherwife, be applied towards her maintenance in child-bed, would ftill leave his wife in as bad a fituation as ever, and no great good would arife: it is difficult to fay what fhould be done; and, while the mind is in that ftate of uncertainty, good fenfe will fay — do nothing.

LETTER LI.

EARLY in the year 1794, I firft had the honour of a conver-fation with Mr. Rofe on the poor-laws: he then preffed me to give my attention immediately to the fubject; and, as foon as poffible, to fend him my fentiments in writing, accompanied with a fketch of what, on the whole, would be moft advifable, in my opinion, to proceed firft upon. In confequence of this requeft, within a few days, I fent him the following two memoirs, accom-panied with a letter; and alfo, by his recommendation, fent a copy of the Hiftory of the Poor to Mr. Pitt, with an offer of my beft fervices.

Memoir I. By 43d Eliz. c. 2. fec. 2. the church-wardens and overfeers fhall, within four days after the end of their year, and other overfeers are nominated, make and yield up, to two juftices, a true and perfect account of all fums by them received, or rated and affeffed, and not received; and alfo of fuch ftock as fhall be in their hands, or in the hands of any of the poor, to work; and of all other things concerning their office.

And alfo, by fec. 4. any fuch two juftices may commit to prifon any one of the faid church-wardens and overfeers which fhall re-fufe fuſe to account; there to remain, without bail or mainprife, until he has made a true account.

And, by 13 Geo. II. c. 38. the ſame officers ſhall yearly, within fourteen days after other overſeers ſhall be appointed, deliver up to the fucceeding overſeers a juſt account in writing, fairly entered in a book to be kept by them for that purpoſe, and ſigned by them, of all ſums of money by them received, or rated and not received, and alſo of all materials that ſhall be in their hands, or in the hands of any of the poor, to be wrought, and of all money paid by ſuch church-wardens and overſeers ſo accounting, and of all other things concerning their office; which account ſhall be verified on oath before one juſtice, who ſhall ſign and atteſt the ſame, at the foot of the account, without fee.

By virtue of theſe authorities, two juſtices iſſue their precepts to the high-conſtables of their diſtricts, to direct their warrants to the petty conſtables, to make out a liſt of houſeholders to be over-ſeers, and to return ſuch liſt on a certain day; that the juſtices may appoint other overſeers, and alſo to give notices to the overſeers to appear on that day to ſwear to their accounts.* At this meeting the high conſtables, as well as the petty conſtables, are preſent.

It

---

* A Specification of the Mode recommended for the annual Account of Totals to be laid before Parliament. — The Sums and Figures are ideal.

1796.	RECEIPTS.			
	1.	2.	3.	4.
Suffolk, Riſbridge-Hundred, Clare.	From the late Overſeers.	Charities: Specifying them.	Poor's Rates.	Labour of the Poor.	Total.
	£24 2 1	Banſon-Farm, one year, Michaelmas, £28 16 0 Gooſecroft, one year, Lady-Day, £14 6 8 ———— £43 2 8	£448 14 2	£14 2 10	£530 1 9

EXPENSES

It is propofed, that, for the purpofe of the intended information, their accounts, which are now kept in a very confufed manner, fhould be reduced under the following heads.

RECEIPTS.— 1. From the hands of the late overfeers.— 2. From eftates in land left for the purpofe of general charity. From ditto, for the purpofe of particular charities, inferting, by name or defcription, any charities, if fuch there be, which are unproductive, and the reafon. From dividends of funded property, or intereft of money out at ufe, for the benefit of the poor of the parifh, if any. — 3. From affeffments to the poor's rate. —4. From the work of the poor.

DISBURSEMENTS.— 1. Application of money to county-purpofes, vagrants, militia, bridges, gaols, &c. Expenfes not concerning the poor, as repairing churches, roads, falaries to minifters, &c. if any.— 2. Ditto, of overfeers in journeys, attendances on magiftrates, &c. Ditto, of entertainments at meetings relative to the poor. Ditto, of law-orders, examinations, removals, appeals.—

EXPENSES.

1. County-Rates, and Expenfes not concerning the Poor.	2. Mifcellaneous Expenfes.	3. Workhoufe, and Number of Poor therein.	4. Poor relieved out of the Workhoufe, and Number relieved.	5. Schools of Induftry, and fetting the Poor to work.	Total.
County-rates, £38　5　4 Raifing one man for navy, £31　10　0 ——— £69　15　4	Overfeer's expenfes attending magiftrates, £3　5　0 Parifh-meetings, £2　2　0 Orders of removal, and law-expenfes, £11　19　0 ——— £17　6　0	Men . . 12 Women . 14 Children, 26 under 14 years of age, £160　12　6	Men . . 22 Women, 13 Children, 68 under 14 years of age. Note. Thefe are all the children at home under 14, belonging to the families relieved. £271　11　10	No fchool of induftry. £6　7　2	£525　12　10

Receipts - - - £530　1　9
Expenfes - - - 525　12　10

Due to the parifh - £　4　8　11

3. Ditto

3. Ditto, of workhoufe, fpecifying the number of men, women, and children, therein, under 14, taken on an average throughout the year. — 4. Ditto, of thofe relieved out of the workhoufe by clothes, food, or money; fpecifying the number of men, women, and children, under the age of 14, fo relieved. — 5. Ditto, in fetting the poor to work.

The overfeer's accounts being thus kept under feparate heads, and the truth of their accounts verified on oath, of *voir dire*, to all fuch queftions as fhall be put to them, touching their accounts, and being figned by two magiftrates.

The high conftables fhall be directed to return, to the clerk of the peace of the enfuing quarter-feffions, a true copy of the feveral *totals* of the receipts and difburfements in the parifhes within their diftrict, which fhall be verified by oath at the quarter-feffions, by the high conftable, to be a true copy; and he fhall receive from the county-ftock, for the account of each parifh fo returned, the fum of——.

That the clerk of the peace be directed to return, within —— days after the quarter-feffions, in a book, a fair copy of fuch totals to the committee of the houfe, appointed for the purpofe of infpecting the fituation of the poor, their rights, duties, and the laws refpecting them.

And that a committee of the Houfe of Commons be appointed for that purpofe.

If an act of parliament could be paffed previous to the next nomination of overfeers, which will this year fall very late, and the attention of the people could be excited to the fubject, by the judges mentioning it on the circuit to the grand juries, or by other means, the firft returns might be made to the Houfe of Commons foon after Eafter; and, by the fame time on the following year, the information of two years may be obtained; which, it is apprehended, may be fufficiently ample and conclufive to form a fpecific plan; which, without touching the corner-ftone of the poor-laws, the 43d of Eliz. may, with great probability of fuccefs, tend to

B b b   diminifh

diminifh the expenfes of the maintenance of the poor between one and two millions annually; and, at the fame time, introduce a fyftem of morality, induftry, and comfort, more congruous with their rights as men, and their duties as fubjects of the Britifh empire.

Memoir II. Since the Houfe of Commons received the laft information on the fubject of the poor, which contained anfwers from all the parifhes in the kingdom to interrogatories applied to the overfeers refpecting the revenue raifed for the relief of the poor, and its expenditure, during the years 1783, 1784, 1785, eight complete years are paffed, during which there is every reafon to believe that the poor-rates have been rifing, throughout that part of the kingdom fubject to the poor-laws, by rapid ftrides; in fome inftances doubling, in others trebling, and, in all, very confiderably increafing, the then amount : the expenfes attending the relief of the poor have, confequently, increafed in a fimilar ratio.

There is alfo reafon to fear, that the mafs of human mifery among our countrymen, which one might conceive would diminifh in proportion as larger fums have been applied to the relief of the miferable, has not diminifhed, but has increafed.

The information alluded to was incomplete, inafmuch as, although it told the Houfe of Commons the fum expended, and fome of the different heads of expenfe, it did not inform them of the number of poor relieved; an information neceffary, to judge of the competence of the fum raifed to the object to which it has been applied.

Nor did it inform the houfe of that part of the revenue, applied to the ufe of the poor, which arifes from eftates, real and perfonal, which have been left by will, or given for charitable purpofes, throughout the kingdom, which is received and diftributed by the church-wardens and overfeers of the poor. This account was

attempted

attempted to be obtained by a fubfequent act of parliament, but the returns were very incomplete.

No particular attention, in the information which was obtained in 1786 upon this fubject, was paid to the incorporated houfes of induftry; inftitutions which then had profited by the experience, in thofe diftricts where they are fituated, of fome years, and now have the experience of an additional number of years. An inquiry into their receipts and difburfements will throw fome farther light on the fubject.

When the propofed information fhall be returned to the Houfe, and rendered as perfect as the nature of a return to an inquiry of fuch magnitude and extent is capable of, it will conftitute a foundation on which fome propofitions may be offered which will tend to meliorate the condition of the poor, and decreafe the expenfes of their maintenance; fome of which may now be curforily hinted at, but not fpecifically dwelt upon.

By a repeal or alteration of that part of the law of fettlements which reftrains the poor from getting their bread where they beft can earn it, at the fame time taking care that fuch liberty fhall not degenerate into vagrancy. The names of Adam Smith, Mr. Hay, Mr. Townfend, and Sir William Young, all fanction this idea.

By inftituting fchools of induftry, on the powers already given by the 43d of Elizabeth, to fet poor children to work, and by adding what other powers are neceffary.

By compelling the overfeers of the poor to find work for the adult.

By encouragement of box-clubs; and by obliging the pauper who removes from his place of fettlement to another parifh to contribute to the box-club where he refides; or, if there is none, or the club there inftituted will not admit him, by obliging him to make a fmall periodical payment, while in health, towards his maintenance in time of diftrefs, to the overfeers of the poor of that parifh, and to fend his children to fuch fchools of induftry.

By

By conftituting fome farther control over the conduct and accounts of the overfeers of the poor.

And by a reduction of the various acts relative to the regulation and relief of the poor, which now are difperfed, through a legiflation of near two centuries, into one or two plain and intelligible acts, fomewhat on the plan of the Highway-Acts, fo that the overfeer may know each article of his duty with as much eafe as the furveyor.

Before the end of the prefent feffions of parliament, it is conceived that fome plan may be digefted, printed, and laid before the Houfe of Commons, containing the outline of fome fuch alterations in the poor-laws as have been here fuggefted; and it may take fomewhat the form of an act, that the alterations may be confidered of by gentlemen during the vacation, and that fuch other lights and fuggeftions may be offered on the fubject, during the next feffion, as may tend to render the fyftem of poor-laws more conducive to the happinefs and comfort of the poor themfelves, and lefs expenfive to the nation at large.

LETTER LII.

WITHIN a few days after my return into the country, I fent another Memoir, farther explanatory of my defign, to Mr. Rofe, of which the following is a copy.

Memoir III.   The information, expected from the Bill recommended, preffes principally on three points:

1. The revenue of the poor.
2. The expenditure of that revenue.
3. The number of the poor relieved.

Therefore,

Therefore, this information, when obtained, will be a *terminus a quo*. The future good which may be reaped from a new modification of the poor-laws may be dated and eftimated.

Confequently, as much exactnefs as can be expected from the extenfivenefs of the inquiry, and the ability of thofe who are to make a return to it, fhould appear in the returns of the overfeers; and that exactnefs or deficiency may, in fome degree, be made apparent, as to the articles of receipt and expenditure, by comparing the returns made to this bill with thofe made in the years 1783, 1784, 1785; any glaring variation, either of receipt or expenditure, being marked as an object of revifion.

And, probably, an office-letter, directed, during the vacation, to the neareft magiftrate to that parifh where fuch manifeft difference appears, requefting him to order the overfeers to attend him with their book of accounts, to revife the totals tranfmitted to the clerk of the peace, and to fend the account fo revifed to the officer appointed to receive the fame, will be the fhorteft and moft effectual means to render the returns perfect before the next feffion of parliament.

An annual check, or control, to be held over the overfeers' accounts, by their return of thofe accounts to, and the infpection of, parliament, is one of the heads of regulation moft likely to operate in the reduction of the poor's rate and expenditure, and the amelioration of the ftate and condition of the poor.

Their conduct and accounts are not fubject, as the laws now ftand, to the revifion of any perfon, fave individuals of the parifh, who are often too much interefted to wifh for any revifion. The magiftrates, if they have the authority to fwear the overfeers to anfwer to the truth of fuch queftions as they fhall afk them touching their accounts, are not generally in the habit of the practice; confequently, their accounts may be kept in a fallacious, defultory, and equivocal, manner.

The

The reduction of the overfeers' accounts under proper heads, fimilar to fuch as are, by the intended bill, made the means of obtaining the information, was mentioned, in the firft Memoir, as a fubject of permanent regulation ; but, poffibly, it will better form a part of the general fyftematic reform of the poor-laws, than become, at prefent, a permanent act.

The fketch and plan contained in the firft two memoirs having been approved of, I was defired to attend Mr. Lowndes, at his chambers in the Temple, that the act of parliament I recommended might be drawn under my infpection as foon as poffible, as it was intended to be immediately propofed to the Houfe of Commons; that, if approved of by parliament, and paffed into a law, the overfeers might have time to make up their accounts, and return anfwers to the queftions in the manner fpecified in the fchedule, at the ufual time of paffing their accounts, before the magiftrates, at the following Eafter.

Accordingly the act was drawn, and I left town in the full belief that, in as fhort a time as might be, it would pafs the two Houfes; and, receiving the royal affent, it would, at the enfuing Eafter, be the rule for paffing the accounts of the overfeers throughout that part of the kingdom fubject to the poor-laws.

But other matters more preffing occafioned the meafure to be poftponed, and it has fince been abandoned, as far as I underftand, on account of the expenfe attending fuch an inquiry.

It would be prefumption to affert, that fufficient information refpecting this important fubject is *not* already collected, and in the poffeffion of thofe from whom the nation expects an amelioration of the prefent fyftem of our poor-laws. A great body of information may be got together by the inquiries of individuals: each one fixing his attention on a particular point may certainly collect fufficient intelligence on that point to be able to form a general rule: it may be fo done; and, if it is fo done, it is well done; but, unlefs fomething of the kind has been done, it can fcarcely be fuppofed but that general principles would be with greater certainty afcertained,

if

if the information of facts respecting the management of the poor
was more complete, and that information collected and applied to
establish certain principles.

For instance, was it necessary to know whether houses of industry should be encouraged or permitted by the legislature to extend
themselves over a greater proportion of the kingdom than they now
occupy? Let the inquiries into the state and condition of the poor
in those districts where they have been established a length of time
be applied, to know whether they have decreased or increased population. If they occasion population to decrease, they should not be
encouraged, because it is a proof that they do not tend to the hap-
piness of the governed: if population is progressive, the answer is
in their favour in that respect. Are the manners of the poor better
or worse in these districts than where no house of industry has been
erected? Are fewer crimes committed, less drunkenness and debauchery in practice? Have houses of industry tended to increase or
diminish the poor's rate? If it appears to be the general tendency
of the information applied to this question, that the morals of the
poor are more correct, that the poor's rate, where these houses have
been instituted, has not advanced *pari passu* with those districts, in
similar circumstances as to the kind of work the poor are employed
in where there are no houses of industry, be it in general agriculture
or manufactures, the answer in this respect is also in their favour;
and all the declamations against them, as being dissonant to the feelings of the poor, fall to the ground; for, in districts where such
measures are pursued with the poor, that population rather in-
creases than decreases, where the moral duties are more generally
attended to, fewer crimes committed, and the poor maintained at
less expense. What can a legislator require more to convince him
that houses of industry, in districts so regulated, are not detrimental, but an advantage, to society?

Information thus obtained throughout the kingdom, and inquiries thus applied to other leading principles respecting the poor,

B b b*   would

would form a folid unerring bafis founded on experience, on which principles of legiflation might be built, which, in all probability, would be attended with the beft effects.

If fufficient information is already obtained, and in the poffef-fion of thofe who have as well the power as the inclination to be of fervice to their country, on this very important point of legiflation, nothing remains but to apply that information properly; and there can be no doubt but thofe, in whofe poffeffion that information re-mains, will fo apply it, if they poffefs it; and it is not too bold an expreffion to affert, that the *falvation* of this country depends on its being fo applied.

There is no doubt but the information received by the Houfe of Commons refpecting the years 1776, 1783, 1784, 1785, is very valuable; but it certainly is vague and diffufive, and cannot eafily be·concentrated fo as to apply to a particular point; and, if it could, it refpects the fituation of the poor in thofe years, not in 1797. How far the queftions in the memoir alluded to would tend to give annually fufficient information, that a perfon at a *coup d'œil* might fee the precife fituation of the poor in every parifh of the kingdom, is not attempted to be ftated; but, fup-pofing it would not *completely* anfwer that purpofe, there is no doubt but, with proper attention, a fchedule, according to which the overfeers might be directed to keep their accounts, could be formed, which would anfwer that purpofe; and it is the meafure at large thefe pages attempt to fupport, not this particular fpecifica-tion of it.

Before this Letter is concluded, it remains to take notice of two acts of parliament which paffed in 1795; by the firft of which the law of removals is confiderably altered; by the other, friendly fo-cieties are farther encouraged, and their powers extended.

The 35 Geo. III. c. 101. after reciting in the preamble the 13 and 14 C. II. cap. 12. repeals fo much of that act as enables juf-tices to remove paupers *likely to become chargeable*, and enacts that no

perfon

perfon fhall be removed to the place of their laft legal fettlement
until they fhall have become *actually chargeable* to the parifh in which
they fhall inhabit.

The fecond fection alfo empowers any juftice of the peace to
fufpend the order of removal, if it fhall appear to him that the
pauper is unable to travel, by reafon of ficknefs or any infirmity;
and that the charges incurred by fuch fufpenfion fhall be paid by
the officers of the parifh to which they are ordered to be removed,
with cofts; but, if fuch charges and cofts exceed twenty pounds,
an appeal lieth to the quarter-feffions. And that this act fhall
not alter the power of juftices to punifh vagabonds, except as to
fufpending the vagrant-pafs on account of illnefs.

The third fection enacts, " That no perfon, coming into any parifh,
townfhip, or place, fhall, from and after the paffing of this act,
be enabled to gain any fettlement therein by delivery of notice in
writing."

The fourth, That no perfon fhall gain a fettlement by paying
public taxes or levies for any tenement of lefs than ten pounds
yearly value: and, by the remaining fection of this act, rogues and
vagabonds are to be confidered as chargeable, and may be removed;
as are unmarried women with child; and, in cafe their removal is
fufpended until after birth, the child is to be deemed and taken as
fettled in its mother's parifh.

No one but muft generally approve of the principles of this
act; but a queftion occurs on the confequences refulting from
the third fection, which enacts, that no perfon fhall gain a fettlement by delivery of notice, which in fact they could not, before the act, without a refidence afterwards of forty days. Is notice, therefore, now neceffary to gain a fettlement? Does not
this claufe virtually repeal the neceffity of notice, and leave an opportunity for a pauper to gain a fettlement by a refidence of forty
days, by virtue of 13 and 14 C.II. cap.12. without notice? — If
it is the meaning of the ftatute that, by notice and refidence of

B b b* 2   forty

forty days taken together, the pauper fhall not gain a fettlement, the claufe ought to have expreffed as much, and no doubt could have arifen : at prefent there appears to remain fome difficulty, as to the legal meaning of the third claufe.

The charges of maintenance during the fufpenfion of the order of removal, and the cofts attending the order and the removal, being faddled upon the parifh to which the pauper is fent as his place of fettlement, is undoubtedly right, according to the prefent principles of the law of fettlements. But are thofe principles founded on the broad bafis of equity ? — They certainly are pregnant with inconvenience and expenfe.

Reimburfement, by the parifh where a pauper is fettled to the parifh in which he has, before his removal, refided, of any fums of money that may have been expended in his maintenance or relief, is a fubject which requires fome difcuffion, as it is attended with expenfe and trouble, and is, in fome degree, open to an expenfive, if not a fraudulent, demand upon the parifh, which has reaped no benefit from the labour of the pauper, by the parifh which has had the advantage of his exertions, while he was capable of any. If it is an *equitable* claim, although it may increafe the aggregate of expenfe, it may be right to fanction it ; if it is *not equitable*, and it can be proved to be inconvenient and expenfive, it ought not to be encouraged by the fanction of law.

It is an acknowledged principle, by the wifeft politicians, that the riches of a country are in proportion to the induftrious exertions of the individuals of a country, and confequently an increment of induftrious population is an increment of riches. The obfervation applies as well to a city, a town, a village, as to a kingdom.

An individual, removing from the place where he was born, has lived in fervice, ferved an apprenticefhip, or, by any means, obtained, under our prefent fyftem of poor-laws, a fettlement, removes,

moves, from the place where he has incurred a debt of gratitude, if not a civil obligation, for the protection received, while
incapable of benefiting in any confiderable degree the place in
which he received it, to another place, for the purpofe of making the moft of his time and labour : the parifh to which he
removes, and where he refides, receives all the benefit arifing from
that time and labour, and, in proportion to the number of fuch
refidents in a parifh, has that parifh increafed in population, and
individuals in it in riches. In the mean time, the parifh where
the labouring-man was fettled, but has not refided, has reaped
none, or very trifling, benefit from its parifhioner : which parifh
then ought, in juftice, to bear the expenfe of the maintenance
of this man, when his ability to labour is diminifhed, and his
expenfes exceed his power to provide for them? There furely
can be no doubt upon the queftion. The conclufion which naturally follows is; that it is a fufficient act of injuftice to the
parifh in which a man is fettled to fend him home to be maintained, when he can no longer earn his own maintenance, without charging his place of fettlement with thofe expenfes which
have arifen, to the parifh which he has benefited by his labour,
in confequence of this humane act of parliament which fufpends
his removal, while, from illnefs or infirmity, it is thought improper by the magiftrate he fhould be removed.

   That expenfes are daily arifing throughout the kingdom, by
this principle of reimburfement being carried into practice, is a
fact; as it is well known, from experience, that the maintenance
of the pauper, after his order of removal is fufpended on account
of illnefs, is not managed, by the overfeers of the parifh where he
remains refident, on that clofe fcale of economy with the maintenance of their own paupers, becaufe they know the order from the
magiftrate will entitle them to reimburfement ; neither is the pauper conveyed to his place of fettlement with that cheapnefs which
his own overfeers would be interefted in attending to ; and, as this

does not arise between a *few* parishes only, but may take place between *almost fifteen thousand parishes*, as to such paupers as may not be resident in their own parishes, among a number of our countrymen liable to become chargeable, amounting, I fear, to six millions; and, it is presumed, the number of non-residents in their own parishes will increase, as the laws are more liberal in allowing of a residence in parishes not their place of settlement; the aggregate of expense saved by annihilating the reimbursement will be very considerable; and will be still a greater object, should the bill now before the parliament pass into a law.

By 35 Geo. III. c. 111. societies established before passing the act of 33 Geo. III. c. 54. for the encouragement of friendly societies, may exhibit the rules, orders, and regulations, for their government at any general quarter-sessions, before or immediately after the Michaelmas session, 1796, and such rules, so being confirmed in the manner recited in that act, shall be valid and effectual.

By the second clause, governors, directors, managers, or members, of any institutions for the purpose of relieving widows, orphans, and families, of the clergy, and others in distressed circumstances, may frame rules and present them for confirmation, in the same manner as societies established by virtue of the Friendly-Society Act.

And, by the third clause, institutions, whose rules shall be confirmed and registered, may appoint treasurers, and be in every respect entitled to the benefit of the Friendly-Society Act, and also of this act.

LETTER LIII.

THE summer of 1795 also introduced this kingdom to the experience of such a scarcity and extravagant price for corn, as the oldest man cannot before remember; nor has the history of the last laft centuries informed us of. The caufes of and the confequences arifing from this moft alarming period of time, which we have now, as far as it refpects the price of all kinds of grain, weathered, fhall not be canvaffed in the following pages, any farther than as they have affected or do ftill affect the poor, and the management of them.

Some lights of information may poffibly be collected from the fcene of diftrefs we have lately paffed; fome obfervations may poffibly be made, fome facts may be ftated, as a foundation for principles of legiflation, on a fubject refpecting which, one may venture to fay, there is not in the kingdom a heart fo cold to the caufe of humanity and of his countrymen, as not to feel an intereft, and not to be willing to offer his mite of information to refcue the poor, as far as may be, from their miferable ftate, and the nation from its ruinous and increafing expenfes on their account.

Without recurring to the numerous facts with which the public prints of the time were filled, which, if individually related or referred to, would occafion this rude fketch of the Hiftory of the Poor to emulate in bulk the hiftory of a great nation in detail; it is prefumed that fome valuable truths may be collected from the whole, which, being made ufe of, may prevent thofe whofe high office it is to give us laws, or to propofe them, from any material deviation from what is right, in the attempt to improve the fituation of the poor, by amending the fyftem which prefcribes the management of them.

The firft obfervation which occurs is, that the impulfe, occafioned by the preffure of fcarcity and the high price of corn, on the minds of the people, excited in them the idea of riot and mifchief, and, in many places, inftigated them to the actual attempt, by taking away the corn brought to market, by threatening the perfonal fafety of the farmers and millers, and deftruction to their property; and, in fome inftances, by carrying thofe laft threats into actual execution.

The

The facts which are stated in the prints of the time gave rife to another obfervation; that, in proportion as the magiftracy of the country were prompt and determined in the execution of their duty, by putting the laws in force, and convincing thofe affembled, that their return to peaceable conduct was the only means to infure relief to them and their families, did the fymptoms of riot and diforder difappear, and our indigent countrymen, by experiencing affiftance from the gratuitous contributions of their more opulent neighbours, together with an allowance from the rate raifed for their relief, vaftly greater than any they had before experienced, or imagined that in any event they fhould have received, paffed through this period of threatened famine and actual fcarcity without any obfervable increafe of human mortality.

A third matter, it is believed, may alfo be ftated as a fact, that, in no inftance, through any breadth of country, did the additional increafe the poor received to their income, from wages, gratuitous donations, and parochial relief, approach the increafed price of bread.

Another fact alfo fhall be taken as granted, that, in proportion as rife of wages formed the principal mode in which relief was given during the times of fcarcity, does diffatisfaction and difappointment now prevail either with the employer or the employed. As there are many inftances in the hiftory of this country of the mifchief done by the populace from the firft impreffions on their minds, whether excited by the actual preffure of diftrefs, as in thofe cafes where dearnefs of provifions has alarmed their attention, as has lately happened; or from the incitements of demagogues to riot and mifrule, from political or party motives; it furely is a ftriking truth, that, whatever can produce a more conftant active infpection as to the management of the poor, and continually imprefs upon their minds, that the watchful eye of fuperior authority is ever over their interefts and conduct, as well to guard thofe interefts from being affected, any farther than direct neceffity impels, from

that

that influence of the feafons and times, which no human wifdom or forefight can avert; and to take care that their conduct, while fuffering under that uncontrollable neceffity, fhall not be fuch as to diminifh, inftead of increafe, the poffible means of affiftance. Such an infpection and control muft tend to the beft effects, as it would, in the late inftance of fcarcity, have prevented a great wafte of time, when that time was more particularly valuable, and many fcenes of riot and mifchief; all of which, like all other natural and political inflammatory diforders, it is a much wifer meafure to prevent than to ftop or allay, after the fermentation is excited: the politician as well as the phyfician will allow this as a maxim, that it is eafier to prevent than to cure a morbid affection.

The fame principle is alfo ftrongly inculcated from the fecond obfervation that has been made, that a prompt attention to the rifing difturbance, and a determination to execute the duties of magiftracy, were attended with the beft effects: but, when the populace were collected, more coercive means on the one hand, and more explanation and perfuafion on the other, were neceffary to diffipate the rifen tumult, than magiftrates, unprotected by any means of defence, were, in every cafe, willing or able to make ufe of; becaufe, in general, a delicacy of fentiment prevails as to calling in the aid of the military, except in thofe cafes where the difpofition of the mob is notorioufly riotous, their behaviour threatening and audacious, and they are in the fact of committing acts of mifchief; befides, on this occafion, the urgent caufe for their alarm and diffatiffaction was obvious to every man's feeling; the price of bread-corn continued rifing, before the harveft of 1796, to a height hitherto unprecedented, and bearing no proportion whatever with the means which labour, by its largeft wages, could procure to purchafe neceffary bread for a family: in many parts of the kingdom, the price of wheat amounted to above twelve or fourteen fhillings the bufhel, which would exhauft the whole gains of an induftrious family of five or fix perfons, where agricultural labour is largely paid, leaving

them

them not a farthing for the other neceffaries of life. Here then was
an emergency which required the beft difcretion of the magiftrates,
who knew and commiferated the diftrefs and alarming fituation of
the poor, and at the fame time felt it their duty, if the voice of perfuafion could not be heard, or would not be attended to, that ftill
the peace muft be preferved. From the inftances of riot which occurred in that diftrict in Suffolk, I was obliged, in the difcharge of
my duty as a magiftrate, to attend to: I am convinced the collected
populace had no conception that the exifting laws, by which they
were accuftomed to receive relief from the overfeer in their diftreffes,
either on immediate application to him, or, being refufed, by application to the magiftrate, could be fo expanded as to admit of an order from the magiftrates for their relief, in the cafe then immediately preffing on their feelings and apprehenfions; becaufe, as foon
as their attention could be fufficiently gained for the voice of reafon
to be heard, and they had been made to underftand the danger
they incurred by riotoufly affembling, with the view to over-awe
and alarm thofe who were difpofed to do every thing the laws
would admit of for their relief, that if they continued affembled,
affiftance from the military would be applied for, but that, if they
difperfed and returned peaceably to their refpective homes, on the
following day the magiftrates of the diftrict would attend, and then
every individual head of a family, applying peaceably and by himfelf,
would undoubtedly receive from the magiftrates an order for relief,
proportionate to what in their opinion the urgency of the cafe and
the individual wants of the poor perfon applying required; the collected mob retired from the fpot to a neighbouring field, where they
talked the matter over among themfelves, and in a few hours all
difperfed.

The next day, four or five of thofe moft preffed by the dearnefs
of corn, from each of the neighbouring parifhes, appeared at the
juftice-meeting which was then held, when the overfeers were recommended to provide flour fufficient for the confumption of their

parifhes

parifhes till harveft, and fell it to the poor of their parifhes at a price which would enable them to procure bread for their families by the earnings they made. And, an equal or fuperior price for corn taking place in the following winter, the poor then applying in a peaceable and orderly manner for relief, the overfeers were then recommended to allow each poor family fixpence a head for each individual compofing the family, weekly, over and above the cafual relief they had before received, and were to continue to receive; which plan was carried into execution throughout the hundred, and every fymptom of riot ceafed, and, except in a very few inftances, this was the only relief the poor in the hundred of Rifbridge, in the county of Suffolk, received through the time of fcarcity, after a fufficiency of wheat for the fupply of the demands of the poor until the harveft in 1796 was procured, by each occupier, engaging to furnifh a proportional part of the wheat he had remaining in hand at a price fixed by confent, which price was to be made good to him out of the poor's rate.

The common day's wages in this county may be ftated at eight fhillings a week in fummer, and feven fhillings in winter, before the fcarcity of 1795; and, except in cafes of illnefs or accidental infirmity, a family, confifting of a man, his wife, and three children, had, in general, no allowance from the parifh: he, therefore, lived upon, and his family was fupported from, his earnings, together with what his wife and children could add to them; which little, whatever it might be, I fear was not increafed in the time of fcarcity; but, fuppofe it amounted to about eighteen-pence or two fhillings a week, during the time of dearnefs, his income was increafed, by the fixpence ordered to each individual of his family, to ten fhillings and fixpence a week, and by the rife of wages one fhilling more, and the earning of his family makes the fum thirteen fhillings or thirteen fhillings and fixpence: but the quartern-loaf was rifen from fixpence, its price when wheat is 12 *l.* a load of five quarters, to a fhilling, at 24 *l.* a load; and, for fome weeks, to fifteen

teen pence; for wheat was fold as high as 30*l.* a load in this county in the fpring of 1796. How then could this addition to his income enable him to fupport his family, when the common allowance of bread, half a peck-loaf to each individual in the family, for a week, cofts him from ten fhillings to twelve fhillings and fixpence? It fhould be recollected, that this computation, being made by day's wages, may be rather low, where the labour is, in general, done by the piece.

In this neighbourhood, barley-cakes and potatoes were the common fubftitute for wheaten bread, a loaf of which was, at times during the fcarcity, bought as a treat; and wheat-flour, from which feven pounds of bran had been taken in grinding each bufhel, was in common ufe with all, both rich and poor: fome ufed the flour without dreffing, as it came from the ftones of the mill. In the northern counties of England, it appears,* that bar-ley-bread and potatoes are the food of the poor, almoft to the exclufion of wheat; or that, where wheat-flour is introduced, it forms but a fmall proportion of the flour that makes the loaf, rye and barley being mixed with it; therefore, the poor, in this part of the ifland, were, by the fcarcity, reduced to live on food fimi-lar to what their countrymen in the North have been, in the cheap-eft times, in the conftant habit of ufing.

The adoption of thefe articles of food in this part of the king-dom, at this preffing time, will, in fome meafure, account for the poor being able to fubfift themfelves and families at the time the price of wheaten bread was more than doubled, while their addi-tional income was not increafed a third, as appears by the inftance taken of a family of five, which is fomewhat of an average-number in a poor man's family.

This fact corroborates an affertion made, in a former part of this tract, that the increafe of the expenfes of the poor does not arife

---

* Sir F. M. Eden's Hiftory of the Poor.

fo

fo much from the increafe of the price of the prime neceffaries of life as from other caufes which have been mentioned; and, poffibly, that man will, in the event, be acknowledged the real friend of the poor, and alfo deferve the good word of his countrymen, who points out in what thofe other expenfes confift, and inftigates the Parliament to an inquiry into the fact, and to an attempt to prevent the continuation of its excefs.

Had bread preferved that proportion in the expenfes of the poor which has been imagined, is it not reafonable to fuppofe that fome of thofe fubftitutes for fine flour, which the fcarcity of the times juft paft by had drawn all conditions of people to, the poor would have continued in the ufe of, with the view either to find money for the other purpofes which they might wifh to indulge themfelves in, or to lay up fomething againft the day of diftrefs, or to preferve themfelves from the neceffity of application to the officers of the poor, or, in fome inftances, to fecure themfelves from the preffure of abfolute diftrefs, where large families receive large allowances from the poor's rate, but yet not fufficient, together with their earnings, to find them the neceffaries of life?

But, it is believed, no fuch prudential favings, in this material article of life, have, in general, been continued in the domeftic economy of the poor. The prefent moderate price of wheat has, although other articles of their confumption have remained as expenfive as ever, brought them back to their former expenditure of bread, from fine flour unmixed with barley, which has alfo been proportionably cheap; and potatoes have nearly, if not entirely, difappeared from their bill of fare.

LETTER LIV.

IT would indicate a blameable degree of apathy to thofe inftitutions, which have equally done honour to our rulers as good to
that country at the helm of which they prefide, were the ufeful at-
tentions of the Board of Agriculture, during the time of fcarcity, by recommendations of, and inftructions refpecting, the cultivation of potatoes, paffed over without being acknowledged. This
Board has been the caufe of introducing, throughout the whole
kingdom, the knowledge and practice of the beft methods of culti-
vating this moft ufeful vegetable, and bringing it into general agricultural ufe: fuch an excellent fubftitute for bread, in a time of
fcarcity, and fo nutritious a root at all times, and of fuch important fervice in the nourifhment and fattening all kinds of farming-
ftock, but particularly fwine and cattle, that there is no doubt but
the cultivation of potatoes will, although the prejudices of the poor
againft the ufe of them for their general food fhould remain, infure
this country againft apprehenfion of any degree of famine in future,
as there can fcarcely be found a farmer who will not raife fome
quantity of them for the ufe of his cattle, which, in cafes of emergency, may become the food of man, and his cattle be fubfifted
as heretofore. But, at prefent, and through this laft winter, although potatoes have been fold at the low price of one fhilling,
and even fo low as nine-pence, a bufhel; but few have been bought
by the poor in this neighbourhood; while the comparative cheapnefs of them, at this price, to a quartern-loaf at fixpence, muft be
evident to every one.

The charitable munificence of our countrymen, that virtue which
has more particularly diftinguifhed Great Britain from all countries
of the globe, and has gained us a character for our humanity almoft at the expenfe of our reputation for political wifdom, was

never

never more remarkably exerted than on the late prefling occafion: but was not that portion of it which expended itfelf in parochial fubfcriptions in fome meafure mifapplied? As to that which privately employed itfelf in alleviating inftances of particular diftrefs, no obfervation, derogatory either to the excellent heart or found head that dictated any of thofe private good acts, is hinted at. But the public fubfcriptions were, in general, an application of this beft trait of our national character in aid of the poor's rate; an effect which was generally perceived after the harveft of 1795 had occafioned the apprehenfions of people to fubfide: and the high price of corn which followed, during a great part of the fubfequent year, was, in general, met by an increafe of the rate for the maintenance of the poor; private charity ftill affifting them by every method that Charity, fkilful, although fecret, in her ways and means, could invent.

The rife of wages, which, voluntarily on the part of the occupiers of land, was in general a concomitant of the late fcarcity, is worth our attention, as to its confequence both to the labourer and his employer; it attended or followed the relief the poor received from public fubfcriptions, private charity, and the poor's rate; and, as far as the high price of corn was the effect of any other caufe than the fmall produce of the crops, high wages rightly accompany high prices; or, if the price increafed in a greater ratio than the produce was deficient, an increafe of wages juftly accompanied an increafe of profit: but, if the price arofe folely, or principally, from the deficiency of produce, and was not increafed by extraneous means; augmented wages, if not voluntary, would be an injuftice to thofe employing the poor; becaufe, in that cafe, deficiency of produce occafioning the increafe of price, no extraprofit would remain for the occupier; but he, having an increafed poor's rate to pay, and his family to maintain from the decreafed produce of his lands, would find himfelf in a worfe fituation than

any

any of the various claſſes of commercial men in this country, whoſe capital and time are not employed in raiſing food for man.

This is mentioned to point out one of the conſequences attendant on any plan, conſtituting a ratio between the price of corn and the price of work ; to demonſtrate that in the proportion wages of agriculture riſe, as there is a deficiency of crop ; while the poor-rate remains as a revenue for the poor in times of diſtreſs, iſſuing, in a great meaſure, immediately from the pockets of the occupiers of land ; it is an unneceſſary act of injuſtice to them, that the means of producing the diminiſhed produce ſhould, at the ſame time, be accompanied with an increaſe of expenſe ; becauſe an increaſe of wages is not called for on the principle of neceſſity, the poor's rate obviating the neceſſity.

But an increaſe of wages is always attended with a decreaſe of labour. Manufacturers have long underſtood this fact, and acted accordingly : every perſon employing workmen, where labour alone, and not the ſkill of the artiſt, is required, finds the truth of this aſſertion from experience : the labouring-claſs, in general, thinks no farther than of immediate maintenance : their own labour ſupplies a part of this ; the pariſh-rate is too often looked at for the remainder, and no man prefers labour to idleneſs, or the intereſts of his more opulent pariſhioners to his own eaſe ; he will not work to diminiſh the poor's rate ; it is therefore found, that increaſed wages do not increaſe either the quantity or the quality of the work done.

And when wages are raiſed, as they have been of late voluntarily, on account of the emergency of the times, to keep up a certain ratio between the price paid for the exertions of labour, and the maintenance of the labourer, which was humanely, but not wiſely, ſubmitted to ; are they eaſily reduced, the emergency ceaſing, and a time of cheapneſs, as to that produce of the earth, on account of the dearneſs of which the wages of the labourer were raiſed, having enſued ? which cheapneſs then falls with double weight on

their

their employers; poor's rates and wages being rifen, and the price
of the produce of the earth being reduced.—Inquire into the fact:—
the anfwer will be, it has not in general been attempted: in thofe
inftances, where the attempt has been made, it has created diflatif-
faction, and, where perfifted in, has occafioned lefs work to be
done; and this, although it may be apparently a paradox, when
coupled with what has been before advanced, is not to be wondered at, as an effect perceived *immediately* on the reduction of the
wages of labour, which *afterwards* may gradually difappear.

While the mind is revolving thofe circumftances refpecting the
conduct of the poor during this time of fcarcity which we have
juft paft by; while we are calling in aid the powers of memory
and reflection, to fix on fome leading principles which may be of
fervice in the amendment or alteration of that fyftem of poor-laws,
under the adminiftration of which the public have expended an
annual revenue, fo confiderable, as would occafion *theory* to declare,
that extreme poverty could not remain where fo much was diftributed; did not *ftubborn fact*, at the fame time, prove, that poverty
and mifery not only remain, but feem to advance, nearly in the
proportion that our expenditure increafes; while idlenefs and diffolutenefs of manners go hand in hand, and the next generation
promifes to be worfe than the prefent. While thefe and fimilar circumftances ftrike the mind, it is difficult to avoid the appearance
of fome degree of prejudice againft the poor, for whofe benefit this
inquiry was firft undertaken, and with a view to whofe *real* and
beft interefts it is continued. Being obliged to ftate matters as they
ftrike the obfervation, and to reafon from facts as they exift; one
is led to doubt the political propriety of increafing the price of
labour by law, as the neceffaries of life increafe in price; although
it may be at the expenfe of that reputation all our countrymen are
defirous to be renowned for,—the reputation of humanity.

And it is a matter of much doubt, whether the character of a
humane man will be preferved in the opinion of many of our ten-

der-hearted patriots, or of our village-politicians, by a recommendation of fchools of induftry and parochial funds, the encouragement of friendly focieties, and a conftant active infpection of thofe
who have the management of the parochial revenue and the conduct of the poor; together with a regular annual parliamentary
inveftigation of this important fubject; inftead of higher wages,
and the prefent unreftrained ftate of idlenefs and diffipation in
which the rifing generation is, I will not fay educated, but, fuffered to remain.

On the other hand, it is too manifeft a truth, for our prefent
comfort and future profpects, that if a wife and well-guided hand
of authority does not, as foon as poffible, ftretch its benign influence over the land, and by fome legiflative line of conduct, which
may couple our interefts with our inclinations; and to which the
poor and the rich, the employer and the employed, will not only
willingly fubmit, but each of them, in their feveral ftations, will
actively coincide to carry into full execution and conftant effect;
were there no external caufe of immenfe expenditure exifting; no
demands for fupplies beyond a peace-eftablifhment neceffary; the
nation could not long bear the increafing expenfes of the poor;
becaufe they fall chiefly on thofe who raife the neceffaries of life;
which neceffaries muft of courfe advance in price, in proportion as
larger burthens fall on the growers of them: this price muft be
paid by the labouring-poor, as well as by the other claffes of the
nation, which will occafion the rates and the price of labour ftill to
rife. Thefe caufes and confequences, reacting on each other, may
ultimately produce a crifis that we muft all dread to think of.

LETTER

LETTER LV.

WHILE all ranks of his majefty's fubjects, by anceftorial pof-feffions, or their own induftry, raifed above the apprehen-fion of want from the prevailing fcarcity, were with a difinterefted benevolence, publicly and in private, by donations and a volun-tary increafe of the wages of the labouring-poor, preferving their more indigent countrymen from the preffure of real want and ap-prehended famine; the legiflature of the kingdom, with a benevo-lence and wifdom worthy of the beft ages, under the happieft governments, by its celerity in enacting thofe laws which were beft calculated for an expeditious relief of the times, nobly difcharged their important duties; and his majefty's minifters, although in the midft of the moft neceffary, important, and expenfive, conteft with its enemies this nation was ever engaged in, with a promptitude of wife and liberal humanity, applied vaft fums of money, which were raifed for our defence from foreign foes, to our prefervation from domeftic famine, by encouraging the importation of foreign grain, by large and, before this time, undheard-of bounties; the payment of which bounties has been one of the means which has exhaufted the Treafury of its riches; while, at the fame time, the payment for the corn imported has affifted to drain the kingdom of its fpecie; a meafure which, although it greatly tended to remove the apprehenfions of the nation, and to reduce the price of corn to a level with the means the poor had, by their own exertions and the affiftance of their neighbours, to purchafe it; yet has not been without certain inconveniences, the preffure of which we now feel. The topic itfelf is new and important, both to the public in-terefts of the ftate, and to thofe of the private individual; but of too extenfive and complicated a nature to be here commented upon, were the knowledge and abilities of the writer equal to the difquifition; who conceives, that it is more within the line of his

purpofe,

purpofe, and his capacity, to make fome few obfervations on the acts which were paffed in parliament this year, which folely refpect the management of the poor.

The firft is 36 Geo. III. cap. 10. and bears date, in the Statutes at Large, Dec. 18, 1795. This act, after a well-adapted preamble, enacts, that directors and guardians of the poor, incorporated by acts of parliament, may, whenever the average-price of wheat at the corn-market, Mark-lane, London, for the quarter, immediately preceding fuch annual, quarterly, or other general, meeting, fhall have exceeded the average-price of wheat at the fame market, during thofe years, from which the average-amount of the poor's rate was taken, upon the paffing of the feveral incorporating-acts refpectively, affefs the feveral parifhes, hamlets, and places, within their refpective hundreds, towns, or diftricts, which now are, or have been, ufually charged to the poor's rates, with fuch fums of money as fuch directors and guardians, &c. fhall think neceffary for the fupport and maintenance of the poor for the current quarter, and for paying the intereft of the money borrowed under the incorporating-acts, and of any debts which may be incurred fince the 1ft of January, 1795, in the maintenance of the poor, notwithftanding fuch fums of money fhould exceed the affeffments limited by the refpective acts : provided, that fuch affeffments, by virtue of this act, are made, collected, and paid, in the fame manner, and fubject to the fame reftrictions, regulations, and powers of appeal, &c. as the affeffments made under the incorporating-acts. And provided alfo, that after January 1, 1798, the fums to be affeffed, by virtue of this act, fhall never exceed double the fum at prefent raifed by virtue of any incorporating-act now exifting.

This act of parliament gave a very neceffary latitude, to the directors and guardians of the incorporated diftricts, to raife the affeffments of the poor's rates, according to the urgency of the occafion; which authority they had abridged themfelves of by the act of parliament incorporating them, and it has been attempted

. tempted to obtain certain information to what degree each of the
houfes of induftry, within the county of Suffolk, has made ufe of
this authority; and for that purpofe letters have been fent to the
fame gentlemen in the diftricts, who, with much obliging readinefs,
communicated that information which is contained in the former
letters in this tract. Anfwers have not been returned to all the
letters; but, as to thofe houfes from which information has been
obtained, it clearly appears, that the poor in them were maintained, through the years 1795 and 1796, with much lefs increafe of rates than in any of the adjoining hundreds, where no
houfes of induftry have been inftituted; and, when the low rates
at which the average of the parifhes was ftruck in the incorporated
hundreds are confidered, there is reafon to believe it is a matter of
pofitive proof, that the maintenance of the poor through the two
laft years has not raifed the poor-rates in the incorporated hundreds to half that affeffment in the pound that their maintenance
has occafioned the rates to be raifed to in the hundreds not incorporated.

And although Sir F. M. Eden's Parochial Reports do not ftate
the accounts of thofe two large incorporated houfes of induftry,
that in the Ifle of Wight and that at Shrewfbury, for either of the
years of fcarcity; yet as he fays generally of the incorporated parifhes in the Ifle of Wight, that one parifh pays two fhillings in the
pound rack-rent; another fifteen pence; another three fhillings and
three pence, on two-thirds of the rent; and of Graffinghall houfe
of induftry, Norfolk, that the average of the rates paid by the incorporated parifhes may be ftated at twenty pence in the pound;
and, by referring to the average of the affeffment of the incorporated
parifhes in the different houfes of induftry, as ftated in a former
Letter of this tract, it will clearly appear, when it is confidered that
the act of parliament only enabled them to double their affeffments,
that it cannot have coft *thofe* parifhes, alfo, half the expenfe to
maintain their poor during the laft two years, eftimating that expenfe

penſe by the poor's rate, as it coſt the pariſhes in the country near
the incorporated diſtricts; moſt of the other pariſhes in Suffolk, if
not all, and many in Eſſex, having expended an aſſeſſment riſing in
different pariſhes from 12s. to above 20s. and one or two pariſhes
to 30s. in the pound.

The cheap maintenance of the poor, in the houſes of induſtry, is a fact I ſhould conceive inconteſtably proved. The
wholeſomeneſs of that maintenance has never been doubted by thoſe
who have viſited them; and if they, by any means, tend to diminiſh the chance of human life, of which ſome doubt has been made
in a former Letter, ſurely it would have appeared, and might be
proved, by a diminiſhed population; as, in moſt diſtricts where they
have been inſtituted, years ſufficient have paſſed for a diminution of
population to be perceived, had that diminution happened. That
queſtion was aſked in the letters ſent: the anſwers returned have
been to this effect: —

There is every reaſon to believe the population has increaſed
much. — It is generally thought that the population, ſince the incorporation took place, has conſiderably increaſed. — The population has certainly increaſed, but in what proportion I cannot ſay.
— Population increaſes among the poor. — We relieve many more
women in child-bed than we did. —— It is to be regretted that
no proof can be collected on this point in thoſe incorporated
pariſhes mentioned in Sir F. M. Eden's parochial reports; becauſe,
an increaſed population being proved with equal probability in thoſe
diſtricts, as it is in Suffolk, there could be no doubt of the fact
throughout the incorporated diſtricts in the kingdom, and one great
objection to theſe inſtitutions would be done away: not that it is,
by any means, the intention of theſe pages to recommend any
means of compelling pariſhes to inſtitute houſes of induſtry; the
wiſh of the writer is, to preſerve the rights of thoſe already inſtituted inviolate in every reſpect, (except that of compelling them to
become ſchools of induſtry, as far as it is compatible with the advantage

vantage and convenience of the parishes incorporated, and subjecting them to a similar infpection and return of their state and condition to parliament, as is expected from the rest of the kingdom,) and alfo to preferve unrepealed the statute of 22 Geo. III. c. 83. and its amendment 33 Geo. III. c. 35. as thofe acts of parliament encourage them, but do not compel the institution of them.

The other act of parliament paffed 24th December, 1795, and is cap. 23 of the fame feffions. Its preamble recites the inconvenience that has arifen from an act of the 9th of George I. empowering parishes to purchafe or hire houfes, and to contract with any perfon for lodging, keeping, and maintaining, the poor; and that the poor, who fhall refufe to be fo lodged, kept, and maintained, fhall not be entitled to receive collection or relief from the overfeers of the parifh. The inconvenience recited is, that this provifion in the act prevents an industrious poor perfon from receiving fuch occafional relief as is beft fuited to his peculiar cafe, as it holds out conditions of relief injurious to the comfort and domeftic fituation of fuch poor perfon; it therefore enacts,

" That the overfeers, with the confent of the parishioners at a veftry, or the approbation in writing of any of his Majefty's juftices of the peace acting in the diftrict, may relieve poor perfons at their own houfes under certain circumftances of temporary illnefs or diftrefs; and that any of his Majefty's juftices of the peace ufually acting within the diftrict may, at his difcretion, order fuch poor perfons to be relieved at their own houfes; provided that the fpecial caufe of ordering fuch relief be written in fuch order given for relief, and that fuch order remain in force for a time not exceeding a month from the date of the order; and that it fhall be lawful for any *two* juftices to make any farther order for a time not exceeding one month, and fo on, from time to time, as the occafion may require, fuch juftice or juftices firft adminiftering an oath as to the need and caufe of fuch relief, in each of the above cafes, and thereupon fummoning the overfeer of the poor of fuch parifh to fhew

caufe

caufe why fuch poor perfon fhould not receive fuch relief as aforefaid : but that this act fhall not extend to places where houfes of induftry are provided under 22 Geo. III. c. 83. or under the authority
of any fpecial act of parliament now in force." To this act of parliament humanity muft give affent, and prudence cannot object.

L E T T E R   LVI.

FROM the time that the firft edition of this publication had
been the occafion of introducing me to the acquaintance of
Mr. Rofe, a correfpondence while in the country, and an inter-
change of fentiments on this important fubject when I was in town,
attended, on his part, with every polite attention and friendly civility, had been continued between us; and, towards the end of
January, 1796, I had the pleafure to receive from him a letter requefting me to meet Mr. Pitt, and feveral gentlemen who had paid
attention to, and had at heart, the amelioration of the fyftem of
the poor-laws, at dinner at Mr. Rofe's on the following Monday.
Accordingly I went to town, and had the honour of meeting Mr.
Pitt, and feveral moft refpectable members of the Houfe of Commons, together with two other gentlemen, one of whom has paid
great attention to the fubject of the meeting, and a profeffional
gentleman, whofe abilities and technical experience are well known.
Soon after the fervants were withdrawn, after dinner, Mr. Pitt
produced a fketch of the heads of a bill which, he faid, he had in
contemplation, and on which he requefted the opinion of the
company prefent; obferving, that, for the purpofe of confidering
each topic individually, we fhould conceive ourfelves a Committee
on the Poor-Laws, and have fome converfation on each head as it
occurred.

Although

Although the confideration of the fubject was continued, without any interruption, till between one and two o'clock in the morning, the fketch had not all paffed under review ; when one of the company, while the converfation was employed about orders of re-moval, remarking the time of the night, Mr. Pitt then obferved, that it was high time for us to remove ourfelves, and our committee broke up.

A day or two afterwards I received a copy of the heads which had been the fubject of our confideration, and a note from Mr. Rofe, fignifying it was Mr. Pitt's defire that I fhould attend, the following day, at eleven o'clock, at his houfe in Downing-ftreet, where I again met the fame gentlemen, and afterwards moft of them, at different times through the month of February, as it fuited Mr. Pitt's convenience.

When all the heads had again been reconfidered, Mr. Rofe fent me a copy of them, as then amended on reconfideration ; and in-formed me it was defired that I fhould, in a pamphlet, fhortly ex-plain to the public the good effects which might be expected from an act of parliament on the plan and principle contained in the heads alluded to ; and that it fhould be prepared for, and paffed through, the prefs as foon as poffible. I then returned into the country to prepare the pamphlet ; but, being prevented fome days by illnefs, I was not able to fend it to town quite fo expeditioufly as was ex pected ; and, about a week after it was fent to Mr. Rofe, I was in-formed, by letter from him, that my pamphlet had been received and approved of ; but that, in the mean time, Mr. Pitt had been indefatigable in his application to the fubject ; that the heads had been reduced to the form of a bill, which was then printing ; that fome alterations had been made, to which the pamphlet could not apply ; that, as foon as printed, a copy fhould be fent me ; and, a few days afterwards, I had the honour to receive, from Mr. Pitt, Heads of a Bill for Amending and Enforcing the Laws for the Relief, Inftruction, and Employment, of the Poor. I then employed my

time

time in making my obfervations on the bill in the form it then was, and tranfmitted them to Mr. Rofe, and foon afterwards went to town ; when he informed me that the meafure was then poftponed for the prefent.

As foon as the bill, as amended by the committee, now before the Houfe, for the better fupport and maintenance of the poor, was printed, I received two copies of it from that gentleman, defiring me to make my obfervations upon the different claufes contained in it, and write them in the margin of one of the copies, which was to be fent back to him, which was accordingly done pretty much at large ; and I attempted to fhew wherein, by its aberrations from the heads fettled by Mr. Pitt and thofe gentlemen, whofe attention to this fubject has been mentioned, the bill had deviated from that plan which was better calculated to do the moft probable good, at the leaft probable expenfe, to the public.

The Heads of the Bill for Amending and Enforcing the Laws for the Relief, Inftruction, and Employment, of the Poor, propofed according to the plan opened by Mr. Pitt to the Houfe of Commons, in the feffion of parliament 1796, having been printed for the benefit of the members, and again by Sir F. M. Eden, in the third volume of his Hiftory of the Poor ; and the bill, as amended by the committee, being printed and difperfed by different editions through the kingdom ; it would be abfurd to reprint them in this publication, as it would increafe to no purpofe the expenfe of a book already too expenfive: but fome good may arife from printing the heads, which I had the honour to affift in fettling, as probably it will be allowed by thofe gentlemen who bear in their recollection the fpeech, in which the Chancellor of the Exchequer gave a fketch of his ideas on the fubject, on the fecond reading of Mr. Whitbread's bill ; that thefe heads more nearly correfpond with the mafterly fketch then given in a fpeech, which it is to be lamented was not heard in a full Houfe, and never has had juftice done it by any minute or report yet printed; and which, in the opinion of fome

good

good judges of elocution, never has been exceeded in this kingdom as an oratorical effort, in point of perfpicuous compreffion of a comprehenfive fubject, terfenefs, elegance of expreffion, and effect; and to the ideas contained in which fpeech, the more clofely any legiflative plan for ameliorating the fyftem of the poor-laws adheres, the more probable will be its good effect. The plan alluded to is, therefore, here introduced; firft obferving, that, in feveral places where the words are in Italic, the matter was not wholly determined on; and alfo where the word OR is ufed, to point out different modes of acting, the precife mode was left unfettled; and as the payment of the county-guardians for their trouble and time was not then *pofitively* determined, either as to the manner or the quantum,. that part of the plan is not inferted.

A SKETCH

OF THE

HEADS OF AN ACT

FOR THE

EMPLOYMENT, INSTRUCTION, AND RELIEF, OF THE POOR,

AS AMENDED, ON RECONSIDERATION, AFTER SEVERAL MEETINGS IN DOWNING-STREET, FEBRUARY, 1796.

PART I. — *Employment and Inftruction of the Poor.*

WHEREAS the laws now in force have not been fufficiently carried into practice, for employing the poor who are able to work, and for inftructing the infant-poor.

Juftices to be authorized within a given time to affociate parifhes to the number or extent of for the purpofe of the act, *in the fame manner as under the* 22d *Geo. III. ch.* 83.

The

The juftices to be authorized and required, within
from the paffing of this act, to make order for the eftablifhment of fchools of induftry in every parifh, or fet of
affociated parifhes; and, for that purpofe, to order a rate to
be made in the firft inftance, and to be paid by inftalments,
for a given period, as they fhall deem convenient, or to authorize a certain fum to be borrowed on the credit of the
rates in the parifh or *parifhes* for purchafing materials
to fet the poor at work, as well grown perfons as children,
and for erecting, hiring, or purchafing, fchools of induftry, for the inftruction of the poor, and for employing
thofe who cannot, when inftructed, conveniently work at
home, either from the circumftances of the families, or
from the nature of the work to be done.

Juftices to be likewife authorized to compel the purchafing, at ftated periods, frefh materials by the officers in
each parifh, or (by fome mode to be provided) within each
hundred, to be diftributed to the officers in each refpective
parifh, for manufacturing articles of clothing, and every
other article of neceffary ufe, for the poor within it, or
fuch other articles for which they can find convenient
fale.

An option muft be given to juftices, to decide on a view
of the circumftances of different parifhes, or with refpect to
different claffes of the poor in the fame parifh.

Whether, 1. Parifhes to maintain, lodge, and board,
the poor employed in the fchools of induftry, taking the
benefit of their earnings.

Or, 2. Parifhes to feed and take care of them during
the hours of their work, taking the benefit of their
earnings.

In both thefe cafes, the poor to be encouraged by rewards.

Or,

OR, 3. Parishes to furnish materials, implements, &c. and to repurchase the manufactures at stated prices, under certain regulations, with an option of the work being done at home or at school.

OR, 4. Parishes to furnish materials, &c. as before, leaving the families to sell the manufactures.

Provision, that if more parishes than one have, with the approbation of the justices, associated for the express purpose of adopting any one of these modes preferably, such agreement shall, in that respect, be binding.

Provision to prevent apprenticing in husbandry for a shorter period than now allowed.

Employment on the roads of separate or associated parishes, or other parish-work.

Labour to be found, according to some one or other of these modes, for all those who are settled in the parish, who cannot find work for themselves.

Provision for cases where substantial householders shall offer *to give a weekly rate for employing children in agriculture*; and such children to be on the same footing as those who attend the schools of industry.

No contracts to be allowed in future for the lodging, keeping, and employing, the poor.

Places of reception, if necessary, in each county for lunatics, ideots, blind, &c. &c. Vide 9 Geo. II. c. 7.

Power to convert the subsisting workhouses into schools of industry.

PART II. — *Removals, Settlement, and Relief.*

No person to be removed as chargeable, if he shall become so only from temporary disability, or sickness; nor shall relief be withheld from him to which he shall be entitled, under this *act*, from the number of his children;

provided

provided that his fettlement fhall be afcertained, as under
the Friendly-Society Act; and that, during his refidence,
he fhall have fubfcribed to a friendly fociety, from
                    after the commencement of this act,
if any is eftablifhed in the parifh or neighbourhood, and
has fent his children, if required, to the parifh-fchool of
induftry, or received work from thence, or employed
them as above-provided.

Provided, that if no friendly fociety fhall be eftablifhed
in the parifh or neighbourhood, or there being one eftablifhed, and the perfon applying fhall not be able on his
application to procure admiffion to it, then, and in every
fuch cafe, his contributing a certain fum to a box, to be kept
by the officers of the parifh, fhall be deemed fufficient. And
in all parifhes or towns, where there are no friendly focieties,
or within   miles thereof, or where application fhall
be made by perfons refufed admittance to friendly focieties,
the parifh-officers fhall be compelled to receive contributions, and to pay weekly allowances proportioned thereto,
during ficknefs, to the contributors, who fhall be placed
in the fame fituation, for the purpofes before-mentioned,
as if they were members of friendly focieties. — Parifhes,
relieving, in the cafes fpecified, perfons not having acquired a fettlement, to recover   .   part of the
fum given in relief, after deducting what the parifh or
the friendly fociety has received.

No relief to be given to perfons not having acquired
fettlements in cafes above-fpecified, except by fetting them
to work.

Every perfon to gain a fettlement who has refided *five
years* in a parifh, and has complied with the above conditions.

                                                        All

All *perfons* having more than *two children*, ages to be fixed, to be entitled to a certain pecuniary allowance weekly, unlefs the overfeers, &c. furnifh them with the means of earning to the fame amount by work, or make competent provifions for their relief, by advancing a fum of money, in the manner to be pointed out by the act.

Power to juftices to order overfeers, &c. to advance a fum of money to any perfon entitled to relief, to enable fuch perfon to purchafe a cow, or other animal, fo as thereby to give them an opportunity of increafing their income to the amount to which they would be entitled to relief.

Perfons not to be excluded from relief in certain cafes, on account of cottages in their own right which they occupy, or other vifible property, not exceeding a certain amount, and of a certain defcription.

No perfon to be entitled to relief, for themfelves or their families, who fhall decline labour offered to them by the overfeers, &c. if able to execute it.

Perfons having fubfcribed to friendly focieties, or contributed to parifh-boxes, as above, for   years, and becoming old or enfirm, to be entitled to a certain extra-relief from the fund raifed for the poor, in proportion as their health and ftrength fhall fail them.

PART III. — *Infpection of Parifhes, and Execution of the Laws.*

Overfeers to be made more permanent in office, and to be bound to anfwer, on oath, *certain* queries to be put to them by juftices, and fuch other queftions as fhall be put to them, relative to the management and employment of the poor.

Power to continue overfeer in office for a fecond year, and for fubfequent ones, if three-fifths of the parifh, in number and value, fhall concur in the meafure; but fuch

F f f   perfon

perfon not to be compellable to ferve : the three-fifths, as before, may, however, agree to give him a falary not exceeding   payable out of the rate.

Additional provifions to compel overfeers to make up their accounts.

Power to be given to the refident clergyman, if rector, vicar, or perpetual curate, or to the officiating minifter, if authorized by the bifhop in a manner to be required, to infpect, from time to time, the *books and accounts* of the parifh, and likewife any houfes or fchools of induftry within the fame; and if, in any cafe, he fhall be of opinion that the laws are not properly enforced, he fhall have like power with that herein-after given to the guardians of the poor to apply to the juftices, at their petty feffions, who fhall proceed in like manner thereon.

One or more guardians of the poor to be appointed for each county, according to its extent, to be chofen by a majority of perfons having freehold-eftates within the county above the amount of £100 a year, and to have an allowance payable out of the *county-rates*.

No perfon to be eligible who is not qualified, by property, to elect as above-defcribed.

To continue in office for four years, unlefs removed by juftices, at the quarter-feffions, for caufe affigned, at the end of which he may be chofen again.

The guardians of the poor to be required, within   calendar-months of his appointment, to vifit and infpect every parifh or place, providing for its own poor, within the county or diftrict for which he is appointed; and afterwards, during his continuance in office, to vifit every parifh again at leaft once in the courfe of each of the three remaining years for which he is elected. To be authorized and required, at every fuch vifitation, to inquire particularly

particularly into the number and condition of perfons fupporting themfelves by labour, and of thofe receiving relief ; diftinguifhing their feveral ages and defcriptions.

The amount and variation of the poor's rate, and the application of the fame, under its feveral heads ; fhewing particularly the fums expended in fetting the poor to work, with the particulars thereof.

The number employed ; diftinguifhing their ages and defcriptions, and the nature and value of the work done, and the manner of difpofing of the fame, and whether they were employed in their own houfes or in the fchools of induftry.

The number of poor receiving pecuniary allowances, or to whom money has been advanced, under the provifions of this act, for their better fupport.

The ftate of the fchools of induftry, *and the houfes of induftry*, (if any,) with the number of perfons lodged, maintained, or inftructed, therein. The number of deaths within the year ; the rules for the management of the faid fchools ; and, generally, all fuch matters as they fhall be required by the juftices, at their quarter or petty feffions, to examine, and report thereupon.

The guardians of the poor to have power, for thefe purpofes, to tranfmit, from time to time, any queftions which they may think neceffary, to church-wardens and overfeers, and direct them to prepare anfwers, in writing, to be verified on oath, and to be authorized, alfo, to call church-wardens, overfeers, and other perfons, before them, at the time of their vifitation, to examine them on oath, and to infpect all books and accounts ; to report the fame to the juftices at a fpecial petty-feffions, to be held as fhall be directed by the act, and then to deliver a fchedule of the foregoing particulars in each parifh, ac-

cording

cording to a form to be annexed, together with fuch obfervations as to the guardians of the poor fhall feem requifite.

And the guardian of the poor fhall be fpecially required, in every cafe where he fhall be of opinion that
all practicable meafures have not been taken for carrying
into execution the purpofes of this act, in fetting the
poor to work, or furnifhing them with additional means
of maintaining themfelves without periodical relief, to
certify the fame to the juftices, and likewife to reprefent
to the juftices what modes of employment and affiftance
are, in his opinion, applicable to the circumftances of
fuch parifh ; and what advances of money, and increafe
of rate, are neceffary for the fame. And, in every fuch
cafe, the guardian of the poor fhall leave, with the officers of the parifh complained of, a copy of fuch certificate   weeks before he fhall deliver the fame to
the juftices of the petty-feffions.

And, in cafe the officers of the parifh fhall not, at the
faid feffions, attend, to fhew caufe why the regulations
propofed fhould not be carried into effect, the juftices fhall
make order for their being carried into effect ; and if the
juftices, on hearing the parifh-officers, fhall be fatisfied
that fuch meafures ought not to be adopted, they fhall
make fuch order as they fhall think fit, recording the reafons why the meafures recommended by the guardians of
the poor cannot be carried fully into effect.

Copies of all the orders made at the petty-feffions, and
copies of all the reports of the guardians of the poor,
together with an abftract, to be tranfmitted to the quarter-feffions.

If either the overfeers or the guardians of the poor
fhall be diffatisfied with the determination of the petty-
feffions,

seffions, power to appeal to the quarter-seffions, having given   days notice thereof, whofe order fhall be final.

Guardians of the poor to tranfmit copies of their reports, and of all orders made thereupon, to the Privy-Council, with a general abftract, according to a form annexed.

The Privy-Council to employ a perfon to prepare abftracts of the general returns of the whole kingdom, and to lay the fame, together with the returns on which they are founded, before parliament, within one month after the firft of January, in each year, if it fhall be then fitting; and, if not then, within twenty days after the firft day of the feffion.

In order to enforce, ftill further, an attention to the due execution of the law, it might be propofed to make a ftanding-order of the Houfe for referring thofe accounts to a Select Committee, to confider and report upon the fame, and that fuch report fhould afterwards be referred to the confideration of a Committee of the whole Houfe, where the refult fhould be ftated in diftinct refolutions, as is now practifed in the India-budget.

Saving claufes, refpecting provifions againft vagrancy, &c.

It would be with a very ill grace indeed, that any perfon, having had the honour of being confulted on a meafure, which the very fuperior judgement and experience of thofe who afterwards reconfidered it have, with the approbation of Mr. Pitt, thought proper to alter, fhould inveigh againft thofe alterations, which more mature confideration has made; on which account a refpectful filence fhall be preferved on every alteration except one, which fo militates with the outline laid down by the Chancellor of the Exchequer, in the
fpeech

fpeech which has been alluded to, as would convict me of a pufilla-
nimous indifference to the good effect of this great meafure, were it
to be paffed by unnoticed.

To prove the affertion, recourfe muft be had to that part of the
Chancellor of the Exchequer's fpeech, which is publifhed by Mr.
Longman, in Paternofter-row, as it is faid, *that* publication is from
the beft authority of any which has appeared in print.

" He fhould wifh, therefore, that an opportunity were given of
reftoring the original purity of the poor-laws, and of removing
thofe corruptions by which they had been obfcured. He was convinced that the evils which they had occafioned did not arife out of
their original conftitution, but coincided with the opinion of Blackftone, that, in proportion as the wife regulations, that were eftablifhed in the long and glorious reign of Queen Elizabeth, have been
fuperfeded by fubfequent enactments, the utility of the inftitution
has been impaired, and the benevolence of the plan rendered fruit-
lefs.

" While he thus had expreffed thofe fentiments which the difcuffion naturally prompted, it might not, perhaps, be improper, on
fuch an occafion, to lay before the Houfe the ideas floating in his
mind, though not digefted with fufficient accuracy, nor arranged
with fufficient clearnefs. Neither what the honourable gentleman
propofed, nor what he himfelf had fuggefted, were remedies adequate to the evil it was intended to remove. Suppofing, however,
the two modes of remedying the evil were on a par in effect, the
preference in principle was clearly due to that which was leaft arbi-
trary in its nature, but it was not difficult to perceive that the remedy propofed by the honourable gentlemen would either be completely ineffectual, or fuch as far to over-reach its mark. There
was of courfe a difference in the numbers which compofe the families of the labouring-poor, and it muft neceffarily require more to
fupport an infant-family. Befides, by the regulations propofed,
either the man with a fmall family would have too much wages, or
the

the man with a large family, who had done moſt ſervice to his country, would have too little. So that were the minimum fixed upon
the ſtandard of a large family, it might operate as an encouragement to idleneſs on one part of the community; and, if it were fixed
on the ſtandard of a ſmall family, thoſe would not enjoy the benefit
of it, for whoſe relief it was intended. What meaſure, then, could be
found to ſupply the defect? Let us, ſaid he, make relief, in caſes
where there is a number of children, a matter of right, an honour,
inſtead of a ground for opprobrium and contempt. This will make
a large family a bleſſing, and not a curſe; and this will draw a
proper line of diſtinction between thoſe who are able to provide for
themſelves by their labour; and thoſe who, after having enriched
their country with a number of children, have a claim upon its
aſſiſtance for their ſupport. All this, however, he would confeſs,
was not enough, if they did not engraft upon it reſolutions to diſcourage the granting relief where it was not wanted. If the neceſſities of thoſe who required aſſiſtance could be ſupplied, by giving
it in labour, or affording employment, which is the principle of the
act of Queen Elizabeth, the moſt important advantages would be
gained. They would thus benefit thoſe to whom they afforded relief, not only by the aſſiſtance beſtowed, but by giving habits of induſtry and frugality, and, in furniſhing a temporary bounty, enable
them to make permanent proviſion for themſelves. By giving effect
to the operation of friendly ſocieties, as had been already hinted at,
individuals would be ſecured from becoming a burthen upon the
public, and, if neceſſary, be enabled to ſubſiſt upon a fund which
their own induſtry had contributed to raiſe. Theſe great points of
granting relief, according to the number and age of children, preventing removals at the caprice of the pariſh-officer, encouraging
ſubſcriptions to friendly ſocieties, and extending as far as poſſible
the means of employing the poor, would tend, in a very great degree, to remove every complaint to which the preſent partial remedy
could be applied. Experience had already ſhewn how much could

be

be done by the induſtry of children, and the advantages of early
employing them in ſuch branches of manufactures as they are capable of executing. The extenſion of ſchools of induſtry was alſo
an object of material importance. If any one would take the trouble
to compute the amount of all the earnings of the children who are
already educated in this manner, he would be ſurpriſed, when he
came to conſider the weight which their ſupport by their own labours took off the country, and the addition which, by the fruits of
their toil, and the habits to which they were formed, was made to
its internal opulence. The ſuggeſtion of theſe ſchools was originally
taken from Lord Hale and Mr. Locke, and upon ſuch authority he
had no difficulty in recommending the adoption of them to the encouragement of the legiſlature. Much might be effected by a plan
of this nature, ſuſceptible of conſtant improvement. Such a plan
would convert the relief granted to the poor into an encouragement
to induſtry, inſtead of being, as it is by the preſent poor-laws, a
premium to idleneſs, and a ſchool for ſloth. There was alſo a
number of regulations to which, on the ſame principle, it would be
neceſſary to attend. The law, which prohibits giving relief where
any viſible property remains, ſhould be aboliſhed. It is neither conſiſtent with policy or humanity to force an induſtrious man, on any
temporary occaſion, to part with the laſt ſhilling of his little capital, and compel him to deſcend to a ſtate of wretchedneſs from
which he could never recover, merely that he might be entitled to a
caſual ſupply. Inſtead of enforcing ſo rigorous a principle, caſes
might, on the contrary, occur, in which, with ſtrict and proper pre-
cautions, ſmall ſums might be advanced by the pariſh to put the
perſons who received them in the way of acquiring what might
place them in a ſituation to make permanent proviſion for themſelves."

The very appoſite quotation from the 14th ſatire of Juvenal,
which the Chancellor of the Exchequer in ſo elegant a manner introduced, is not mentioned in this ſketch of his ſpeech; but that

quotation

quotation was fo aptly applied as to explain, to the greateft precifion, the prevailing idea which may be fuppofed then floating in
his mind, that its introduction requires no apology:

> Gratum eft quod patriæ civem populoque dedifti,
> Si facis, ut patriæ fit idoneus, utilis agris,
> Utilis et bellorum et pacis rebus agendis.

The queftion that naturally flows from thefe pages in Mr. Longman's publication, combined with this quotation, is; whether a fketch
of an act of parliament which enforces fchools of induftry, and an
annual parliamentary infpection of, and control over, the management of the poor, by obligatory claufes, which, if not carried into
execution, befpeak an inattention to, and difobedience of, a pofitive written law of the land, and not any fault in the declaratory
part of the law itfelf; which principle is alfo enforced by another
obligatory claufe, with refpect to finding employment for the poor,
viz. that where fuch employment is *not found* by fome of the means
pointed out, *an allowance fhould be made from the parochial rates to
the poor in a certain proportion, for fuch of them and their children as are
permitted to live in idlenefs, by fuch an inattention, on the part of the
officers of the parifh, to the law of the land?*

Or, heads of an act of parliament which, in the firft inftance,
oblige a payment to the poor in refpect of their number of children,
and leave it a matter of option in the diftrict, whether fchools of
induftry fhould be inftituted or not; and alfo, whether an annual
parliamentary infpection and control fhould or fhould not be enacted; are moft in conformity with that part of the fpeech of the
Chancellor of the Exchequer, on the fecond reading of Mr. Whitbread's bill, which has been alluded to, as explained by this quotation from Juvenal? without which infpection into, or fome control
over, the management of the poor, of a *higher* nature, and more
effective powers, than the prefent, over which we have long flept,
we fhall be foon awakened to certain ruin, as to the morals of the
poor, and the property of thofe who maintain them.

Any

Any other deviation from the plan, which that fpeech gave a glimpfe of to the Houfe of Commons, it is by no means my intention to obferve upon ; nor am I bold enough to affert, that the plan referred to is now the beft policy, and replete with the wifeft humanity ; but, on the contrary, believe, more knowledge of local facts and circumftances may be neceffary, before a bill of this extreme importance is paffed into a law; and it may be no improbable conjecture, that the inveftigation of the management and conduct of the poor, their morals, habits, economy, and feelings, being left open, the ftream of practical information and theoretic knowledge being kept running, will refine itfelf ; and the real ftate and fituation of the poor in fociety, and the rule of conduct with refpect to them, that is moft likely to benefit them, and the nation itfelf, will more clearly appear ; confequently, that a law made in the *maturity* of fuch an inveftigation will be more likely to approach perfection than one enacted in its infancy.

While this is going through the prefs, Mr. Whitbread has again urged the Chancellor of the Exchequer to bring forward the debate on the bill now before parliament ; declaring, at the fame time, that, unlefs the fenfe of the Houfe is taken on that now before them, he will himfelf introduce fome propofition on the fubject.

Without doubting, in the leaft, the abilities of Mr. Whitbread to offer a propofition in favour of the labouring claffes of men, or his wifh to ftand forth in the eyes of ·the nation as their protector and friend ; it may with truth be afferted, that, if his propofed plan be of the nature of his laft effort, it ought not to be the law of the land : becaufe, as has been proved, it has not neceffity, juftice, or convenience, for its bafis ; and, if it is, in this refpect, like moft of the late acts on the fubject of the poor, that it applies itfelf only to fome *fmall* part of this capacious field of legiflation, it ought not to fuperfede a *general* inveftigation of the fubject, now it has the light of the Chancellor of the Exchequer's abilities thrown fteadily upon the whole fyftem ; but ftill Mr. Whitbread's

intention

intention is no bad fymptom in the cafe, which wants information, and ftands in need of the cleareft lights of practical experience and theoretic ability; and every other light which may prevent ftumbling at the threfhold of an intricate fubject of this importance is of confequence. A good act of parliament, a few months later, is better than a doubtful one a few months fooner; and, when all fufficient information is obtained, we feel ourfelves fafe in Mr. Pitt's application of it to every wife and humane purpofe. The prefent fyftem already too much refembles a thing of fhreds and patches, to bear more bolftering ftatutes; and, probably, a total repeal of every act of parliament fince the 43d of Elizabeth. A ftrict and active execution of that act alone might be attended with better effect than the prefent fyftem, as at prefent executed, al-though affifted with every additional bill, which each member in the Houfe of Commons might think it expedient to propofe, and the parliament to pafs.

In the mean time, it is probable, that fuch a return of the annual accounts of the overfeers to parliament, as has been recommended, being tried fomewhat more than one year, every neceffary information would be obtained. By fuch an act, for the overfeers keeping their accounts under certain heads, and thofe accounts to be returned to parliament in the manner as was firft propofed, the information of two years would be col-lected by Eafter, 1799, if the act was to pafs by Chriftmas; the number of claimants for the weekly allowances to the children of the poor, together with the total expenfes attending that hu-mane meafure propofed by the bill, before the Houfe of Commons, would be known; as alfo the effect occafioned by fchools of in-duftry, in thofe parifhes where they have been inftituted, as far as the morals and the earnings of the children have been meliorated and increafed, would be feen; whence the propriety of a general inftitution of them throughout the kingdom might be eftimated; and, during this time, the effect of a parliamentary inveftigation

into,

into, and control over, the management of the poor might be judged of, by the proof of a greater circumfpection in the conduct of the overfeers, and of the poor themfelves, when confcious that the eye of the greateft authority in the kingdom is conftantly over their conduct. Thefe and many other important articles of information might in this fhort time be obtained on the fubject, as well as a probable amendment of conduct in the parifh-officers, and of morals and manners in the people, without any very confiderable addition of expenfe.

L E T T E R   LVII.

THE exertions of the Rev. Mr. Bouyer, in the caufe of induftry and the poor, by the inftitution, continued patronage, and fupervifion, of the fchools of induftry in Lincolnfhire, which have been mentioned in an early part of this tract, occafioned me to wifh much for the correfpondence of that gentleman on the fubject ; which honour I have very lately obtained by the kind interference of my valuable friend Mr. Spranger, a mafter in Chancery ; who, at my requeft, informed Mr. Bouyer of my wifh to have an anfwer to a few queftions refpecting the fchools under his direction, which he was fo obliging to comply with, by favouring me with a very polite letter on the fubject, full of important information.

1ft. In anfwer to my queftions, Mr. Bouyer fays, That fchools of induftry are, when properly adminiftered, certainly very profitable to parifhes: the average abfolute numerical profit, clear of all expenfes, except the firft building and furnifhing, may be eftimated, by the loweft computation, at a fhilling a week each for all the children admitted into them : — at a much larger, though

lefs

lefs certainly eftimable, fum, in the importunate applications for relief which they prevent; — but if they were generally enforced, regulated, and fuftained, by legiflative authority, at a rate of profit (arifing neceffarily out of the melioration of principles and habits) perfectly incalculable.

2d. That the honorary and intrinfically valuable rewards to meritorious children are fully kept up, and indeed rather increafed, in proportion to the prefent ftate of the fociety's funds; and the friends and promoters of the inftitution have never feen any reafon to depart, in any material particular, from the manner of their application and diftribution.

3d. In fome places, the poor are become fully fenfible of the benefits of the inftitution; and, in a neighbouring market-town, abfolutely importuned the perfons who had formed the poor-houfe to open in it a day-fchool of induftry, for the employment of the children of the town; a benefit of which they this year lament the privation, occafioned by the felfifhnefs and indolence of the perfons into whofe hands the management of that houfe has now fallen; but that much impreffion has not been made on the minds of the poor in general.

4th. That knitting and fpinning jerfey are the only objects to which the fchools can now attend; and that thefe were the principal, but by no means the only, objects he had in contemplation, had he been favoured with more univerfal and more perfevering fupport.

Mr. Bouyer's letter contains alfo many very conclufive reafons why thefe fchools, in Lincolnfhire, have not in general hitherto met with that full fuccefs, that every friend to humanity expected, and had reafon to hope, that part of the kingdom would have received from the experiment; but, at the fame time, the following pleafing account of the good effects arifing from them has been extracted from his very friendly and valuable communication.

That

That he has the heart-felt pleafure of feeing a general tenor of regularity and good conduct mark the lives of thofe young people who have received the favours of the fociety; and of *particularly* remarking, that thofe, who have been honoured with the *higheft* rewards, are *equally* diftinguifhed by the commendation of the mafters whom they ferve, and that fome of them are advantageoufly fettled in life, through the affiftance of this inftitution; and be- coming, as hufbands and wives, fathers and mothers, happy, ufe- ful, and virtuous, members of fociety.

That the plan is ftill purfued of rewarding meritorious youth, in proportion to the fcale to which the funds of the fchools are narrowed; and every day's experience, whether of fuccefs or incon- venience, ftill confirms the expediency of fchools; which, in the few places where they are kept up, materially contribute to the good order of the parifh, and the diminution of its burthens; whilft the only difficulties of their prefent adminiftration arife from the comparative uncertainty of the work of thofe candidates who are not collected under one regular government, and whom, for want of fchools, they are forced to admit to a participation of the premiums.

The knitting trials, reftrained to children under eight years of age, caufe as early exertions as human nature is capable of. They had one of them on April 27th : there were twenty-feven candi- dates, under eight years old, for fifteen premiums. The trial con- fifted in their knitting up each feventeen yards in length of worfted, as part of a ftocking, upon middle-fized needles; and the child who finifhed it, the fecond of the whole number, was only five years old, and performed that tafk without one fingle flip, or miftake, in twenty-nine minutes : that work was well worth a halfpenny; and, according to the proportion which practice teaches to fettle with fome certainty between a fingle hour's exertions and a common day's work of eight hours only, that little child could, without any fort of fatigue or hindrance from proper play and ex- ercife,

ercife, earn a fhilling a week at this moft unprofitable employment; and when it is coufidered that, without fuch encouragements as are held out by the fociety, the eldeft child there would
never have learnt any work at all, we may, from fuch inftances,
eftimate, in fome degree, the value of all fuch public rewards.

The fociety, which feemed to be at its loweft ebb laft year,
is now apparently gaining frefh vigour, and the fpirit of it plainly
reviving. This appeared at the adjudication-meeting, on April
27th, by a confiderable increafe in the number of candidates, in
the proportion of one-fourth more than laft year. Befides this,
four neighbouring parifhes have intimated their intention to build
a central fchool on a large plan. This revival may be attributed
partly to Mr. Pitt's having declared his intention of introducing
fchools of induftry into general practice.

In fome other counties, and parts of counties, the plan of
fchools of induftry has been more fuccefsfully tried than in Lincolnfhire: no where more fo, in Mr. Bouyer's opinion, than
in the county of Rutland, which began very foon after thofe
in Lincolnfhire, and literally adopted all their proceedings and
forms. From thefe they have fince only departed in very few
inftances; fome of which variations are happy confequences of
the fpirit with which they are fupported, and apply to objects
highly proper and beneficial. That fociety flourifhes exceedingly, and is honoured, not only by the countenance and patronage, but alfo by the cordial co-operation, of the firft noblemen
and gentlemen of the county.

Mr. Bouyer wifhed to return the moft explicit anfwers to the
queftions which were fent him, but, in fo doing, a very confiderable difficulty arofe from the fear of mifconception. He fays,

The Society of Induftry may be confidered in two different
afpects. *Firft,* as a trial of the general plan of affembling, under
proper government, the poor children of the parifh, from the
earlieft part of their infancy at which they are capable of any
exertion,

exertion, till they fhall be old and ftrong enough for fervice, or
labour in hufbandry; and giving them, in that important interval, a public education, by means profitable to themfelves and
parents, and capable of kindling honeft ambition and emulation
in their minds. *Secondly*, as a local eftablifhment in that part
of the county where the plan originated. — The fuccefs of the undertaking, in thefe two views of it, has been extremely different: flattering and encouraging, beyond defcription, in the *former*; but, in the *latter*, obftructed by various difficulties, which
have tried the patience and perfeverance of its friends and well-
wifhers very feverely.

Mr. Bouyer alfo wifhes to have it obferved, that this is no new
reprefentation of the matter; in proof of which he begs leave to
refer to his Statement, p. 96, 97, and 98, of the laft Edition of the
Society's Pamphlet, publifhed eight years ago, part of which may
be feen by the reader in the 34th Letter of this Series: and, as a
farther proof of this obfervation, the pamphlet alluded to then goes
on to ftate,

" That, in the mean while, the Society of Induftry feems to
have made fome little progrefs in its humble walk, as a pre-
paratory ftep to a more general and comprehenfive eftablifhment; but the Editor cannot refrain from obferving, that many
non-refident proprietors of large eftates in thefe parts, whofe
goodnefs of heart and charitable difpofition cannot be quef-
tioned, appear to have been negligently, or perhaps induftrioufly, kept from the knowledge of the efforts for reformation made by the fociety, of the fuccefs of thofe efforts in
part, and of the much greater efficacy which would have accrued to thofe falutary meafures from *their benefactions* and *fubfcriptions*, and ftill more from *their influence* and *authority* properly
exerted.

" Among the many ill confequences which attend the annual
change of overfeers, the fociety has fuftained a very confiderable

rable diminution of its income by the ignorance, neglect, pre-judices, or perfonal refentments, of new-comers into office, who have often withdrawn the periodical fubfcriptions after having received the greateft benefits from the fociety; and, in many inftances, to the bitter difappointment of many deferving children, whom, by thefe means, they difqualified from becoming candidates for the fociety's premiums." His Letter then continues to ftate,

That, after the experience which has fince been had, and although the fund for rewarding merit, and the circle of its influence, have now been reduced to one-third of their original extent; although the operation of the laws above-recited, and of many other local difadvantages, which it would be tedious, and, in fome degree, invidious, to enumerate; yet none of thefe difappointments have had the fmalleft tendency to invalidate the evidence which the trial has procured of the general utility of the meafure, if not of its abfolute neceffity, as affording the only probable means of national reform.

But it feems to be the opinion of my correfpondent, that its fuccefs in that view muft depend on legiflative fupport; and, to make that fupport effectual, there muft be,

1. A general uniformity in the outline, to give not only ftability to the regulation, but a proper direction to the efforts of the inferior agents in it.

2. A permanent adminiftration, by fkilful and refponfible perfons, fubftituted to the rotation of overfeers; which is the moft confpicuous blemifh of our poor-laws; for, they feem to be enacted on the abfurd fuppofition that fkill, honefty, and perfeverance, were transferrable, from one farmer to another, with the parifh-books.

3. A proper inducement to perfons, who are able and refponfible, to give up their whole time, or a much greater portion of it that can be expected gratuitoufly; efpecially, if the prin-

H h h   ciple

ciple of rotation is, as he apprehends it muſt be, totally relinquiſhed.

4. A very particular care ſo to place ſuch appointments that
they ſhall not degenerate into patronage, jobs, penſions, and ſinecures. Offices, and, to a certain degree, lucrative ones, muſt be
created; but they ſhould be much fewer, more effective, and more
reſponſible, than in any plan that has yet appeared. Perhaps the
greateſt objection to that which is now under public contemplation
is, the multiplicity of offices, by rotation, ſlower indeed than that
of the preſent overſeers, and depending upon a general activity
in public buſineſs, which has never yet exiſted but in ſpeculation;
inſtead of putting the execution into the hands of fewer perſons,
who ſhould continue in office, *quamdiu ſe bene geſſerint,* and be
held to their duty by the only tye which can ſecure the performance of it, a reſponſibility proportioned to the value of the employment. The utmoſt expectation that can be formed, by per
ſons acquainted with human nature and the preſent ſtate of ſociety, is this, — that as many patriotic and public-ſpirited men
may be found, in each county or diſtrict, as ſhall be ſtrictly
neceſſary to enforce that reſponſibility, and to examine into the
diſcharge of thoſe purchaſed duties, looking for no other reward
than the conſciouſneſs of their own integrity and zeal, and prepared, at the ſame time, to hear their good qualities, and the
exertions by which they diſplay them, oftener queſtioned, or
miſrepreſented, than thankfully, or even candidly, acknowledged.

Such is the opinion of a gentleman whoſe exertions, and con
ſequently experience, in the regulation of theſe ſchools of induſtry, are well known; and whoſe well-founded judgement, and
prediction of the probable advantages ariſing from an inſtitution
of them by legiſlative authority, merit great attention. It would
be preſumptuous were the writer of theſe Letters, whoſe experience, in this moſt uſeful line of regulation, is ſo trifling as to
confine

confine his judgement to that of a mere theorift, to add any obfervations to thofe contained in this Letter, or to prolong it by any animadverfions on what his correfpondent has written : he will only venture to fuggeft, that, probably, as to the *general* management of the poor, in the parifh, the inftitution of overfeers, by the 43d of Elizabeth, was not quite fo replete with abfurdity as his correfpondent reprefents; and conceives that they are, even in *thefe times*, the propereft perfons to be entrufted with the management of the poor, a perfon of longer durability in office, and more particularly qualified for the purpofe, having the fupervifion of the fchools of induftry : befides, it appears as fomewhat tending to injuftice, that the overfeers of the poor, who are in rotation, thofe from whofe pockets the rates for the maintenance of the poor are taken, fhould not be entrufted with the difburfement of the money they collect, were that difburfement but fubject to the fupervifion and control of Parliament.

LETTER LVIII.

DEAR SIR,.

AS moft of thefe Letters originally were fent to you for your very ufeful publication, the Annals of Agriculture; as they took their rife from fome of thofe friendly converfations in which we have fo frequently agitated the interefts of Agriculture, and the humbler votaries to her fhrine, the labouring-poor ; with great propriety may the laft of the Series be addreffed to you ; more efpecially as it affords the writer an opportunity of acknowledging publicly the fatisfaction he has received from the long habits of correfpondence and friendly intercourfe which have fubfifted be-

tween

tween us, and the real pleafure he takes in feeing you placed in that fituation where your abilities, and indefatigable application to the interefts of agriculture, have proved, and have the greateft chance of continuing to prove, an honour to yourfelf, and an advantage to your country.

We have often lamented together,

> Non ullus aratro
>
> Dignus honos.

That caufe of complaint has now been fometime removed by the inftitution of a Board which has been of the greateft fervice, as well as honour, to the caufe of agriculture; for, during a war which has increafed our expenditure of money and men beyond all former experience or calculations, we have feen nothing of that impoverifhed condition of our fields, fo elegantly lamented by our favourite Georgical poet, in the continuation of the quotation :

> Squalent abductis arva colonis,
>
> Et curvæ rigidum falces conflantur in Enfem.

But, on the contrary, agriculture has flourifhed with a vigour which even peace itfelf can fcarcely increafe.

In the courfe of thefe Letters which have been addreffed to you, it has been the view of the writer to preferve the fubject of the poor as near as poffible what Sir Jofiah Child calls it, *a calm fubject* : it certainly ought to be fo; but it is not at all times that militating interefts, contending opinions, and information of dubious certainty, will admit it to remain fo : thus far, at leaft, I have refolved, — that not an atom of the controverfy of general politics, or the ill temper of party prejudice, fhould be fuffered to fall from my pen. The Letters profefs an Inquiry into the Hiftory of the Poor, their Rights and Duties, and the Laws refpecting them. No collateral fubject has been agitated which may tend to interrupt that philofophic coolnefs with which even our *deareft* interefts are beft canvaffed ; and your friend ftops his expreffions of approbation, at this point, folely with the view of preferving thefe pages, which

are

are dedicated to the fervice of the poor, free from any affertion that may lead to a difcuffion of general politics.

After having been obliged, in the correction, and, in fome inftances, alteration, of his former publication, to perufe again what he had before written, and to connect with it the new matter which has fince arifen, it is probable that, while the whole is frefh in his recollection, the mind may be able to judge more accurately than after the impreffion of facts and reafons have, by time, become in fome meafure effaced, of what would be the real and fubftantial practical improvements which may be introduced in the management of the poor; and he confeffes that, of the various ameliorations of the fyftem contained in the Bill now before the Houfe, two feem to your correfpondent particularly prominent;—fchools of induftry, and parliamentary infpection and control. The other parts of the propofed fyftem, although very probably productive of good, have not that good fo unmixed with fome contiguous evil, which may adulterate the mafs, as have thefe two great objects; and Mr. Bouyer's information, as contained in the laft Letter, corroborates the opinion ftrongly as to the effect of fchools of induftry when under the control of the legiflature; which control alfo muft be an active principle in all the departments of this bufinefs, and will be more efficacious than a thoufand ftatutes whofe enforcing fanctions are penalties never fued for. The laws of certificates and removals, and thofe which enabled the overfeer to hold out the parifh work-houfe to the diftreffed pauper as a bugbear to deter him from afking for relief, require no additional freedom from reftraint, fince the paffing thofe acts of parliament which have been mentioned in the Letters continuing this publication; and the law of fettlements (that omiffion being corrected which has been pointed out as the confequence of the act of parliament which, rumour fays, the public ftands indebted for to the attention and humanity of Mr. Eaft) will probably remain a harmlefs, but, were the principles rightly underftood, I think an unneceffary, mode of

identifying

identifying the parifh which muft ultimately fupport the needy
pauper; although that mode may ftill continue to be attended with expenfes of law. Some hints received from my friends
have occafioned me to confider the probable confequences of a total
repeal of all acts of parliament fince the 43d of Elizabeth, and the
addition of two acts of parliament as aifles, or wings, to that
excellent edifice; an act for the education of the children of the
poor in induftrious habits; and another, inftituting a comprehenfive and cheap fyftem of parliamentary infpection and control.
To judge of the propriety of fuch an idea, it would be neceffary
to examine into what would be the real ftate and condition of the
poor, in every bearing and dependency, fuppofing the magiftrates
and overfeers had no rule of law by which to regulate their conduct, except that ftatute; an inveftigation which would require
much attention and reflection; and, it is to be feared, if any explanation or additional regulation might be thought neceffary,
each individual, who might turn his attention to the fubject,
conceiving the rule, which ftrikes his mind, as effential, and that
the fyftem would be imperfect without it, more auxiliary claufes
would be propofed than are contained in all the acts which have
been paffed fince the reign of Elizabeth.

But it is time to conclude the fubject, which, thank God, is now
before the Houfe of Commons; and is brought before them in
the beft manner, by the only individual in the nation, who, from
every concurrent circumftance favourable to the full inveftigation
of this important regulation, except the political anxiety of the
times, could with the greateft and moft favourable propriety introduce a law which will affect the internal regulation and comfort
of the *whole kingdom*, fubject to the poor-laws. This is a regulation which affects *no particular* clafs or defcription of men in parliament, confined neither to the interefts of thofe on the right or
on the left of the Speaker's chair, but equally concerns every individual in the Houfe; and, when the fubject comes before the

Houfe

Houfe of Lords, every peer will feel that the deareft interefts of his country are in queftion; and I cannot help anticipating, in idea, the fatisfaction his Majefty will experience, when the royal prerogative ftamps the fanction of law on an act which is calculated to educate millions of his fubjects, the rifing and the future generations of the labouring-poor of this kingdom, in habits of induftry and moral economy, fure preludes to a greater chance of comfort in this life and happinefs in the next.

If thefe pages have in any degree been the means of introducing or accelerating this meafure, your friend will have no reafon to regret that he has, although in a rough and unpolifhed ftyle, ventured to publifh the Hiftory of the Poor, their Rights and Duties, and the Laws refpecting them; which, by laying open to the public the diftreffes of that valuable and numerous branch of our countrymen, and the great expenfes of the other claffes of the ftate in their maintenance, have induced thofe in power and authority to make ufe of the advantages of their fituation in the behalf of their diftreffed fellow-fubjects.

T. R.

May 11th, 1797.

THE END.

INDEX.

33 Geo.

I N D E X.

INDEX.

INDEX.

INDEX.

INDEX.

Parents

INDEX.

INDEX.

ERRATA.

Page   31, line 27, *water*, not *waters*.
    65, laſt line, *reſidents*, not *his majeſty's ſubjects*.
    66, line 5, *were*, not *was*.
    82, line 11, *country*, not *county*.
  141, line 8, *have*, not *has*.
  210, line 21, *it* omitted.
  221, line 29, *ſixty*, not *forty*.
  222, line 29, *prevents*, not *prevent*.
  224, line 8, *than*, not *that*.
  238, line 2, in the note, *country*, not *county*.
  292, line 2, in the note, the ſame miſtake.
  310, laſt line, *to* ſhould be omitted.
  342, line 15, *country*, not *county*.
  343, line 18, *the* omitted, viz. to *the* elegant, &c.
  413, line 14, *farmed*, not *formed*.
  417, line 3, *their*, not *the*.

.